Manpower and employment in Arab countries

Manpower and employment in Arab countries
Some critical issues

Selected papers and reports
of the ILO/ECWA Seminar
on manpower and employment planning
in Arab countries,
Beirut, May 1975

International Labour Office   Geneva

ISBN 92-2-101535-1

First published 1976
Second impression 1977

ILO publications can be obtained through major booksellers or ILO local offices in many countries, or direct from ILO Publications, International Labour Office, CH-1211 Geneva 22, Switzerland. A catalogue or list of new publications will be sent free of charge from the above address.

Printed by the International Labour Office, Geneva, Switzerland

P R E F A C E

Until recently very few studies were concerned with problems of manpower and employment promotion in Arab countries. This gap could not be motivated by the absence or slightness of such problems. Indeed, most Arab countries are faced with serious employment problems, of one type or another. Thus, while the poor countries suffer from unemployment, underemployment, low incomes and income inequality, development in the oil-rich countries is slowed down by shortages of skilled and high-level personnel as well as of unskilled labour in several cases. Other problems, such as rural-urban migration, urban congestion and educated unemployment, are also met in many Arab countries. At the regional level, more or less spontaneous large-scale migrations often result in manpower imbalances and seem to call for a better regulation of the workers' movements.

Both the complexity of these problems and the absence of clear policies for dealing with them led the ILO and ECWA to the conclusion that a systematic effort must be made to promote a better understanding of the nature of the employment problems now confronting Arab countries, of the policies needed to cope with them, and of the kinds of assistance desired from international and regional organisations for that purpose. The first step was the organisation of a joint Seminar for Arab States on Manpower and Employment Planning which was held in Beirut in May 1975, with the financial assistance of the UNDP.

The Seminar provided an opportunity for the exchange of views on the above subjects between the various Arab countries concerned. Papers were presented by consultants on such topics as the relationships between population, employment and development; the definition of sectoral priorities, choice of technology and employment; education and the labour market; trade policies and employment and inter-Arab migration patterns. Besides, various aspects of the problem were illustrated by case studies covering respectively Egypt; Iraq and Syria; Lebanon; Algeria; Kuwait, Saudi Arabia and Libya (oil-rich countries), and the Yemen Arab Republic, the Democratic Republic of Yemen, and the Sultanate of Oman (considered the least developed countries).

The present volume, edited by L.J.Berouti and W.Keddeman (ILO) contains a selection of the above papers. In most cases, the papers were abridged for publication purposes. They are preceded by an introduction analysing the broad context of employment problems and policies in the Arab countries. The final report of the above Seminar, as well as the plan of action adopted by it have been included. It is hoped that this collection will not only lead to a better understanding of manpower and employment problems and policies in the region, but will also stimulate further research designed at improving the patterns of human resources development and utilisation.

CONTENTS

INTRODUCTION

EMPLOYMENT PROMOTION PROBLEMS IN ARAB COUNTRIES

by

L.J. Bérouti[1]

Most Arab countries offer the image of societies in transition. Indeed, major changes are taking place in their traditional socio-economic patterns. These are paralleled by even more rapid changes in their demographic, manpower and employment structures. Hence a double tension. First, Arab economies have to go over the test of modernisation and overcome many constraints of a socio-economic nature. Secondly, they have to watch that modernisation does not disrupt their social set-up and create imbalances in the utilisation of human resources which could jeopardise development efforts themselves.

An attempt will be made here to analyse manpower and employment patterns, trends and prospects in Arab countries as well as the major problems which they involve. Subsequently, major policy issues and approaches for dealing with these problems will be reviewed. The analysis will draw upon the material presented at the Seminar for Arab States on Manpower and Employment Planning (Beirut, May 1975), most of which is published in the present volume.

Part One

Basic aspects of manpower and employment patterns, trends and prospects

Growth and structural aspects of Arab economies

Of course, growth patterns in Arab countries differ between countries, with different endowments of natural, human and financial resources and varying degrees of development. As expected, in oil-rich countries, such as Algeria, Bahrain, Iraq, Kuwait, Libya, Qatar, Saudi Arabia and the United Arab Emirates, economic growth rates are generally higher than in countries relatively poor in natural resources, such as Egypt, Jordan, Morocco, Sudan and Tunisia, not to mention the countries considered as the least developed, i.e. Oman[2], the Yemen Arab Republic and the Yemen Democratic Republic. However, on the whole, it seems that most Arab economies are growing rapidly, as illustrated by available data on Gross Domestic Product (GDP). Table 1 presents estimates showing that GDP_3 has increased during 1960-70 at the annual rates of 7.0 per cent in South-West Asia[3] and 5.5 per cent in Northern Africa (at constant prices), and is expected to grow until 1990 at the annual rate of 8.0 per cent in both regions.

Indeed, important economic and social progress was achieved during the last 15 years in most Arab countries. The availability of oil resources and increases in oil prices in some eight countries, with the resulting accumulation of gold and foreign exchange reserves, and new possibilities for development financing, were important factors. Other factors include improvements in agricultural methods, the growth of manufacturing industries, the introduction of modern transportation and communication systems and the expansion of basic physical and social infrastructures (e.g. water, electricity, schools, hospitals, etc.).

---

[1] International Labour Office.

[2] Although with some oil resources.

[3] Which, however, includes not only Arab countries, but also Cyprus, Israel and Turkey.

Nevertheless, the basic structure of the economy remains largely traditional. The national production capacity is limited as compared to requirements, in view of the lack of manufacturing industries and of insufficient infrastructures. This results in heavy dependency on imports. These weaknesses are themselves compounded by rapid growth of the population and of the labour force with low proportions of economically active persons (i.e. high dependency ratios), low literacy and school enrolment rates (in spite of recent improvements), manpower shortages leading in some countries to heavy immigration, lack of skills coexisting with surpluses of unskilled labour and low levels of productivity and living in most countries. The manpower and employment aspects of this situation are further detailed hereunder. They raise the critical problem of finding ways of mobilising Arab populations for development, i.e. for activating natural and other resources.

Population and labour force[1]

Population in Arab countries is characterised by rapid growth. Table 2 presents estimates in individual countries showing that annual rates of growth during 1970-75 were close to (or even exceeding) 3 per cent. However, country differences can be observed, linked with differences in natural rates of increase and migration patterns. Thus, growth rates are lowest in Tunisia (2.27 per cent) and Egypt (2.41 per cent), due to declining fertility, and highest in Kuwait (7.38 per cent), due to immigration.

In a majority of Arab countries, birth rates are very high, although some slowdown can be noticed in countries such as Egypt, Lebanon and Tunisia (in the latter, the rate has decreased from 46.2 in 1960 to 36.1 in 1970). High fertility levels seem to be linked with relative poverty, traditional culture and values, and the limitations of family planning institutions. On the other hand, mortality rates are still high, with a high incidence of infant mortality and a low expectation of life at birth, although they are decreasing in some countries, with development and improvements in health systems.

Considerable external migrations are taking place in the Arab world, from within the region and from outside, thus influencing the size of the population, particularly in the Arab Gulf States, and favouring the development of subregional labour markets.[2] Important internal migrations, especially rural-urban migrations resulting from demographic pressure in predominantly agricultural economies and the attraction of major cities, also affect population distribution. While the emigration of skilled personnel often aggravates manpower imbalances in sending countries, rural-urban migration seems to lead to various forms of labour under-utilisation and poverty in urban areas.

Rapid population growth in Arab countries creates a pressure on natural resources and influences their economic patterns and levels of living. Regarding land pressure, it is worth noting that, although population density is generally low (except in Lebanon and Bahrain, see table 2), it is uneven and only a rough measure, since it includes land which is not or cannot be populated. Thus, in Egypt, only 3.55 per cent of the total territory is populated, which raises the density ratio in this part from 35 to 1,000 inhabitants per square km.

As concerns levels of living, they are generally low. In 1973, the per capita GDP was estimated at US$400 in South-West Asia and only US$200 in Northern Africa (at 1960 constant prices, see table 1). Of course, these averages cover wide differences between countries (e.g. between Kuwait - around US$4,000 - and the Yemen Arab Republic - only US$100). However, even oil-rich countries with high per capita income still present the characteristics of economically less developed countries (e.g. as regards the level and structure of production and employment, educational levels and qualifications of the labour force, etc.). This points to the need, not only for moderating population growth in many Arab countries, but also for overcoming existing structural socio-economic constraints to development. This can be done through more active national policies but also better regional co-operation schemes pooling to some extent economic, financial and human resources.

---

[1] Much of the information included here is due to M. Rasevic. See his paper: "Population, employment and development in Arab countries", E/ECWA/ILO/WG.4/2, Seminar on Manpower and Employment Planning in the Arab Countries, Beirut, 12-24 May 1975.

[2] See A.M. Farrag: "Migration between Arab countries" (published in this volume).

Table 1

Estimates of population, labour force, employment,
unemployment and GDP in South-West Asia
and Northern Africa, 1960-90

Indicator	1960	1970	1973	1980	1990	Annual growth rate (%)			
						1960- 1970	1970- 1973	1973- 1980	1980- 1990
South-West Asia[1]									
Population ('000)	58 370	77 109	84 260	104 301	140 283	2.8	3.0	3.1	3.1
Labour force ('000)	22 200	27 376	29 310	34 962	45 938	2.1	2.3	2.5	2.8
Employment ('000)	20 850	25 996	28 080	33 600	44 400	2.2	2.6	2.7	2.9
Unemployment ('000)	1 350	1 380	1 230	1 362	1 538	-	-	-	-
Unemployment rate (%)	6.1	5.0	4.2	3.9	3.3	-	-	-	-
Employment (%):									
- Agriculture	53.0	40.0	36.0	29.0	20.0	-	-	-	-
- Manufacturing, mining, energy and transport	13.8	18.5	20.0	23.0	26.0	-	-	-	-
- Services, banks, financial institutions	16.9	19.8	21.0	23.0	26.0	-	-	-	-
- Construction, commerce, undetermined	16.3	21.7	23.0	25.0	28.0	-	-	-	-
GDP (US$ million/ 1960)	13 900	27 300	33 700	57 800	122 500	7.0	7.3	8.0	7.8
Per capita GDP (US$ 1960)	240	355	400	555	875	4.1	4.2	4.8	4.6
Northern Africa[2]									
Population ('000)	65 392	86 606	95 200	119 385	163 230	2.9	3.3	3.3	3.2
Labour force ('000)	18 882	23 600	25 560	30 965	41 850	2.3	2.6	2.7	3.0
Employment ('000)	17 527	20 880	23 580	28 600	38 700	1.8	3.1	2.8	3.1
Unemployment ('000)	1 355	1 820	1 980	2 365	3 150	-	-	-	-
Unemployment rate (%)	7.2	7.7	7.7	7.6	7.6	-	-	-	-
Employment (%):									
- Agriculture	63.2	56.6	54.0	44.0	30.0	-	-	-	-
- Manufacturing, mining, energy and transport	10.1	12.7	14.0	18.0	24.0	-	-	-	-
- Services, banks, financial institutions	13.7	14.9	15.0	18.0	21.0	-	-	-	-
- Construction, commerce, undetermined	13.0	15.8	17.0	20.0	25.0	-	-	-	-
GDP (US$ million/ 1960)	9 100	15 500	19 100	32 700	70 600	5.5	7.0	8.0	8.0
Per capita GDP (US$ 1960)	140	180	200	275	430	2.6	3.8	4.6	4.0

[1] Includes Arab countries (Bahrain, Gaza Strip, Iraq, Jordan, Kuwait, Lebanon, Oman, Qatar, Saudi Arabia, Syria, United Arab Emirates, Yemen Arab Republic and Yemen Democratic Republic), Cyprus, Israel and Turkey.

[2] Includes Algeria, Egypt, Libya, Morocco, Sudan, Tunisia, Ifni and ex-Spanish North Africa and Sahara.

Source: Extracted from Yves Sabolo: "Employment and unemployment 1960-90", International Labour Review, Vol. 112, No. 6, December 1975, pp. 401-417. Revised estimates and projections of the labour force are being prepared by the Statistical Bureau of the ILO.

Table 2

Estimates of population size in 1970 and 1975,
population growth rates and population density
in Arab countries

Country	Population[1] (in thousands)		Annual growth rate (%)	Density ratio[2] (per square km)
	1970	1975		
Algeria	14 330	16 792	3.22	6
Bahrain	215	251	3.14	360
Egypt	33 329	37 543	2.41	35
Gaza Strip	501	594	3.47	-
Iraq	9 356	11 067	3.42	23
Jordan	2 280	2 688	3.35	25
Kuwait	760	1 085	7.38	51
Lebanon	2 469	2 869	3.05	285
Libya	1 938	2 255	3.07	1
Morocco	15 126	17 504	2.96	35
Oman	657	766	3.12	3
Qatar	79	92	3.09	4
Saudi Arabia	7 740	8 966	2.98	4
Sudan	15 695	18 268	3.08	7
Syria	6 247	7 259	3.05	36
Tunisia	5 137	5 747	2.27	33
United Arab Emirates	190	222	3.16	2
Yemen Arab Republic	5 767	6 668	2.94	31
Yemen Democratic Republic	1 436	1 667	3.03	5

[1] United Nations Population Projections, Medium Variant, ESA/P/WP.56, October 1975.

[2] United Nations Demographic Yearbook.

High fertility levels and low expectation of life at birth help to explain the young age structure in Arab countries, characterised by large proportions of children (aged 0 to 14), and small proportions of the aged (65 years and over). This structure involves a high dependency ratio as well as heavy pressures on social services. Also, the relatively high proportion of the 15 to 24 age group raises the delicate problem of absorbing into the labour market new entrants, often without the required skills and motivations.

Rapid population growth during the last decades has also implied rapid growth of the population of working age (15 to 64 age group). Table 3 presents estimates showing that the annual growth rates of the working age population during 1970-75 ranged from 2.7 to 3.5 per cent. It was highest in Algeria. However, activity rates remained low (between 21 and 28 per cent), mainly due to low female participation (between 2 and 13 per cent). The latter (although underestimated mainly due to inadequate reporting of family workers) seems to be linked not only with generally low levels of manpower demand, but also with such factors as early marriage, large numbers of children, limited educational attainments and other cultural and institutional factors (e.g. negative attitudes of men towards female activity outside the home, etc.).

Table 3

Estimates of rates of growth of working age population and crude activity rates in Arab countries

Country	Annual growth rate of working age population (1970-75)[1]	Crude activity rate[2]			
		Year	Male	Female	Both sexes
Algeria	3.5	1966	42.2	1.8	21.7
Bahrain	-	1971	49.0	3.3	27.9
Egypt	2.7	1973	49.3	3.1	26.4
Iraq	3.4	-	-	-	-
Jordan	3.2	1971	43.1	2.6	23.1
Kuwait	5.9	1970	53.8	5.2	32.8
Lebanon	3.2	1970	43.8	9.5	26.9
Libya	2.9	1964	46.6	2.7	25.6
Morocco	3.2	1971	44.5	8.0	26.3
Saudi Arabia	2.7	-	-	-	-
Sudan	3.0	-	-	-	-
Syria	3.4	1973	38.5	10.0	24.3
Tunisia	3.5	1971	41.2	12.9	26.8
Yemen Arab Republic	2.7	-	-	-	-
Yemen Democratic Republic	2.7	1973	42.4	9.4	25.8

[1] United Nations Population Projections, quoted in Rasevic, op. cit.

[2] ILO Year Book of Labour Statistics, 1975.

Rapid growth of the working age population was accompanied by similar increases in the labour force (i.e. the proportion of the working age population which is economically active). Table 4 presents estimates showing that the annual growth rates of the labour force during 1970-75 ranged from 2.23 per cent (in Saudi Arabia) to 2.95 per cent (in Iraq).[1] If we except oil-rich countries, generally under-populated, where high labour force growth rates could stimulate production, such rates can have adverse effects in countries overpopulated and without important natural resources (e.g. Egypt). In the latter countries, labour force pressures tend to produce an increase in unemployment and underemployment (especially among the 15 to 24 age group), as well as a deterioration in living standards, in view of the difficulties of their economies to absorb the growing numbers entering the labour market.

Table 4

Labour force estimates and projections in
Arab countries, 1970-85

Country	Labour force projections (in thousands)				Annual growth rate (%)		
	1970	1975	1980	1985	1970-75	1975-80	1980-85
Algeria	3 369	3 894	4 545	5 362	2.94	3.14	3.36
Egypt	9 174	10 357	11 741	13 426	2.46	2.54	2.72
Iraq	2 395	2 770	3 224	3 784	2.95	3.08	3.25
Jordan	564	641	737	857	2.59	2.83	3.06
Kuwait	282	431	637	911	8.85	8.13	7.42
Lebanon and Gaza Strip	864	986	1 112	1 264	2.68	2.43	2.60
Libya	488	550	625	721	2.42	2.59	2.90
Morocco	4 161	4 782	5 543	6 516	2.82	3.00	3.29
Oman, Bahrain, Qatar, UAE	290	331	381	441	2.68	2.85	2.97
Saudi Arabia	2 109	2 355	2 649	3 025	2.23	2.38	2.69
Sudan	5 065	5 830	6 760	7 938	2.85	3.00	3.26
Syria	1 574	1 817	2 109	2 466	2.91	3.03	3.18
Tunisia	1 273	1 457	1 685	1 964	2.74	2.95	3.11
Yemen Arab Republic	1 689	1 911	2 178	2 512	2.50	2.65	2.89
Yemen Democratic Republic	347	388	436	498	2.26	2.36	2.69

Source: Compiled from ILO Labour Force Projections, Parts I and II, Asia and Africa, Geneva, 1971.

---

[1] We except Kuwait, where the growth of the labour force was greatly determined by immigration movements.

   To what extent will present trends in population and the labour force continue up to 1990? Demographic projections prepared by the United Nations seem to indicate that, despite decreases in birth rates, population in Arab countries will continue to grow rapidly, due to its young age structure and further declines in death rates. Table 1 estimates future annual growth rates at 3.1 per cent in South-West Asia and 3.2 per cent in Northern Africa.

   Most significant increases will take place in the working age group and in the labour force. Indeed, table 1 suggests that the annual growth rates of the labour force would considerably increase during 1973-80 and 1980-90[1]: from 2.5 to 2.8 per cent in South-West Asia and from 2.7 to 3.0 per cent in Northern Africa. While such rates might represent an advantage in Arab countries rich in natural resources and with low population densities (most oil-producing countries), they could raise serious labour absorption problems in the other countries.

Employment, unemployment and underemployment

   Concern about future labour absorption is justified by the traditional structure of most Arab economies. In spite of variations, one can notice the general preponderance of the agricultural sector, with relatively low proportions of the active population in the secondary sector, and relatively high proportions in the tertiary sector (see table 5). It seems that, mainly due to the insufficient development and low labour intensity of the secondary sector, rural migrants enter numerous service activities.

Table 5

Structure of economically active population in Arab countries

Country	Year	Sector of activity		
		Primary	Secondary	Tertiary
Algeria	1966	56.7	14.1	29.2
Egypt	1966	53.3	16.2	30.5
Libya	1964	37.1	19.0	43.9
Morocco	1971	53.1	17.2	29.7
Tunisia	1966	42.6	19.3	38.1
Bahrain	1971	6.7	34.5	58.8
Kuwait	1970	1.7	34.2	64.1
Lebanon	1970	18.9	25.3	55.8
Syria	1971	58.2	16.9	24.9

Source: Calculated by Rasevic, op. cit., on the basis of data included in Year Book of Labour Statistics, ILO.

---

[1] The labour force during these periods is not affected by decreases in birth rates, since persons of working age at that time are already born.

Will these patterns continue in the future? Estimates of employment growth during 1973-90 presented in table 1 have assumed considerable changes in the economic structures of Arab countries. Thus, the proportion of persons employed in agriculture would decrease during that period from 36 to 20 per cent of total employment in South-West Asia, and from 54 to 30 per cent in Northern Africa (less industrialised than the former). Conversely, the proportions of persons employed in the secondary and tertiary sectors would considerably increase. Such changes would go together with a strengthening and greater diversification of the productive capacity of the countries concerned. They would enable employment growth to match, and even slightly exceed, the growth of the labour force. As a result, unemployment rates would drop from 4.2 to 3.3 per cent in South-West Asia and from 7.7 to 7.6 per cent in Northern Africa.

However, for these changes to materialise, considerable action will be needed to remove the structural constraints which are behind the employment problem. For the time being, this problem manifests itself in different ways. It can firstly take the shape of open unemployment, i.e. queues of workers, outside labour exchanges or in the market place, seeking but unable to find jobs. The extent of such unemployment is usually misrepresented, since all job seekers do not register at employment exchanges and the latter tend to limit their coverage to urban areas. Thus, in 1973, only 4,060 job seekers were recorded in Sudan's Employment Office Statistics, as compared with 76,500 job seekers registered in the Syrian Labour Force Sample Survey![1] Nevertheless, it exists and affects particularly the educated youth in urban areas, in view of the lack of employment opportunities in the modern sector which could match the aspirations of young workers. This form of unemployment has to be carefully watched, since it could create dangerous socio-political tensions.

Besides open unemployment, many forms of underemployment obtain in Arab countries. Seasonal underemployment in agriculture is quite usual (e.g. in Egypt). A less visible form of labour underutilisation exists in the tertiary sector, where considerable numbers of persons can be found performing jobs with low productivity and incomes, or which do not conform with their qualifications and experience (e.g. university graduates performing clerical jobs which require only secondary school certificates). Such underemployment seems to be frequent in the public sector (e.g. in Egypt, but also Syria, Iraq and other countries), crowded with persons contributing little to a truly defined social product. It can also be observed in the informal service sectors (e.g. in Tunisia), where rural migrants but also new entrants into the labour force accept low-income jobs awaiting better earning opportunities in the modern sector. Finally, market distortions in favour of high wages in the latter, strengthened by various institutional factors (e.g. government policies, minimum wage legislation, organised trade unions, etc.), tend to create a situation of wage dualism aggravating existing income inequalities.

Labour surpluses in Arab countries often coexist with labour shortages. Indeed, in many countries, the composition of the demand for labour does not match the structure of manpower supply, with resulting excess supply of certain categories of skills and excess demand for other categories. These imbalances cannot be fully corrected in the short term by wage movements, since wage signals take time to influence the educational qualifications of the labour force and Arab labour markets are relatively fragmented (e.g. a white-collar worker might not accept, nor be suitable for, manual jobs). Individual job preferences, little affected by existing labour market mechanisms (e.g. employment information system, labour exchanges, vocational guidance and training activities, etc.), tend to reinforce labour market rigidities.

Of course, the Arab world is not homogeneous. Despite common cultural, social and political features, Arab economies are diverse. There are differences in cultivable land (soils are fertile in some countries, arid in others), mineral resource endowments (eight countries are rich in oil, while others have only scant minerals), financial resources including reserves of gold and foreign exchange, levels and structure of income and employment, physical and social infrastructure, institutional features (e.g. forms of government, fiscality, land tenure systems, etc.), size, population and density, fertility and mortality rates, migration patterns, literacy, educational and skill levels, etc. Hence differences in their employment patterns.

---

[1] See ILO, Year Book of Labour Statistics, Geneva, 1975.

In this connection, one can distinguish three groups of countries.[1] A first group includes oil economies with relatively small populations and meagre non-oil resources (Bahrain, Kuwait, Libya, Qatar, Saudi Arabia and the United Arab Emirates). These countries do not suffer from open unemployment; on the contrary, they experience low participation rates and labour shortages, which they tend to compensate through imports of expatriate labour force. However, the availability of important financial resources seems to encourage an overmanning of government services and disguised underemployment in the tertiary sector. Government policies of absorbing in the public service new entrants into the labour force stimulate themselves the rise of employment expectations which do not match the economy's manpower requirements. Hence the risk of seeing labour surpluses coexisting with skills shortages.

A second group of Arab countries includes economies with relatively large populations as related to land and other natural resources (Egypt, Jordan, Morocco, Tunisia, the Yemen Arab Republic and, only to some extent, Algeria). These are labour-surplus economies where population pressures result in underemployment in agriculture[2], rural-urban migration, open unemployment in the modern urban sector and disguised underemployment in the informal urban sector. Government policies involving significant absorption of redundant labour into the public service (e.g. in Egypt) represent only a relief operation since they tend to perpetuate work aspirations which also do not match the economy's requirements. On the other hand, emigration policies followed by Algeria, Morocco and, more recently, Egypt, risk creaming off their best workers, thus impoverishing the human capital stock at their disposal.

A last group of countries includes economies with more favourable land/man ratios than the second (e.g. Sudan), and even oil revenues, although with larger populations than the first (e.g. Iraq and Syria). These countries share some of the employment characteristics of the first group, including labour over-absorption in a public sector which enjoys good wages, with resulting skills shortages in the other sectors.[3] However, capital resources are less abundant (especially in Sudan), which also implies a certain amount of labour redundancy.

To conclude, it seems that the employment problem is mainly caused by structural imbalances in the socio-economic structure, i.e. in resource endowment (land, capital and labour) and in the skill composition of the active population. Thus, Egypt's problem is basically its land/man ratio, while Saudi Arabia's problem seems to be the shortage of skilled manpower in relation to capital funds. Labour market imperfections and rigidities, and slow development of demand, tend to aggravate these initial imbalances. Although government policies may attempt to remove these weaknesses, in particular through educational policies influencing the composition of manpower supply, through direct recruitment to the public service influencing the structure of labour demand and through wage determination, these interventions often create incentives which, unfortunately, work in the opposite direction. Hence the interest of turning now to policy instruments which could lead in the future to economic structures and markets more favourable to employment promotion. We shall limit our analysis to the general policy issues and approaches which were examined at the Beirut Seminar.

---

[1] We are following here the distinction made by R.E. Mabro in his paper entitled: "Employment, choice of technology, sectoral priorities" (published in this volume).

[2] See A. Mohie-Eldin: "Underemployment in Egyptian agriculture" (published in this volume).

[3] See K. Hameed: "Manpower and employment planning in Iraq and the Syrian Arab Republic" (published in this volume).

Part Two

General policy issues and approaches

Population and migration policies

Firstly, population and migration policies can be utilised to influence economic and employment patterns. However, such policies will have to adapt to the diversity of conditions existing in Arab countries. While rapid population growth and selective immigration might be desirable in the first group of countries defined above, i.e. those with rich natural resources and small populations, the reduction of fertility and birth rates seems to be a must in the second group, i.e. labour-surplus countries with large populations as related to land and natural resources.

This diversity of conditions indeed is reflected in the population and immigration policies of the countries concerned. Thus, Kuwait, Libya, Qatar, Saudi Arabia and the United Arab Emirates, which belong to the first group of countries, aim at significantly larger populations, either through natural increase or through immigration. On the contrary, Egypt, Morocco and Tunisia, which belong to the second group, have official family planning programmes designed to reduce fertility rates. They also encourage the emigration of their nationals. Governments of most of the other countries either support family planning activities within the framework of their health and social welfare programmes (e.g. Algeria, Iraq, Sudan and the Yemen Democratic Republic), or encourage the activities undertaken by private associations (e.g. Lebanon and Jordan). Only a few countries have no position.[1]

Thus, family planning presents particular importance in labour-surplus Arab countries. In their case, it seems that existing programmes, if they were expanded and made accessible to the rural and poor sections of the population, would, in the long run, help to slow down the growth of the labour force and ease the employment problem. In the short run, the dependency burden would be reduced.

Concerning migrations, one should distinguish between rural-urban and inter-Arab movements. Very few Arab countries have really attempted to check urban population increase, with all its resulting problems. However, balanced demographic growth between urban and rural areas is in the interest of both economic and employment growth. The solution seems to lie in the design of comprehensive rural development strategies, to be complemented by appropriate urbanisation and regional development policies.

As regards inter-Arab workers' movements, mainly affecting skilled manpower, they tend to be more or less spontaneous. No permanent regional or bilateral institution exists for regulating such movements in the light of information on respective manpower needs. The same lack of co-ordination obtains within the countries concerned, where responsibilities for migration tend to be fragmented between different agencies often pursuing inconsistent policies. The situation results in an aggravation (a) of skill shortages in manpower-exporting countries, already affected by the "brain drain", in favour of the richer (e.g. oil-producing) countries, and consequently (b) of development inequalities. On the other hand, expatriates do not always enjoy equality of treatment in the manpower-importing countries, where they often fill the undesired jobs.[2]

To remedy this situation, more co-ordinated migration policies seem to be called for at the regional level, which could stimulate development in both sending and receiving countries, and also facilitate regional economic integration. In particular, thought should be given to developing an information system through

---

[1] See IPPF: "Family planning and population policies in Middle East and Northern Africa region", First Regional Population Conference, Beirut, 1974.

[2] See A.M. Farrag, op. cit.

which (a) both categories of countries would exchange information on their manpower and working conditions and (b) the impact on both of the proposed migrations would be assessed. Such information could greatly facilitate the timely rotation of certain categories of manpower whose work presents important seasonal variations (e.g. construction and agricultural workers), as well as the formulation of agreements covering such movements. It could also assist in the planning of regional education and training facilities (e.g. training of instructors, fellowships, etc.). It was felt at the Beirut Seminar that the establishment in the region of a team of employment experts could help in the promotion of such a system.

Education and training policies

The education and training system can also be oriented towards more dynamic economic and employment structures. For the time being, it seems in many Arab countries to perpetuate traditional imbalances. Rapid developments in education have taken place. However, these have mostly implied quantitative expansion along lines inherited from former regimes, to the detriment of quality. Lack of efficacy is evidenced by increasing costs with high repetition and drop-out rates. National imbalances are aggravated by lack of balance between regions, urban and rural areas, males and females, and social groups (better enrolment rates can be observed for the urban, male and well-to-do categories). Of even more concern is the maladjustment of the output of the system and the labour market, with symptoms such as the arts graduates surpluses and educated unemployment, the "brain drain" and shortages of technicians and skilled manpower. This mismatch is aggravated by the weaknesses of existing labour market mechanisms (e.g. wage structure, manpower information, vocational guidance, recruitment, training and placement of the workers, various obstacles to occupational mobility, etc.).[1]

In the light of the above, it seems that a new look is needed at the structure and contents of Arab education and training systems. In particular, it was felt at the Beirut Seminar that a proper balance should be established between the development of primary education, to be generalised, and the development of secondary and higher learning. Secondary schools could usefully combine general teaching with practical skills preparing young people for adult life. However, more adequate vocational preparation could mainly be achieved through the expansion of technical education and vocational training facilities as compared with general education. In this regard, appropriate balance will have to be found between government-sponsored institutions and private apprenticeship or in-plant training and upgrading programmes. With respect to higher education policies, they should be reviewed with the aim of achieving a better match between the supply of university graduates and their demand on the labour market.

At all the above levels, particular attention needs to be devoted to the qualitative aspects of education, including teachers' and instructors' training and improvements in teaching methods. Educational planning should also take into account the special needs of less privileged groups (e.g. females, needy students, the rural poor, etc.). It should be complemented by appropriate action on labour market mechanisms, including the revision of the structure of wages, salaries and other incentives which induce people to select certain courses of education in numbers that exceed the labour-absorption capacity of the economy, and a better organisation of vocational guidance, training and placement activities. Finally, education, training and labour market policies need to be based on a permanent system of data collection and analysis which could provide the information and understanding required for their intervention.

Sectoral priorities and choice of technology

Employment growth in Arab countries will greatly depend upon the priorities assigned in their development plans and programmes to various sectors of economic activity. It will also depend on the choice of techniques which will be actually utilised in these sectors. In this respect, it can be noted that, although most Arab development plans gave during the last years high priority to industrialisation, industrial development did not lead to high employment gains, nor to noticeable changes in their employment structures. On the contrary, the tertiary sector, enjoying relatively low priority, showed the greatest employment expansion.

---

[1] See M. Debeauvais: "Employment and education in the Arab countries: The data and their interpretation" (published in this volume).

The reason seems to lie mainly in the choice of labour-saving technologies in the modern sector. In oil-rich countries, the abundance of primary resources coupled with manpower shortages makes the choice of sophisticated technologies both feasible and necessary. Even in other countries, some sectors present limited flexibility in the choice of technology: investment in heavy industry, a priority in many countries, generally requires the use of advanced technologies. In other sectors, there is more scope for adopting appropriate labour-intensive technologies. However, it seems that Arab countries prefer to depend in their choice on imported advanced technologies, more prestigious but also labour-saving, expensive and pre-senting problems of handling and maintenance. Foreign consultants as well as local engineers trained abroad usually recommend such technologies. This often results in the creation of enclaves of modernity in an ocean of backwardness, involving not only limited employment creation but also considerable labour-displacement in the traditional sector.[1]

For correcting these biases, it is important that technological choices take place within a well-defined development framework. In particular, fiscal and investment policies and legislation should avoid favouring systematically capital-using technologies and the creation of excess capacity of production. In addition, opportunities for applying labour-using technologies should be identified on a project-by-project basis, and attention given to the possibility of subdividing individual projects into processes, some of which may lead to labour-intensive technologies. In the case of basic industries, efforts should be made to develop linkages and complementarities with other industries.

Possibilities of improving existing local technologies to fit the socio-economic conditions of Arab countries also need to be explored. As to training facilities, they will have to adapt to the coexistence of various types of techno-logies. In order to facilitate these interventions, it was suggested at the Beirut Seminar to create a regional centre responsible for identifying, adapting or developing appropriate technologies, and for disseminating among Arab States such information. It was hoped that such a centre would not only stimulate employ-ment creation in new activities but also avoid labour displacement in existing ones.

Trade policies

Commercial policies (e.g. tariffs, quantitative restrictions, export taxes and subsidies) often have an adverse impact on employment. Indeed, protection measures can induce negative distortions in the price relationships among sectors and parti-cular goods. Thus, higher real protection given to industrial goods, including the farmers' inputs, can create a bias against agricultural products and, consequently, employment in agriculture. High tariffs on finished consumer goods tend to encourage the development of a modern sector (often multinational companies) with high money wage rates and advanced technology, which employs little labour and has negative effects on employment in competing labour-intensive small-scale activities. Low duties (or no duties at all because of special investment incentive laws) on imports of equipments and industrial inputs (which besides are subsidised through artificially low interest rates) favour the introduction of sophisticated labour-saving technologies and also discourage the domestic production of these goods. Such a protection system (as well as some forms of foreign aid) may make it more profitable to process foreign raw materials and intermediate inputs than to export locally processed domestic raw materials, with adverse effects on the employment situation.[2]

Planning of the foreign sector should, therefore, integrate employment considera-tions and attempt to correct the above price distortions. For that purpose, improve-ments are needed in the collection and analysis of information on the profiles and effects of tariffs and other commercial policy measures. On the other hand, one can contend that developing Arab countries should not attach exaggerated weight to inter-national prices in their process of decision-making. They could as well adopt internally oriented development paths, taking mainly into account their basic needs, including the need for diversifying their economies.

---

[1] See R.E. Mabro, op. cit.

[2] See H.H. Bell: "Trade policy, relative prices and employment" (published in this volume).

However, such policies should be selective and minimise the negative implications mentioned above. To avoid the dangers of excessive competition between Arab countries, more co-operation is also called for at the regional level. Better economic integration would indeed generate wider markets for Arab goods as well as promote regional specialisation in the processing and trade of local materials, resulting in improved levels and structures of production and employment.

Employment planning frameworks

More dynamic co-operation at the regional level will imply a strengthening of the national systems responsible for employment planning, as well as a certain degree of harmonisation between their policies. For the time being, these are diverse. In some countries (e.g. Algeria, Egypt, Syria and Iraq)[1], the public sector is the major employer and plays a dominant role in development and employment policy formulation and implementation. Special emphasis is laid in these countries on industrialisation and development of technical education, and surplus labour, including university graduates, tends to be absorbed in the public sector. Measures imposing on the young graduates periods of service for the Government, restricting the workers' movements from the public to the private sector and discouraging the emigration of critical skills, are sometimes adopted (e.g. Syria). Although such systems generally permit a greater control of the State on employment mechanisms, they also involve a certain amount of labour underutilisation in the public sector, skills shortages in the private sector and delicate problems of over-all co-ordination. It seems that this basic problem of balanced allocation of human resources calls, in the countries concerned, for comprehensive employment reviews of the type organised with the assistance of the ILO within the framework of its World Employment Programme.

In other countries (e.g. Lebanon[2], Jordan, Morocco, Tunisia, etc.), the private sector tends to be more active than the public sector and the local labour market freer of government restrictions. However, the very indicative character of development planning, the weaknesses of planning institutions, and the lack of clearly defined employment policies tend to favour the perpetuation of existing manpower imbalances (e.g. rural-urban migration, open unemployment in the modern urban sector and underemployment in agriculture and informal activities). Similar weaknesses in administrative structures and planning capabilities can be observed in oil-rich countries (with problems of skills shortages and regulation of expatriate labour) and the less-developed countries (with serious labour surpluses). Here again, the solution seems to lie in a strengthening of manpower and employment planning mechanisms as well as in the formulation of over-all development strategies giving due consideration to human resources objectives and policies.

Conclusion

To conclude, it is clear that most Arab countries have serious employment problems to contend with. The nature of these problems varies considerably between them, ranging from situations of absolute manpower shortage necessitating large-scale immigration of workers, to problems of chronic unemployment, underemployment and poverty. In a number of countries, the latter problems coincide with shortages of skilled and technical personnel for the modern sector, and these are in some cases made more acute by emigration of such personnel to the oil-rich countries. Because by and large all Arab countries have made the modern sector the cornerstone of their future development, there is, everywhere, a keen awareness of the crippling effect that these shortages have, or could have, on the further growth of the modern sector and this explains the emphasis placed, both in national policies and during the discussions at the Beirut Seminar, on identifying the shortages and on the development and improvement of education and training facilities for meeting skill requirements.

On the other hand, surprisingly little attention seems to have been given hitherto in many Arab countries to the problems of unemployment, underemployment and low incomes, despite their acknowledged prevalence. Little effort has been made to

---

[1] See the papers of A. Mohie-Eldin and K. Hameed, op. cit., and the paper of A. Remili: "Employment and planned development of the Algerian economy" (published in this volume).

[2] See J.F. Audroing and M. Vernières: "The working of the labour market in Lebanon" (published in this volume).

measure them or to follow their evolution. There seems to be an implicit assumption that modern sector growth will gradually absorb the whole population and redound to the general benefit. Yet the evidence from many parts of the region is that, as in other parts of the developing world and except in the small oil-rich countries, employment growth in the modern sector fails to keep pace with the rapidly growing labour force; that the income gap between people working in the largely urban modern sector, and people in the traditional sector, especially rural people, is widening; that this gap feeds a continuing rural-urban stream, mainly to the larger centres, which is in excess of the opportunities for stable and remunerative employment and which accentuates the dualism, in those centres, between a relatively prosperous class of workers integrated in the modern sector and the large and growing numbers who find only casual employment or eke out a living in various small-scale, informal sector activities. This evolution, contrasting with the stated objectives of full employment and equity, can only generate social tensions which could eventually bring development to a halt. Yet it seems an inevitable consequence of present patterns of development.

The setting is of course totally different in the smaller oil-rich countries, with their abundant resources and chronic over-all manpower shortage. Yet the stratification of jobs between nationals and non-nationals is likewise beginning to cause concern for its longer-term social implications.

Thus, despite their differences, Arab countries seem to have a common need to reappraise their development strategies using as a criterion not only their success in achieving high rates of GNP growth, but the extent to which such growth benefits all strata of the population (including, in oil-rich countries, non-national workers whose employment even in menial tasks contributes to over-all development). Such a reappraisal involves a review of sectoral priorities in development, e.g. the emphasis to be placed on agriculture or industry, on large- or small-scale enterprises, on primary or higher levels of education, on preventive or curative medicine, or generally the rural-urban balance in providing a number of services. It involves also a review of macro-economic policies in the fiscal, financial, monetary or trade fields which may restrict the expansion of employment (e.g. by encouraging the introduction of labour-saving equipments) or adversely affect the incomes of certain categories of workers and the development potential of the sectors employing them (e.g. through the maintenance of artificially low agricultural prices).

A major purpose of the Beirut Seminar was to further awareness and discussion of this multidimensional nature of the employment problem and of employment policy, and several of the papers reproduced in this volume highlight it. The variety of situations encountered in the Arab world has also been illustrated, since no uniform solutions are applicable to all countries. At the same time, the large and growing movements of manpower taking place between Arab countries have been analysed together with the measures needed to develop, beyond the necessary frame of national manpower and employment policies, regional co-operation designed to avoid serious distortions on the regional employment market. The conclusions adopted by the Seminar, which are reproduced at the end of this volume, reflect the consensus reached on this wide range of issues, and the directions in which the participants felt that future action should go both at the national level and through regional and international co-operation.

I. APPROACHES

EMPLOYMENT, CHOICE OF TECHNOLOGY, SECTORAL PRIORITIES

by

R. E. Mabro*

INTRODUCTION

The subject of this paper is wide and open to many different interpretations. Treatises could be written on the employment problem and on choice of technology, and the ill-specified issue of sectoral priorities draws in the whole topic of planning. The geographical reference is also wide. Arab countries are numerous. Despite common cultural, social or political features, Arab economies are diverse - more diverse perhaps than any random sample of LDCs and certainly more diverse than any group of industrialised countries. The reason is that natural resource endowments and structural characteristics, always very heterogeneous matter more for the study of an LDC than an industrialised country. The distribution of natural resources is very uneven in Arab countries. Some have the most fertile soils of the world, others the most arid. Some have considerable oil wealth, others scant mineral resources. Some are among the most over populated countries of the third world: others have very small populations scattered over large areas of land. The structural characteristics (composition of GDP and employment), the institutional features (forms of Government, fiscality, tenure systems etc.), and the stage of development as measured by real indicators (literacy, skills, health, infrastructure etc.) are all very diverse.

We cannot possibly do justice to such a vast subject and bring in the analysis all the variations warranted by differences in the economic structure of the countries concerned within the limits of a short paper.

I thus had to make painful choices. The treatment of the issues is necessarily selective and my hope is that my particular selection will not disappoint too many. I have been consciously blunt and unqualified on some points not for the sake of sterile controversy but in order to stimulate a debate which may throw new light on difficult problems.

The paper is divided into two main sections. In the first, the nature of the employment problem is discussed. In the second section I looked at theoretical and policy issues related to choice of technology and sectoral priorities.

The main themes of the paper are the following: a) the employment problem in Arab countries manifests itself in different ways. It need not arise merely as open unemployment. Many disguised forms of under employment obtain. The coexistence of labour shortages and labour surpluses in different parts of the economy is a common occurence; b) the employment problem is attributed to imbalances in the economic structure. The imbalances are so pronounced that they may not be completely removed by the normal operations of markets, imperfect as they usually are; c) the employment problem is part of a global development problem; d) in most LDCs, industry is the planner's favourite sector. But industry makes small contributions to employment. In practice, the tertiary sector which does not rank high in planner's priority is the leading employment sector; e) choice of technology is restricted by technical, economic and socio-political factors; f) the structure of aggregate demand is a neglected but perhaps significant register to be considered besides choice of technique and sectoral planning.

A. EMPLOYMENT AND UNEMPLOYMENT

Employment is the main concern. A meaningful study of sectoral strategies and choice of techniques presupposes an analysis of the employment issue. A few remarks on the nature of the problem in LDCs in general, and in Arab countries in particular, are a necessary preamble. The issues, however, are not simple and we may run from the outset into serious difficulties.

Despite the new, and much welcome, emphasis on employment and income distribution in development economics, and despite the considerable amount of work recently undertaken on these topics, there is little consensus on the definition of the employment problem, its significance, the causes and features of the phenomenon.

The definitional issue is complex because unemployment in LDCs does not only manifest itself in an open and visible way: queues of workers, outside labour exchanges or in the market place, seeking but unable to find jobs. However important, open unemployment is not the whole of the story. In many LDCs seasonal underemployment and disguised unemployment are found in the two largest sectors of the economy, namely agriculture and the services.

But how to define or how to identify underemployment? It tends to take a variety of forms. It may not be easily isolated as a self-contained phenomenon with clear-cut

---

* Oxford University

features, nor can it be attributed to independent causes.   Underemployment is an integral element of a global economic, social and institutional context characterised by structural imbalances and rigidities, market distortions, lack of complementary resources to labour, deficient modes of labour utilisation and organisation and, in many instances, by widespread poverty.

Some economists prefer to restrict the definition of unemployment and underemployment to situations in which workers are willing to supply more hours of work at the going wage but are unable to do so because of deficiencies in the demand for labour.   These definitions, however, fail to do justice to the problem.   Manpower resources may be grossly underutilised when workers are physically but voluntarily underemployed in LDCs.   A worker may voluntarily supply short hours because the expected reward from an additional unit of labour time fails to compensate him for the required effort.   To argue that he is not underemployed because he voluntarily and rationally adjusts to a very constrained situation would miss the essence of the problem.

Other economists, aware of these limitations, tend to relate underemployment to low earnings and low productivity jobs.   The approach has obvious merits but suffers from a lack of rigour and may cause confusion.   Is underemployment synonymous with poverty? These concepts have different contents and ought to be distinguished, even though the dividing line may be blurred by a significant overlap.

We shall adopt another approach and attempt to identify a number of different phenomena loosely subsumed under the generic term "employment problem".   This approach recognises that the problem has several dimensions that can be usefully distinguished for both analytical and policy purposes.

One aspect of the employment problem, already mentioned, is open unemployment.   Its incidence varies from country to country, and from time to time in the same country.   Open unemployment is not exclusively an urban phenomenon, as it may arise in rural areas as well especially during the seasonal trough.   Open unemployment may be found among the educated and the non-educated.   Its extent is usually misrepresented by official statistics in LDCs, because of incomplete or faulty reporting systems.   Thus, seasonal open unemployment in agriculture seldom comes within the catchment area of labour exchanges.   Construction is a sector where demand for labour tends to fluctuate sharply from period to period.   Unemployment statistics which relate to that sector are difficult to interpret.   The point is that open unemployment, though referred to as 'visible' unemployment, may often escape the observer.

LDCs are said to suffer from 'disguised' unemployment.   This type of unemployment or underemployment is not made invisible by defective statistics, but because it is concealed by false appearances.   The concept has several meanings.   The original meaning - Joan Robinson's[1] - though least used in development economies, is perhaps the most apt.   The 'disguised unemployed' is somebody who performs a job which does not conform with his qualifications and experience, simply because he can't find any other.   Joan Robinson had the Great Depression in mind.   The concept conveys the idea of qualitative - rather than quantitative - underutilisation of labour.   The engineer who worked as a taxi-driver during the Depression was not physically unemployed or underemployed.   He may have worked harder and longer hours as a taxi-driver than as an engineer, but his specific skills were under-or-not-at-all-utilised.   Disguised unemployment in the sense of qualitative underutilisation may exist in LDCs, especially in the Government sector.   In some countries graduates perform menial clerical jobs which elsewhere are left to employees with secondary or primary school certificates.   It is true that a different phenomenon also obtains in LDCs: the manning of skilled jobs by underqualified personnel.

The classical meaning of disguised unemployment in development economies is the Nurkse-Lewis definition.[2]   There is disguised unemployment when the marginal product of labour is zero.   Disguised unemployment in this sense was thought to exist in many agrarian economies with large populations and scarce supplies of land.   A long controversy has revealed that

[1]   J. Robinson, Essays in the theory of employment, McMillan, London, 1937.

[2]   W.A. Lewis, Economic Development with unlimited supplies of Labour, The Manchester School of Economic and Social Studies, Vol.22, No.2, May 1954 and R. Nurkse, Problems of capital formation in underdeveloped countries, Blackwell, Oxford, 1953.

the concept rests on implausible assumptions about the behaviour of economic agents - peasants or farmers. Empirical research revealed that the marginal product of labour time is seldom zero in agriculture. To conclude that there is no 'employment' problem in agriculture in labour-surplus economies would be wrong. Labour may be quantitatively under-utilised because of a shortage of complementary factors. In my view the test of a disguised unemployment is whether labourers would supply more labour inputs if endowed with more land, not whether they apply their effort right up to the margin at which productivity falls to zero.

Disguised unemployment may exist in the tertiary sector. A marginal productivity definition raises further problems when applied to this sector. The reason is that the net output of services is difficult to measure independently of wages. In Government service, for example, a man's output is defined as his earnings. He may be doing nothing in his job, or he may be performing unnecessary tasks invented by him or his employers to keep up the pretence. Yet disguised unemployment may truly exist. The criterion is neither low income nor hours of work, but the absence of contribution to a truly defined social product.

Disguised unemployment in the Robinsonian sense may exist in the informal service sector. The disguised unemployed may be a migrant to the town or an entrant to the labour force bridging a waiting period for a job in the modern sector. Here, neither earnings, nor output, nor hours of work provide the criterion, simply under-utilisation of skills.

A final word on a different aspect of the 'labour utilisation problem' in LDCs may be called for. In many LDCs participation rates to the labour force are low by comparison with advanced industrial countries. The discrepancy does not merely relate to differences in age-composition or to other demographic or institutional factors. It is not just a matter of tradition which, say, keeps women at home. Participation rates are influenced by the aggregate demand for labour. Low rates are a manifestation of physical, if not qualitative, under-utilisation.

Different interpretations of the phenomena just described, not necessarily inconsistent with one another, have been put forward. One interpretation focuses on market distortions. An excess supply of labour at the going wage rate simply means that wages are above the equilibrium level. Some put the blame squarely on trade unions, Government policy, minimum wage legislation or other institutional factors responsible for placing a high floor under wages in the modern-urban sector of the economy. Recently, Michael Todaro has gone further and linked urban unemployment, internal migration and wage distortions in a formal model. The existence of a wage differential between agriculture and the modern sector attracts migrants even in conditions of surplus labour in the towns, manifested by a pool of unemployed workers. The behavioural assumption is that migrants compare the present value of expected life earnings in rural and urban occupations, and include in their calculations the probability of remaining unemployed for a while in the towns. This probability is related to the ratio of modern employment to the total urban labour force, consisting of both employed and unemployed. The system is in equilibrium, that is migration ceases, when this ratio becomes equal to the agricultural/urban wage ratio. Todaro's model expresses and elaborates, in the framework of a two-sector economy where labour markets are linked by migration, the basic economic proposition mentioned earlier, namely, that unemployment or excess supply of a resource at a going price means that this price is too high.

All that may be valid and interesting but does not take us very far. It is true that a removal of institutional constraints in labour markets would facilitate wage adjustments and, ceteris paribus, a reduction of unemployment. But the policy is seldom practicable and it is wrong to infer, even in theory, that a purely competitive labour market is cleared automatically. A perfect adjustment may be prevented by the existence of a subsistence floor, the minimum supply price which just compensates workers for the disutility of effort. An artist or an intellectual may be induced to work free, because of non-monetary rewards. In general, however, the supply price of labour is correctly assumed to be always positive. Situations in which the demand for labour is lower than total availabilities at the minimum supply price are not difficult to imagine. Such situations are common in agrarian economies where markets for wage labourers - landless peasants or members of small family farms - operate almost as perfectly as in text-book models. They occur especially during the seasonal trough, when demand is slack and supplies infinitely elastic at a very low wage rate. Open unemployment may thus obtain in systems free from institutional rigidities.

As market imperfections are but an aspect of the problem, it is natural to look at other elements for a more complete explanation. Keynes's familiar theory comes to mind. The crucial variables are aggregate demand and its determinants. But this theory is of limited relevance to many developing countries. Keynesian unemployment relates to short-term situations (the short-term being defined in terms of a fixed capital stock) characterised by excess supply of both labour and productive capacity. To concentrate on aggregate demand, and to recommend policies which attempt to resorb unemployment through shifts in the components of the aggregate demand curve, makes sense in such situations, precisely because they are assumed to be free from supply bottlenecks. In reality the issue is more complex as reflationary policies may have early repercussions on the rate of price increases and on the external balance. The unemployment problem in LDCs is often of a different nature though at times, and in certain places, Keynesian unemployment may also obtain. It typically arises in a context riddled with supply constraints. After all, the essence of under-development is the paucity of means, a poor and imbalanced endowment of factors of production complementary to labour. Unemployment then tends to be a chronic feature of the economy rather than a short-term aberration. And limiting factors on the productive or supply side of the economic system are likely to be more significant than a deficiency in aggregate demand.

A third interpretation subsumes these supply inelasticities under the broader concept of structural imbalances. As different meanings are attached to the word 'structure', and as the term 'imbalance' is not always defined with precision, the concept is sometimes dismissed on the grounds of loose thinking. Yet some of the perceptions it expresses are fundamentally correct. A few 'distinguos' may help.

One aspect of the economic structure is the composition of the resource endowment. Common sense often recognises imbalances in the composition of primary factors. Egypt, for example, is said to have too little agricultural land in relation to its agrarian population. Saudi Arabia, like some other oil-exporting countries, clearly suffers from inadequate supplies of skilled labour in relation to capital funds accruing in the form of free foreign exchange. The economist will seek stricter definitions. An imbalance in factor endowment must be revealed by significant divergences between the marginal products of two factors of production. How significant is a given discrepancy, or how symptomatic of serious imbalances, becomes again a matter of judgement. Common sense is the ultimate criterion, though it is worth recalling that the analytical detour from an initial hunch to the final reasoned judgement may not be avoided without grave risks of error. An imbalance in resource endowment need not always entail unemployment. Some primary factors - capital and labour, for example - are theoretically mobile. International migration of labour, and investment of funds abroad, can improve domestic factor proportions and yet contribute to the national income via remittances and national appropriation of profits earned in foreign placements. These considerations, however, should be heavily qualified and interpreted with caution, as they are too often misused to dismiss embarrassing issues. An imbalance in resource endowment, notwithstanding the developmental successes of countries such as the U.K. and Japan, is a disadvantage. The economy remains vulnerable to changes in external conditions which could stop or reverse the migration flow, or threaten the safety and returns of its investments abroad. An imbalance in the endowment of primary factors is a source of serious problems for the modern LDC, even in the rare instances when it does not entail unemployment of a major resource. These problems have names: possible unemployment in the future, retarded development due to constraints on absorptive capacity, risks of foreign dependence.

Another known objection to the significance of structural imbalances in resources relates to factor substitutability. Structuralists often sin in ignoring the considerable flexibility involved in production. Neoclassicists sin in believing - or, more subtly, in suggesting or implying - that the structural problem would vanish if substitutability were properly taken into account. It is true that capital scarcity may be compensated for, and is often compensated for, by an intensive recourse to labour. In the XIXth century Egypt's canals were not dug by labourers armed with shovels and spades, but virtually with bare hands. It is equally true that land scarcity can be compensated for by increased applications of capital and labour. In Egypt again, multi-cropping doubled the effective supply of land from a given restricted acreage; but multi-cropping involves a rise in both the manhour/land and the capital/land ratios. There is always some room for manoeuvre, even when the supply of a factor of production appears to be very inelastic and other resources are relatively abundant. But the flexibility is not infinite and there are circumstances when the abundant resources cannot be fully used. There is a limit on the divisibility of the scarce factor, whether it be labour, land or capital. It can be spread thin in the economy but sooner or later a point is reached when the marginal product of the complementary resource falls virtually to zero. In Sudan land is in excess supply, given present capital and labour endowments of the country. Large tracts remain uncultivated. Structural imbalances manifest themselves in the 'unemployment' of a major resource.

A strict definition of structural imbalances that would satisfy the purist may be coined. There is imbalance (given the production function) when the factor proportions are such that the marginal product of one factor is zero (or, more generally, lower than its marginal costs in use). This situation usually leads to unemployment. The Nurkse-Lewis views on disguised unemployment in agriculture involve this definition of structural imbalances.

Imbalances in factor endowments are but one aspect of the structuralist interpretation. Imbalances in the skill and educational composition of the labour force constitute another important aspect. Over the past thirty or forty years, Government policy in LDCs, people's aspirations and a host of other factors have combined to significantly increase the supply of secondary school leavers and graduates on to the labour market. In many countries the composition of the demand for labour does not match the structure of supply. Excess demand for certain categories of skills co-exist with excess supply of other categories. These disequilibria are not easily corrected in the short-term by relative wage movements. First, supply responses are delayed by perception lags and by the schooling interval - years elapse between the time a decision on the desired type of education is made and the completion of the course. Secondly, labour markets tend to be fragmented. The unemployed white-collar worker may not want to consider a manual job; conversely, he may not be recruited to such a job even if he applies for it. Put differently, labour is not perfectly mobile between jobs with different specifications. Thirdly, workers may not respond to the inducement of immediate employment opportunities in job X, if they have set their sights on job Y. That there is excess demand for X and excess supply for Y is not the relevant consideration, if X is an inferior job to Y. The worker may prefer to remain unemployed for a while, and queue for Y, rather than take on X, if this latter course of action jeopardises his future chances of getting job Y. Such behaviour is rational because the worker's objective is to maximise income over a long stretch of time.

We would thus conclude that the employment problem in LDCs is the result of a combination of factors. Deficient demand is one factor. Labour market imperfections attributable to the play of institutional forces (trade unions, government policy, legislation), concentration of buyers (monopsony), to imperfect labour mobility and to segmentation on the supply side (labour is not a homogeneous factor of production, and the substitutability of one category for another is not infinite in the short-term) are singled out by many economists as the main culprits. Such an interpretation is both true and short-sighted. Labour markets in LDCs are not more imperfect than elsewhere and yet the employment problem seems to be much more intractable. The reason is that the markets in LDCs are under considerable strain, having to cope with large initial imbalances in factor endowment and in the composition of the labour force. High rates of population growth, educational and developmental policies continually recreate these imbalances. Markets do not perform miracles. They send signals, provide opportunities for arbitrage, ease certain pressures, etc. But they cannot match the unmatchable, nor can they equilibrate the supply of, and demand for, labour below minimum supply prices, nor can they induce lagged responses at the appropriate time by sending advance signals. The Neoclassicists who believe that markets, if left unhindered, would always produce the correct adjustments, are wrong. Fortunately, few hold such extreme views. The view that most of us undoubtedly share is that markets operate within a given economic structure which often hinders more than it helps their operations. No policy-maker concerned with results can afford to ignore either element: the market and the structure. He will want to act on both.

Another conclusion may be drawn from our discussion of the employment problem. At several stages of the argument we have recognised that many LDCs could simultaneously suffer from unemployment/underemployment and labour shortages. Both are constraints on economic development, both have distributional effects, both are a source of worry to Governments and planners. It is legitimate to include these apparently contradictory phenomena in the same box, as both are manifestations of the same fundamental problem: structural imbalances which markets can ease but generally fail to remove.

The employment problem in Arab countries involves both aspects. Most suffer from shortages of certain categories of skilled manpower and most are affected by excess supply of labour in certain occupations. In some, however, the first problem is much more acute than the second, while in others labour surpluses are more in evidence than shortages. We would distinguish three groups of Arab economies.

a) Oil economies with relatively small populations and meagre non-oil resources. This group includes Libya, Kuwait, Qatar, the Emirates and, perhaps, Saudi Arabia. Open unemployment is virtually unknown in most of these economies. The aggregate domestic supply of labour seems to fall significantly short of demand. Casual evidence is provided by the size of the expatriate labour force relative to that of the national labour force. Yet in all these countries participation rates tend to be low, a situation usually attributed to Islamic traditions, which restrict the employment of women. In many of these countries Government services seem to be over-manned, and the presumption is that the tertiary sector may well be affected by disguised unemployment. The oil-economy faces a typical structural problem: lags and difficulties in the adjustment of the manpower structure to the new requirements of an economy suddenly endowed with huge financial resources for economic development. An added difficulty is due to the expectations which the oil-boom raises among the population. All naturally want to acquire some share

in the new wealth.   Those with entrepreneurial skills - a minority in any
society - will find their opportunities in private business ventures.   A
much larger group, however, will seek a secure job with the Government.   The
demand for secondary and university education, the qualifications required for
the better-paid Government jobs, increases.   And the Government cannot but
absorb in the public service school leavers and graduates as they enter the
labour market.   To leave them unemployed is politically unwise.   The
budgetary constraint does not apply in oil-economies.   On the contrary,
Governments may find that the expansion of public employment is a convenient
method of distributing to the population part of the oil income that accrues
directly to the State.   These forces further reduce the narrow scope for
adjusting over the long term the structure of labour supply to demand requirements.   The co-existence of labour surpluses and shortages may remain a
fundamental feature of these oil-economies for many decades to come.

b) Economies with large populations relative to land and other natural
resources.   At present this group comprises Egypt, Morocco and, in spite of
oil and gas, Algeria.   Whether smaller countries such as Jordan and Tunisia
belong to this category is an open question.   These countries generally
conform to the general description of the labour-surplus economy.   Population pressures against inadequate supplies of land may produce some form of
disguised unemployment in agriculture and/or induce strong movements of
population from rural areas to the towns.   Internal migration is usually the
dominant phenomenon.   It transforms disguised unemployment in agriculture
into open unemployment in the modern urban sector, or into disguised unemployment of the Robinsonian type in the informal urban sector.   The size of the
potential employment problem in these countries is often marked by (a)
Government policies which, in Egypt for example, lead to significant absorption of redundant labour into public service; and (b) external migration,
which has been very significant during the past fifteen or twenty years in
Algeria and Morocco, and which has recently been gaining momentum in Egypt.
The Egyptian policy of providing jobs in the public sector as an automatic
right to any graduate is a relief operation, not a long-term solution to the
employment problem.   The policy creates, via the demand for education/job
aspirations nexus conditions favourable to the perpetuation of the state of
affairs it purports to correct.   External migration entails costs as well as
benefits.   Migration is selective.   It tends to cream off the best workers
from each professional category.   It may create additional structural
imbalances in the composition of the labour force.   Benefits arising from
learning and acquisition of skills, or from foreign exchange remittances,
must be set against the social costs to the economy of new imbalances which
impede the process of economic development.

c) The third group comprises countries such as Iraq, Syria and Sudan.   The
common feature is a more favourable land/man ratio than in the labour-surplus
economies mentioned above.   They are widely different in other respects.
Iraq enjoys considerable oil-revenues and may share some of the employment
characteristics of oil-states described in paragraph 'a'.   The Government
absorbs more labour than it requires.   It also tends to offer good wages,
and hence influences job preferences in society in its favour.   This absorption
of labour where it is not needed aggravates shortages in sectors where labour
could make a positive contribution to the social product.   In Sudan, the problem
is a shortage of capital which hinders an efficient utilisation of both labour
and land.   A relative abundance of land does not necessarily mean that labour
is fully employed.   Diminishing returns to labour inputs may set in very
quickly because of capital scarcity.   In other words, labour which may seem
scarce in relation to land availabilities could at the same time be abundant
in relation to the capital endowment, and hence be partly unemployed or under-
utilised.

This rapid survey of the employment problem in Arab countries enables us to add to the
conclusions drawn earlier from the more general discussion on unemployment/underemployment
in LDCs.   Government policy appears to have an importance influence on labour markets.   It
influences (through education) the composition of supplies.   In many Arab countries (rich
oil-exporting as well as poor economies), the Government has been willing to shift artificially to the right the demand curve for labour, in order to prevent the manifestation of
unemployment.   Finally, Governments influence the labour market by setting wage and salary
scales for a significant proportion of the labour force (their own employees).   They partially determine the wage structure in the economy and hence weaken, to some extent, market
adjustment mechanisms.

To place an emphasis on the role of Governments may be taken as a serious qualification to the earlier emphasis on structural imbalances. This is not entirely correct. Governments are not perfectly free agents. Their policies may be attributed in part to pressures and tensions provoked by these imbalances. There is always some room for manoeuvre but the margin may be narrowly limited by severe constraints.

Having discussed aspects of the employment problem both in general terms and in the context of certain Arab economies, we are in a better position to assess remedies offered by sectoral planning and choice of techniques. The fundamental question is whether the effects of structural imbalances in resources can be minimised by adapting both the structure of the economy (sectoral priorities and balances in planning) and the technology to a lop-sided endowment.

B. SECTORS AND TECHNIQUES

a) Sectoral priorities

Economic development is associated with regular patterns of structural changes. (Structure, here, refers to the sectoral composition of GDP total employment and other macro-economic aggregates). The Clark-Fisher law is familiar.[1] It postulates a regular sequence as income grows. The share of the secondary sector (industry) in GDP and employment begins to rise at the expense of the primary sector and at a later stage the tertiary sector assumes the leading role. Simon Kuznets'[2] monumental work on the quantitative economic history of the world provides some evidence for this law. Further, Hoffman,[3] Chenery[4] and others have established a marked correlation between the share of industry in GDP and per capita incomes. The recent experience of LDCs reveals marked divergences from this behaviour. For obvious reasons, oil economies follow a pattern of their own. We cannot ignore these exceptions. In oil economies the primary sector leads the growth of incomes. On the employment side, the tertiary sector tends to lead. In other LDCs, the sequence 'primary large but declining/secondary small but rising' generally obtains, with the proviso that the tertiary sector often accounts for a very large (if not the largest) share of GDP, even at low levels of income. In employment the sequence is not always clear. The tertiary sector usually increases its share while the economy is still in the 'secondary' stage and sometimes the tertiary sector dominates the employment picture at a very early phase of the country's development.

The question is whether the Clark-Fisher law wrongly associates economic development with a given sectoral sequence, or whether the law is correct as actual deviations can be accounted for by special circumstances. One could argue, for example, that oil economies do not fall under the coverage of the Clark-Fisher law because income growth, temporarily at least, is dissociated from economic development. The actual sectoral sequence in oil economies simply reflects the source of income growth and its accidental occurrence. A process of economic development generated from within would have given rise to the 'normal' pattern of structural changes. In fact, this pattern will become increasingly apparent in the future, when oil economies start to transform their financial wealth into productive investment within the domestic economy. The divergence between the Clark-Fisher law and the behaviour of non-oil economy may be interpreted with subtler arguments. The observed pattern of structural changes in employment simply reflects the transfer of disguised unemployed workers from agriculture to the service sector. Changes are more apparent than real. An advanced stage of economic development is associated with the expansion of genuine tertiary activities, not with the creation of a pool of disguisedly unemployed labour, now in agriculture, now in the services. A pattern of structural changes that indicates economic progress involves changes in the composition of tertiary employment and tertiary activities. These changes are not easy to identify. But the application of any other criterion, given the pathology of labour-surplus LDCs today, could be grossly misleading.

---

[1] Colin Clark, Conditions of Economic Progress, end ed., London, McMillan, 1951.

[2] S. Kuznets, Economic Growth and Structure - selected essays, London, Heinemann, 1966.

[3] W. G. Hoffmann, The Growth of Industrial Economies, Manchester, 1968.

[4] H.B. Chenery and L. Taylor, Development Patterns - Among Countries and Over Time, Review of Economics and Statistics (Cambridge), November, 1968. Also: Patterns of Industrial Growth, American Economic Review, September, 1960.

If patterns of historical behaviour in advanced countries are a guide to sectoral priorities in LDCs, we would safely infer that industrialisation will always be the planner's favourite. The aspiration to industrialise, however, has deeper roots and motivations than this argument may suggest. The belief is that economic power today largely depends on a society's ability to adopt and master modern technology. Technology is a cultural world which involves knowledge, habits of mind, modes of organisation and social behaviour, education and research. Industry is the privileged technological domain. If offers significant opportunities for productive applications, learning by doing, innovations and inventions, all of which lead to economic advances. This belief has a strong rationale which does not absolve planners from the many disastrous mistakes committed in its name. The desire to industrialise is as plainly manifested in most Arab countries as in other LDCs. Rich oil economies are as eager to industrialise as poor and over-populated agrarian countries. Saudi Arabia is currently considering a massive programme of industrial investment. The small Gulf Emirates are concerned with industrialisation. Algeria, since independence, has put her economic hopes in an industrialisation strategy involving very capital-intensive investments in petrochemicals and related activities. Egypt, since 1930, has continually attempted - though with varying degrees of success - to diversity an economic structure dominated by agriculture. Iraq is industrialising at a fast rate; and Lebanon, despite its small size, an economic structure geared to the provision of services and the absence of significant tariff protection, has been able to sustain a 6-7 per cent real rate of growth of manufacturing output.

Bringing together the threads of the analysis suggests the following conclusions. (a) The long-term sectoral priority for most LDCs is likely to be industrialisation, but it should be recalled that the efficient pursuit of this objective may sometimes involve long detours and indirect preparations. (b) The preferences of Government and planners, as revealed in declarations, official planning documents and often in actual policy decisions, are usually loaded in favour of industry. (c) These priorities, even when they have determined investment patterns over a long stretch of years, do not seem to have a marked influence on patterns of structural changes in employment. In many LDCs, and particularly in most Arab countries, the tertiary sector seems to absorb the largest part of the incremental labour force. If sectoral priorities were only revealed by their employment effects, we would have legitimately inferred that the top priority is always given to the services rather than to industry.

This apparent contradiction may be explained by two remarks. First, modern industry generates less employment per unit of investment than most other sectors of the economy. Thus industry could well be the priority sector in economic development, attracting the lion's share of investible resources, and yet be outdistanced from the point of view of employment generation by the tertiary sector. Secondly, the growth of employment in the services (though reduced by Government policy in both oil-exporting economies such as Kuwait or Libya and in labour-surplus economies such as Egypt) is the effect of transient measures applied to alleviate structural imbalances, not the sign of a sectoral priority for long-run development.

These explanations, however, do not dispose of a difficult dilemma. However, expressed or however approached, (and you will find a score of different formulations in the literature) we always face the same stubborn problem: how to reconcile a growth or development objective with an employment objective? The problem has troubled development economists since the invention of their discipline. It arises whether the discussion focuses on choice of techniques or sectoral priorities in planning or any other policy. It has often bothered planners and policy-makers. It may be harder to solve in some of the countries with which we are concerned than elsewhere in the third world, because of special features of oil-economies. We shall come back to this conflict later.

b) Choice of techniques

In a sense, the choice of technique problem is a particular application of cost-benefit analysis. The selection of an investment project and the selection of the specific technical characteristics of that investment are related aspects of the same exercise. Economists are not short of recipes and algorithms for cost-benefit calculations; but to review them all here would not make much sense.

We shall instead concentrate on a few important issues. One of these relates to the choice of the maximand. The apparent conflict between growth and employment objectives, mentioned in the previous section, emerges here again.

This conflict is revealed with startling simplicity in Sen's 'corn made of corn and labour' model.[1] Assume that corn is both the capital goods (as seeds) and the output

---

[1] A.K. Sen, Choice of Techniques, Blackwell, Oxford, 3rd ed., 1968.

(whether as seeds or as food); land is in fixed supply; labour is the variable factor; wages are paid in corn; diminishing marginal returns obtain in production when labour inputs are applied beyond a certain point. The apparent conflict between three objectives - maximum surplus, maximum output and maximum employment - is clear. Less employment is generated when the aim is to maximise the reinvestible surplus, than when output or employment are the goals. Since the amount of corn used as capital in any period is fixed, the labour intensity of the technique is directly related to the volume of labour inputs. The maximisation of the surplus entails a more capital-intensive technique than the maximisation of output or employment. One implication of the model is that maximum employment (defined as the point where the wage bill absorbs the whole output) is a self-defeating objective. No corn is left for production in the next period. Maximum employment today means no employment tomorrow. One may, of course, be able to borrow and gain some lease of life. The fundamental point, however, remains unaltered: there is no long-term future for an economy which fails to save. Another implication is that the reinvestible surplus criterion which produces less employment today than other criteria, maximises employment in the long run.

Sen's presentation of the issues exaggerates, however, the nature of the conflict. First, the room for choice may be narrower than is apparent in the model. If the wage rate is close to subsistence, there is often no option but to maximise output. Attempts to maximise the surplus would be self-defeating when society or the Government are under an obligation to keep the unemployed alive. In a closed economy (no transfers of resources from abroad) the subsidy is bound to come out of the potential surplus. The economy would be better off if it adopted maximum output as its goal. Secondly, in situation where the wage rate is above subsistence, and where the Government is not entirely deprived of fiscal instruments, the conflict between maximum surplus and maximum output could be largely illusory. Maximum output may be sought and a surplus equivalent to that obtained under the alternative objective extracted through taxation. More employment would thus be achieved than under the maximum surplus criterion and long-term interests would be safeguarded. The distributional implications are clear: more employment is obtained but the standard of living of the employed falls.

Many economists are sceptical about the ability of Governments in LDCs to tax certain segments of the population. Institutional forces - such as trade unions - may resist attempts to lower the real wage of workers in employment for the benefit of the unemployed. When fiscal or administrative inefficiencies, or institutional rigidities, prevail, the conflict of objectives re-emerges. In such situations I would be inclined to adopt a method of technique-appraisal similar to the Little and Mirrless criterion. The maximand is the present value of the net social product; and the shadow wage of labour takes into account its opportunity cost (i.e., its marginal product in the alternative occupation) but also the cost of the labourer's increased consumption in terms of future growth. If labour is in abundant supply in the economy, the criterion tends to favour relatively labour-intensive techniques (because the opportunity cost or marginal product element in the shadow wage will probably be low). The second element in the shadow-wage calculation pulls the choice of technique in the other direction. Other things being equal, the greater is the worker's extra-consumption (i.e., the higher the wage differential between the worker's old and new occupations), the higher the cost in terms of future growth. The criterion will tend to select a relatively more capital-intensive technique in this case than when the costs of extra-consumption are low or heavily discounted.

Possible conflict of objectives is not the only important issue which arises in this context. The choice of techniques is more an issue of political economy than of positive economics. As Sen puts it, albeit only in a footnote, we can neither assume that technological choice has no consequence outside the field of economics nor that economics provides all the criteria for technological choice. There is a suspicion in many LDCs which suffer from an employment problem that recommendations in favour of labour-intensive techniques, intermediate technology or of a special output-mix heavily weighted with traditional goods serve neo-imperialistic objectives. Those who come up with these recommendations may be perfectly innocent but their advice is seen as potentially dangerous. The danger is to condemn the LDC to perpetual technological backwardness. Whether this danger is real or imaginary is a difficult question to answer. The fact, and it can prove to be a considerable obstacle to the communication of advice and ideas, is that the danger is perceived as real in many quarters, and deep resentment may build up.

An honest economist would recognise that the issue is not entirely emotional and extra-economic (recourse to those arguments is the economist's preferred way of dismissing an embarrassing problem). The issue is one of external economies. Different techniques may have different external effects, that is contribute in different ways to the training of labour, to its familiarisation with the technological culture, to the development and application of technical progress, etc. As economists know very little, about external effects, that is amenable to quantifications, they tend either to talk in the superlative about their importance or to dismiss them entirely as irrelevancies. The fact is that externalities seldom enter into their cost-benefit calculations in an explicit way. For all we know, all choice of techniques recommendations may be seriously misleading, especially if externalities happen to be significant.

If the economist's assessment is incomplete in its own terms of reference, how much does it leave to be desired on broader criteria? Technological choices influence social behaviour and social relationships. They have political implications through their distributional effects, their impact on the class structure, their influence on ideas, the educational system, expectations, tastes and aspirations. The trade-off between employment, profit, and output is but an aspect of the story; externalities but another aspect. Cuation is called for. The apostles of hand-looms and intermediate techniques are probably as misled as those who believe that capital-intensive, technologically advanced monuments will necessarily produce development. We know that much, because we know that in issues which involve different aspects unilateral conceptions are likely to be wrong.

c) Sectors and techniques

The relationships between structural changes and choice of techniques may now be explored. In essence the issue is simple. Employment in an economy may be varied by altering either the technical characteristics of the various activities, or by altering the weights attached to these activities in the economic structure, or, of course, by altering these two parameters.

Assume that an economy comprises n activities, each charactertised by a degree of labour intensity $a_i = li/ki$, and that the weight of each activity in the economy is its share $w_i = li/K$ of the capital stock. Average labour intensity in the economy is given by

$$L/K = \sum a_i \, w_i \qquad (1)$$

and total employment $\qquad L = \sum K \, a_i \, w_i \qquad (2)$

Equation (2) can be adapted for incremental changes as

$$\Delta L = I \sum a_i \, w_i \qquad (3)$$

where I is the volume of investment, a_i the labour-intensity in activity i, and w_i the investment share of activity i.

Planners concerned with an employment problem could attempt to attain a given target ΔL by juggling with two vectors: the set of technical parameters a, and the set of weights w. (We are assuming that I is fixed because of budgetary constraints.) The notion that as much flexibility is perhaps afforded by the weighting system as by choice of techniques has been recently emphasised by economists irritated with widespread scepticism is due to the realisation that technological choice is often rigidly constrained by the very narrow range of techniques extant at any time on the market, by engineering biasses in favour of the most up-to-date (often the most capital-intensive) technology, by imperfections in international trade which restricts the number of sources from which capital goods can be imported, and a host of similar factors.

Well, the argument goes, you can always try to achieve through variations of the output-mix what you can't achieve with technological choice.

The problem, however, is not as simple as it appears because a) employment is not the sole factor taken into consideration in determining sectoral priorities, and b) the sectors which planners may want to favour for economic growth, potential linkages and external effects, prestige or other political reasons, may turn out to be among the more capital-intensive activities.

We know that typical degrees of capital intensity tend to differ between various sectors of an economy. Not that the average capital-intensity of a sector could not itself vary considerably from country to country, or from time to time in the same country, because of differences in both techniques and the activity-mix. But a broad hierarchy, an ordinal scale of sectoral capital intensities, tends to obtain. Thus the petrochemical industry in LDCs is usually significantly more capital-intensive than agriculture. Assume a two-sector economy with a large agricultural sector and a nascent petro-chemical industry. A priority to petro-chemicals, which may be rationally justified on developmental grounds, would rigidly constrain the pursuit of any employment objective. First, the rising weight of the capital-intensive petro-chemicals reduces the 'employment potential of the structure'. Secondly, choice of techniques would offer very little scope in this particular economy because a poor agriculture can seldom be made more labour-intensive than it already is and the options for petro-chemicals are usually limited to a narrow capital-intensive range of techniques. I have intentionally taken an extreme example to highlight a common and familiar difficulty encountered by most planners.   The sector they want to expand, which I have called petro-chemicals but which is generally industry, is usually much more capital-intensive than the sector which tends to shrink in relative importance as development proceeds (that is, agriculture).   But it is important to recall that room for manoeuvre tends to increase with the number of activities.   In our model we only included two, hence the excessive rigidity.   Interesting implications follow.   First the real world is likely to have more flexibility in it than our models, because it involves many more parameters than we care to consider.   Second, a diversified economy is generally better equipped to cope with the employment problem than an economy with a lop-sided structure.

d) Planning

All that may sound terribly pessimistic.   Planners, however, have practical problems to solve and may ask for operational suggestions.   The general principle is that planning is an iterative process which goes back and forth from the micro-decision (project selection and choice of techniques) to the macro-framework (global objectives, sectoral priorities, aggregate balances).

As mentioned earlier, any good method of cost-benefit analysis will usually do for the micro-decisions.   Despite all the fuss that academics like to make about their inventions, it remains true that there is not much difference between, say, the Little-Mirrless[1] method or the UNIDO guidelines.[2]   In practice, most planners will use cruder methods, because of constraints on their time and on the availability of data.   A proper understanding of the sophisticated techniques, even when they are never applied, remains essential.   The skill and effectiveness with which the cruder methods are used largely depends on this understanding.   A good dose of common sense is also necessary.   There is no point advising certain governments that they should industrialise on the hand-loom pattern when it is known that the whole developmental strategy is oriented the other way.   A planner or an adviser worth his salt would, however, attempt to contradict decisions which seem unnecessarily or excessively costly.   The least he can do is to assess these costs.

Other tools are available for macro-planning.   The employment potential of output growth in different sectors may be assessed, for example, with the help of Verdoorn's law.[3]   In essence the law postulates a relationship between output growth and productivity growth.   This necessarily implies a relationship between output and employment growth.   Thus, if

$$y = a + bp$$
$$\text{then} \quad y = a + b(y - o)$$
$$\text{or} \quad y = a(1 - b) - eb(1 - b)$$

where y, p and e are rates of growth of output, productivity and employment respectively, and a and b are coefficients.

The rationale behind Verdoorn's law may be interpreted in different ways.   One explanation is that a high rate of output growth favours high productivity growth because of economies of scale and technical progress.   Another explanation suggests that productivity growth may be an exogenous variable (relating, for example, to education and other characteristics of the labour force) and that productivity growth stimulates output growth via demand.

The utility of Verdoorn's law to planners depends on the empirical strength of the relationship and on the stability of the coefficients.   All that, of course, is a matter of controversy.   It is certain, for example, that sectoral estimates of the coefficient will

---

[1]   Little, I.M.D., and Mirrless, J.A., Manual of Industrial Project Analysis in Developing Countries, Vol.II, Social Cost Benefit Analysis, OECD, Paris, 1969.   Also: A Reply to some criticisms of the OECD Manual, Bulletin of the Oxford Institute of Economics and Statistics, Vol.34, 1972.

[2]   UNIDO, Evaluation of Industrial Projects, United Nations, New York, 1968 and UNIDO Guidelines for Project Evaluation, United Nations, New York.

[3]   First reported in P.J. Verdoorn, Fattori che regolano lo suiluppo della produttività del lavoro, Industria, No.1 1949 and further developed in P.J. Verdoorn, On an empirical law governing the productivity of labour, paper presented to the Varese Meeting of the Econometric Society, September 1950, see Econometrica, Vol.19, April 1951, p.209-210.

be more reliable than aggregate estimates.   The relationship could also be given different specifications and the slope of the function made a variable.

A feature of empirical estimates that is most relevant to our concern with sectoral priorities and employment planning is that the values of the coefficients tend to differ markedly from one sector to another.   A given rate of output growth relates to different rates of productivity growth in various economic activities.   The employment effects are different.   This may sound trite but an approximate idea of orders of magnitude is useful to planners.   One possible use of Verdoorn coefficients in planning is a crude check on the employment effects of a given vector of sectoral output growth.

Sabolo[1]/ estimated employment functions which would also provide planners with coefficients for macro-economic exercises.   Sabolo applied normal regression techniques to relate the share of a sector in total employment to a set of independent variables, income per capita, investment per capita, private and public consumption as well as exports per capita.   The equations chosen are logarithmic of the quadratic form.   Every independent variable is taken separately in an independent equation.   The exercise provides sectoral estimates of elasticities (the proportionate response of the dependent variable, i.e., the sectoral share in employment, to changes in the independent variable, i.e., income, investment, consumption, etc.).   The elasticities themselves are not constant as their values depend on the logarithm of the independent variable.   Here again the Sabolo estimates (or similar estimates calculated with a more comprehensive or more up-to-date sample) could help the planners in assessing, a priori, the employment responses to changes in important macro-economic parameters.

Empirical estimates of Verdoorn coefficients or Sabolo elasticities are in fact historical indicators.   Their primary value is that they describe quantitatively an 'average' pattern of historical behaviour.   Sabolo's findings are interesting in this respect. They confirm that part of the Clarke-Fisher law which relates to the decline of agricultural employment as development proceeds.   They also confirm our suspicion that mining behaves erratically (which means that oil-producing economies should always be treated as a separate group).   They suggest, rather surprisingly, at first, that the behaviour of employment elasticities for non-agricultural sectors other than construction does not display significant differences.   In other words, there is no way of distinguishing a phase of structural changes led by the secondary sector from a phase led by the tertiary sector.   But this is essentially one of our earlier qualifications to the Clark-fisher criterion.

Last but not least, Sabolo's results indicate that changes in the composition of final demand (public and private consumption, investment and exports) have a significant influence on employment creation.   This point is not often emphasised.   If the 'average' historical behaviour of a sample of countries is of any relevance, we would infer that the relationship between the structure of final demand and employment has important implications for planning and economic policy.   It provides us with a third register, besides choice of techniques and structure of output, on which to play in attempts to solve the employment problem.

Sabolo found, for example, that the employment elasticity of private consumption tends to be high in all sectors except agriculture, where it is negative.   The operation of Engel's law is easily recognised in this phenomenon.   Thus private consumption is a sensitive variable; but the complicating factor which we rediscover here under a new guise, is the possible conflict between employment today encouraged by an increase in private consumption and employment tomorrow adversely affected by a concomitant drop in investment. Sabolo's results on public consumption, on which he does not comment, are of particular interest to us because public consumption is such an important factor in many Arab economies - especially oil-exporting countries, but also Egypt.   The employment elasticities of public consumption per capita are higher for all non-agricultural sectors, and for all values of the independent variable, than the elasticities of private consumption.

In countries like Egypt, increases in public consumption are cripling to the development effort.   The economic history of Egypt in the past fifteen years provides ample evidence,   If we disaggregated the components of public consumption growth, we would find that it includes growth in (a) defence expenditures which can have a relatively high employment potential, and (b) public employment itself.   There is some circularity.   Increases in public consumption are partly generated by increases in public employment; it is misleading to say that they have employment generation effects.   In oil-exporting countries, increases in public consumption may not adversely affect the development effort, insofar as availabilities of investment funds are concerned.   These may be sufficiently abundant in

---

1/ Y. Sabolo, La croissance sectorielle de l'emploi, BIT, Genève, 1969.

any case. But development is not a matter of funds only. Incentives and attitudes play a significant part. Absorption of a large segment of the labour force in Government employment where rewards are both high and dissociated from the supply of effort may well solve employment problems in the short-run. It is not conductive to long-term development.

e) Policies

We have drifted from a discussion of technical coefficients, criteria and methods for planning to that of more substantial issues. This is natural and calls for no apologies. Coefficients are meaningless without interpretation, and interpretation often takes us away from the quantitative to the qualitative. Planning is an exercise in quantitative consistency which presupposes an understanding of the substantive issues. The exercise is incomplete unless supplemented with an analysis of possible policies.

We have analysed in an earlier section the nature of the employment problem in Arab countries. The a priori discussion of (a) sectoral priorities in output and employment planning, (b) choice of techniques and (c) possibilities to play with the composition of aggregate demand in attempts to solve the employment problem may have generated more scepticism than hope. If Governments and their people were willing to accept that harmonious economic development - that is, economic development which either takes positive advantage of structural imbalances, or corrects them - is a very long affair, there would be grounds for more hope than scepticism. But impatience fostered by demonstration effects, strong links between middle classes all round the world, homogeneisation of cultures and tastes, is both a fact and a force. It has to be reckoned with. Without impatience, the choice of technique problem would be easier, because Governments might not have put such a negative valuation on labour-intensive or intermediate technology. The learning process could start with basic skills and be allowed to move slowly from the simple to the complex. This is not acceptable because waiting involves costs and perhaps risks of falling under new forms of foreign dependency. The price paid for impatience is either an aggravated employment problem or technological dualism (the co-existence of a small sector of very advanced technology and a relatively primitive economy without significant links between the two). Without impatience, the sectoral register would probably provide more room for manoeuvre. Why accelerate, for example, the inevitable decline in the relative importance of agriculture by neglecting investment opportunities because of industry? The rule is not that one should invest in agriculture at all costs (paradoxically, some oil economies with the least profitable prospects in agriculture seem to take this line); no more than one should invest in industry at all costs. It remains true that Egypt who has never entirely forgotten its agriculture, Algeria, Iraq and almost all non-desert Arab economies could do infinitely more in agriculture than they have cared to achieve in the past. It is absurd, for example, that the drainage project in Egypt, the need for which was recognised as early as in the 1920s, did not receive attention until the 1970s. The relative decline of agriculture in economic development need not be associated with an absolute decline nor with a lower rate of productivity growth than economically feasible. Without impatience, more could be done to ease structural imbalances with a judicious manipulation of aggregate demand. The priority would go to investment. Increases in public consumption would be geared first towards developmental services such as education and health which are both productive and labour-intensive. The greatest difficulty arises in this context. The educational policies ought to contribute significantly to the solution of the employment problem (by increasing the supply of skilled workers for which there is excess demand relative to the supply of unskilled workers whose numbers tend to be in excess of requirements anyway). In many LDCs - and especially in Arab countries - the educational policy seems to aggravate structural imbalances. It responds to society's demands - especially to middle class demands - for a classical type of education which may lead in some instances to the acquisition of higher professional qualifications. But technical education and middle-level professional qualifications are not adequately supplied by the system partly because of a deficiency in private demand. No doubt, some market or institutional imperfection explains the gap between the private and the social benefits of technical education. Government employment policies, social values, the salary scales and the promotional structure, all favour the literate graduate and put the skilled foreman at a disadvantage. Yet, the former is often disguisedly unemployed while the latter may contribute to the development of his country.

We are driven to the conclusion that an effective employment strategy is necessarily comprehensive, involving a wide range of planning and policy instruments. The reason is that the employment problem in LDCs is a global problem difficult to dissociate from the wider development problem. The employment problem arises as a chronic feature because of structural and institutional flaws on LDCs demographic pressures, market imperfections and policy failures; also because of inadequate or unbalanced endowment of resources, poverty and maldistribution of income. The problem may thus be tackled at any of these points. A population policy may not help immediately because of long lags between implementation and effects but may contribute to the solution of the long term problem. Redistribution of income may help if an improvement in the lot of the poor raises the level of domestic demand for labour-intensive consumer goods. Indirect effects could cancel however some of these advantages. All policy measures which increases the flow of information in labour-markets, enhances the flexibility of their operations and magnify their signals are not a panacea but they do help. As governments are very significant employers in most Arab countries, their own wage and recruitment policies matter most. I have argued in a study on Libyan employment problems that the apparent shortage of labour in agriculture was largely induced by the Government wage and employment policy which attracted labour in relatively well paid, secure and unproductive jobs. There is no doubt that similar situations prevail in most oil producing countries. In Egypt, the government employment policy may not create visible or significant shortages elsewhere. It may be viewed as a direct remedy to a serious potential unemployment problem. But it has locked the economy into a vicious circle in which expectations of a job in the Government influence demand for education and thus increase the supply of those who seek a Government job. The short-term remedy has become an open-ended commitment and entails a significant drain on resources. Economic development is put in jeopardy.

The submission of this paper has been that though choices of technology and reshuffling of sectoral priorities may help, the main thrust on the employment front may only be effected with a broad development package designed to fulfil a balanced set of objectives.

APPENDIX : Comments on sectoral employment policies
in Arab countries

a) Agriculture: The choice of technique problem in agriculture often involves a choice
between mechanisation and cultivation methods with hand tools and animal power.   In countries like Egypt which suffer from an acute employment problem the case may be against mechanisation. But the issue is not simple. The use of tractors enables deeper ploughing,
economies in the use of seeds, better levelling and alignment.   Higher output per acre of
land, the scarce factor, is an important benefit.   Mechanisation also increases the efficiency of livestock production.   At present, the draught animal is used for both power and
livestock products.   Dairy and meat production from a given stock would undoubtedly increase.
A reduction in total is consistent with an increase in livestock production.   Such a reduction may release cropped area used for clover for more profitable uses.   The substitution
problem is however complex because of technological complementarities between cotton and
clover cultivation and higher requirements for feedstuff entailed by a shift towards livestock production.   Finally a greater specialisation of cattle for dairy and meat production
has positive employment effects which ought to be assessed.   The point is that there is no
prima facie case.   A complex cost-benefit analysis is required in each situation.   Its
conclusions may be very sensitive to variations in relative factor and product prices.

Some oil producing countries with medium population and poor land endowments (such
as Libya or Saudi Arabia) face difficult choices in agriculture.   On the one hand, agriculture still retains a large share of the working population; on the other hand, considerable
investment and large subsidies would be necessary to check a very significant shift away
from the land.   Agriculture is always at a strong disadvantage in oil economies because
wage levels and average incomes tend to be very high in the non-agricultural sector.   This
exerts a pull on the rural population which may not be affectively checked unless agricultural incomes are allowed to rise very significantly.   Agriculture, which suffers in any
case from strong natural disadvantages (water scarcity, low soil fertility), is unlikely to
become competitive, except in few areas and in certain specialised activities, without considerable subsidies.   Whether this is worthwhile is a political question.   The economist's
recommendation would be: i) maximise the retention potential of agriculture by concentrating investment and extension resources in the areas where development possibilities may turn
out to be economical in the long-run and ii) prepare a slow transition from agriculture to
other occupations for the rest of the population using investment funds that the romantic
would spend on unprofitable agricultural projects in other sectors of the economy.   The
transition is bound to be slow and necessarily involve subsidies.   But this is one of the
many manifestations of the structural problems in oil-producing countries.   Its solution is
a very long affair which can be further delayed by the pursuit of inappropriate policies.

In agrarian economies - such as Morocco, Egypt etc. - the output/employment conflict
can be partly resolved by changes in the agricultural output mix rather than changes in
technique (already very labour-intensive).   In both Morocco and Egypt the composition of
agricultural output has changed significantly in recent years.   The share of fruit and
vegetables, for example, has increased in relation to field crops.   Export promotion and
the growth of domestic demand for these goods have stimulated these developments.   In general, value-added in fruit and vegetables is higher than the value-added of most field crops.
There are output gains.   There are also employment gains because the cropping frequency of
vegetables is higher and their cultivation is labour-intensive (there are less seasonal
fluctuations in the demand for labour and greater total requirements).   Indirect employment
effects in processing, food manufacturing and trade may obtain.

b) Construction: A common economic fallacy is that construction can make a significant
contribution to the solution of disguised unemployment problems in agriculture.   The notion
is that construction employs unskilled workers who are in abundant supply.   It is true that
some expansion of construction activity may help.   But the potential contribution is limited
by these factors.   a) Construction is a small employment sector relatively to agriculture
in labour-surplus economies.   The relative order of magnitude is 1:10.   A high rate of
employment growth in construction would be necessary to absorb significant numbers.   Such a
high rate of growth presupposes increases in the rate of investment which may not be sustain-
able for very long by a poor economy.   It is often forgotten that most construction works,
apart from digging canals and trenches, is material-intensive.   b) Unskilled labour is not
a homogenous category.   Construction work of the unskilled type (such as mixing and carrying
concrete) requires physical strength and endurance to an unusual degree.   Having worked on
building sites, I talk from experience.   These attributes are a scarce resource in LDCs.
The relative scarcity of unskilled construction workers is best manifested by the behaviour
of wages in times of rising demand.   Rising wages in construction cannot be attributed to
institutional factors because the labour market is typically unstructured.   Data from Iran
and Egypt suggest that real wages for unskilled construction workers tend to rise fast when
the sector expands.   In other words, there seems to be a correlation between increases in
real wages and sectoral employment growth.   We can but assume that the supply of unskilled

labour to construction is <u>not</u> perfectly elastic. In oil economies such as Libya and Saudi Arabia, there is a marked reluctance on the part of unskilled workers, even when unemployed, to work in construction. These differences in preferences reveal a lack of homogeity on workers' tastes. c) Construction tends to draw unskilled labour from agriculture or to attract new migrants in the towns. It rarely contributes to the solution of the urban under-employment problem which is the most severe in many countries.

c) <u>Educational services</u>: Education is a labour-intensive activity. There is a case, on employment grounds, to expand this sector. The trouble is that an educational policy which does not provide the economy with the appropriate mix of skills can exacerbate the employment problem. Education absorbs labour as an input but its output may add significantly to the pool of redundant or potentially redundant labour. This is not an argument against the provision of education. I do believe, as I assume most of us do, that education is an extremely valuable and valued good. The problem is àwhat type of education?'. This problem cannot be successfully tackled on the supply side only (say by educational planning based on manpower forecasts). Demand is all important and the determinants of demand though comprising tastes and social factors are also economic. To attract students to technological institutes it is necessary to provide both the educational facilities and the appropriate salary and career structure. Most Arab countries need much larger numbers of 'engineers' in the British sense than graduates in arts or law, more skilled manual workers with a good level of basic education than secondary school graduates. The balance of supply is biassed in the opposite direction. To change this state of affairs is a long and arduous task. Society's perception that the engineer has a subordinate and inferior job to the graduate will not change overnight. But these perceptions will slowly evolve if engineers are well paid, if they are given better promotional prospects than the average or the poor quality and if they are given access, through merit, to managerial jobs. This may sound utopian. Yet, the failure or success of industrialisation may partly depend on that.

EMPLOYMENT AND EDUCATION IN THE ARAB COUNTRIES:

THE DATA AND THEIR INTERPRETATION

by

Michel Debeauvais[1]

PREFACE

The main points underlying this study are the following:

1.   Education policies and employment policies have been studied mainly in terms of quantitative expansion, whereas the problems increasingly regarded as deserving priority are of a different kind: qualitative shortcomings, regional or socio-economic imbalances, failure to match supply and demand in the educational system and on the labour market.

2.   The theoretical concepts hitherto accepted are now undergoing a process of critical reassessment, which implies taking a new look at the analytical methods used to study the education and employment situation, and at the techniques of human-resources forecasting.

3.   Generally speaking, the Arab countries are not at present in possession of the minimum of manpower data essential for a knowledge of the employment situation and its mode of development; this being so, there is little prospect of arriving at more reliable employment forecasts, even less of assessing the inter-relationships between the educational system, the labour market and the economy, while projections are very unlikely to be realistic.

4.   The setting up of a system of basic data on education and employment is a sine qua non for the elaboration and application of a human-resources development policy embracing educational policy and employment policy.

5.   The data already available for the countries in the region may serve as a basis for the exchange of information about relevant data on human resources, the drawing up of a list of social indicators for the region (to be kept up-to-date), and possibly the setting up of a regional data bank.   Furthermore, the experience of other countries where conditions are different may be used so that benefit can be derived from all available international experience.

6.   The significance of statistics in the formulation of a human-resources policy (both short-term and for planning purposes) can often be shown more effectively by means of graphs rather than by tables of figures.   In this survey an attempt is made to illustrate this point of view, using examples drawn from statistics about countries in the region or, failing these, about countries with more exact or more detailed data.

In the first chapter, we shall review the kind of data which are adapted to educational policy requirements.

The second chapter will be more particularly dedicated to data concerning the educational structure of the labour market.

---

[1] Professor at the University of Paris. Abridged version.

CHAPTER I

A DATA SYSTEM ADAPTED TO EDUCATIONAL POLICY REQUIREMENTS

It is impossible to formulate an educational policy or a human resources policy that will place education and employment problems within the framework of over-all social and economic development policy, without a minimum of data through which aims and means of action can be based upon the knowledge of the present state of the educational system, the way in which it is evolving, the results it is producing and its relationship with the employment market.

With this in mind, a growing number of countries are seeking to determine what significant statistics (already available or yet to be set up) are required for future action. These efforts fit into the wider context of the new tendency to give a genuine place in development policies to social aims such as equality of opportunity. An attempt is therefore being made to define "social indicators", some of which relate to the educational system:

(a) as a producer of services (educational, public and private, in-school and out-of-school) made available to the community;

(b) as a consumer of financial and skilled manpower resources;

(c) as a producer of professional knowledge and skills which are put to use on the labour market;

(d) as a means of achieving other aims such as equalisation of opportunity in employment, income distribution, social mobility.

Three sets of data may be singled out from the significant statistics required to illustrate these different aspects:

(a) basic indicators, which make it possible to define the main aspects of the educational system: quantitative data on volume, types and quality of educational services, the use made of them by those for whom they are intended, costs and financing, development trends;

(b) indicators of aims, expressing in figures the results aimed at in order to give a concrete significance to the objectives chosen and the priorities established;

(c) indicators of means, which define the measures adopted or proposed in order to achieve the aims of educational policy; direct and indirect costs of such measures, allocation of trained staff, goods and equipment;

(d) indicators of results, whereby it is possible to assess the effectiveness of the measures applied in relation to the aims set, and to take timely corrective action where necessary.

Such a collection of data is an ambitious undertaking, considering the statistics at present available[1], but there must be a vision of the final objective if priorities are to be established for adapting each country's statistical machinery.

---

[1] The Statistical Yearbooks of UNESCO indicate the progress made from year to year in the systematic collection of some global data on educational systems, but there are very big gaps even in these basic statistics, e.g. as regards expenditure on education. The OECD, in its Yearbook of Educational Statistics (Vol. 1, International Tables, 1974), admits that of 46 indicators selected, 20 "are probably too complicated to be usable", and that others are not yet available (those on out-of-school vocational training, for instance). An earlier inquiry into educational expenditures had shown similar gaps, for example on private school resources and resources specific to state schools.

The experience of the more advanced countries can be put to good use; at the same time, the establishment of regional indicators can be of help to national bureaux of statistics by supplying them with material for international comparisons.

Some action has already been taken at international level to lay the foundations for a co-operative effort to adapt statistical machinery to the new demands being made on it.

UNESCO has drawn up an international system of classification of the levels and types of education of the population, which member States will be asked to use in the censuses of the 1980s.[1]

The OECD has set out to establish a system of classification of educational systems based on a "conversion key" which will permit of international comparisons of the highest possible degree of accuracy.[2]

The OECD has also[3] put forward a suggestion for classifying the aims of educational policy in six different fields (covered by 46 indicators):

- the contribution of education to the transmission of knowledge;

- the contribution of education to the development of the individual;

- the contribution of education to the transmission and progress of values;

- the efficient use of resources in each of these three spheres.

As we cannot go into these questions with any thoroughness, we shall indicate below a few characteristic data for which it would seem possible to collect a body of comparative statistics on the Arab countries, either immediately or in the near future.

The examples described are meant to show how graphs can be used to illustrate significant indicators constructed from sets of statistics already available. We believe that graphic indicators of this kind, which could be brought up-to-date periodically, would provide a data bank in a form which could be readily interpreted and utilised to meet the requirements of national users.

1. SCHOOL ENROLMENT RATES

The advantage of this indicator is that it supplies a measurement in figures of the level of enrolment reached, and this is why it is the one most used for quantifying national educational aims and for international comparisons.

---

[1] Draft International Classification of Education (ICDE), UNESCO, 1971.

[2] "A Classification of Educational Systems", OECD (7 volumes published in 1972 and 1973 covering 19 countries).

[3] "A system of education indicators as guidelines for government action", OECD, 1973. Cf. also "educational policies for the decade 1970/1980", OECD, 1971.

In spite of the UNESCO recommendation on standardising methods of calculating rates,[1] national practice in the matter continues to vary from country to country, with the result that international comparisons are often inaccurate.

Attempts have often been made to establish a balanced relationship (or an optimum one) between the level of school enrolment and the level of economic development. Graphs I and II, based on adjusted enrolment rates for primary and secondary schools, show that there is no significant relationship between these two indicators for the countries of the Arab group; this is certainly due to lags between economic development and social development. These lags appear more marked than when a wider group of countries is being studied: F. Harbison had found correlations of 0.455 between per capita GNP and the primary school enrolment rate, and 0.809 for the secondary school enrolment rate. We cannot establish any rule from these negative findings, but they do indicate the need to be wary of the over-simplifications that have often served in the past to justify a choice of social aims according to standards based on over-hasty international comparisons.

The same statistical data on the population by age and the numbers enrolled in school can also be used to work out indicators measuring regional disparities. Graph III shows regional inequalities in male and female school enrolment. The different distances from the dots to the bisector show that there is not the same degree of inequality between the sexes in all the provinces, and that there is no systematic relationship between the development of education and female school enrolment: the situation in the Oases and Tizi-Ouzou provinces is close to the national average with regard to the level of school enrolment, but there is greater disparity between the sexes there than elsewhere; the inverse is the case in the province of Tiaret.

For more exhaustive qualitative analyses, education pyramids by year of age, sex and school level provide a means of presenting synthetically a large number of data in figures (as many as 40 in Graph IV). Most of the Arab countries have sufficiently detailed demographic and educational statistics to make up pyramids similar to the one in Graph IV on Iraq, which represents school enrolment rates for ages 6-15 for each sex, in the primary school level which is a six-year one.

---

[1] The recommendation adopted in 1958 by the member States advocates relating the total number of pupils at a given level to the age group corresponding to the number of years of study at that level. In many countries, however, other methods are still being used; for the sector of the population eligible for primary school, the age-group 5-14 is often taken, or else an age-group going one year beyond the number of years in the course to compensate for the number of pupils having to repeat a year, or again, a group corresponding to the "normal age", which is usually higher than the number of years in the course. Such practices lead to a systematic under-estimation of enrolment rates, in so far as the index of 100 is taken as the limit at which complete enrolment is achieved.

Another and more recent practice is to count only children of "normal" age as constituting the school population; this also means that enrolment rates will be under-estimated, as compared with those of other countries not using this method.

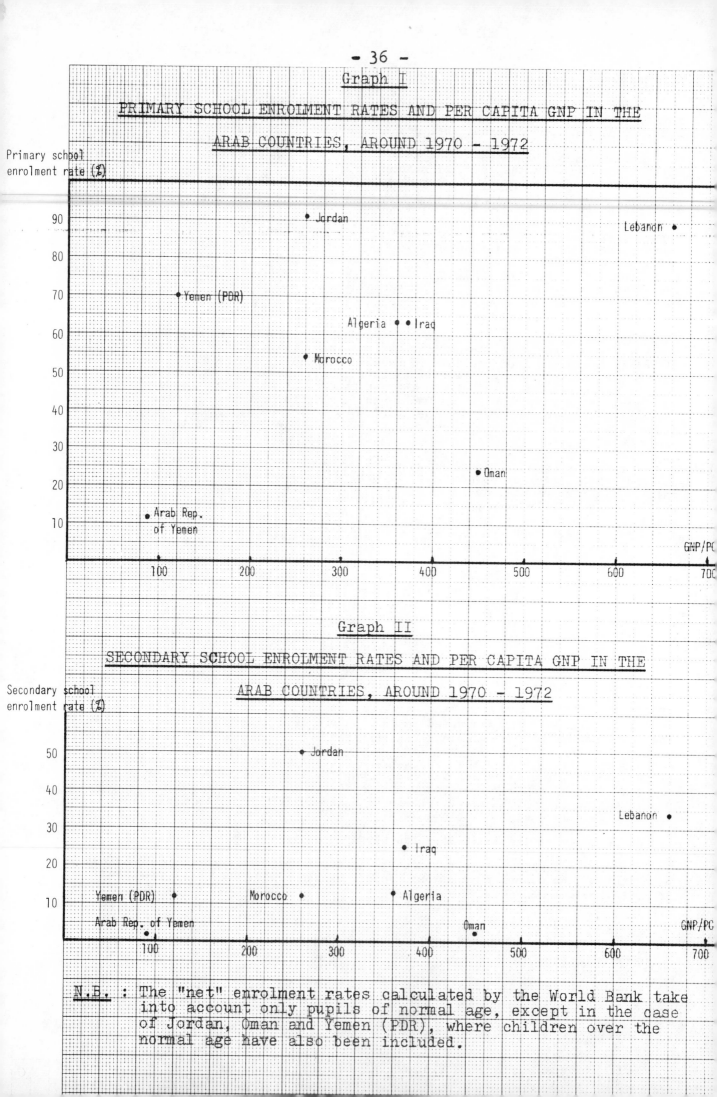

Graph I

PRIMARY SCHOOL ENROLMENT RATES AND PER CAPITA GNP IN THE

ARAB COUNTRIES, AROUND 1970 - 1972

Graph II

SECONDARY SCHOOL ENROLMENT RATES AND PER CAPITA GNP IN THE

ARAB COUNTRIES, AROUND 1970 - 1972

N.B. : The "net" enrolment rates calculated by the World Bank take
into account only pupils of normal age, except in the case
of Jordan, Oman and Yemen (PDR), where children over the
normal age have also been included.

Graph III

<u>ALGERIA - PRIMARY SCHOOL ENROLMENT RATES BY SEX AND</u>

<u>BY WILAYA, AS OF 1 JANUARY 1973</u>

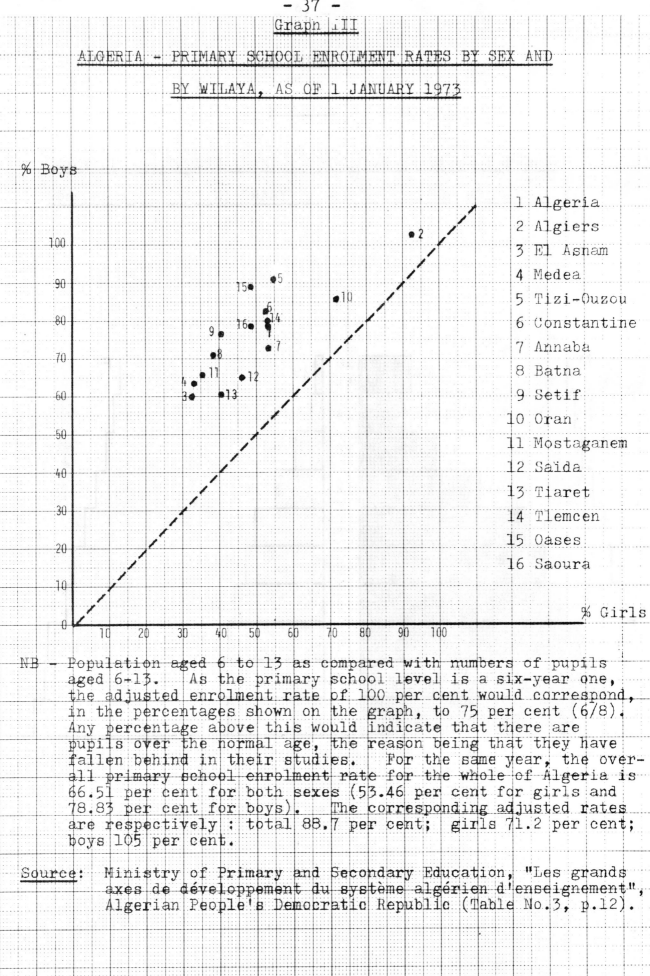

% Boys

1 Algeria
2 Algiers
3 El Asnam
4 Medea
5 Tizi-Ouzou
6 Constantine
7 Annaba
8 Batna
9 Setif
10 Oran
11 Mostaganem
12 Saida
13 Tiaret
14 Tlemcen
15 Oases
16 Saoura

% Girls

NB - Population aged 6 to 13 as compared with numbers of pupils
     aged 6-13.   As the primary school level is a six-year one,
     the adjusted enrolment rate of 100 per cent would correspond,
     in the percentages shown on the graph, to 75 per cent (6/8).
     Any percentage above this would indicate that there are
     pupils over the normal age, the reason being that they have
     fallen behind in their studies.   For the same year, the over-
     all primary school enrolment rate for the whole of Algeria is
     66.51 per cent for both sexes (53.46 per cent for girls and
     78.83 per cent for boys).   The corresponding adjusted rates
     are respectively : total 88.7 per cent; girls 71.2 per cent;
     boys 105 per cent.

Source: Ministry of Primary and Secondary Education, "Les grands
          axes de développement du système algérien d'enseignement",
          Algerian People's Democratic Republic (Table No.3, p.12).

Graph IV

I R A Q

SCHOOL POPULATION IN PUBLIC PRIMARY EDUCATION AND TOTAL

POPULATION AGE GROUPS 6 - 15 YEARS IN 1971 in thousands

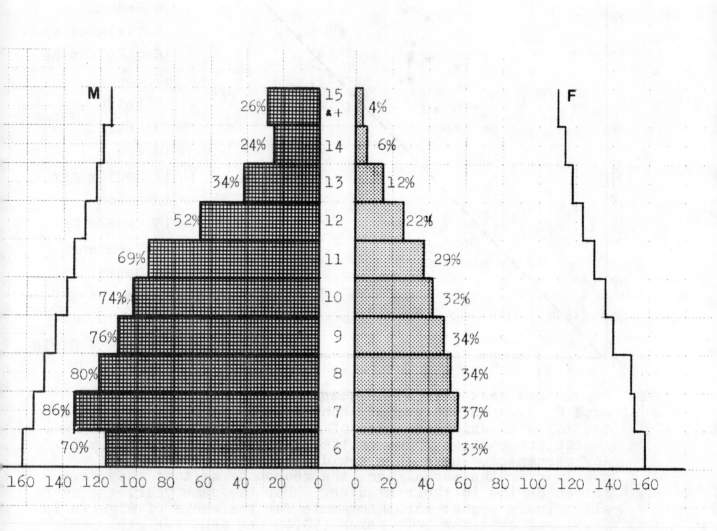

Source : Statistics of Iraq Ministry of National Education.

2. DYNAMIC INDICATORS MEASURING THE DEVELOPMENT OF THE SCHOOL SYSTEM

The global indicator most widely used to illustrate school enrolment trends is the average annual growth rate of numbers in school, the advantage of which is that it offers an easy way of measuring development and readily lends itself to comparisons with, say, population growth rates.

Illustration by semi-logarithmic graphs brings out the regularity of exponential growth rates and the differences in development as between levels and between the sexes, and makes it possible to differentiate between the various periods by giving the annual growth rate for each.

The subsequent graphs show school enrolment trends in Algeria and Sudan, for various levels of education. Their purpose is not to analyse the dynamics of the school system, but merely to serve as an example of the use of graphs to show dynamic indicators of school enrolment, in such a way as to facilitate the clear interpretation of tables of chronological statistics, bringing out the trends that are of value for planning purposes.

In the case of Algeria, Graph V is clear evidence of the considerable and sustained effort being made in the domain of education.

Graph VI shows school enrolment trends in the Sudan for the twelve years of the educational course. The effects of the reforms carried out after the Revolution of May 1968 are apparent: the 4-4-4 system is replaced by the 6-3-3 system. These changes make it impossible to express the over-all trend in terms of average annual growth rates, but as in the case of other countries expansion is seen to be greater in the higher sectors; the increase in primary school enrolment makes itself felt everywhere by increased pressure on the subsequent courses, and these changes are not always the result of decisions or forecasts made by the planners. At all events we can see from the graph that the increase in numbers of pupils in the first year of primary school (5.9 per cent per year since 1959) has not been affected by the reforms, whereas numbers in the ninth year of studies have increased three times as rapidly (17.5 per cent per year).

It would seem that these differences in the rhythm of development between the various educational levels, which we note in the cases studied, can be ascribed far more to "social demand" for education than to government decisions, for in all the Arab countries in which there is not yet universal primary school enrolment, the achieving of this goal is one of the top priorities. This applies, for instance, to Sudan, where in 1973 the proportion of children aged 7 to 12 who were not enrolled in school was officially estimated at 38 per cent in the towns and 80 per cent in rural areas.

The examples quoted seem to indicate that in actual fact (whatever priority aims were set forth in the official plans) priority has been given to the higher levels of the educational system, which are at the same time the ones involving the highest cost per student and the greatest regional and social disparities. The probability is, therefore, that this uneven expansion of the educational system has not brought about any reduction in disparities between the various regional or social groups. The purpose of the Second Development Decade, with its stress on reducing inequalities, implies a re-consideration of educational policies in this light. Plans for quantitative expansion of enrolment will have to be supplemented (and modified) by plans for reducing inequalities. Before measures of this kind can be drafted and implemented, it is essential to decide on suitable indicators to measure the inequalities and see how they are changing: inequality between the sexes, regional inequalities, inequalities between social classes or income groups, urban/rural inequalities. The redistributional effects of education between the social categories which finance it and those which benefit from it will also have to be taken into account.

Graph V

<u>ALGERIA</u> : <u>SCHOOL ENROLMENT TRENDS FROM 1962/63 TO 1972/73</u>

<u>elementary, intermediate and secondary</u>

<u>schools (including technical schools)</u>

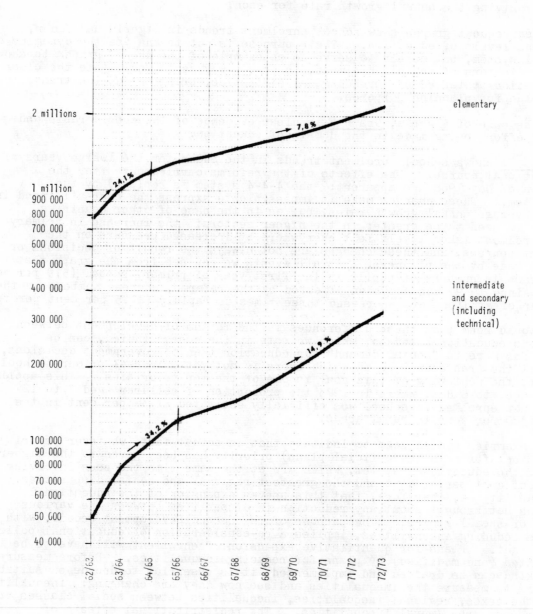

<u>Source</u> : Ministry of Primary and Secondary Education,
"Les grands axes de développement du système
algérien d'enseignement", Algerian People's
Democratic Republic (Table No.1, p.11)

Graph VI

SUDAN — SCHOOL ENROLMENT TRENDS BY YEARS OF STUDY FOR

PRIMARY, INTERMEDIATE AND SECONDARY

SCHOOLS, FROM 1959/60 TO 1973/74

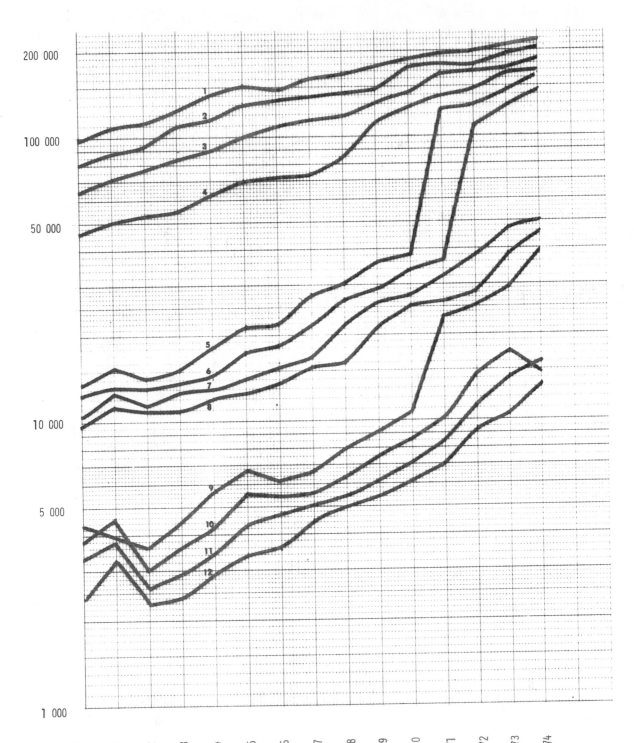

Source: Higher Education and Employment of Graduates –
The Case of the Sudan, by Bikas C. Sanyal and
El Sammani A. Yacoub, IIEP, International Institute
for Educational Planning, IIEP/RP/13-C.S.
(Rev. 1), Sept. 1974.

3. MEASURING THE REDISTRIBUTIVE EFFECTS OF EDUCATION

The purpose of analysing the redistributive effects of education is to compare the financial contributions paid to the community in the form of direct or indirect taxation by the various categories of families, with the services they receive from it, using global estimates of school enrolment rates or of per capita public expenditure on education, with indications as to who finances the public educational system and who benefits by it; the social transfers brought about by making available to all a free or virtually free public service are then taken into account. The analysis can distinguish between socio-professional categories (or income groups), and can also indicate transfers between regions or between urban and rural areas.

This system of analysis has recently been applied in Colombia.[1] The tax contributions (direct and indirect) of 14 different income groups (a distinction being made between urban and rural areas) were compared with the public subsidies received by each group in the form of educational services, taking into account their respective school enrolment rate at the three levels (public primary, secondary and higher education) and the expenditure per pupil from public funds. Another analysis was carried out at regional level, comparing expenditures on primary education per province (taking into account local and regional funding, and central government subsidies) with regional enrolment rates.

The results show that public funding acts as a compensating factor for the lowest income groups only in primary education, because these groups are little affected by enrolment in secondary and higher levels; as for central government subsidies to the provinces, they do little to rectify the disparities in school enrolment.

We can see how this type of analysis, which is little used as yet although comparatively easy to carry out, can be of value in leading to a restatement of educational policies by linking up the aims of educational expansion at the various levels with such social aims as selective assistance to the different social categories and the providing of equality of opportunity between urban and rural areas or between different income groups.

It would therefore appear advisable to supplement indicators of educational expenditure (public and private expenditures, unit costs, and changes in these within a given time-span) with indicators measuring the extent to which the various categories of the population share in educational services.

One essential feature of the human resources policy is the assessment of educational policy as it affects the labour market, yet this is the very field in which there is the greatest lack of the necessary information. Most of the data on education collected by statistics departments relate only to numbers enrolled, while employment statistics very rarely include information on the educational levels of the workers, much less on out-of-school training. In recent years many governments have taken decisions aimed at avoiding imbalance in the supply of and demand for particular skills, but without having at their disposal a data system which would provide accurate knowledge of the quantitative dimension of such problems as skilled manpower requirements, graduate unemployment or the "brain drain".

In the same way, the majority of educational reforms have been aimed at adapting the system to the requirements of economic development and to the labour market's capacity for absorption, but these reforms were carried out as the difficulties arose, and could not be based on an over-all perception of the relationship between the educational system and the labour market.

---

[1] J.P. Jallade, "Public expenditures on education and income distribution in Colombia", World Bank Staff Occasional Papers, No.18, J. Hopkins University Press, Baltimore, 1974.

Thus we find a general tendency in many current or projected programmes of educational reform to encourage reorganisation of the curricula, methods and structures of primary and intermediate education with a view to preparing the pupils for non-wage-earning employment, particularly in agriculture. Up to now, great difficulties have been encountered in implementing reforms of this type, and also in putting into effect some out-of-school innovations[1], at all levels: high costs, recruiting of pupils, employment prospects afterwards, failure to use the occupational skills acquired, pressure from pupils wishing to go on to a higher level of studies instead of starting work, and so on. While we shall not go into the educational aspects of these reforms here, it may be pointed out that it seems essential to set up a data system hitherto lacking, from which to assess:

(a) the extent of the phenomena on which it is hoped to produce an effect through the reorganisation of education, and

(b) the effectiveness of the reforms undertaken.

The relevant data relate to:

(a) outflows from the educational system at the various levels, as estimated from statistics on the school system.

There are simple models available for forecasting at national level the annual figures for successful students and dropouts, based on the rates of upgrading, repeating and dropping out for each year of the course. To use these models it is only necessary to know the number of students repeating each year of studies, and this information is available in more than half the Arab countries.[2] They can be used as simulation models to forecast the consequences of various hypothetical flows of new school entrants and spontaneous or deliberate changes in school outputs on the numbers of students successfully completing the course and the numbers of dropouts.

(b) Inflows into the labour force, according to the main levels and types of education. To this end global estimates can be made at national level from population censuses (or national employment surveys), in an attempt to reconstitute annual inflows and outflows.

(c) Data, even incomplete, on the professional career of former students, particularly students from specialised technical training centres and new-type centres set up as a result of educational reforms.

We shall go on to consider a number of points relating to methods of forecasting manpower supply, and to follow up survey methods dealing with former graduates.

---

[1] Ph. Coombs and M. Ahmed, "Attacking Rural Poverty. A World Bank Publication". The Johns Hopkins University Press, London 1974. Twenty programmes of out-of-school training are analysed with the help of comparative studies aimed at assessing the results of these experiments.

[2] I. Verdelin et al. "A Statistical Panorama of Education in the Arab Countries", Regional Centre for Educational Planning and Administration, Beirut 1972. Rates of educational returns are shown for eleven Arab countries.

CHAPTER II

THE EDUCATIONAL STRUCTURE OF THE LABOUR MARKET

Human resources development policies in the sixties consisted largely in forecasting manpower needs by occupation and levels of skill; this led to greater emphasis being laid on methods of forecasting than on the analysis of past and present conditions. It was partly due to the lack of statistical information, but also to the fact that the shortage of skilled workers at all levels was regarded as the main obstacle to development, in the developing countries as in the industrial countries. At the same time, the General Censuses of Population were looked upon as the main source of information, providing a starting-point for long-range projections of what appeared to be limitless skilled manpower needs.

This meant that insufficient importance was attached to such problems as the efficient use of existing trained manpower, occupational mobility, adult education, the wage structure, employment in the non-modern sectors and, generally speaking, labour market adjustment mechanisms.

If these new problems are to be given their rightful place, a greater variety of information will be needed than in the past; priority must also be given to the analysis of present conditions, for an improvement in methods of forecasting can only derive from a better knowledge of the relationships observed between employment and the educational system.

As regards employment data relevant to the needs of human resources policy, we shall discuss the following fields, in which there seems to be a possibility of speedily improving the amount and the quality of information on the Arab countries:

- the education stock in the economically active population, and how it is evolving;

- the occupational structure and skill levels of the economically active population;

- forecasts of the supply of young educated people in the labour market; the influence of education on female participation rates;

- forecasts of the demand for skills, based on international comparisons;

- adjustment between supply and demand; replacement needs; job mobility.

1. THE EDUCATION STOCK IN THE ECONOMICALLY ACTIVE POPULATION

The concept of "education stock" and the complementary concept of "education flow" are linked with the macro-economic research studies of the sixties, which sought to assess the proportion of economic growth attributable to qualitative improvement in the labour force due to a higher level of education among the workers.

The following tables, covering some fifteen industrial countries, show three types of indicators of this kind, which measure the educational levels of the adult population between the ages of 25 and 64 (Table A) making a distinction between the three different levels of the educational system, which differ in their respective costs and in their contribution to the economy. Table B gives the same information for the younger age group (25-34), and from this we can see how quickly the educational levels of the active population are being transformed, one of the leading factors for change in the employment market in all countries. Table C shows a projection of levels of education up to 1980, based on present trends and forecasts of school enrolment figures in the countries concerned.

These measurements of education stock and flows in the adult population and in the active population could very well be carried out at the present time in several Arab countries, using census data on the educational levels of the population and the available school statistics.

Table A

Average number of years of schooling of the 25-64 age group,

around 1970, by level of education

(latest available data from censuses or surveys,
supplemented by estimates)

			Total No. of years of schooling	in: Primary	Secondary	Higher
+ Belgium	a	1971	9.9	6.0	3.4	0.49
+ Canada		1971	9.9	5.8	3.8	0.31 d
+ Denmark	a	1971/2	9.4	5.0	4.1	0.36
France		1968	9.1	5.0	3.8	0.35
Germany		1970	9.2	4.0	5.1	0.18
Greece		1971	5.9	4.5	1.2	0.21
Ireland		1966	9.4	6.0	3.2	0.37
+ Italy		1971	6.4	4.3	1.9	0.19 d
Japan		1970	10.0	6.0	3.6	0.35
+ Netherlands	b	1970	8.6	6.0	2.3	0.35
+ Norway	c	1970	8.7	7.0	1.4	0.29
+ Portugal		1970	3.6	2.5	1.0	0.15
Spain		1970	5.1	3.4	1.5	0.16
Sweden	b	1967	8.3	6.0	2.0	0.31 d
+ United Kingdom		1971	10.2	6.0	3.9	0.23
United States		1970	11.1	5.8	4.5	0.76

a   Age group 20-59

b   Economically active population

c   Age group 25-59

d   Excluding non-university higher education

+   Estimates

Source: Yearbook of Education Statistics, vol.1, OECD, 1974.

Table B

Average number of years of schooling of the 25-34 age group, around 1970, by level of education

(latest available data from censuses or surveys,
supplemented by estimates)

			Total No. of years of schooling	in: Primary	Secondary	Higher
+ Belgium	a	1971	11.3	6.0	4.3	0.93
+ Canada		1971	11.0	5.8	4.7	0.52 d
+ Denmark	a	1971	10.2	5.0	4.5	0.64
France		1968	10.1	5.0	4.6	0.53
+ Germany		1970	9.4	4.0	5.2	0.21
Greece	b	1971	8.0	5.6	2.1	0.31
Ireland		1966	9.8	6.0	3.3	0.47
+ Italy		1971	7.9	4.6	3.0	0.28 d
Japan		1970	11.1	6.0	4.7	0.49
+ Netherlands	c	1970	9.7	6.0	3.1	0.54
+ Norway		1970	9.6	7.0	2.1	0.51
+ Portugal		1970	5.3	3.1	1.8	0.40
Spain		1970	5.6	3.6	1.8	0.21
Sweden		1967	9.6	6.0	3.0	0.53 b
+ United Kingdom	c	1971	11.0	6.0	4.6	0.37
United States		1970	12.0	5.9	5.1	0.98

a   Age group 20-29

b   Age group 25-29

c   Economically active population

d   Excluding non-university higher education

+   Estimates

Source: Yearbook of Education Statistics, vol.1, OECD, 1974.

Table C

Estimates of the growth of the schooling levels of the adult population (25-64 years) between 1970 and 1980

(in annual rates of growth)

		Total school enrolment	in: Primary	Secondary	Higher
Belgium	(a) 1971-81	0.9	0.0	1.6	4.8
Canada	1971-81	1.0	0.1	1.8	5.5
Denmark	(a) 1971-81	0.6	0.0	0.8	4.9
France	1968-78	1.0	0.0	1.6	6.1
Germany	1970-80	0.2	0.0	0.1	4.1
Greece	1971-81	-	1.1	4.9	-
Italy	1971-81	1.6	0.5	3.6	3.6
Japan	1970-80	0.8	0.0	1.7	3.8
Netherlands	1970-80	1.0	0.0	2.7	3.7
Norway	(b) 1970-80	1.2	0.0	4.4	8.2
Portugal	1970-80	3.2	1.6	5.2	10.3
Spain	1970-80	2.2	0.4	4.7	9.3
Sweden	1967-77	1.2	0.0	3.3	6.8
United Kingdom	(c) 1971-81	0.6	0.0	1.1	4.9
United States	1970-80	0.9	0.0	0.9	5.6
Average		1.2	0.2	2.6	5.8

(a) Total No. of persons aged 20-59

(b) Total No. of persons aged 25-59

(c) Excluding Northern Ireland

Source: "Inégalités de distribution de l'éducation entre pays, sexes, générations et individus", OECD, Nov. 1974, SME/CA/74.91 (85 pp. - roneo).

Illiteracy

The over-all illiteracy rate, reckoned from a given age (higher than the primary school enrolment age) is a global indicator frequently used in international comparisons of levels of social development, the relevant information being taken from population census results. To meet the needs of a policy aimed at fighting illiteracy, census figures make it possible to calculate rates by sex, age group and area. Graph VII shows 54 particulars taken from the Syrian census of 1970, in the form of illiteracy profiles by age and sex, and for urban and rural areas. Similar graphs could be prepared for each province from the same source, to form a groundwork of information from which future developments could be forecast in relation with school enrolment of young people and adult literacy campaigns.

Moreover, if we again take the Syrian census figures and compare school enrolment rates (61 per cent for the 10-14 age group) and illiteracy rates (33.3 per cent for the same age group), we find that 6.7 per cent of young people have become literate without going through school, or have left school before the age of 15 but had learned to read and write. By comparing the 1960 and 1970 census figures, both available, it would be possible to measure the fall in the illiteracy rate for cohorts of adults, and from there go on to assess the results of adult education campaigns.

2. THE STRUCTURAL CHARACTERISTICS OF MANPOWER

The structures which have been most studied hitherto are the distribution of manpower by occupational categories and, to a lesser degree, distribution by levels of education or, less frequently still, by type of education. Here again, the population census figures are the primary source of information that can be used to relate educational policy to employment policy.

Programmes for census data processing should, in our view, make systematic provision for cross-tabulation of occupations with educational levels, by age groups and economic sectors, and if necessary by regions. Naturally it would be advisable for the degree of detail of these cross-tabulations (and the cost of each additional table, which would not be high) to be in keeping with the goals of human resources policy. Such tables would provide the facts required both for assessing the situation on the labour market and for making forecasts based on a quantitative and qualitative judgment. This would obviate the over-hasty generalisations which have sometimes resulted from attempts to establish a direct relationship between high-level personnel (or university graduates) and the economy.

It can be seen, for instance, from the published tables of the 1970 Syrian census that of the 65,200 employed persons of both sexes classified as "managerial and professional workers", 61 per cent are teachers (most of them in primary schools) and 12.7 per cent health services personnel; only 3.8 per cent are in production sectors (manufacturing industries, building and public works, mining). Moreover, the 31,600 active persons with a university degree are mainly concentrated in the towns (92 per cent are town-dwellers), particularly in Damascus (45 per cent) and they represent only 14 per cent of the total active population. The 22,600 holders of technical diplomas, on the other hand, are less unevenly distributed, since three quarters of them live outside the capital.

Indications such as these are of course much too superficial to form an adequate foundation for a human resources policy; that would call for correlated variables and not simple distributions according to a single characteristic. There are also other sources of information besides the census figures which could supply data on the qualitative characteristics of manpower: a case in point exists in Iraq, where statistics are available showing (for the year 1972) 62,000 civil servants with college diplomas, distributed by sex and year of graduation, for five levels of diploma.[1]

---

[1] Census of government employees on 31 May 1972, Ministry of Planning, Central Bureau of Statistics, Baghdad (in Arabic).

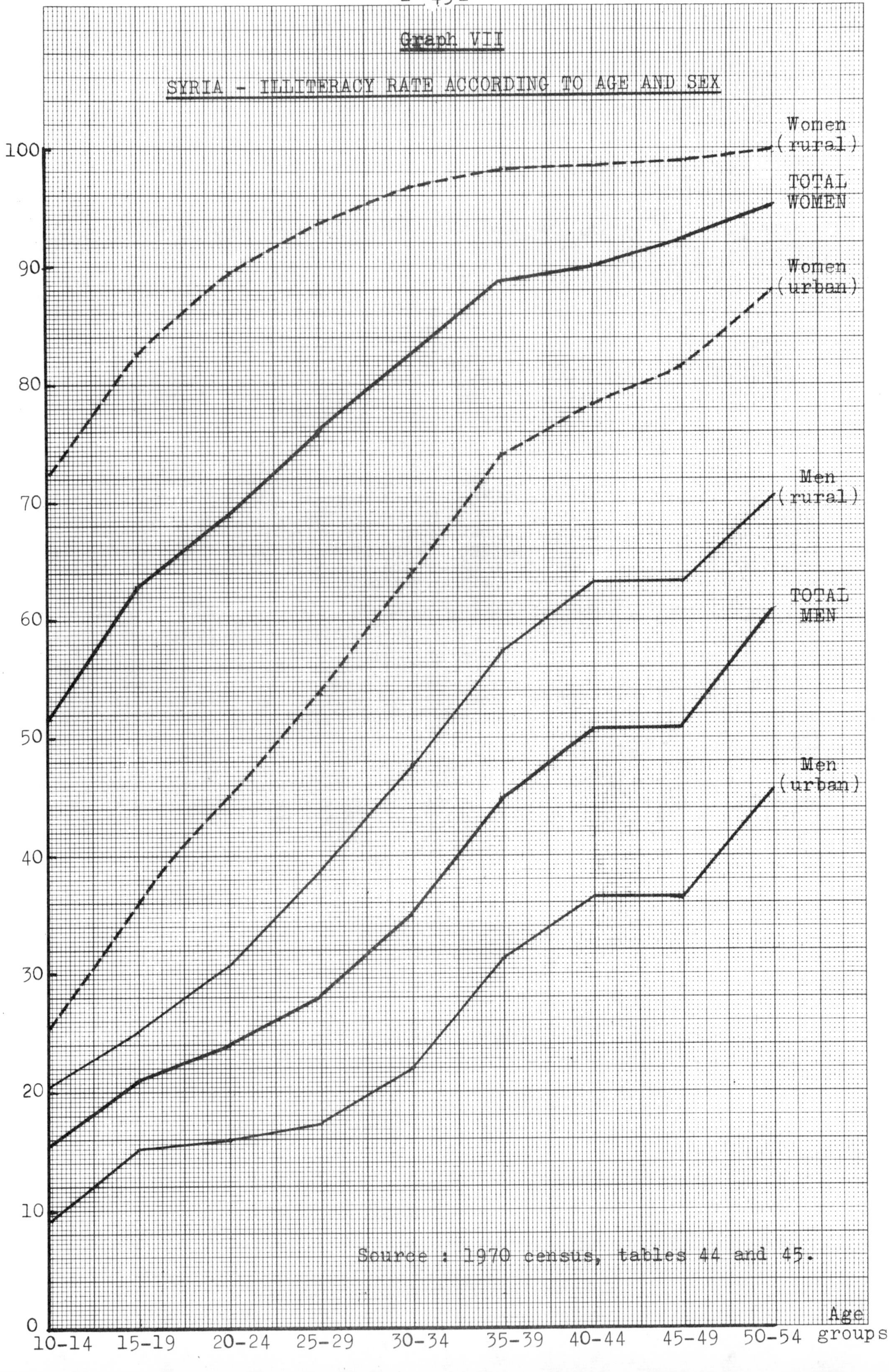
Graph VII
SYRIA - ILLITERACY RATE ACCORDING TO AGE AND SEX
Women (rural)
TOTAL WOMEN
Women (urban)
Men (rural)
TOTAL MEN
Men (urban)
100
90
80
70
60
50
40
30
20
10
0
Source : 1970 census, tables 44 and 45.
10-14
15-19
20-24
25-29
30-34
35-39
40-44
45-49
50-54
Age groups

In Syria[1], annual employment surveys (using representative samples) have been collecting data since 1969 on employment, occupational categories, levels of education, earnings and hours of work, but there do not appear to be any descriptive or analytical studies of the labour market arising out of these data. There is every reason to believe that the data already published (or available though unpublished) would even now be adequate for an initial assessment of qualitative manpower characteristics in the majority of the Arab countries. Even if they are incomplete, existing data have not been fully exploited.

However interesting these structural characteristics of the economically active population may be, they have to be used where they are most adequate, namely for jobs in the modern sector. New tendencies must also be taken into account, however, where we find the emphasis being placed on the other sectors, variously described as traditional, unorganised or informal, to indicate a group of economic activities which do not fit into the standard categories and which are identified not so much by any positive definition as by contrast with the modern sectors and occupations. The reports of the World Employment Programme missions have made a considerable contribution to this development by showing that if goals of full employment were to be effectively sought, it was essential to supplement manpower policies aimed at expanding the modern wage-earning sector and improving conditions in it, with an economic and social policy directed towards upgrading the other sectors which had hitherto been treated as residual.

The World Employment Programme report on Iran suggests that special attention be devoted to the sector composed of goods and services production, in which firms using modern technology and the traditional crafts sector are engaged side by side. The report gives concrete examples indicating that public development aid, both direct and indirect, favours the modern sector to the almost complete exclusion of the rest, thus contributing to a worsening of the situation in the informal sector. A better knowledge of employment trends in this sector would help towards a better appreciation of the indirect effects of government action, which usually takes into account only direct results.

The report on Kenya, like those on Colombia and Ceylon, showed how economic policy could be re-directed so as to take into account the needs and potentialities of the informal sector. There must, however, be a parallel reorientation of the information system so that these informal sectors can be measured and their patterns of change observed. For a start, the modern sector would have to be distinguished from the rest in every field of activity and in every group of occupational categories, and an adequate system of classification would be needed for the professional activities in these informal sectors, incomes, products manufactured, production units, etc.

A project of this kind would certainly call for a good number of case studies and monographs to fill in the gaps in the knowledge of everything outside the modern sector and modern-type employment. As things are at present, existing statistics obtained from censuses, periodical employment surveys or industrial and trade censuses do no more than make it possible to identify wage-employment and thus arrive at an estimate of the non-modern sectors by subtraction from the working-age population.[2] For example, in the preparatory studies for the Second Algerian Four-Year Plan[2], an attempt was made to reconstitute from the 1966 census and the other incomplete information available the pattern of development of non-agricultural employment in the modern sectors during the First Plan (1970-1973); estimates for the other sectors were arrived at by subtraction from the male population of working-age.

---

[1] Results of Employment, Wages and Hours of Work Survey, Central Bureau of Statistics, Damascus, March 1973.

- Statistical Abstract, Central Bureau of Statistics, Damascus, 1974.

- The Annual Statistical Bulletin of the Ministry of Social Affairs and Labour, Damascus, 1972.

[2] Second Four-Year Plan 1974-1977, State Planning Secretariat, Algiers, May 1974.

These estimates obtained by subtraction cannot be regarded as entirely satisfactory, but it is nevertheless worth-while to assess the relative strengths of the sectors concerned instead of simply ignoring them. We can thus bring out the contradictory aspects of the school enrolment policies which are affecting an increasingly large segment of the population and one which is everywhere in excess of the numbers likely to find jobs in the modern sector. In Egypt, the Government decided in 1968 on the basis of estimated capacity of the modern sectors to absorb managerial personnel, to limit to 35,000 per year the numbers of students admitted to centres of higher learning, 60 per cent of them on the scientific and technical side and 10 per cent in teacher training. Similar estimates could be made for each of the Arab countries for the period 1975-1980-1985, in order to arrive at a clear idea of the quantitative dimension of the relationship between education and employment, in relation to openings in the modern sector and trends in the other sectors.

This kind of estimates of labour market trends could be supplemented by structural aspects, for example changes in the occupational structure of graduates and their distribution over the various sectors of the economy. Some recent publications suggest interesting working hypotheses to be used in the analysis of labour market structures.

P. Doeringer[1] has suggested making a distinction between two sectors of the labour market, one of them privileged as regards initial level of education, subsequent training, job mobility and careers profile; these advantages are considered to have a cumulative effect and to tend to increase the distance between the privileged sector and the so-called "secondary" sector throughout professional life. Furthermore, it is suggested that this dualism corresponds largely to a distinction between the recruitment, promotion and training policies of two types of business concerns: firms with an open "internal labour market" would tend to have recourse to the external market to fill the various posts, while those with a "structured" internal market would be more likely to recruit at a low level and apply a policy of career planning, vocational training and within-firm promotion to meet their skilled manpower needs.

This is not the place to discuss the relevance of these theoretical concepts to labour market analysis in the industrial countries which have been the basis for them (mainly the United States, and to a lesser degree Britain, Sweden and Japan), but it would be interesting to see how they could be applied to employment conditions in developing countries; there is every reason to believe that the structural characteristics of employment in rural areas, and in the informal sector in the towns, the importance of which has been stressed in the World Employment Programme mission reports, are very different from those of the modern sector. In addition, the informal sector is bound to be undergoing far-reaching changes as a result of the changes in the modern sector whose products are in direct competition with its own.

The relationship between the modern and the informal sectors could also be studied by testing the recent models which seek to give an account of the drift from the countryside in terms of wage differentials between town and country and urban unemployment rates.

At the present stage, the main obstacle in the way of expanding this kind of study is constituted by the lack of empirical data. That is why we believe that priority should be given to the use of existing but unexploited data, and to deciding on the new data that will be essential if we wish to have a fuller knowledge of the non-traditional sectors and the main characteristics of the workers, their activities and their incomes.

---

[1] See for instance P.B. Doeringer and M.J. Piore, "Internal Labor Markets and Manpower Analysis", Lexington Books, Lex., Mass., 1971, and P.B. Doeringer, "Travailleurs à salaires modestes, caractère dualiste du marché du travail et systèmes de relations industrielles", in "Détermination des Salaires", OECD, 1974, pp. 3-48.

3. FORECASTING ENTRY FLOWS INTO THE LABOUR FORCE

Dynamic manpower analysis is a sine qua non for the planner, who cannot be content simply to forecast the pattern of change in the total labour force. He has to take into account the annual inflow into, and outflow from, the active population, and in making forecasts by occupation, he has also to study each group of occupations from the point of view of age structure and job mobility.

One factor he must take into account is that workers with a higher educational level come on to the labour market later, and also leave it later. Thus replacement rates vary from one occupational category to another, and from one time to another. They do not simply correspond to the inverse of the duration of working life, as has often been assumed in the planning of developing countries, since the higher the birth-rate, the more unstable are demographic structures in time.

In Jordan, H. Rizk[1] has estimated that the ratio of the numbers leaving working life to the numbers entering it had gone from 1 to 3.65 in 1950 to 1 to 5.28 in 1960 and 1 to 6.42 in 1970. Taking into account the age structure, the ratio in 1980 would thus be 1 to 7.48.

In Algeria, the demographic forecasts for 1972 to 1990 show an estimated replacement rate of 1 per cent per year for the total active population.[2] Of course this does not mean that the average length of working life would be 100 years, but that the high proportion of very young people in the working population signifies a much lower retirement rate for workers already in active life in 1973.

In France on the other hand, with an almost stable population, the annual replacement requirements up to 1980 were estimated at 3.3 per cent in the Fifth and Sixth Plans.[3] In the United States[4], the replacement rate forecast up to 1985 is 5.4 per cent per year for the whole of the active population, but it is 6.55 per cent for the higher level group (professionals).

These significant variations, which emerge when many factors specific to each country are taken into account, underline the importance of paying more attention than the planners have hitherto done to structural analysis by age and occupation, so that replacement needs forecasting can be based on the most accurate and detailed data possible. Population census figures contain the basic information required, provided the necessary cross-sections are made.

---

[1] H. Rizk, "Population Policies: Scope, Goals, Means and Problems", in Population Bulletin of the U.N., ECWA, No.7, July 1974.

[2] J. Timar and O. Bertrand: "Les méthodes de prévision des besoins en main-d'oeuvre: le cas de l'Algérie", in "Tiers Monde", 1974.

[3] J. Begué, in "Projections tendancielles des besoins français en main-d'oeuvre par professions 1968-1975-1980" (INSEE, D 8,1970), describes in detail the two methods used to assess replacement needs on the basis of two different assumptions, one taking into account job mobility in the light of trends noted between the 1962 and 1968 censuses.

[4] Estimates taken from the projections presented by Neal H. Rosenthal, "The U.S. Economy in 1985: Projected Changes in Occupations", in Monthly Labor Review, Vol. 96, No.12, Dec. 1974.

Another point is that within one occupational category the younger workers have often spent much more time in school than the older generations, as a result of the recent expansion of secondary and higher education.[1] If we look at the forecasts by occupation (demand) alongside the forecasts by level of education (supply), we can realise better that levels of education are rising rapidly in most occupations. It is the dynamic analysis of school careers that makes it possible to estimate the flow of young people reaching the labour market each year, according to levels of education and certificates or diplomas.

Where trends, developments and variations in time are to be shown, the instrument most commonly used (and the one which best lends itself to comparisons) is the average annual growth rate over the period under consideration. These geometrical rates are based on the implicit assumption that growth has been exponential and regular during the relevant period, which is often the case in the short and medium term. This is the procedure used to show changes in world population, or the demographic growth rate of the various countries. We have indicated elsewhere[2] how calculations can be made easier by using average annual growth rates when trying to identify the different factors that account for trends in the various occupational categories or their educational profiles.

It must not be forgotten, however, that this is an assumption made for purposes of simplification, and that in some cases the normal pattern of change has been disturbed by special demographic factors: wars, mass migrations, etc. In such cases it may be worthwhile to reconstitute the fluctuations that have occurred between censuses. When the detailed results of the 1970 censuses are known, it will be possible to compare them with those of the 1960 censuses, by occupational categories, levels of education and economic sectors, but allowance will have to be made for migration trends which will cause irregularities in the ten-year pattern of development.

There are quite extensive migration movements in many of the Arab countries: the emigration of skilled manpower (Lebanon), the immigration of skilled manpower (Kuwait, Bahrain), the emigration of unskilled manpower (Algeria) or of skilled and unskilled manpower (Tunisia), and so on.

The construction of indicators of inflow and outflow, if possible by educational levels and/or degree of skills, forms an essential statistical basis for drawing up national and regional programmes of action with a place for migrations in human resources policy. The establishment of a set of significant indicators, periodically brought up-to-date, would also make it possible to allow for migration movements in projections of active population, by sex, education and skill levels.

4. THE EDUCATIONAL LEVEL OF WOMEN AFFECTS THEIR PARTICIPATION
    IN THE LABOUR FORCE

The usual practice in projecting the supply of active population is to assume stability or slow growth in the participation of women in working life. It would seem that insufficient importance has hitherto been attached to the developmental factor constituted by the rapid rise in the educational level of women in all countries, and the influence educational attainments have on their attitude to the labour market. We shall begin by showing that in general, national and international projections are conservative.

_____

[1] The phenomenon is not peculiar to the developing countries, for the intensified expansion of educational systems has been more or less general throughout the world since the fifties, as was shown above for 16 industrial nations by comparing the average number of years of schooling of the 25-34 age group (Table B) with the total active population aged 25 to 64 (Table A).

[2] M. Debeauvais, "Les niveaux d'éducation de la population active dans les Recensements de 1970 - analyse comparative des relations éducation-emploi", 191 pp. (Typescript study submitted to UNESCO in 1974 - to be published at a later date).

In most countries, forecasts of female active population are based on the extrapolation of earlier trends in female labour force participation rates, with possible adjustments to allow for specific factors: lowering of the retirement age, reduced participation of women in the agricultural labour force, longer attendance at school, etc., but the positive relationship between the female participation rates and the level of schooling or diplomas is not usually taken into account.

A comparison in twelve OECD countries between the period observed (1965-1970) and the projection period (1970-1975-80-85) shows that extrapolations forecast either a slowing down in the trends observed (Sweden, United Kingdom, France, United States, Denmark), or the stabilisation of rates at their present level (Germany, Netherlands, Switzerland, Italy), or a reduction (Finland, Japan). If the rise in levels of women's educational attainments had been taken into account, the projections would have been much higher.

Similar comments may be made regarding the labour force projections made by the International Labour Office. Two graphs show labour force participation rates by age groups for Jordan and Tunisia, bringing out the very slight or even negative changes expected up to 1990. This appears to us to run counter to the data (which all point the same way) showing the close link between female activity rates and level of education, and the increase in school enrolment of girls, which has everywhere been more rapid than for boys. There is thus every reason to believe that the tendency to give women greater equality of educational opportunity will increasingly find expression in a call for equal opportunities on the labour market, accompanied by a complete change in women's attitudes to employment.

These graphs bring out more clearly than the tables of figures used in drawing them up, the main characteristics of forecasts prepared from that particular model, and also make it possible to assess their usefulness in the planning of human resources. Indeed, we can see that the model has taken into account the expected effects of increased school enrolment of girls, which means lower participation rates for the 10-14 age group and to a lesser extent for the 15-19 age group. Of the others, only the 20-24 age group shows a noticeable increase in the participation rate, but it is a very limited one. For the female active population as a whole, the over-all rate of participation remains more or less stationary throughout the projection period. It is this assumption that female participation will stagnate at its present abnormally low rate which seems to us open to question and in need of reconsideration.

We shall now show the influence of the level of education on female labour force participation rates, with examples drawn from the countries for which we were able to find the required data.

All population censuses which include educational questions offer the possibility of analysing that relationship. Unfortunately, the data published often do not permit calculating participation rates by levels of schooling: these are important for comparing the data of female active population by levels of education or diplomas with similar data for the total economically active population, preferably by age groups.[1] For a more detailed analysis it would be useful to have statistics by provinces, urban and rural areas, etc.

The following graphs show the over-all female participation rates (population over the age of 9) according to levels of schooling, for Egypt in 1960 (Graph X) and for Syria in 1970 (Graph XI). It can be seem that beyond a certain level of schooling (senior secondary education in Egypt, technical and higher education in Syria), the great majority of women form part of the labour force whatever their age.

_____

[1] Nothing is said here about variations in male participation rates, which have less significance because practically all males old enough and fit to work are registered as members of the labour force; very few of the non-active males are likely to enter the labour market.

Graph VIII

FEMALE PARTICIPATION RATES BY AGE GROUPS

IN JORDAN (1950-1985)

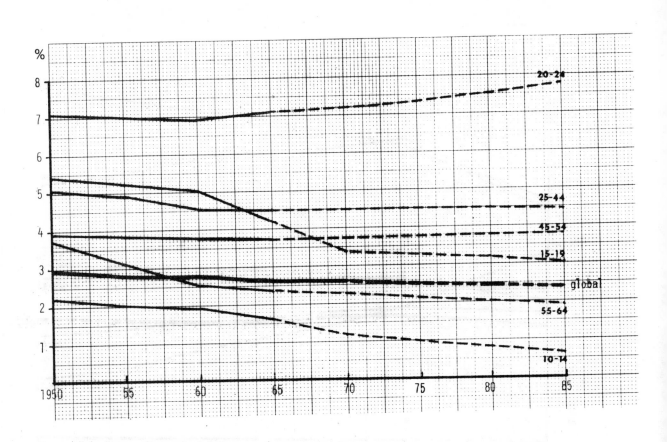

<u>Source:</u> **Labour force projections 1965-1985, Part 1, Asia, ILO, 1971.**

N.B. According to the particulars given by the ILO, the participation
rates for 1950 and 1960 are calculated from population censuses,
with the definitions of active population made comparable.
Failing censuses, the rates are "estimates based on participation rates in the remainder of the region". For the period
1965-1985, the extrapolations "are based very largely on the
results of very detailed comparative analyses for which statistical, graphical and electronic calculating techniques have
been used".

Graph IX

FEMALE PARTICIPATION RATES BY AGE GROUPS

IN TUNISIA (1950-1985)

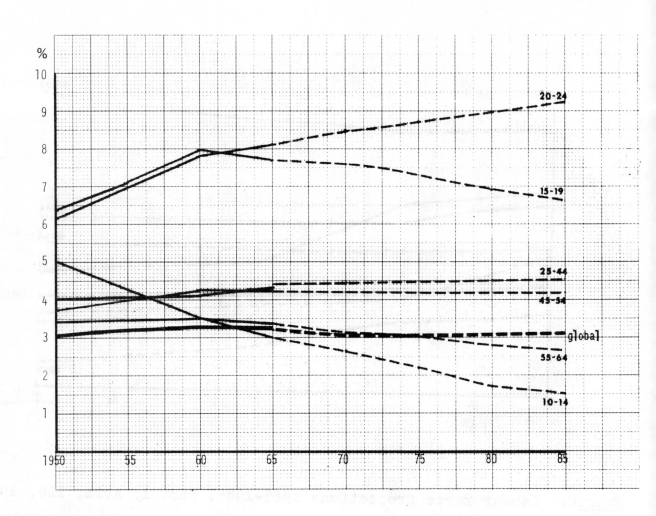

Source: Labour force projections 1965-1985, Part 2, Africa, ILO, 1971.

N.B. According to the particulars given by the ILO, the participation
rates for 1950 and 1960 are calculated from population censuses,
with the definitions of active population made comparable.
Failing censuses, the rates are "estimates based on participation rates in the remainder of the region". For the period
1965-1985, the extrapolations "are based very largely on the
results of very detailed comparative analyses for which statistical, graphical and electronic calculating techniques have
been used".

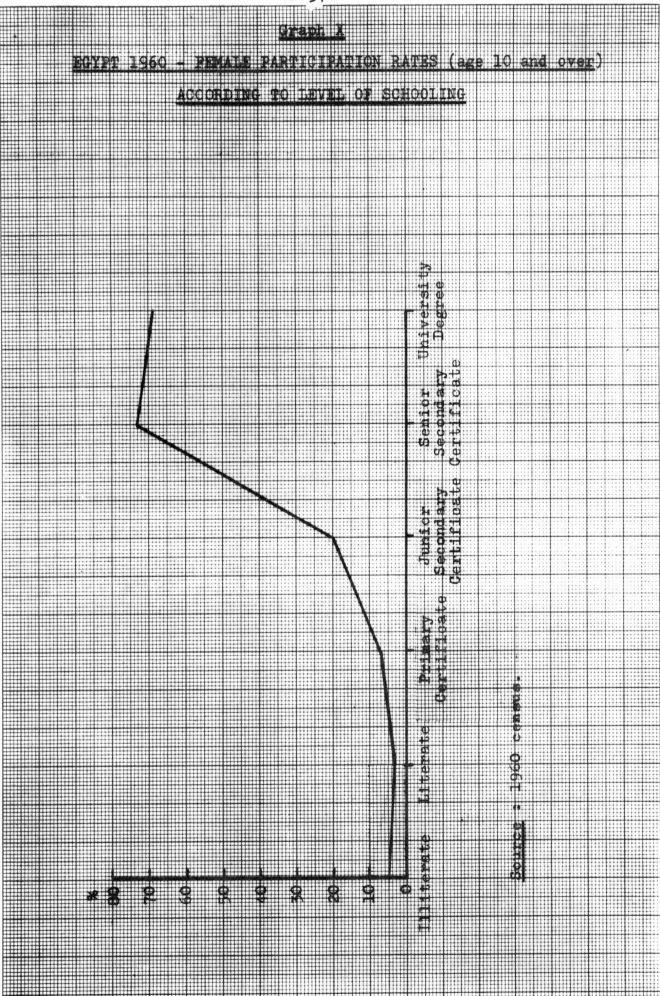

Graph X

EGYPT 1960 - FEMALE PARTICIPATION RATES (age 10 and over)

ACCORDING TO LEVEL OF SCHOOLING

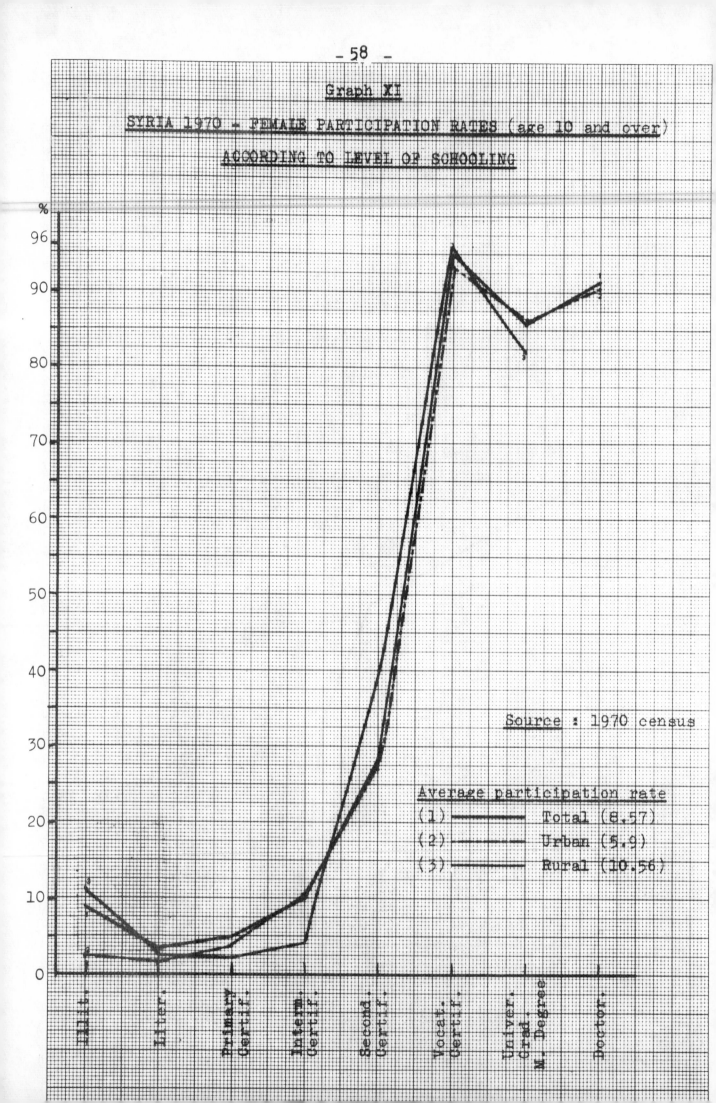

Graph XI

SYRIA 1970 - FEMALE PARTICIPATION RATES (age 10 and over)

ACCORDING TO LEVEL OF SCHOOLING

Source : 1970 census

Average participation rate
(1) ——————— Total (8.57)
(2) ——————— Urban (5.9)
(3) ——————— Rural (10.56)

Using the data from a number of successive censuses, we can compare the age profiles of participation rates by levels of schooling so as to see whether attitudes to labour force participation remain stable or are changing.   In France, participation rates for the same levels of schooling increased between the 1962 and the 1968 censuses.

Thanks to demographic forecasts and projections of female participation rates by levels of schooling and by age, forecasts of the expansion of school enrolment for girls can be used to prepare projections of female labour force participation according to educational attainment.   However, it is true that the level of schooling is not the only factor which influences female labour force participation. The US Department of Labor Statistics show that women with one child or more under the age of six have participation rates almost twice as low as the others, for all levels of schooling.   It will also be observed that the rates are not stable in time, showing a noticeable increase between 1968 and 1972, except for the eight years' schooling level.

For a more detailed analysis, then, allowance would have to be made for family status (married or single, one child or more, etc.) but the census data, which contain these particulars, are not usually available with such extensive cross-tabulations.   Arrangements would have to be made for these information requirements to be taken into account in census data processing programmes.

The examples quoted stress the significance of the relationship between educational attainment and the attitude to employment.   It would, therefore, be advisable to undertake systematic analysis of national data with a view to the revision (upward) of female economically active population forecasts, taking into account participation rates by levels of schooling (and possibly according to the number of children), probable increase in school enrolment of girls, and changes of attitude to wage-employment observed with the passage of time.   Studies of this type would be particularly valuable in the Arab countries, where female participation rates are especially low at present because of historical and sociological factors which are likely to change in the future.   The effects of these changes are sure to make themselves felt on the wage-employment market in particular, which is more limited and which can expand only to the extent that new jobs can be created in the modern sector.

CONCLUSION

The various questions dealt with in this paper do not by any means constitute an exhaustive list of aspects to be considered in working out a human resources policy.   They do not go beyond the quantitative and global aspects, but they have been selected for attention here because improvements in the domain of basic data are at once fairly easy to achieve, by fuller exploitation of existing sources, and a deciding factor for progress in other domains: analysis and projections, even rough ones, of skilled manpower supply and demand should make it possible to place in their order of importance other problems such as the capacity of the modern sectors to absorb graduates, and generally speaking the inter-relationships between decisions on the educational system, employment and the development of the economy.

That is why we believe that alongside the basic information system, however modest, to be set up at national and regional level, a list of priorities should also be drawn up for representative case studies or even monographs on the main problems connected with supply and demand adjustment policy measures.   Data on the structural aspects of manpower or quantitative data on the educational system do not provide an adequate approach to these problems, and must be supplemented by data on the dynamics of the labour market.

We consider that three types of data are essential for an analysis of these questions:

(a)   data on job mobility, which are needed in order to adjust initial training and adult education curricula.   Censuses (or post-census surveys) can supply information regarding past trends, when those questioned are asked to state how they were employed several years earlier;

(b)   data on earnings by levels of schooling and types of diploma, to allow analysis of wage structure, levels and distribution by age, occupation, economic sectors, sex, etc.   This information can be obtained through additional questionnaires to be filled in only by graduates at a census (as done in India), or by post-census surveys carried out on representative samplings by interview.   Follow-up studies of former pupils of various institutions to trace their professional career can supply partial data on both the prospects offered by the educational system and the workings of the labour market for young people, and disparities in income;

(c)   data on unemployment and under-employment, taking into account the various levels and types of education.   Apart from population censuses (which have not proved very suitable for measuring unemployment, particularly in developing countries), employment surveys or specific inquiries into unemployment could include questions on the levels and types of education of those concerned.   This would show how education affects unemployment,

(d)   data on employment and income size and characteristics in the non-modern sectors.   Before even collecting nation-wide statistics, there seems to be a need for monographic studies to define appropriate concepts and terminology.

It may appear over-ambitious, or premature, to mention data of this kind when there is still an absence of basic information on job mobility (even geographical), incomes, employment, under-employment and unemployment in nearly all the Arab countries.   It should not be forgotten, however, that without this minimum of data there can be no adequate grasp of the size and nature of the problems involved, no progress towards efficient use of human resources and no appraisal of results. Also, it seems likely that new trends in development policies will lead to a more systematic attempt to determine exactly what significant data must be collected concerning employment, under-employment, earnings and the traditional sector. Once the plans of work of the national statistical offices have undergone revision in this sense, it will become easier to introduce into questionnaires, survey plans and schedules the necessary features relating to professional activities and levels and types of education.

TRADE POLICY, RELATIVE PRICES AND EMPLOYMENT

by

Harry H. Bell*

I. Introduction

This paper is concerned with the most conventional aspects of trade policy--notably "protection"--in the belief that these will remain relevant to problems of structural unemployment and underemployment in the area long after most of the "excess" oil revenues are dissipated on imports or otherwise absorbed by the international balance-of-payments adjustment mechanism. Indeed, most of the Arab population lives in countries likely to suffer from the chronic unemployment and/or under-employment 1/ of unskilled labour considered by many to be typical of dualistic societies. Whether or not one accepts the theoretical model of the labour-surplus "economy" or its applicability to the Middle East, 2/ very high population growth is expected to continue to be reflected in rapid growth of the labour force, which will also have to absorb the prospective rise in the presently low female participation. ILO projections indicate that annual growth of the labour force in the coming decade will range from 2.6 per cent in Egypt to as high as 3.2 per cent in Algeria and Iraq, as compared with 2.3 per cent in all developing countries and only 0.7 and 1.5 per cent, respectively, in the EEC and North America. 3/

As compared with the relatively sparsely populated desert countries that account for most of the "excess" oil funds, several of the principal Arab countries suffering from chronic employment problems have little if any control over their own terms of trade and the others have perhaps reached the limit of such control. Like most countries, Egypt, Syria, Lebanon, and Tunisia are mainly "price-takers." World price relationships for most of their exports, and all their imports, are "given." However, like other independent countries, they are free--within wide limits--to use tariffs, subsidies, non-tariff barriers, and other protective measures to determine their array of relative prices on tradable goods with respect to the set of world prices they face at their borders. This differentiated profile of relative prices affects incentives in agriculture, export trade, and import-competing industry with effects on employment that, as often as not, may be perverse. Somewhat less directly, it also affects incentives in the non-trade sectors of the economy--notably construction and services--which play particuparly important roles in the absorption of redundant manpower.

The key relative prices that affect employment and income creation at the macroeconomic level are, of course, wages, the rate of interest, and the exchange rate. Increasingly, the procedures of national economic planning and project selection now take account of calculated "shadow" values of these variables, which are believed to reflect the true relative scarcities of factor resources better than the observed money wage rates, the prevailing market rates of interest, and the official exchange rate.

Without questioning the primordial importance of distrotions in these macroeconomic relative prices, the present survey is mainly concerned with the implications for employment of protection-induced distortions in the price relationships among particular categories of

---

* ILO Consultant

1/ There is apparently little agreement on the definitions or measurement of either "open unemployment" or "underemployment," but there is general agreement on the prevalence of the phenomena themselves. Cf. David Turnham, The Employment Problem in Less Developed Countries: A Review of Evidence (Organization for Economic Co-operation and Development, Development Centre, Paris 1971), pp.41-71. See also Appendix 1 on "Appropriate Measurement of Employment Situations in Less Developed Countries," in D.J. Turnham and E.K. Hawkins, "The Employment Problem and World Bank Activities" (I.B.R.D., Bank Staff Working Paper No.148, March 1973), William H. Bartsch, "Unemployment in Less Developed Countries: A Case Study of a Poor District of Tehran," International Development Review, (1971/1), pp.19-22.

2/ See below, pp.29-31. As far as Egypt is concerned, the existence of a labour surplus, or significant "disguised unemployment in agriculture, industry, or services, has been denied by Bent Hansen in "Economic Development of Egypt," Ch.2, Charles A. Cooper and Sidney Alexander, Economic Development and Population Growth in the Middle East (New York: American Elsevier Publishing Co., 1972), pp.26-30.

3/ Source: Table 1, Turnham and Hawkins, op.cit.

goods and as among sectors. The discussion will concentrate on the characteristic bias of tariff structures of many developing countries against agriculture, the bias against export-ing, and the apparent tendency of systematic relative under-pricing of imported capital goods and industrial inputs to favour sophisticated labour-saving technologies. These have been major themes in the literature on development economics of the past five to ten years. Most of the empirical work has been based on the experience in Latin America and South Asia. The lessons learned and the implicit policy prescriptions are perhaps completely irrelevant to those of the oil-producing Arab states whose development is at present constrained by neither a surplus of labour nor a shortage of finance. The degree to which they may be applicable in the other Arab countries is a matter for case-by-case study in the context of their particular problems. Some price relationships are of more crucial importance to some countries than to others.

II. Relative Prices and Profiles of Protection

A. Measurement in Terms of International Prices

All prices are ratios expressed in relationship to some standard. Current money prices are usually measured in terms of the domestic currency as standard or numeraire. World prices, including the posted price of oil, have usually been expressed in an international currency such as the U.S. dollar or the pound sterling. Now that these currencies are floating, other more or less artificially constructed accounting units can be used, depending on the purpose. Much economic analysis (as distinguished from financial analysis) is con-ducted in terms of "real" prices, i.e., the implicit ratios at which goods are exchanged against other goods. Finally, when the index for one basket of goods is related to that for another basket, we obtain the "terms of trade".

For purposes of evaluating effects of tariffs and othe protective measures, it is convenient to take as reference the current international price of each commodity. In this case, we do not mean the "world price" of, say, wool in London or sugar in New York or oil in the Persian Gulf, but rather the price of any tradable product at the customs frontier of the country under consideration. Thus, in considering the tariff protection on products that are imported or could be imported into Lebanon, the CIF price in dollars at the Lebanese border is taken as unity (100 per cent), and an ad valorem tariff of, say 15 per cent implies that the whole-sale or ex-factory price inside Lebanon is expected to be about 115 per cent of such border price times the exchange rate. On the other hand, when referring to products that are normally exported from Lebanon, one takes the FOB price at the border as the rele-vant international price. If there is an export duty of 10 per cent, the domestic price of the commodity is expected to be only 90 per cent of the border price times the exchange rate. Similarly, a 20 per cent subsidy on exports is presumed to permit a domestic-to-foreign ratio of 120 per cent to prevail.

Why should one take the interrelationships of prices in the world market as a standard of reference against which to measure the so-called "distortions" in national markets? The relative prices in the world market always are bound to be considered inequitable and "distorted" from the standpoint of the overwhelming majority of countries and sectoral interest groups. (It is never human nature to be satisfied with one's own terms of trade.) Regardless of justice, however, international prices exist objectively and, with rate excep-tions, they are largely outside the control of most individual countries. Moreover, at any given moment, they reflect a temporary competitive equilibrium which takes account of all the available information on relative gluts and scarcities; and they comprise the set of oppor-tunities which permit a country, if it wishes, to benefit from foreign trade.

This is not to say that international prices are easy to identify and measure. It has been questioned whether the notion has much meaning now that large transnational firms are increasingly resorting to discriminatory "marginal-cost-pricing" practices (or out-right "dumping") for market-penetration purposes, and to "transfer-pricing" for tax-minimisation purposes. 1/ Be that as it may, all ad valorem tariffs assume the existence of an inter-national price and, as a practical matter, customs officials are usually able to determine what it is. For import substitutes and other goods that do not actually cross frontiers, the difficulty in identifying an international price is only one of a number of problems of measurement that complicate analysis of protective structures.

1/ Helen Hughes, "Trade and Industrialization Policies: The Political Economy of the Second Best" (I.B.R.D. Development Economics Staff Working Paper No.143, February 1973), pp. 2-6.

B. Definition of Nominal Protection

An ad valorem import duty has been pictured as a sort of wedge driven in between the level of the local-currency equivalent of the CIF border price and the domestic price, lifting the latter a certain percentage higher than it would have been if there were unrestricted trade and no tariff. Analogously, an export subsidy or export duty is also a wedge that pushes the domestic price up or down, as the case may be, with respect to the FOB border price.

More generally, what tariff theorists have come to call the "rate of nominal protection" of a particular product is defined as the percentage excess of the domestic price over the local-currency equivalent of the international border price, but only to the extent that this results from application of protective measures, i.e., measures that discriminate between domestic and foreign goods. 1/ The rate of nominal protection is sometimes negative, when the protective measures involve a subsidisation of imports or a tax on exports and thereby cause the domestic price to be lower than the foreign price at the prevailing rate of exchange. The same concepts of positive and negative nominal protection apply not only to normal ad valorem duties, but also to the tariff-like price effects of quantitative restrictions and other non-tariff barriers (NTB's) that may supplement or take the place of tariff protection.

The profile of nominal protection depicts the array of differentiated disparities between domestic prices for particular products or groups of products, on the one hand, and the set of international prices facing the country, on the other hand, evaluated at the prevailing exchange rate. The notion of "profile" stresses that protection characteristically involves differentiation. A perfectly "smooth" or "flat" profile of protection on all imports and exports would be virtually indistinguishable from free trade under a system of dual exchange rates. Indeed, rates of nominal protection can be expressed in terms of the corresponding implicit exchange rates instead of in terms of the percentage deviation from international prices. (This way of looking at tariffs reminds us that they perform part of the function of the exchange rate and that high average tariffs on importables permit retention of an over-valued official exchange rate, usually at the sacrifice of potential export trade.) Conversely, a system of multiple exchange rates discriminating among various kinds of goods, such as in Egypt's parallel-exchange market arrangements, is as much a part of the structure of protection as the tariff of customs duties.

Protection measured by price disparities is, moreover, multi-dimensional. It involves not only a product-by-product differentiation of protective rates, but also geographical discrimination. As far as most Arab countries are concerned, the greater part of their trade probably does not occur under so-called "most-favoured nation" (MFN) conditions, but rather within the framework of bilateral trade agreements with the socialist countries and a number of developing countries, the "association" or other special-preference agreements under the EEC's Mediterranean policy, and various regional arrangements in the context of economic integration, such as the Arab Common Market. Currency factors are also a source of preferential differentiation of trade-policy treatment, although the Franc Zone arrangements may play a lesser role in the Maghreb than formerly.

The temporal dimension of protection is also important, not only because of the accelerating rate of political evolution or the phasing-in of new preferential agreements, but especially because a number of Arab countries have come to depend more on quantitative import restrictions, exchange allocations, and state trading monopolies for the determination of levels of protection than on the tariff proper, which is relegated to a revenue role. When this is the case, the tariff link to international prices is severed and the rates of nominal protection may even fluctuate from day to day, at the mercy of domestic demand and supply factors. Thus, analysis of protective rates should also be conducted by time series indexes.

C. Statutory Tariffs Compared with Nominal Protection

One must begin the analysis of protective structure somewhere, and it is normal to start from the conventional tariff profile and then make successive adjustments in order to

---

1/ Cf. Bela Balassa and Associates, the Structure of Protection in Developing Countries (Baltimore and London: John Hopkins Press, 1971, p.4; W.M. Corden, The Theory of Protection (Oxford: Clarendon Press, 1971), pp.21-27; Ian Little, Tibor Scitovsky, and Maurice Scott, Industry and Trade in Some Developing Countries: A Comparative Study (London: Oxford University Press, 1970), pp.2-3.

obtain something like a profile of relative prices, i.e., of nominal protection.   Table I
compares average tariff rates of Morocco in 1968-69 1/ with Latin American tariff structures
that are representative of the type of profile found in countries whose trade policy has
been dominated over a number of years by the development strategy of import-substituting
industrialisation.   The first column shows composite averages of the national legal customs
duties plus various surcharges of the original five countries of the Andean Group (Bolivia,
Colombia, Chile, Ecuador, and Peru) as of May 1969, just before the Andean Group's programme
of trade liberalisation and tariff harmonisation began to be implemented. 2/   The second
column shows estimates of the common external tariff rates of the Central American Common
Market that were theoretically applied by four of the five Member States of that grouping in
in 1972. 3/ (Costa Rica, El Salvador, Guatemala, Nicaragua, Honduras did not even theoretically apply the common tariff).   The products are grouped in categories showing end-use,
economic origin, and levels of processing according to a classification system widely used
in Latin America. 4/   The choice of Morocco as the Arab country for illustrative comparison
with the Latin American countries was dictated mainly by the convenience and simplicity of
the Moroccan legal tariff.   Along with Lebanon, Tunisia, and Jordan, it is among the
countries where the tariff still appears to be more important than quantitative restrictions
and state trading as a determinant of relative prices.   Moreover, because of the Act of
Algeciras, the Moroccan tariff is not complicated by preferential rates.

It is observed immediately from Table I that the Moroccan statutory tariffs in almost
all categories are much lower than those of the Central American common external tariff,
which in turn tend to be generally lower than the tariffs of the South American countries.
(Also, although this is not brought out in the table, the Moroccan tariffs are much less
differentiated within the categories.)   Nevertheless, further observation shows that the
general profile of the three sets of tariffs is remarkably similar, at least at the levels
of aggregation of the categories shown.   Indeed, the rank-correlation coefficients of
Morocco with respect to Central America (0.84) and with respect to the five South American
countries (0.81) are highly significant statistically and even somewhat greater than the
rank-correlation between the two sets of Latin American countries, (0.74).   Alcoholic
beverages and tobacco, which almost universally bear high duties, have a counterpart in high
domestic excise taxes and are motivated largely by revenue rather than protective considerations.   Among the other product groups, clothing and other finished textile products bear
the highest tariffs, followed by the remaining categories of consumer goods, including
directly-consumed primary food products.   Intermediate goods (except semi-finished textiles
and, to some extent, semi-processed foodstuffs) have relatively low tariffs, and capital
goods have much lower rates than other manufactured products.   These relative patterns are
characteristic of the statutory tariffs of many and perhaps most countries of the world,
including the post-Kennedy-Round tariffs of the principal industrial countries, 5/ although

---

1/   Calculated from Bulletin International des Douanes (International Customs Journal),
No.132 (8th edition), Morocco (Kingdom of),(Brussels: International Customs Tariffs Bureau,
October 1968).   Averages are based on a 400-item sample and weighted according to the same
composite trade weighting used for the data on Central America.   Rates include customs duty,
special tax, and stamp duty, but exclude purchase and sales tax.   Note that the rates shown
are somewhat out of date and do not take account of the duty reductions negotiated with EEC,
effective 1 September 1970, which reportedly lowered Morocco's MFN tariffs by 25 per cent on
products accounting for about 7 per cent of imports from the Community.

2/   Calculated from various documents compiled by the Junta del Acuerdo de Cartagena
(secretariat of the Andean Group in Lima).   Based on 500-item sample and weighted by a trade
weighting reflecting typical Latin American import patterns and the OECD trade pattern.
Note that the tariff levels and structures of the five countries included in the composite
average were widely divergent.   This is shown by the following comparison of the over-all
averages given by the sample for the national tariffs: Bolivia 50%, Ecuador 98%, Colombia
60%, Chile 152%, Peru 79%, composite average 88%.

3/   Mixed specific and ad valorem duties taken from official documents compiled by the
Common Market secretariat, were converted into ad valorem terms according to unit values
estimated by the author from 1972 trade statistics.   Total tariffs shown here include the
tariff proper plus the 30% surcharge applied to most imports under the Protocol of San Jose.
Averages are based on 400-item sample, weighted by a composite trade pattern reflecting total
Central American import structure and the trade pattern of OECD countries.

4/   E.C.L.A., document E/CN.12/739/Corr.1, 8 November 1965, "Classification del comercio
exterior segun uso o destino economico" (CUODE).

5/   Cf. UNCTAD document TD/6/Rev 1, The Kennedy Round: Estimated Effects on Tariff
Barriers (New York: United Nations, S les No. E.68.II.D12, 1968), Chart I, p.46.

TABLE I

COMPARISON OF AVERAGE TARIFFS: LATIN AMERICA AND MOROCCO
(Statutory Tariffs, Including Surcharges)

	(1) 5 South American Countries (1969)	(2) Common External Tariff, Central America (1972)	(3) Morocco (1969)
	(in percent _ad valorem_)		
1. Non-Durable Consumer Goods:			
Food products	130	148	72
Beverages, tobacco	203	297	121 (+)
Clothing	232	181	75
Other	129	65	55
2. Durable Consumer Goods:			
Personal vehicles	220	62	40
Other	131	83	65
3. Fuel and Lubricants	47	10	11
4. Raw Materials and Intermediate Inputs for Agriculture:			
Feed for animals	100	20	10
Other	62	9	8
5. Raw Materials and Intermediate Inputs for industry:			
Foodstuffs	73	96	16
Agricultural origin, non-food (incl. textile fibres and intermediates)	97	72	28
Mineral origin	61	27	14
Chemicals and pharmaceuticals	68	45	16
6. Construction Materials	85	65	19
7.) 8.) Capital Goods for Agriculture and Industry	49	15	17
9. Transport Equipment (excl. personal vehicles)	86	27	27
Over-all Average (Weighted)	88	57	30
Levels of Processing:			
Primary	67	62	14
Semi-Manufactures	69	39	13
Manufactures	102	61	39
Of which: Capital goods for Agriculture and Industry	49	15	17
Other	125	72	44

Source: See notes to text.

the absolute height of the latter is usually much lower than that of developing countries. Since most of the other major Arab countries apparently have higher and more differentiated protective structures than that of Morocco, it appears that illustrative examples from Latin American experience with the import-substitution type of trade policy are also relevant in the Arab world.

Table II uses the example of the Central American external tariff to show that the profile of nominal protection measured by actual relative prices is likely to be very different from the profile of statutory tariffs.

Once one has established what the average statutory rates--including surcharges, etc.-- are in terms of ad valorem equivalents (col.1), it is necessary to calculate to what extent these are actually applied (col.2). In Latin America, many customs exemptions are provided, on a systematic or ad hoc basis, for special categories of importers (such as governments, diplomats, religious and charitable institutions, etc.); for certain basic foodstuffs and other goods deemed to be particularly essential for mass consumption; and in the context of legislation authorising fiscal incentives for approved industrial investment programmes. The latter affect mainly capital goods and intermediate inputs that are not locally produced. (Temporary-import arrangements and industrial free-trade zones to encourage exports such as those established in Egypt under Law No.65 of 1971 are a special case within the framework of these industrial incentives.) In Central America, it is extremely difficult even to inventory the various types of exemptions, since each Member State has different lists and policies. Even where an up-to-date inventory of these measures exists, it is still neces- sary to estimate whether and to what extent they lower the incidence of protection on the price of (a) goods actually imported and (b) domestically-produced import-competing goods. Such derogations from the basic tariff schedule appear to be almost as prevalent in Arab countries as in Latin America. As will be shown later, there are reasons to believe that any immediately favourable effects of the investment incentives on employment may well be more than offset in the long run by their choice of technology toward capital-intensiveness.

Thus far, we have been looking at import tariffs, but these do not determine the rela- tive prices of export goods. Traditional or "strong" exports (like oil, natural gas, and wine in Algeria, phosphates in Morocco and Jordan, and long-staple cotton in Egypt) are usually subject to export duties, quantitative export controls, or outright governmental export monopolies. Assuming for the moment that there are no quantitative controls or state-trading monopolies, one can use the scheduled export taxes, or their ad valorem equiv- alents, as a measure of the negative nominal protection on these goods and to substitute this for the positive nominal protection normally applied with respect to importable goods. On the other hand, the protection-induced price disparity on those exports (normally non- traditional exports) that are not subject to export duties is assumed to be zero with respect to FOB border prices, except to the extent that cash subsidies or customs drawbacks are given as export-promotion measures. In any case, the positive rates of nominal protection result- ing from the subsidies are unlikely to be as high as the tariff that would be applied if the identical product were imported. A corresponding adjustment should, therefore, be made in the tariff profile, as illustrated by col.3 of Table II, in which the protection affecting Central America's typical export products such as beef, bananas, coffee, cotton, and wood is shifted from an import to an export basis.

The most difficult adjustments are those to take account of redundancy ("water in the tariff"), when tariffs are prohibitively high, and of the excess domestic-price disparity that results when non-tariff barriers such as quantitative import restrictions supersede the tariff's role as the dominant instrument of protection. Since quantitative restrictions were believed to have relatively few price effects in Central America in 1972, the substan- tially lower figures shown in col.4 as compared with col.3 are attributable mainly to the fact that so many tariffs were largely redundant. This was especially true of a number of primary foodstuffs, such as fruits and vegetables, which were given high tariffs for appar- ently symbolic reasons though the local production was so abundant and competitive that no significant import flow could have been expected to occur in the absence of protective meas- ures. Indeed, astronomical tariffs are often legislated for a country's characteristic exports, which is an extreme case of redundancy. Central America's import duties on bananas were apparently equivalent to about 465 per cent ad valorem; and Morocco levied a duty of 120 per cent on tinned fish, its most successful manufactured export product. However, many other cases of redundant tariffs apply to industries that are still on an import-substitution basis and uncompetitive at international prices, but in which domestic competition keeps domestic prices well below the maximum theoretically permitted by the tariff. The higher the levels of the tariff, the greater the proportion likely to be unutilised, except when the exchange rate is very overvalued because of domestic inflation.

Neither prohibitive tariffs nor tariffs superseded by import prohibitions or other restrictive non-tariff barriers give information about relative prices. For all products

TABLE II

CENTRAL AMERICAN COMMON MARKET: ESTIMATED NOMINAL PROTECTION, 1972
(Compared with Statutory Tariffs)

	Statutory Import Tariffs	Adjusted for Exemptions	Adjusted for Export Products	Adjusted for Redundancy Excise Taxes and NTB's
				(in per cent _ad valorem_)
1. Non-Durable Consumer Goods:				
Food products	148	121	98	14
Beverages, tobacco	297	94	94	0
Clothing	181	116	116	63
Other	65	49	49	34
2. Durable Consumer Goods:				
Personal Vehicles	62	62	62	62
Other	83	76	76	73
3. Fuel and Lubricants:	10	6	6	6
4. Raw Materials and Intermediate Inputs for Agriculture:				
Feed for animals	20	3	3	2
Other	9	7	7	7
5. Raw Materials and Intermediate Inputs for Industry:				
Foodstuffs	96	75	56	6
Agricultural origin, non-food (incl. textile fibres and intermediates)	72	56	53	28
Mineral origin	27	17	17	16
Chemicals and pharmaceuticals	45	14	14	8
6. Construction Materials:	65	48	45	9
7.) Capital Goods for Agriculture and 8.) Industry	15	11	11	10
9. Transport Equipment (excl. personal vehicles)	_27_	_25_	_25_	_23_
Over-all Average (Weighted)	57	41	38	21
Levels of Processing:				
Primary	62			3.3
Semi-Manufactures	39			6.4
Manufactures	61			29.8
Of which:				
Capital Goods for Agriculture and Industry	15			9.9
Other	72			34.6

Source: Estimated by the author from fragmentary information.

where one of these situations exists, the statutory duties are useless for estimating rates of nominal protection. Preferably, the international price disparities should be measured directly by price survey techniques. If this is prohibitively costly or otherwise not feasible, it may still be possible to develop judgmental estimates from fragmentary information, if a relatively small proportion of the products sampled are found to be affected by restrictive import regimes or super-high tariffs. In the cases of Morocco, Lebanon, and Jordan, it should not be too difficult to calculate reasonable estimates of nominal protection, based mainly on the tariff. The statistical problems are much more formidable with respect to the apparently much more complicated trade and exchange regimes of Egypt, Syria, and Iraq, and especially the comprehensive state-trading regime of Algeria. Problems arising from geographic differentiation of protection under Franc Zone and EEC association arrangements might affect particularly the evaluation of the Tunisian and Algerian protective profiles, although Egypt and Lebanon also give reverse preferences to the Community under the latter's Mediterranean policy. Detailed study would be required in order to determine the extent to which the pattern of relative prices is also affected by the numerous bilateral clearing accords, by the Arab Common Market, and by ad hoc measures.

D. Effective Protection

The reason for insisting so much on the definition of nominal rates of protection, and on the difference between statutory tariffs and nominal protection, is that estimation of "effective" rates of the protection presupposes a correct concept and measurement of the nominal rates, in terms of relative prices. Indeed, the notion of "nominal" protection only originated (in the early 1960's) in connection with development of the theory of effective protection, and in contradistinction to the latter.

It is recalled that the effective rate of protection measures the net incidence, positive or negative, that tariffs and other protective measures have on the value added generated by a particular productive activity. It takes account of the nominal protection on output less the nominal protection on the inputs (sometimes just the internationally-traded inputs) going into the industrial process. This net protection is expressed as a percentage of the value added that would have been obtained in the absence of protective measures.1/

The amount of net protection depends on the escalation of the tariff structure; the tendency for nominal rates on outputs to be substantially higher than the nominal protection contained in the inputs going into the product. The escalation of the Central American tariff structure is illustrated in the comparison at the bottom of Table II, which shows somewhat higher nominal rates for semi-manufactures than for primary products and much higher rates for manufactures than for semi-manufactures.

There is disagreement among theorists regarding the degree to which the allocation of resources among industries can be predicted from the relationships of their effective rates of protection. 2/ Nevertheless, the extreme peaks and valleys in the protective profiles of many developing countries (including, presumably, most of the major Arab countries) are generally considered to reflect strong incentives and disincentives that are likely to pull resources away from the pattern that would reflect comparative advantage, with effects that can hardly be neutral with respect to employment. No claim is made here that there is necessarily a precise relationship between these incentives and disincentives and the profile of effective protection. Ambiguities in the concept and content of "value added", analytical problems resulting from substitutability of factors and inputs in production as a result of changes in relative prices, and innumerable statistical problems make effective rates very imperfect indicators of the production effects of protective measures. In conjunction with

---

1/ Cf. Harry G. Johnson, "The Theory of Tariff Structure, with Special Reference to World Trade and Development" (lecture, Geneva, 1964), reprinted in Aspects of the Theory of Tariffs (Cambridge, Mass.: Harvard University Press, 1972), pp.307-30; Balassa and Associates, op.cit., Appendix A, pp.315-39; Corden, op.cit., pp.28-64; Herbert G. Grubel and Harry G. Johnson (eds.), Effective Tariff Protection (Geneva: GATT/Graduate Institute of International Studies, 1971), passim.

2/ A number of recent articles have challenged the realism of the rigid assumptions under which it had been asserted that the effective rate of protection is the best or most practical measure of resource pulls resulting from protection. Cf. J.N. Bhagwati and T.N. Srinivasan, "The General Equilibrium Theory of Effective Protection and Resource Allocation," Journal of International Economics (Vol.3, No.3, 1973), pp.259-282; Lance Taylor and Stephen L. Black, "Practical General Equilibrium Estimation of Resource Pulls under Trade Liberalisation," Journal of International Economics (Vol.4, 1974), pp.37-48; Bent Hansen, "Effective Protection: A Probabilistic Argument" Journal of Economics (Vol.4, 1974) pp.207-11.

nominal rates, they, nevertheless, provide a helpful tool for diagnosis of serious distortions of tariff structure, since they call attention to the interaction of protection on inputs and outputs.

Despite the imprecision of most numerical estimates of effective protection, the basic pattern of relative incentives and disincentives generally reflected in sectoral averages is characteristic of the import-substitution stage of commercial policy, which is now found in most countries emerging from colonialism and in the process of industrialisation.

III. Employment Implications of Import-Substitution Policies

A. Import Substitution vs. Policies of Import-Substituting Industrialisation.

It is important to distinguish between, on the one hand, import substitution as empirically observed fact and, on the other hand, the complex of development strategies and associated trade policies that has come to be known as import-substituting industrialisation (or "ISI"). Observed import substitution is measured by various objective statistical criteria (e.g., in terms of a reduction of the total import coefficient with respect to total supply [1]), and it is at least as likely to be the effect of development as the cause.[2] As a development strategy, import-substituting industrialisation involves, inter alia, conscious efforts to replace imports through imposition of a combination of protective measures. It is well known that, after these policies are pushed beyond a certain point, they tend to be increasingly frustrated by a rise in imports of components for assembly, raw and intermediate materials, and capital goods, so that the import coefficient can no longer be compressed except at the cost of an interruption of growth brought on by the "import constraint". A reductio ad absurdum is reached in those cases where value added becomes negative at international prices, i.e., more foreign exchange is expended on inputs than it would cost to import the product itself. [3]

The main characteristics of import-substituting patterns of protection, already exemplified in Tables I and II in the preceding chapter, can be recapitulated as follows:

(1) High average levels of nominal protection, reflecting high statutory tariffs (including surcharges) and/or high implicit tariffs resulting from direct trade controls and/or multiple exchange rates;

(2) Differentiation of nominal rates within categories, especially as between locally produced and non-competing goods ("Tailor-made" protection);

(3) Sharp or erratic escalation of nominal rates by stages of processing, except that capital goods tend to be exempted from protective measures or have relatively low rates;

(4) Very low or negative rates of real nominal protection for agriculture and other primary sectors as compared with the manufacturing sector (internal terms-of-trade discrimination against agriculture);

(5) Negative protection (deliberate) on the country's strongly competitive traditional exports;

(6) Implicit but unintended discrimination against diversified non-traditional exports at the prevailing exchange rate and in the absence of subsidisation; and

(7) Revenue role of tariff structure relegated to a secondary consideration relative to industrialisation objectives.

---

[1] Cf. Hollis B. Chenery, "Patterns of Industrial Growth", American Economic Review (L., Vol.4, September 1960) pp.624-53.

[2] Donald B. Keesing, "Outward Looking Policies and Economic Development", Economic Journal (June 1967), pp.30-305; Gordon C. Winston, "Notes on the Concept of Import Substitution", Pakistan Development Review (Vol. VII, Spring 1967), pp.107-17.

[3] Stephen E. Guisinger, "Negative Value Added and the Theory of Effective Protection, Quarterly Journal of Economics (Vol.3, No.3, August 1969), pp.415-33.

Historically, import-substituting industrialisation policies emerged as a body of doctrine in publications of the Economic Commission for Latin America (ECLA) when it was headed by Dr. Raul Presbisch. 1/ In the Arab region, Egypt embarked on import-substitution policies in 1952, with what appear in retrospect to have been relatively moderate increases in tariffs on manufactured consumer goods, a lowering or abolition of tariffs on machinery and non-competing intermediate inputs, and exemption from duty of essential foodstuffs to restrain the rise in living costs and money wages. 2/ By the end of the decade, Egyptian protection policy was mainly implemented by manipulation of import-licensing controls and an ever-shifting series of measures in the field of multiple exchange rates. In other major Arab countries, import-substitution policies began to be applied in varying degrees in the 1960's, when the restraints of colonial trade preference systems and of membership in the Sterling Area and Franc Zone weakened or were cast off.

Many of the justifications for import-substituting strategies in developing countries are identical to those adduced for protectionist policies in industrialised Western countries, especially the classic infant-industry argument and the pragmatic argument that in balance-of-payments crises it is easier to raise tariffs, impose surcharges, and tighten quotas than to devalue explicit exchange rates or compress domestic demand. As in developed countries, it later seems impossible to dismantle the emergency measures because the adverse, direct and immediate effects on employment are more visible than the indirect, more generalised, and possibly deferred advantages. However, there are a number of special rationales applicable only in developing countries. Some are political and sociological: to destroy the power of an absentee--and frequently foreign--landed oligarchy on which was based the earlier primary export-oriented society, or to stimulate an emerging entrepreneurial middle class with the promise of a guaranteed and subsidised domestic market. Another element of the justification is export pessimism with respect to the trade barriers in dustrial countries and instability of demand in world markets. Then there is the whole complex of reasons for favouring industry over agriculture. Prospects of rapid growth rates in the former are compared to what appear to be stagnant rates in the latter (leaving out of account the differences in the size of the respective bases). Planners also feel that inward-looking industrial development speeds up creation of input-output linkages a la Hirschman 3/, thereby raising the multiplier effects of demand on income and employment (but perhaps at the cost of making the economy more vulnerable to inflationary and deflationary shocks).

There is a whole family of justifications for the import-substituting-industrialisation strategy based on an assumed institutionally-based higher cost of labour in the urban sector relative to the rural sector that should be corrected by tariffs on industrial goods. This so-called "Manoilesco argument", which appeared between the wars 4/, was subsequently transformed into an extremely sophisticated model in a famous article by W. Arthur Lewis 5/ which

---

1/ See, especially, The Economic Development of Latin America and its Principal Problems (New York: United Nations, 1950, reprinted in Economic Bulletin for Latin America, Vol. VII, No.1, 1962).

2/ For an economic history of Egypt since World War II, in which much attention is paid to policies and developments affecting relative prices, see Bent Hansen and Girgis A. Marzuk, Development and Economic Policy in the UAR (Egypt) (Amsterdam: North-Holland Publishing Co., 1965), especially pp.149-53, 159-65, 191-210, 235-45, 285-94.

3/ Alfred O. Hirschman, The Strategy of Economic Development (New Haven: Yale University Press, 1958), ch.6 Hirschman recognised, however, that import-substituting policies may tend to discourage backward linkages, since entrepreneurs making final products have a vested interest in importing their inputs. See "The Political Economy of Import Substituting Industrialisation in Latin America", Quarterly Journal of Economics (Vol.LXXXII, No.1, February 1968), pp.17-24.

4/ M. Manoilesco, "Arbeitsproduktivitat and Assenhandel", Weltwirtschaftliches Archiv (Vol.XLII, 1935), pp.13-43. See also E.E. Hagen, "An Economic Justification for Protection", Quarterly Journal of Economics (1958), pp.497-8, and rebuttal by H. Myint, "Infant Industry Arguments for Assistance to Industries in the Setting of Dynamic Trade Theory", in Roy Harrod and Douglas Hague (eds.), International Trade Theory in a Developing World (proceedings of a conference held by the International Economic Association, 1963), pp.175-80.

5/ W.A. Lewis, "Economic Development with Unlimited Supplies of Labour", The Manchester School of Economic and Social Studies, (Vol.22, No.2, May 1954), p.140.

was followed up in a number of studies by Fei and Ranis.1/ Lewis assumed that a number of developing countries are characterised by an unlimited supply of labour in the form of disguised unemployment in subsistence agriculture, where the marginal product of labour is zero. He specified that this is "obviously the relevant assumption for the economies of Egypt, of India, or of Jamaica". By turning the domestic terms of trade against agriculture in favour of industry, and using inflationary credit creation for finance, the capitalist sector attracts the surplus labour into industry and, through reinvesting in new productive capacity the profits derived from use of the otherwise idle resources, creates the savings required to bring the inflationary process to an end. Ultimately, the labour surplus will be fully absorbed. One of the problems with this scenario has to do with the initial assumption of an unlimited supply of labour having zero or negligible marginal productivity in agriculture and which is available to the industrialists at a constant real wage. The factual basis of the assumption has been challenged, not only with respect to Egypt 2/, but also with respect to several other countries where it had alleged to apply.3/

It is interesting that some of the principal exponents of this dualistic labour-surplus justification for protectionist industrialisation have subsequently changed their emphasis. As President of the Caribbean Development Bank, Sir Arthur Lewis has recently stressed international competitiveness and measures in the field of devaluation, appropriate trade policies, productivity, and incomes policy as a prescription for better employment in that area.

Fei and Ranis are still analysing development in terms of labour-surplus model, but have nothing good to say for the land-or raw-material based "import-substitution syndrome"4/, except as an historical stage that dualistic countries go through on their way to an outward-looking "export-substitution" stage based on utilisation of labour and skills in manufactured exports. All the emphasis has shifted to elimination of distorted relative prices resulting from overvalued exchange rates and excessive protection, on correcting the neglect of agriculture, and on making more use of relative prices in planning the transition to more open economies.

From the beginning of the 1960's Prebisch 5/ and the ECLA economists also evolved away from their earlier doctrines, since it became clear that the easy stage of import substitution, aimed at taking over the national markets for consumer goods, soon led to stagnation when these markets were saturated and it was impossible to take advantage of economies of scale except in the very largest countries. The strategy of import substitution was not repudiated, however, but rather transferred from the national to the regional level in the context of regional integration, within which there could be more "balanced" substitution of imports of intermediate inputs and capital goods.

B. The Bias Against Agriculture

About 60 per cent of the economically active labour force of Arab countries was engaged in agriculture as of about 1970.6/ Substantially less than 10 per cent was in protected manufacturing industry. Regardless of controversies over definition of disguised

---

1/ J.C.H. Fei and G. Ranis, Development of the Labor Surplus Economy (Homewood, Ill.: Richard D. Irwin, Inc., 1964).

2/ Cf. Bent Hansen, as noted above, and Doreen Warriner, Land Reform and Economic Development (Cairo, 1955), pp.25-6, cited by Myint, op.cit., p.178.

3/ Dale W. Jorgenson, "Testing Alternative Theories of the Development of a Dual Economy", in I. Adelman and E. Thorbecke (eds.), The Theory and Design of Economic Development (Baltimore: John Hopkins Press, 1966), pp.45-66; Lloyd G. Reynolds, "Economic Development with Surplus Labor: Some Complications" (Yale University Economic Growth Center, discussion Paper No.45, February 8, 1968).

4/ G. Ranis, "Relative Prices in Planning for Economic Development", op.cit.

5/ Towards a Dynamic Development Policy for Latin America (New York: United Nations, 1963, E/CN. 12/680/Rev.1), pp.67-73.

6/ Elias H. Tuma, "Population, Food and Agriculture in the Arab Countries", Middle East Journal (Vol.28, No.4, Autumn 1974), table on p.392.

unemployment and the extent of a surplus of workers having zero marginal productivity, subsistence agriculture is the ultimate source of the underemployed persons who accumulate in marginal occupations in the traditional sectors of cities. Since the high growth rates of value added in modern manufacturing industry are not accompanied by equivalent growth in employment, especially of the unskilled, a major focus of employment policy (if not the major focus) must be on protecting the labour-retaining capacity of agriculture. The problem is complicated, however, by the equal need to increase agricultural productivity to expand food output.

Referring to Latin America, Professor Rosenstein-Rodan,1/ has summarised the commercial-policy aspect of this issue as follows:

...Output and employment in agriculture are at present below equilibrium; they have to be increased, although in the longer run the percentage of labour force in agriculture will fall. The main reason why agricultural development is "lagging" in most underdeveloped countries is due to the fact that the domestic terms of trade between industrial and agricultural products are even more unfavourable to agriculture than the international ones. Infant industry protection raises the prices of industrial products, while agricultural prices are at the world market level. If it takes twice as many bushels of wheat to buy a ton of fertilizer, a farmer acts as a homo economicus and does not buy it. The tariff policy must be changed to create lower industrial prices if full employment is to be reached. Various forms of regional and subregional integration are as essential for that purpose as are other measures to improve the international division of labour by facilitating and promoting exports.

To what extent is this applicable to Arab countries, or at least those whose economies are not so dominated by oil that unemployment is, for the time being, an irrelevant concern? Having insufficient knowledge of agricultural trends and policies in the region to hazard an answer myself, I simply cite the view of Professor Hansen, based on his many years in Cairo.2/

An issue that has gained importance during recent years is the relationship between industrial and agricultural prices. There has been a clear tendency to let the terms of trade of agriculture deteriorate as a means of financing industrialisation...(fn) Before World War II, fertilizers were imported duty free. Although this policy was dictated mainly by the wishes of the landlords, it obviously had positive allocation effects. Since the 1950s the government has sold fertilizers to the peasants at prices generally above import prices, probably as a device to tax agriculture....In other (particularly Communist) countries, this policy has had detrimental effects on agricultural development and has led to compulsory deliveries of certain minimum quantities at official prices. In Egypt the results seem to be much the same. If agriculture is to expand more rapidly than in the past, price policies have to be more favourable to agricultural production.....

The strong tendency of commercial policy in developing countries to be biased against agriculture (as contrasted with the equally strong opposite tendency in developed countries) often reflects a deliberate policy, on social-political as well as economic grounds, of taxing the exports of plantation agriculture. To the extent that these traditional exports face relatively inelastic foreign demand and supply, moreover, it may be possible to "make the foreigners pay the tax", through terms-of-trade effects. The Egyptian policies with respect to export taxes, buffer stocks, special exchange rates, etc. for long-staple cotton illustrate such a strategy, carried out over a number of years with varying degrees of success and/or frustration.3/

However, the notion of "bias against agriculture" is subject to various interpretations. The price comparisons in the profile of nominal protection have the virtue of being conceptually straightforward, and it is not clear whether the allegedly greater insight into incen-

---

1/ P.N. Rosenstein-Rodan, Planning for Full Employment in Latin America (Ottawa, Carleton University, School of International Affairs, Occasional Papers No.20, April 1972), p.10.

2/ Hansen, "Economic Development of Egypt", in Cooper and Alexander, op.cit., p.83.

3/ See Hansen, Development and Economic Policy in the UAR, op.cit., pp.95-108, for a concise history and evaluation of cotton marketing policy.

tive and resource-pull effects provided by the effective-protection approach compensates for the practical and theoretical problems of applying it. From the point of view of employment policy, moreover, other types of measurement might be more relevant; for example, computation of the domestic terms of trade would highlight more directly the income transfer imposed on agriculture by the industrial sector. Here again, however, all kinds of statistical problems arise, not least of which is the lack of data on what the sectors purchase from each other and at what prices.

The literature has adequately documented the importance of relative prices, including those for fertilizer and other inputs, in expanding agricultural output. The disincentives resulting from the frequent underpricing of food aid under PL 480 and similar programmes have been pointed out. The most backward peasants respond rationally to output prices and costs of production and adjust proportions of factor inputs to their relative prices.[1] Non-tariff barriers may also have disincentive effects additional to those that are reflected in higher costs in money terms. For example, it was reported in Tunisia that licensing delays and irregular supply of spare parts under barter agreements and tied loans have discouraged use of agricultural machinery at various times.[2]

Econometric studies have indicated that factor-substitution elasticity between capital and labour may be fairly high in developing countries' agriculture. This raises the question of capital/labour ratios, and it has been suggested that protection-induced or other distortions of factor prices--such as possible under-pricing of tractors--might have adverse effects on employment in agriculture comparable to those noted in industry. On the other hand, the increased productivity resulting from mechanisation may be urgently needed to raise food output or to keep export crops internationally competitive. Depending on circumstances with respect to land tenure, etc., the mechanisation may also stimulate an absolute increase in employment.[3] Our lack of knowledge regarding total effects in this as in many other areas suggests that the more neutral the protective system the better. Since agricultural products tend to be priced close to world-market levels anyway, this is an argument for applying zero tariffs and complete freedom from quantitative controls for agricultural equipment, fertilizer, and other inputs. If rising capital/labour ratios appear to be speeding up the displacement of labour from agriculture, it seems more appropriate for corrective action to take the form of subsidised programmes of labour-intensive rural public works (feeder roads, etc.) requiring little or no sophisticated construction equipment, rather than tampering with input prices. In principle, effects of an eventual devaluation should be passed through so as to affect more or less equally both agricultural producer prices and prices for agricultural machinery and inputs. This would admittedly be difficult to implement politically.

C. Industrial Employment Effects

1. The employment lag and the production functions

The observed failure of the rate of growth of employment in industry, especially in manufacturing, to keep pace with that of output, let alone significantly contribute to absorption of the excess labour supply being generated by demographic forces, has disappointed the original hopes of proponents of import-substituting industrialisation. It has already been noted that, even if employment rose proportionately, it takes a great deal of growth to make a substantial employment impact, given the relatively small share of the labour force involved in modern industry. In any case, employment does not rise proportionately. During the 1950's and early 1960's, the ratio of employment growth to output growth (roughly an employment elasticity) was on the average about 0.62 for all developing countries[4]

---

[1] Cf. Theodore W. Schultz, _Transforming Traditional Agriculture_ (New Haven: Yale University Press, 1964), pp.36-52.

[2] Abdessatar Grissa, _Agricultural Policies and Employment: Case Study of Tunisia_ (Paris: O.E.C.D. Development Centre, Employment Series: No.9, 1973), pp.66-67.

[3] Cf. Helen Hughes, "The Scope for Labor Capital Substitution in the Developing Economies of Southeast and East Asia. A Sectoral Approach" (I.B.R.D., Economic Staff Working Paper No.140, January 1973) pp.15-20.

[4] Source: Gene M. Tidrick, "Wages, Output and the Employment Lag in Jamaica" (Williams College, Center for Development Economics, Research Memorandum No.40, December 1970; Werner Baer and Michael E.A. Herve, "Employment and Industrialization in Developing Countries", _Quarterly Journal of Economics_ (February 1966), p.91.

It may or may not be significant that the indicated elasticities for Latin America (.43) and India (.49), which were already import-substituting areas par excellence, were substantially below the over-all average. Argentina actually showed a negative ratio of -.45, while Egypt was at the higher end of the range (.71).

The functional relationships behind the employment lag are imperfectly understood despite all the econometric work that has been done in the analysis of production functions, especially in measuring capital/labour ratios and the inter-factoral elasticities of substitution.1/   One can identify two schools of thought regarding the explanation of the employment gap: some economists -- esepcially in Latin America -- stress structural factors, such as the capital intensity of technology itself, reinforced by the tendency of foreign firms to impose their familiar production methods all around the world: others are market-oriented, emphasising that technology can be relatively flexible and will depend on the relative prices of the factors of production.2/

It is perhaps possible to be eclectic in this matter: to recognise that structural and even psychological or sociological reasons may be important, e.g., that engineers and directors of multinational firms and (until recently) of international aid institutions may well have a strong prejudice in favour of advanced labour-saving technology3/ and, indeed, that, in some industries, the technical coefficients may be very rigid. However, there are enough reasons to believe that commercial and other policies contribute seriously to the problem.   Recent econometric research, moreover, indicates that relative factor prices do matter, that earlier estimates of very low substitution elasticities were biased downward by incorrect specification of the equations or by deficient data, and that the true elasticities of substitution are likely to be 0.5 or higher.4/

Let us consider some of the ways that the typical import-substituting protective profile may operate to lower the relative labour content of production in non-agricultural sectors.

2. High protection on import-competing consumer goods

The highest levels of nominal and effective protection normally apply to finished durable and non-durable consumer goods.   Assuming that the protection is non-redundant, and in the absence of strict wage and price controls, one of the most important effects is to provide a monopoly shelter over payment of abnormally high money wage rates.   If unions are strong and the higher wages are supported by minimum wage legislation, wage rates for unskilled and semi-skilled labour will also be raised sooner or later in the other modernised branches of the economy, including mining, transport, construction, services, and the less protected part of manufacturing.5/   Various estimates have been made of the employment increase that might have been achieved had real wages been held constant (Tidrick) or if labour-market distortions were eliminated (Tyler).   According to Tyler, this would have meant an increase of 232,000 jobs in Brazil in 1968 as compared with actual employment of

---

1/ Much of the econometric investigation is now based on the CES (constance elasticity of substitution) production function, developed by K.J. Arrow, H.B. Chenery, B.S. Minhas, and R.M. Solow, "Capital-Labor Substitution and Economic Efficiency", Review of Economics and Statistics (XLIII, No.3, August 1961).

2/ W.G. Tyler, "Labor Absorption with Import Substituting Industrialization: An Examination of Elasticities of Substitution in the Brazilian Manufacturing Sector", Diskussionsbeitrage No.24 (Kiel: Institute of World Economics, October 1972), pp.1-2.

3/ Cf. Louis T. Wells, Jr., "Economic Man and Engineering Man: Choice of Technology in a Low Wage Country", SEADAG Papers 73-1 (New York: Southeast Asian Development Advisory Group of the Asia Society, 1972).

4/ See, for example, D. Schydlowsky and M. Syrquin, "The Estimation of CES Production Functions and Neutral Efficiency Levels Using Effective Rates of Protection as Price Deflators" (Harvard University, Center for International Affairs, Development Research Group, Economic Development Report No.194, June 1971); Tyler, op.cit.; Gordon C. Winston, "On the Inevitability of Factor Substitution" (Williams College, Center for Development Economics, Research Memorandum No.46, April 1972); Howard Pack, "The Employment-Output Trade-Off in LDC's - A Micro-economic Approach" (Yale University, Economic Growth Center, Discussion Paper No.179).

5/ Cf. Tidrick, op.cit., pp.39-54.   Tidrick and others point out that strong export-oriented extractive industries (like bauxite mining in Jamaica, copper in Chile, and oil in the Middle East) may lead the way to higher wages, along with the protected manufacturing industries.

unskilled labour in manufacturing amounting to 982,000.1/ Obviously, not all wage distortions are attributable to high effective rates of protection, but it is reasonable to assume that a large proportion are, at least in countries where private enterprise is free to bid for labour and where institutional political forces strengthen the bargaining power of the labour unions. The argument may not apply in countries like Egypt, where so much of industry is socialised and the tendency for wages and prices to rise has been repressed.

Economic dualism exists within urban society as well as in rural society and between the rural and urban societies.2/ High protection in consumer-goods industries probably raises the over-all capital/labour ratio through displacement and discouragement of small-scale traditional manufacturing activities by more modern protected firms. The two technologies continue to co-exist, however, because the labour-intensive artisanal enterprises are more adapted to local conditions and do not have to pay high wages.3/ A stage is reached, however, at which the national market is saturated. The more modern firms, blocked from exporting by their high labour costs and high profit expectations, compete more and more vigorously with the small producers, and selling prices gradually come down from the protected level (increasing the amount of the tariff that is redundant). The high sheltered profits are eroded and unemployment begins to appear in the modern organised sector; while underemployment and misery build up in the informal sector, where many of the producers are self-employed. (This model applies in many Latin American countries and has been observed by the author in Cyprus. It might well be applicable in Lebanon.)

Luxury goods are usually subject to extra high tariffs and/or import prohibitions, rationalised by austerity considerations. Unless domestic import substitutes are also penalised, say, by internal excise taxes, this results in lucratic local production. Whether or not capital-intensive, such production often employs very little local labour. A high proportion of the inputs are typically imported and much of the value added by processing is remitted abroad in the form of profits and royalties on the brand names.

It has been seen that protectionist policies have important effects on the intersectoral distribution of income and that these appear to have adverse employment effects on balance. Income distribution is also obviously affected within sectors. Besides making possible payment of higher wages in favoured industries, the increased margin of value added permits still larger profits and other property income in the protected firms, especially those which --like cosmetics--enjoy the highest rates of protection. Other firms and industries, such as exporters, may see their value added reduced by the pattern of protection. There thus appears to be no clear a priori basis on which to predict the direction in which the high protective rates will skew the income distribution. High prices on consumer goods used mainly by low-income groups are, to be sure, a form of regressive taxation, but this may be offset by special exemptions for basic mass-consumption items, especially those important in the cost-of-living index.

Even if the protective system's effects on income distribution are correctly analysed, it is not obvious what the latter's employment effects will be. Savings ratios as well as expenditure patterns are relevant, and one should distinguish between the short and long

---

1/ Tyler defined "distortion" as the difference between the minimum wage and the opportunity cost of unskilled labour, measured by its estimated marginal product in agriculture in Southern Brazil. Harberger's measure of the opportunity cost of labour, based on wages in the unprotected urban sector, would seem to be a preferable shadow wage rate and would yield a lower estimate of the employment cost of distortions. A.C. Harberger, "On Measuring the Social Opportunity Cost of Labour", in Fiscal Measures for Employment Promotion in Developing Countries (Geneva: ILO, 1972), pp.3-24.

2/ For a definition of economic dualism and classification of countries by this criterion, see Irma Adelman and Cynthia Taft Morris, "An Anatomy of Income Distribution Patterns in Developing Nations--A Summary of Findings" (I.B.R.D., Economic Staff Working Paper No.116, September 23, 1971), Appendix A. Iraq, Libya, Morocco, Sudan, and Tunisia are classified among the "countries in which there is a sharp and pervasive sectoral or geographic cleavage between an important exchange sector and important traditional nonmonetised sector". Lebanon (like Israel, Greece and Japan) is among the countries in which "traditional and modern production methods exist side by side in almost all sectors of the economy".

3/ Cf. Tibor Scitovsky, "Prospects for Latin American Industrialization with the Framework of Latin American Economic Integration: Bases for Analysis" in The Process of Industrialization in Latin America (Washington: Inter-American Development Bank, Guatemala Round Table, 1969), pp.40-41. On four-sector dualism, see also Reynolds, op.cit. pp.2-4.

terms. Various studies exist on the labour-intensity of expenditure at different income levels, for increments to income, and for specified income redistributions, but the results are remarkably inconclusive 1/ and it is difficult to link the findings to trade policy, even though we know it cannot be neutral with respect to income distribution.

3. Underpricing of capital goods

Virtually all tariff structures in developing countries, with the notable exception of Argentina, have low duties on imported capital equipment. In Lebanon, the normal rate is 1 per cent; in Egypt 2 per cent. Investment incentive laws, like Egypt's Law No. 43 and its predecessors, give systematic or ad hoc exemption from even these low duties. Licensing is normally for planning, not for protective purposes. The liberal tariff and non-tariff treatment of capital goods imports is usually combined with other fiscal measures to attract foreign and domestic investors: complete tax holidays for a number of years or rapid write-off provisions with respect to depreciation of fixed assets; preferentially low interest rates from state-owned development banks; free entry of raw materials and intermediate goods; guaranteed transfer of profits and royalties to parent companies; and, in some cases, direct cash subsidies. In any case, where average protection in the rest of the tariff structure is high, permitting a substantially over-valued exchange rate, the low or zero-duty treatment of capital goods is equivalent to subsidisation.2/

ILO and World Bank missions,3/ as well as numerous academic economists, are increasingly calling attention to the anomaly of this bias of tariff structure in favour of capital-intensive technology in countries that consider capital to be the scarce and labour the abundant factor. To be sure, the question of the extent to which capital is the scarce factor in the Arab world as a whole may be debatable, although most of the Arab population is still living in capital-deficit countries.

The same empirical studies of substitution elasticities that have documented the influence of high labour costs on the capital/labour ratio are at least equally applicable on the capital side. In conjunction with theoretical analysis, they indicate the strong probability that an increase in tariffs on imported equipment relative to other goods will tend to increase employment. This can occur either through an absolute rise in nominal protection on the capital goods themselves or through a combination of devaluation and trade liberalisation measures that would reduce rates of effective protection in other sectors.4/

One series of recent studies has emphasised the variety of ways in which changes in the user costs of equipment vary the labour intensity of its utilisation despite the apparent fixity of technology. Ex ante substitutability is clearly much greater than ex post substitutability; but, even after capital equipment is in place, it can be "stretched", e.g. by working several shifts.5/

Subsidisation of interest rates has effects on capital intensity similar to those of

---

1/ The most relevant to conditions in the Arab region is a study by Ronald Soligo for A.I.D., "Factor Intensity of Consumption Patterns, Income Distribution and Employment Growth in West Pakistan" (Yale University, Economic Growth Center, November 1972). It concluded that rural households consume a more labour-intensive basket of goods and services than urban households, and that lower income groups' consumption has a higher direct and indirect labour input than that of higher income groups. However, if the labour required to produce capital goods, such as housing, is included, and Mexico had the same income distribution as the UK, there would be a 4-1/2 per cent favourable impact on employment. The Potential Effect of Income Redistribution on Economic Growth in Six Latin American Countries (New York: Praeger Publishers, 1972).

2/ Cf. Ian Little, Tibor Scitovsky, Maurice Scott, Industry and Trade in Some Developing Countries: A Comparative Study (London: Oxford University Press, 1970), pp.87-88.

3/ E.g., Employment and Income Policies for Iran (Geneva: ILO, 1973), pp.89-94; Employment in Trinidad and Tobago (Washington: I.B.R.D., March 1973), p.67; see also papers by Cosciani, Lent, Fine and others in the Geneva symposium of ILO in January 1971, Fiscal Measures for Employment Promotion in Developing Countries, op.cit.

4/ Cf. James McCabe, Tariff Policy, Equipment Production and Employment in Developing Countries (Yale University, Economic Growth Center Discussion Paper No.170, January 1973).

5/ See Gordon C. Winston: "The Theory of Capital Utilization and Idleness", Journal of Economic Literature (Vol.XII, No.4, December 1974), pp.1301-16; "Capital Utilization: Physiological Costs and Preferences for Shift Work" (Williams College, Center for Development Economics, Research Memorandum No.42, October 1971); "On the Inevitability of Factor Substitution", op.cit.

the underpricing of capital goods by the tariff and trade-control system.[1] In countries where the private sector still prevails, it favours the large capital-intensive firms, especially the multinationals. (This is not to imply that such capital subsidies may not be justified in particular projects, but this should be a conscious governmental policy decision based on a cost-benefit exercise in which appropriate discount rates and shadow prices are applied.) It is also noted that the capital side of the capital/labour ratio includes the use of plant structures as well as of equipment goods like machinery. In retail trade, on the other hand, inventories and other working capital may be the important elements,[2] and these are not significantly affected by the structure of protection. Thus, commercial policy with respect to what are normally classified as capital goods is only one of a number of interrelated variables that affect the bias of technology toward capital intensity. However, the fact that giant road equipment is almost always imported duty-free and, therefore, at a preferential implicit exchange rate creates a major distortion between social and market costs in construction. Duty exemptions for tourism projects have also contributed to the over-building of excessively luxurious hotels around the Mediterranean and Caribbean.

Finally, the underpricing of capital goods for the sake of so-called industrialisation policies has discouraged a justified substitution of imports of capital goods in the countries concerned. Aside from the fact that domestically produced equipment tends to be complementary to labour-intensive technology, its manufacture is also usually high on the labour-intensive scale.[3] That a significant proportion of equipment needs can be locally produced when stimulated by relative prices is shown by the experience of Argentina, the unique example of a developing country that gives substantial protection to this sector, although in this case the policy may have been overdone to the point of inefficiency and misallocation of resources.[4] In Turkey, the domestic share in the total purchases of equipment increased substantially after the 1958 exchange-rate adjustment, together with greater availability of internal as compared to external credit, reduced the implicit subsidy on imported capital goods, with the apparent effect of increasing both aggregate employment and value added.

4. Protection on inputs

In developing countries, the tariff treatment of primary raw materials other than foodstuffs need not raise serious issues. If based on local resources, they are likely to be strong export products. Any import tariff will be redundant; actual nominal protection will be zero or negative even at the going exchange rate and effective protection will be negative. If there is no resource base for significant local production, there will be no argument about importing them duty free or at a rate that is negligible in comparison with the rest of the tariff.

On the other hand, the tariff treatment of intermediate products above the primary level raises some of the most difficult practical issues of commercial policy. (It should be noted, however, that the greater the spread between the upper and lower levels of the protective profile, the more difficult these problems will be.) The objective of extending import substitution to a wider gamut of ever more sophisticated products and of developing backward linkages conflicts head-on with the interests of the manufacturers of finished products, especially those who are beginning to overcome the bias against exporting or those protected producers for the local market whose own margin of effective protection is not as wide as they would like.

---

[1] A. Berry, "The Rate of Interest and the Demand for Labor" (Yale University, Economic Growth Center Discussion Paper No.144, August 1972).

[2] A.S. Bhalla, "Economic Efficiency, Capital Intensity and Capital-Labor Substitution in Retail Trade" (Yale University, Economic Growth Center Discussion Paper no.94, September 1, 1970).

[3] Howard Pack and Michael Todaro, "Technological Transfer, Labor Absorption, and Economic Development" (Yale University, Economic Growth Center Discussion Paper No.65, May 1, 1969).

[4] Constantine Michalopoulos, Relative Prices, Capital Goods Imports and the Foreign Exchange Constraint: A Case Study of Argentina (Washington: AID Discussion Paper No.23, November 1971).

It may be that project-selection criteria justify the creation of the new linkages, with benefits shown to exceed any higher costs imposed on subsequent stages of processing, even when these are for export. (Indeed, EEC and other preference-granting countries may require integration of several stages of processing for compliance with their rules of origin.) A major consideration is, of course, the size of the potential market and whether the paper mill, glass plant, or petrochemical complex is intended to compete internationally, within a regional integration grouping, or only nationally. Employment implications are likely to be ambivalent. Spinning and weaving mills are relatively labour intensive, but if the clothing industry is forced to depend largely or entirely on high-cost domestic intermediates, it may lose its international market at the cost of more jobs than have been created. A full assessment of the labour intensity of an activity requires a great deal of work with the input-output table. A petrochemical complex, which is definitely capital intensive, may make an otherwise viable synthetic-textiles or plastic-fabricating industry uncompetitive, at a very great sacrifice of employment. This raises the kind of political problem that makes regional integration schemes stagnate or even come apart.

The temptation is to make more and more special arrangements in the framework of industrial incentive schemes or export promotion programmes: tariff-free quotas tied to particular end users; import-entitlement schemes giving special access to a "parallel" exchange market; temporary import arrangements for re-export; free-trade zones. The dilemma is real. It is considered necessary to develop manufactured exports, especially when these are very labour-intensive but this may be literally impossible if inputs have to be bought at domestic prices. A free-trade zone is, therefore, established, and--in effect--a piece of the national territory is expatriated. Such labourers as are employed there become virtually _frontaliers_ if not _Gastarbeiter_. There are administrative problems in controlling the duty-free intermediate goods and keeping them out of a domestic black market. Domestic inter-industry linkages are at least partly ruptured, and it seems ironic to plan regional customs unions when--as in Chile--the integrity of the national customs area cannot be maintained. There is no easy solution to the problem, but it is possible to live with it if the basic protective system has moderate levels.

Protection on semi-manufactured inputs that are not produced at all locally is likely to be zero. This is good for international competitiveness, but as in the case of capital goods, it means that these inputs are relatively subsidised at the current exchange rate if the average levels of the protective system are high. There are analogous implications if the inputs are linked to sophisticated capital-intensive technology, since the using industry is assured a wide margin of effective protection. Also the possible development of a local import-substitute is discouraged.

Interesting questions have been raised whether there are possible favourable long-term side effects from higher energy prices in some developing countries, at least insofar as these might tend to counter inappropriately capital-intensive technology based on cheap energy.[1] In this connection, the question also arises as to what shadow prices for oil are in fact being used in (1) oil-importing and (2) oil-exporting Arab countries.

5. The bias against exporting

The notion of the "bias against exporting" is rather ambiguous. Balassa defines it "as the percentage excess of domestic value added obtainable as a result of protection in producing for domestic markets over that obtainable for exporting", [2] and applies it narrowly within a particular industry or even with respect to a particular product or group of related products. In effect, this gives a measure of the difference in incentives between selling the product in the domestic market at protected prices and exporting it at international prices (FOB) plus any subsidies (including drawbacks of duties paid on inputs actually imported) and minus any explicit or implicit export taxes (including requirements to sell

---

[1] _Cf._ Dudley Seers, "Here Lies the Strategy", _Development Forum_. (March 1974), pp. 1-3.

[2] Balassa and Associates, _op.cit._, p.332.

export proceeds at an unfavourable exchange rate and the adverse price effects of quantitative export controls). Since allowance also has to be made for the cost of protection on inputs, whether the product is sold domestically or exported, the bias against exporting is expressed by comparison of the _effective_ rate for the product in import substitution with that in exporting. On the other hand, one can also speak of the bias against exporting in a more macroeconomic inter-sectoral sense, comparing the value added from using domestic resources in all import-competing sectors with that obtainable in traditionally export-oriented sectors. In this sense, the term is closer to the notion of the bias against agriculture, already discussed, and the effective rates compared are sectoral averages.

As already brought out, the bias against traditional exports is a normal feature of the structure of protection in countries having high concentration of export trade in a few primary commodities that are strongly competitive internationally.[1] Obvious examples are petroleum in the Persian Gulf countries, Libya, Iraq, and Algeria; cotton in Sudan, Egypt, and Syria, and phosphates in Morocco may also fall in this category. Such commodities have such a strong comparative advantage that they can bear heavily discriminatory taxation. Depending on the foreign demand and supply elasticities, the export tax can turn the terms of trade dramatically in favour of the exporting country, as has been shown by the successes of OPEC and the _Office Cherifien des Phosphates_. Also, discrimination in the protective structure against export of such commodities in primary form is used to favour increased local employment and value added by "downstream" processing. This is the original meaning of the term "export substitution", which, however, has come to be used to include any substitution of non-traditional labour-based manufactured exports for traditional resource-based primary exports.[2]

It may be noted, of the two principal traditional exports of the Arab region, oil is capital intensive and cotton is labour intensive, _par excellence_. Fortunately, most of the oil-dominated countries, with the principal exception of Algeria, do not suffer from labour surplus. The combination of specialisation in raw cotton production with forward linkage into an export-oriented cotton-goods industry has also been fortunate for Egypt. Cotton is a good example of the self-limiting nature of a commercial-policy bias against traditional exports. Despite the area's near-monopoly of long-staple cotton, export price policy and acreage-control policy have had to be manipulated flexibly in view of the availability of substitutes and the vagaries of world demand. At the same time, attention has also had to be paid to the input needs of the domestic textile industry, which has been handicapped by prohibitions or the import of cheap short-staple cotton. At times, Egypt has even applied export subsidies or subsidised exchange rates simultaneously with export duties, apparently because of price and exchange-rate anomalies arising in connection with bilateral clearing deals, which sometimes resulted in undesired triangular switch operations.[3] This is an example of the additional complications caused by the geographically-discriminatory differentiation of protection.

Quite different problems are raised by the protective bias against non-traditional or diversified manufactured exports. If there is no export subsidy, nominal protection on the output is zero and costs are burdened by the price effect on the protection on inputs; therefore, effective protection on the exported product is likely to be negative. At the same time, however, the import-substituting policy has provided for high nominal and effective protection when the same product is marketed domestically. As long as this situation is allowed to prevail, there are unlikely to be substantial exports of such products unless the

---

[1] In Fei and Ranis' theory of stages of development of the labour-surplus economy, the export-substitution stage historically follows the stage of import substitution, which was "fuelled mainly by traditional land-based exports". See, for example, Gustav Ranis, "Industrial Sector Labor Absorption", _Economic Development and Cultural Change_ (Vol.21, No.3, April 1973), pp.387-408. When this stage ("the switching point") is reached, distortions in relative prices begin to be eliminated, efficiency increases throughout the economy, and there is better utilisation of the excess supply of unskilled labour. Finally, after becoming a net food importer, the "commercialisation" point is reached, when the labour-surplus condition is completely absorbed by the industrial sector. Fei and Ranis have traced this sequence of stages in Japan, Taiwan, and Korea.

[2] Hansen and Marzouk, _op.cit._, p.104.

[3] The role of "domestic absorption" as a constraint on exporting manufactures is among the questions investigated by Henry J. Bruton, "Export Growth and Import Substitution", (Williams College, Center for Development Economics, Research Memorandum No.22, July 1968).

producer can act as a discriminating monopolist, exporting at marginal cost in order to take advantage of economies of scale. Even then, he is obtaining less value added per unit sold from exporting operations than from domestic sales. Eventually, to be sure, the internal market will be saturated. Competition may then bring internal prices down, reducing the bias and the degree of domestic absorption,1/ but an unrealistic exchange rate and the burden of input protection will still discourage exporting until--or unless--exporters obtain a subsidy and/or a change in their exchange rate and/or access to duty-free imported inputs. Such remedies may be long delayed. Thus, export pessimism is not just the result of problems of access to developed-country markets, but also a natural concomitant of high protection for import-substitutes in some of the developing countries that are trying to export.2/

From the employment standpoint, one can look at the promotion of diversified manufactured exports in two ways. First, viewing export substitution as an alternative to import substitution, one can compare the employment content of a country's industrial exports with that which would be involved in replacing its industrial imports with domestic production. Such a comparison, which necessitates taking account both of direct and indirect utilisation of capital and labour, indicated that in Mexico in 1968 investment in export industry would on the average create more employment of unskilled labour than equivalent investment in replacement of imports.3/ The situation would certainly be different in some other countries (for example, the oil-rich Arab countries), but the Mexican result was in accordance with a priori expectations based on the Heckscher-Ohlin theory of factor proportions in foreign trade. Leaving out oil, but taking account of processed fruits and vegetables, wine, tinned fish, etc., it seems clear that the marginal exports of most Arab countries would contain more labour than production of marginal import substitutes. (Although food processing industries have relatively low value added and directly involve relatively little labour, their primary inputs generally have high labour content.)

One can also look at the employment effects of an expansion of exports in an absolute sense (not just in comparison with import substitution industries) in those countries where import substitution has already run out of steam and excess capacity exists. A study 4/ of South Korean experience has analysed the employment-creating impact of exports as consisting of (1) direct employment effects, (2) backward and forward linkage effects, and (3) multiplier effects (due to consumption expenditures of employed workers). In addition, there may also be (4) foreign-exchange effects through elimination of bottlenecks due to a foreign-exchange "gap" constraint; however, this is an employment-facilitating rather than an employment-creating effect. According to the estimate, $1 million increase in Korean manufactured exports would create 500 jobs in export industries, 150 in supporting industries, and 150 in consumer goods and service industries, in the short run. This was considered an underestimate. A similar calculation exists for Egypt, although the data are 20 years old. It has been estimated, on the basis of direct and indirect labour requirements to produce manufactured exports in 1954, that the unemployment of the labour force (assumed to be 10 per cent) could have been absorbed by an 80 per cent increase in existing manufactured exports.5/ This implied that it would require $1,238 in exports valued in

1/ The role of "domestic absorption" as a constraint on exporting manufactures is among the questions investigated by Henry J. Bruton, "Export Growth and Import Substitution," (Williams College, Center for Development Economcis, Research Memorandum No.22, July 1968).

2/ Cf. Hal B. Lary, Imports of Manufactures from Less Developed Countries (New York: National Bureau of Economic Research, 1968), pp.10-11; Richard C. Porter and Charles P. Staelin, "The Rediscovery of Exports by the Third World", Foreign Trade Review (January-March, 1972), pp.14-17.

3/ John Sheahan, "Trade and Employment, Industrial Exports Compared to Import Substitution in Mexico" (Williams College, Center for Development Economics, Research Memorandum No.43, December 1971). Another study of the Mexican exports has nevertheless found them to be less labour intensive than they might have been expected to be. See Susumi Watanabe, "Constraints on Labour Intensive Export Industries in Mexico", International Labour Review (Vol.109, No.1, January 1974). Watanabe attributed the relatively poor manufacturing industry to" (1) the high degree of protection enjoyed by material-producing home industries, which raises the costs of inputs considerably, and (2) the social legislation". Mexican capital-intensive exports, on the other hand, were artificially encouraged by measures linking access to imported inputs to export performance.

4/ Susumu Watanabe, "Exports and Employment: the Case of the Republic of Korea," International Labour Review (V 1.106, No.6, December 1972), pp.501-514.

5/ William G. Tyler, "Employment Generation and the Promotion of Manufactured Exports in Less Developed Countries: Some Suggestive Evidence" (mimeo, paper prepared for Kiel Conference on "Problems of the International Division of Labor,"July 12-15, 1973, based on unpublished paper by Maurice Girgis, Kiel Institute of World Economics).

constant 1969 dollars to create one job.

More and more countries are now convinced of the necessity of export expansion, for employment, growth, and balance-of-payments reasons. They are also aware of the export-inhibiting effects of their high levels of protection on the import side, but they often consider the latter to be politically and institutionally untouchable. Therefore, they attempt to offset the protection effects with subsidies and other export incentives, including access to special parallel exchange markets and other arrangements to link exports to import payments. The consideration of labour intensity is often important, or ostensibly important, in determining the liberality of the special incentive. The most modest subsidies are those aimed at merely offsetting the negative effective protection on exports: ex-post drawbacks of import duties actually paid or implicitly paid (by the latter I means the protective element in the price of domestically produced inputs), temporary admission schemes and ex ante exemptions from import duties and import prohibitions, and establishment of free-trade zones. "A second level of subsidy through income tax exemptions and cheap credit may balance the general excess cost of domestic factors and goods due to protection generally.1/ Finally, one can conceive of subsidies intended to eliminate completely the bias against exporting by offsetting the full amount by which the domestic price is raised by nominal protection. In practice, export subsidies are given either on a uniform or ad hoc basis in accordance with some rough judgement of what is needed to stimulate exporters to make adequate efforts to penetrate foreign markets.

All of these forms of export subsidisation, which are used by Egypt, Lebanon, and other Arab countries, can be shown to be inferior to a reduction of high rates of import-substiting protection on outputs as well as inputs, accompanied by exchange-rate devaluation. First, there is the increasingly serious legal risk that destination countries will impose countervailing duties, regardless of any question of moral justification, and despite the fact that countervailing duties have been rarely used against developing countries in the past. Secondly, and more important from the present standpoint, there is the fact that the exporting country is likely to be ignorant of the true costs and price incidence of either its import-protection structure or of its export subsidies. Citing the case of Korea, Balassa points out that, "just as import substitution, exports may also be carried too far. This will be the case if subsidies induce producers to expand exports to the point where the domestic resource cost of additional dollar in export earnings exceeds the resource cost of saving a dollar through import substitution."2/ This has happened not only in Korea but has also been well documented in Pakistan,3/India,4/ and a number of other countries. Moreover, it appears that there has been a perverse tendency to subsidise relatively capital-intensive more than labour-intensive exports. In any case, there is no reason to believe that employment benefits from irrational allocation of resources.

> "The higher and the more unequal protection, the higher and more complex
> will the subsidy system have to be, and the less likely is it to lead to an
> optimal allocation of resources. Sound export policies do not thus merely
> require the imposition of a subsidy system to match protection; a decline
> in over-all protection, and a reduction in its variability, are essential".5/

Finally, excessive subsidisation constitutes a gift via the terms of trade from the exporting country to the consumers in the importing countries. Indeed, it has been shown by theoretical reasoning that an export subsidy reduces the real-income level of the exporting

---

1/ Hughes, "Trade and Industrialization Policies...," op.cit., p.19.

2/ Bela Balassa, "Industrial Policies in Taiwan and Korea", Economia Internazionale

3/ Ronald Soligo and Joseph J. Stern, "Some Comments on the Export Bonus, Export Promotion and Investment Criteria", Pakistan Development Review (Spring 1966), pp.38-56.

4/ Charles P. Staelin, "The Cost and Composition of Indian Exports" (University of Michigan, Center for Research on Economic Development, Discussion Paper 22, May 1972).

5/ Hughes, op.cit., p.20.

country by more than would a tariff of equivalent terms-of-trade effect imposed by the outside world against its imports.[1]   On the other hand, a number of econometric studies have shown that, for non-traditional manufactured exports, both foreign demand and domestic supply are quite elastic with respect to exchange-rate adjustments.[2]   Also, exports of small countries and minor exports of large countries face the greatest prospect of success.[3]

Little mention has been made of the bias of developed countries' protective regimes against labour-intensive imports from developing countries.   That is another story, well told in a number of UNCTAD and ILO reports.   It is an additional reason for preferring realistic exchange rates to subsidisation as a technique of export promotion, since the former are less vulnerable to counter-measures.   Generalised preferences schemes openly discriminate against "sensitive", i.e., labour-intensive imports and against Hong Kong and other Far Eastern countries most competitive in them (although Hong Kong, Singapore, Taiwan, and South Korea can no longer be considered labour-surplus countries).   Taking account of the origin rules, the special-preference arrangements of the EEC in the Mediterranean region are not much better in this regard, especially with respect to textiles and processed agricultural products.   In any case, the small Far Eastern countries, whose protective structures are least influenced by import-substitution objectives, still have the best records both for successful export growth and for employment growth.

IV. Summary and Conclusions

The survey opened with a review of the role of protective measures in determining the differentiated relationship between domestic and international prices of various kinds of goods ("nominal" protection), as well as the net incidence of the protective measures affecting both products and their inputs relative to the value added obtainable in various productive activities ("effective" protection).   Latin American statutory tariff rates and estimated rates of nominal and effective protection were used to illustrate the typical patterns of protective structure found in many countries, including the major Arab countries (other than the desert oil countries), and which are associated with the development strategy of import-substituting industrialisation.

The remainder of the paper was devoted to a discussion of the price distortions inherent in many import-substituting commercial policies and which appear to operate against absorption of redundant labour.   These include the bias against agriculture, excessively high protection on import-competing consumer goods, the under-pricing of capital goods, and the bias against diversified manufactured exports.   More complicated problems arise in connection with the pricing of intermediate goods, because of the ambivalent effects of linkages with respect to employment creation, on the one hand, and competitiveness, on the other hand.

Trade policy interacts with employment policy in many ways.   The relationship is usually indirect and the policy implications frequently ambiguous, given the existence of other objectives such as growth, nationalism, etc.   The fact that protection is a multi-dimensional phenomenon complicates the analysis.   The geographical dimension (preferences, integration groupings, bilateral deals with state-trading countries) is especially important in the Arab countries, so that the price effects of protective régimes are further obscured, let alone their impact on employment.

In any case, there is no evidence that high and erratic profiles of nominal and effective protection, such as have characterised the policy of import-substituting industrialisation in many developing countries, will contribute any more successfully to the absorption of excess unskilled labour in Arab countries.   Theory and experience indicate the contrary.

---

[1] D.J. Horwell, "On Export Subsidies and Import Tariffs", Economica (November 1966), pp.472-74.   See also Gottfried Haberler, "Import Taxes and Export Subsidies: A Substitute for the Realignment of Exchange Rates", Kyklos (Vol.XX, 1967), pp.17-23.

[3] Barend A. DeVries, The Export Experience of Developing Countries (Washington: I.B.R.D., World Bank Staff Occasional Papers No.3, 1967), Ch.III.

[2] Cf. Jonathan W. Eaton, "Effective Devaluation as an Export Incentive in Less Developed Countries" (Harvard University, Development Research Group, Economic Development Report No.221, July 1972); Bruton, op.cit.; Porter and Staelin, op.cit.

One cannot expect trade policy alone to solve the problem of chronic underemployment in dualistic societies characterised by high population growth, but one can try to avoid compounding the problem through price incentives biased toward unnecessarily capital-intensive technologies. In general, the lower and less differentiated the profile of nominal protection, the narrower is the scope for perverse effects.

Availability of new sources of capital finance in some countries of the Arab world has not freed the relatively overpopulated countries from the problem of capital-biased technology. To the extent that development finance may now be easier to obtain throughout the region, the probability may indeed increase that inappropriate technologies will be embodied in the new investments. Shadow-pricing cost-benefit exercises may decrease this risk in the project-evaluation process, but it would be preferable (especially in private-enterprise economies) if protection systems did not give systematically wrong signals about the relative prices in markets for goods and factors of production.

Arab régimes of protection at present include some of the most liberal in the world and some of the most restrictive. Several countries, notably Syria and Egypt, have recently taken important steps toward liberalisation. Nevertheless, there is a presumption in favour of further reforms throughout the region. (Almost all protective systems in the world are the product of historical accidents, embodied in out-of-date legislative frameworks, rigidified by administrative inertia, and defended by sheltered vested interests, so that it is no wonder that their implied price relationships reflect little coherent purpose.)

The most essential pre-condition of reform of the protective system is to make relative price implications visible and explicit, so that any biasing of incentives can be recognised. Such visibility can be facilitated by:

-- replacement of specific and mixed customs duties by ad valorem rates;

-- absorption into the tariff system, to the extent feasible, of quantitative restrictions, surcharges, and multiple exchange rates which discriminate among different categories of goods;

-- investigation of the amount of redundancy in the tariffs and of the price effects of non-tariff barriers, preferably by calculation of indexes measuring actual disparities between domestic and international prices (such indexes should ideally be disaggregated by product categories and by preference zones, and if possible calculated in time series);

-- estimation of rates of effective protection at the most disaggregated levels possible.

The prevalence of state-trading practices in the region presents unusual problems for estimation and evaluation of protective profiles, but in principle there appears to be no incompatibility between Arab Socialism and taking account of relative prices in the planning process. In this respect, the Arab countries may be able to profit from the experience of Eastern European countries.

The fact that exchange rates are floating all over the world offers unusual opportunities to take those tariff-reform measures that have exchange-rate implications. For example, instead of having to devalue in order to absorb some of the tariff system into the exchange system, a country could simply refrain from an otherwise justified upward revaluation against other countries.

The formation of regional integration groupings normally begins with efforts to investigate the real levels of protection of the member countries, preparatory to elaboration of programmes of mutual trade liberalisation and tariff harmonisation. It is understandable that the current strategy for the Arab Common Market has apparently de-emphasised the custom-union goal temporarily in favour of priority for utilisation of surplus oil funds within the region.[1] This is undoubtedly a politically realistic step, but it appears to postpone further the coming to grips with the relative-price disciplines that successful integration groupings had to face.

---

[1] Source: Ma. A. Ziadeh, "The Arab Common Market -- A Dream Come True", The Arab Economist (Vol.VI, No.61, February 1974).

MIGRATION BETWEEN ARAB COUNTRIES

by

Abdelmegid M. Farrag[*]

Introduction

Today's Arab population is estimated at around 130 million people, living on an area of about 13 million square kilometres. This area suffers from no lack of natural resources (e.g. oil, iron, phosphate, etc.), agricultural land, capital, labour and technical personnel and it disposes of a large enough market which could absorb the total production of the area as a whole. One-third of the world's oil is produced by Arab countries, where also one-half, or more, of the world oil reserves can be found. About one-quarter of the world phosphate is produced in Arab countries. But out of the total arable area only 20 per cent is exploited.

Almost all factors conducive to economic development exist in Arab countries. The income accruing to the oil-producing Arab countries is reported at around 9 billion dollars for 1972 and is estimated at more than 67 billion dollars for 1974. The foreign currency and gold reserves are estimated also for 1972 at around 12 billion dollars and are expected to reach 50 billion dollars in 1980. Manpower is abundant with an adequate supply of high-level qualified personnel.

Arab funds deposited in Western banks stand at about 51 billion dollars, the surplus capital accruing to oil-producing Arab countries amounts to 19 billion dollars, whereas the amount needed for development projects in all Arab countries is estimated at around only 10 billion dollars.[1]

The need for regional co-operation among Arab countries arises from the diversity of resources in the individual countries. Those rich in capital are relatively poor in manpower as is the case with Saudi Arabia, Kuwait, Libya and the United Arab Emirates. Others rich in manpower are relatively poor in capital as is the case with Egypt, Syria, Lebanon, Jordan, etc. Even when equally endowed with say agriculture, there is diversity in the types of crops grown in each country.

The free movement of labour has long been recognised desirable. The first article of the agreement approved by the Council for Arab Economic Unity (CAEU) on 3 June 1957 called for a complete economic union to guarantee, inter alia, the free movement of Arabs among Arab countries, the right of residence and of employment, the right of ownership of real estate, etc. The agreement was put into effect on 30 April 1964.[2]

The decision to set up an Arab Common Market, taken in 1965, likewise stipulated that by the end of five years all obstacles facing the movement of workers between Arab countries would be totally removed and that Arab frontiers would be crossed by any Arab without visa upon presentation of his national identity card.

---

[*] The present paper is an abridged and updated version of the paper entitled Employment and Regional Co-operation (including Migration), E/ECWA/ILO/WG.4/4, Beirut, May 1975, prepared by Abdelmegid M. Farrag, Faculty of Economics and Political Science, Cairo University. The original version was revised by W. Keddeman.

[1] Council for Arab Economic Unity: Report of the Secretary-General, 21st Session, July 1973, p. 14 (in Arabic).

[2] It has been ratified by Kuwait (9 June 1962), Egypt (25 May 1963), Iraq (20 January 1964), Syria (22 February 1964), Jordan (1 June 1964), Yemen AR (16 May 1967), Sudan (19 November 1969), Yemen PDR (2 June 1974), United Arab Emirates (18 December 1974), Somalia (6 January 1975) and Libya (2 March 1975).

The purpose of this paper is to find out the magnitude and characteristics of inter-Arab migration. The main sources of data about non-nationals working in Arab countries are the censuses, the manpower sample surveys (where available), and the records of the Ministry of Labour.

Data from all these sources when they co-exist are not and need not necessarily be identical. Censuses and sample surveys often provide data on a proportion of non-nationals without showing their cause of residence. On the other hand, data on the cause of residence are not always cross-classified by nationalities. Most cross-classifications are made by dividing non-nationals into Arabs and non-Arabs without indicating individual nationalities.

Data available at the Ministries of Labour rarely show any stocks. They merely provide information on the number of work permits issued during certain periods of time. These are, however, sometimes classified into renewals on one side and newly issued permits on the other.

Variations in classificatory practices of these data among Arab countries are such that any effort to elaborate comparable tables would inevitably be frustrated. Existing data are either incomplete, irregular or full of gaps. They can rarely be checked for accuracy. Moreover, discrepancies exist between stock statistics and flow statistics, and between immigration and emigration statistics for paired countries. In some cases, the data are not published being considered either provisional, inaccurate or confidential.

The inevitable result is that no meaningful analysis of flows is possible. The best that can be attempted, under the circumstances, is to describe the structure and/or to trace short-term trends of foreign residents in a given country. Even in undertaking this limited task, the data are not always free from defects.

The paper is divided into two parts. The first part consists of a series of country profiles which pull together available existing information on foreign workers living in the main manpower-importing countries. The second part examines some of the general issues relating to migration.

PART I

COUNTRY PROFILES

1. Kuwait

Relatively abundant information is available from the 1965 and 1970 censuses, during which period the total population in Kuwait increased from 467,000 to 739,000; the number of Kuwaitis increased from 220,000 to 347,000, i.e. the growth rate of Kuwaiti population is the same as that for non-Kuwaitis.   In 1970 Kuwaitis formed 47 per cent of the total population; Jordanians and Palestinians constituted the biggest group of non-Kuwaiti population, about 20 per cent of the total population in 1970, followed by Iraqis (5.3 per cent), Egyptians (4.1 per cent) and Syrians (3.7 per cent).   Non-Arabs form 10.6 per cent of the total population.

While Kuwaitis represent 47 per cent of the total population of Kuwait in 1970, they represent only 25 per cent of the labour force.   The distribution by economic activity is as follows:

Table 1:   Labour force by nationality and economic activity, 1970

Economic Activity	Percentage shares of			Labour Force	
	Non-Kuwaiti Arab	Non-Arab	Kuwaiti	Number	%
Agriculture	52.2	28.1	19.7	4 060	1.7
Mining and quarry-ing	57.1	19.6	23.3	7 171	3.1
Manufacturing	57.1	23.9	19.0	32 089	13.7
Construction	53.7	39.8	6.5	33 669	14.4
Gas, electricity, water	59.3	11.3	29.4	7 252	3.1
Commerce	54.4	23.5	22.1	33 006	14.1
Transport	49.3	31.3	19.4	12 136	5.2
Services	47.4	17.0	35.6	104 103	44.7
All	51.7	22.9	25.4	233 486	100.0

Source: Tables 14 and 52 of the Population Census of Kuwait, 1970, Part I, March 1972.

Thus, while Kuwaitis constitute 25 per cent of the total labour force, they are spread more or less proportionately over the different sectors with two notable exceptions.   In the services sector, where more than half of all Kuwaitis are employed, they constitute 35 per cent whereas in the construction sector they form 6.5 per cent only.   Of the two categories of foreigners distinguished above, Arabs numbering 120,500 are represented in all sectors with little variation in their shares.   Non-Arabs, who number 53,500, on the other hand are heavily concentrated in construction and transport.

More detailed information on the nationality distribution of the foreign labour force by economic sectors exists for the different Arab nationalities. Thus, the largest group, Jordanians and Palestinians, is concentrated in manufacturing and public utilities with relatively few in construction and services; Iraqis show a higher than average share in mining and construction, Lebanese in manufacturing and construction, Omanis in agriculture and services, Syrians in manufacturing and commerce, Yemenis in commerce and Egyptians in construction and services.

The occupational picture clearly shows the predominance of non-Kuwaitis in professional as well as in skilled and unskilled workers categories, as illustrated in the following table:

Table 2: Labour force by nationality
and occupation, 1970

Occupation	Percentage shares of			Labour Force	
	Non-Kuwaiti Arab	Non-Arab	Kuwaiti	Number	%
Professional	70.2	15.2	14.6	25 621	10.8
Managerial and administrative	44.1	21.6	34.3	1 780	0.8
Clerical	47.6	11.7	40.7	28 202	12.0
Sales workers	50.3	18.7	31.0	21 090	9.0
Service workers	42.7	17.0	40.3	57 713	24.5
Agricultural workers	56.2	21.1	22.7	3 941	1.7
Production process workers	53.4	32.7	13.9	96 953	41.2
All	51.7	22.9	25.4	235 300	100.0

Source: Tables 21 and 53 of the Population Census of Kuwait, 1970, Part I, March 1972.

Non-Kuwaitis make up 85 per cent of professionals and of production process workers. Kuwaitis, on the other hand, have relatively high ratios in clerical and service worker occupations. Among the categories of foreign manpower, Arabs have higher than average ratios in professional occupations while non-Arabs are mostly found in the category of production process workers.

The detailed picture for the different (Arab) nationalities shows that Egyptians, Jordanians and Palestinians have above-average shares in professional, managerial and clerical occupations, Iraqis in the agricultural and production process workers' categories, Lebanese as sales and managerial workers, Omanis as service workers, Yemenis and Syrians as sales workers.

Compared with the earlier censuses of 1957 and 1965, the number of foreign workers has remained more or less proportionate to that of Kuwaitis between 1957 and 1970, increasing between 1957 and 1965 but decreasing between 1965 and 1970. The following table shows the number of foreign workers per Kuwaiti worker for the different years as well as for the different sectors:

Table 3: Foreign workers per Kuwaiti worker
by sector in 1957, 1965 and 1970

Sector	1957	1965	1970
Agriculture	0.7	2.5	4.1
Mining	3.5	4.2	3.3
Manufacturing	5.4	8.8	4.3
Construction	21.2	21.8	14.4
Electricity, etc.	*	3.2	2.4
Commerce	1.0	3.5	3.5
Transport, etc.	1.4	2.8	4.1
Service	2.0	2.2	1.8
All	2.0	3.5	2.9

* Included in manufacturing
Source: Calculated from census figures.

Two factors presently of some importance exert a negative influence on the number of foreign workers. First, some of the manpower-exporting countries, in particular Iran, Iraq and Egypt, are themselves in need of certain categories of manpower and are making attempts to attract their nationals back by offering various incentives. Second, the Gulf countries further south are competing with Kuwait for manpower and are offering similar, if not better, conditions of work, including higher wages, right to naturalise, property ownership, etc. Whether these factors are strong enough to make substantial numbers of people (re) migrate is not known. However, it cannot be claimed that manpower shortages, in Kuwait, have become more serious in the recent past.

Wages and other conditions of work are reported to be more favourable to Kuwaitis than to non-Kuwaitis.[1] On the legal side, all foreigners are subject to a system of work permits, requests for which have to be initiated by the employer. Foreigners, as yet, have no right of permanent residence nor of naturalisation. However, attempts are underway to permit certain categories of foreign workers to acquire permanent residence while other categories, in the past, have been given citizenship. The 1964 Trade Union Law, finally, allows non-Kuwaitis who have resided in Kuwait for at least 5 years to apply for membership in the trade unions.

Manpower projections indicate that foreign manpower will continue to be needed to sustain further growth and will increase at a rate more or less equivalent to that of Kuwaiti manpower. Lower increases in foreign manpower can only be achieved at the expense of economic growth. However, with increased training of Kuwaitis, their share of higher-level occupations increases, leaving lower-skilled and manual jobs for foreigners.[2]

2. Libya

Provisional tabulations of the 1973 census indicate the total population of Libya to be 2.291 million, about 203,000 of which, or 8.9 per cent, are non-Libyans. Compared with the results of the 1964 census, there has been a very rapid increase in total population, averaging about 4.3 per cent per annum over the period 1964-1973. The increase in non-Libyan population has been very high, about 17 per cent per annum, starting however from a low base of 49,000 persons in 1964. The natural rate of increase of the Libyan population, about 3.6 per cent per annum, is equally high by international standards but some of this may be due to under-enumeration in 1964 or unofficial immigration during the inter-census period.

Preliminary results of the 1973 census indicate a labour force of about 540,000 persons, 118,000 of whom (22 per cent) are non-Libyans. Several estimates of non-Libyan employment have been made by different agencies. Thus, the plan estimates the number of non-Libyans in 1972 to be 80,000[3], while a study by the Manpower Planning Committee estimates non-Libyan employment in September 1972 in the public sector alone at 86,600[4]; the Ministry of Labour reports a total number of 41,600 work permits to have been issued to the private sector during the period August 1971 - September 1972 as well as estimates total non-Libyan employment in the private sector in 1973 at 87,700.[5] A third source, that of residence-cum-work permits issued by the Ministry of Interior, puts the number of work permits

---

[1] See, for example, Kuwait Planning Board, Central Statistical Department, "Statistics of Employment, Wages and Hours of Work", January 1969.

[2] C.A. Sinclair: "Manpower Demand and Supply Projections: Kuwait", n.d. (mimeographed).

[3] Ministry of Planning, "The Three-year Plan for Social and Economic Development, 1973-1975", (in Arabic), Tripoli, 1973, p. 134.

[4] Ministry of Planning, Manpower Planning Committee: "Report on the Manpower Situation, 1972", (roneo), Tripoli, December 1972, pp. 3-5.

[5] Ministry of Labour, "Annual Report on Foreign Labour in the Private Sector, 1973", (Arabic, roneo).

at 173,000 in July 1974. The latter, though excluding illegal immigrants, is probably the most comprehensive figure and is more or less in line with the provisional results of the 1973 census. In spite of the uncertainty over the exact figures, they do very clearly indicate the extremely rapid increases in non-Libyan employment, particularly in the more recent past. Estimates of the increases in non-Libyan employment, based on the two censuses and on the Ministry of Interior's statistics, are presented below:

Table 4: Non-Libyan employment, different years

1964	17	100
September 1971	68	500
September 1972	86	600
December 1972	90	400
July 1973	118	400
December 1973	140	200
May 1974	165	000
December 1974	193	700
July 1975	223	000

Clearly the increases are very high; between December 1972 and December 1973 the percentage increase amounts to 55 per cent; between December 1973 and December 1974 it is 38 per cent. Employment of Libyan nationals, at the same time, grew at relatively slow rates, between 1 and 2 per cent per annum over the years of the inter-census period.

The nationality composition of the non-Libyan labour force is as follows:

Table 5: Percentage distribution of non-Libyan labour force

Nationality	1972	December 1973	1974
Egyptian	49.3	60.4	62.3
Tunisian	20.2	18.3	18.5
Jordanian	5.0	3.9	3.3
Lebanese	10.4	5.3	4.1
Palestinian	6.0	4.0	3.4
Syrian	5.6	5.7	6.3
Other Arab	3.5	2.4	2.1
Total Arab (%)	100.0	100.0	100.0
Total Arab ('000)	73.4	119.4	165.8
Non-Arab ('000)	17.0	20.8	27.9
Total ('000)	90.4	140.2	193.7

Source: Department of Immigration, Ministry of Interior

The predominance of two nationalities, Egyptians and Tunisians, is clear and increasing. Other nationalities show declining or roughly constant shares. The relative concentration of employment by economic sectors for Libyans and non-Libyans is shown in the following table:

Table 6:   Labour force by nationality
and economic activity, 1973

| Economic activity | Percentage share of | | Labour force | |
	Libyans	Non-Libyans	Number (000s)	Per cent
Agriculture	89.5	10.5	129.0	24.0
Crude petroleum and gas	73.5	26.5	10.2	1.9
Other mining and quarrying	56.9	43.1	5.1	0.9
Manufacturing	64.1	35.9	25.9	4.8
Electricity, gas and water	84.3	15.7	10.2	1.9
Construction	35.4	64.6	90.4	16.8
Trade, restaurants, hotels	90.3	9.7	39.3	7.3
Transport, storage, communication	95.6	4.4	45.0	8.4
Finance, insurance, business services	80.0	20.0	6.5	1.2
Public administration and defence	96.1	3.9	63.6	11.8
Educational services	84.7	15.3	45.8	8.5
Health services	79.1	20.9	23.5	4.4
Other services	79.1	20.9	43.6	8.1
Total	78.0	22.0	538.1	100.0

Source: Preliminary Results of Population Census, July 1973.

The relative concentration of non-Libyans in the construction, manufacturing and mining sectors is remarkable.   These are precisely the sectors where the increases in employment of non-Libyans have taken place.   A great number of Libyans continue to be employed in agriculture but, as compared to the situation in 1964, increases in the employment of Libyan nationals have taken place almost exclusively in the services sectors (in particular education, health and other services), in public administration and in transport.   The number of Libyans in mining, manu-facturing and construction has actually declined between 1964 and 1973.   The broad occupational distribution of employment of Libyans and non-Libyans is as follows:

Table 7:   Labour force by nationality and
occupational category, 1973

| Occupational category | Percentage share of | | Total Number (000s) | Per cent |
	Libyans	Non-Libyans		
Professional	44.1	55.9	22.9	4.3
Technician	79.8	20.2	44.0	8.2
Clerical	86.2	13.8	31.1	5.8
Skilled and semi-skilled	81.2	18.8	271.6	50.5
Unskilled	75.5	24.5	168.5	31.2
Total	78.0	22.0	538.1	100.0

Source: Preliminary Results of Population Census, July 1973.

The relative concentration of Libyan nationals in the clerical, skilled and semi-skilled as well as in technician occupations is to be noted. Compared to the situation at the time of the 1964 census, the over-all improvement in the employment of Libyans, in the sense of having increased their share in the professional and technician occupations is remarkable. Indeed, in absolute numbers, employment of nationals has only marginally increased in the skilled, semi-skilled and unskilled occupations, while the other occupational groups have shown considerable increases. In contrast, the bulk of the new immigrants between 1964 and 1973 are employed in the lesser skilled occupations. At a more detailed occupational level, the pre-dominance of foreigners in engineering occupations (80 per cent), and among medical doctors and dentists (90 per cent) is to be noted as well as their slight partici-pation in such occupations as lawyers and jurists (26 per cent), primary school teachers (16 per cent), other clerks (7 per cent), drivers (3 per cent), farmers (1 per cent) and sales workers (4 per cent).

Though different attempts to forecast manpower requirements have been made in the past and though the data-base for making such projections has been greatly expanded and improved, forecasts continue to be extremely difficult to make and are subject to considerable margins of error. On the supply side, the slow rate of growth of the Libyan labour force over the last 10 or 15 years has been noted. This rate is bound to go up in the future and approach the level of the population growth rate, which is well in excess of 3 per cent per annum. Furthermore, the presently extremely low participation rate, just over 20 per cent, cannot decline any further. Already, there are indications that at least two of the underlying causes of the low participation rates, i.e. non-participation of females and very young population, will be of lesser importance as educated females tend to be employed and the age structure is shifting slightly in favour of the above 15 age groups. How fast the participation rate will rise in the future is difficult to forecast as too little is presently known about the rate of change in the under-lying causes. In addition, government policies do have some influence on these rates although, again, the precise effect is not known.

The structure of manpower supply is changing rapidly under the influence of the phenomenal expansion of education and training. The consequent shift in the occupational structure of the Libyan labour force, already evident for the period 1964-1973, will become even more pronounced and a future where no Libyans will take up unskilled and semi-skilled occupations can be envisaged.

The real problem in forecasting manpower requirements lies in determining the demand for manpower. Very heavy investments in the recent past have induced the Libyan share in the labour force to drop below 70 per cent. The numbers of non-Libyan workers have increased at annual rates of 30 to 40 per cent, a rate which, however, is declining and will continue to decline as the initial investments in new industries make way for investments in the improvement of existing industries. Moreover, under the pressure of increasing numbers of Libyan graduates, a stage is likely to be reached where educated immigration will stop and may turn into a net emigration while unskilled immigration accelerates. At present, neither the phasing nor the magnitude of such migration streams can be forecast with any degree of precision.

3. Saudi Arabia

Statistical and other information on migration to and from Saudi Arabia is extremely scarce. Population censuses have not yielded satisfactory results and comprehensive surveys of the employment and manpower situation do not exist. However, a number of government agencies collect and publish statistics related to employment and manpower matters. Among these are the Passports and Nationality Department which keeps track of arrivals and departures of foreigners, cross-classified by nationality and occupation, the Civil Service Commission which keeps records of government employment, again by nationality and occupation and the Ministry of Labour which is responsible for the issuing of work permits. The latter also carries out employment surveys in the private sector which are, however, restricted to a limited number of establishments. Finally, ad hoc studies and surveys have been undertaken by various outside consultants, including UNDP/ILO and, more recently, the Central Planning Organisation has prepared employment and man-power estimates for the periods 1970-1975 and 1975-1980.

It was estimated that approximately 400,000 non-Saudis were employed in 1970, equivalent to about 32 per cent of total employment (estimated at 1.2 million).[1] The estimate is very tentative and uncertain, in particular caused by the large numbers of Yemenis living in Saudi Arabia. Migration of the latter is both easy and frequent and some Yemeni sources indicate the number of Yemenis having migrated abroad to amount to as many as 1.5 million. The majority of these are thought to live in Saudi Arabia where, however, they may well have been counted as Saudis. Apart from Yemenis, 200,000 other non-nationals are estimated to be working in the country, including some 50,000 Jordanians, 40,000 Syrians, 30,000 Lebanese and several thousands of Egyptians, Omanis, Qataris and Sudanese.

Recent immigration statistics show the following:

Table 8: Foreigners entering and leaving Saudi Arabia - 1972

Country of origin	Entering	Leaving	Increase	Decrease
Egypt	26 482	27 580	-	- 1 098
Bahrain	32 717	31 225	1 492	-
Jordan	50 015	48 457	1 558	-
Kuwait	50 562	40 741	9 821	-
Lebanon	21 629	20 764	865	-
Oman	5 166	6 276	-	- 1 110
Qatar	27 906	26 475	1 431	-
Syria	24 229	23 548	681	-
Yemen AR	68 162	53 639	14 523	-
Other Arab countries	35 842	38 475	-	- 2 633
Non-Arab countries	107 668	105 585	2 073	-
All	450 378	422 775	27 603	-

Source: Statistical Yearbook, 9th issue, 1,393 H (1973), p. 195.

Work permits issued by the Ministry of Labour numbered 7,009 during 1971/72.[2] However, work permits are neither necessary for everyone, as some people will work on the strength of temporary visas or of permits issued by others than the Ministry of Labour, nor will every non-national obtain one. The number of non-permit holders is difficult to assess. Thus, while 7,009 work permits were issued during 1971/72 and 23,629 non-nationals were working directly for the Government, 246,147 permanent residence permits were issued during the same year. Even after allowing for non-working dependants, the gap between the two figures might well amount to some 100,000 persons. The same discrepancy may be illustrated by the figures on work permits issued and the number of persons entering the country having a particular occupation, e.g. construction workers.

---

[1] O.J.C. Francis, Report to the Government of the Kingdom of Saudi Arabia on Manpower Assessment and Planning, ILO/TAP/Saudi Arabia/R.7, ILO, Geneva, 1971.

[2] Kingdom of Saudi Arabia, Central Department of Statistics, Statistical Yearbook, 9th issue 1,393 H (1973), p. 174.

Table 9: <u>Number of construction workers entering and work permits issued to construction workers, 1967 to 1972</u>

Year	1967	1968	1969	1970	1971	1972
Number of entrants (000)	38.9	72.6	51.8	65.0	80.9	87.0
Number of work permits	783	1 434	188	129	206	258

Information on employment by economic activity can be obtained from Ministry of Labour statistics covering the private sector; the latest such available information pertains to 1965.

Table 10: <u>Employment by economic activity, private sector, 1965</u>

Activity	Total	Non-Saudi	Per cent
Agriculture	75	72	96
Mining, quarrying	234	118	50
Manufacturing	26 529	14 664	55
Construction	9 965	4 812	48
Electricity, gas, etc.	2 472	501	20
Commerce	43 676	17 972	41
Transport, etc.	3 588	1 818	51
Services	18 059	12 053	61
Total	104 598	52 010	50

Source: Kingdom of Saudi Arabia, Ministry of Labour and Social Affairs, Department of Research and Statistics: Statistical Bulletin on Employment in the Private Sector in 25 Saudi cities, 1,388 H (1968).

The table shows the high share of non-Saudis employed in private sector establishments. The sectoral picture is more or less the same for each of the sectors with the exception of public utilities where only 20 per cent of all persons employed are foreign(agriculture should not be considered representative). Non-Saudi employment in Government for that year is probably much lower. A recent more limited survey of manufacturing industry puts the share of non-nationals in total employment at 39 per cent.[1]

The estimated number of non-Saudis (in 1973) in government employment is about 29,000 whereas total government employment amounts to 150,000, yielding a share of 20 per cent of non-Saudis to total employment.

Table 11: Government employment, 1970-1973

Year	Category	Total	Non-Saudi	Per cent
1970-1971	Officials	70 781	17 937	25.3
	General service	46 497	2 339	5.0
	Both	117 278	20 276	17.3
1971-1972	Officials	81 086	22 223	27.4
	General service	52 996	1 406	2.7
	Both	134 082	23 629	16.9
1972-1973	Officials	94 044	26 266	27.9
	General service	55 009	3 023	5.5
	Both	149 053	29 287	19.9

Source: Saudi Arabia Civil Service Commission: "Statistical Bulletin on Government Employment", 1,393 (H) (in Arabic), p. 20.

---

[1] Industrial Studies and Development Centre: "Techno-economic Industrial Structure and Growth Prospects in Saudi Arabia, Part I, Report and Recommendations", February, 1973, p. 88.

Some indication of the occupational concentration of non-Saudis is given in Table 11 above.   Non-Saudis in Government employment are mostly found among the higher-skilled officials; few are found in the general service category.   A more detailed breakdown by type of post shows that a majority of the officials (68 per cent) worked in the educational sector in 1973; a further 20 per cent was employed as craftsmen/technicians.[1]

The Ministry of Labour private sector employment survey for 1965 indicates an over-representation of foreigners in professional occupations (83 per cent of all professionals) and in the group of service workers (67 per cent).[2]   The 1970 ISDC survey of manufacturing industry shows over-representation of non-Saudis in particular in engineering and technician occupations.

There is a rather widespread belief that nationals from particular countries concentrate in particular occupations.   Thus it is considered that Yemenis work as unskilled workers in agriculture, construction and manufacturing and as skilled craftsmen and artisans; Egyptians as teachers, Jordanians, Syrians and Lebanese in white-collar jobs in industry and commerce, Jordanians also as skilled workers, Omanis as unskilled workers in construction and Sudanese in blue-collar jobs and in domestic housework.   While some concentration of certain nationalities in particular occupations may be inferred from the statistics, the latter are nevertheless too scattered and incomprehensive to allow more detailed observations to be made.

Manpower projections for Saudi Arabia indicated a total demand for manpower during the period 1970-1975 of about 460,000 persons, which is more than double the estimated supply through the natural increase of the labour force.[3]   The shortfall of 250,000 persons was expected to be met from immigration.   Shortages were estimated to occur in particular in the professional, managerial and skilled workers categories.

More recent estimates and projections show the total demand for the period 1970-1975 to have been much lower, at around 200-250,000.   Projections for 1976-80 range between 300,000 and 475,000[4], with supply estimated at between 325,000 and 335,000.[5]   Breakdowns of supply and demand by occupational/educational levels indicate shortages at all levels except unskilled to continue, though declining, well into the 1980s.   Shortages appear to be more severe at the secondary level and total estimated required (net) immigration ranges between 125,000 and 300,000 persons for the five-year period 1976-1980, which would raise the share of non-Saudis in the non-agricultural labour force to close to 50 per cent.   At the same time increases of nomadic and other uneducated population are likely to become heavy enough to require special measures for the creation of appropriate jobs for these sections of the population.

4.   Bahrain

Among the Gulf states Bahrain is probably the country with the most complete information on its employment and manpower situation.   Bahrain has had three censuses (1959, 1965, 1971) and a comprehensive manpower study was completed in 1974.[6]

---

[1] Statistical Bulletin on Government Employment, op. cit.

[2] Statistical Bulletin on Employment in the Private Sector in 25 Saudi Cities, op. cit.

[3] O.J.C. Francis, op. cit.

[4] These and subsequent figures are quoted by James A. Socknat, "Labour Market Conditions and Prospects in the Gulf States and Saudi Arabia", paper prepared for a seminar in Amman, Jordan, June 1975.

[5] Supply excludes nomads; estimates of total supply increases, including nomads, amount to 600,000 over the period 1975-1980.

[6] James A. Socknat, the Ford Foundation,"Projections of Manpower Demand and Supply 1971-1986 and Policy and Program Suggestions for Bahrain", Manama, Bahrain, February 1974.

The share of non-Bahrainis in the total population is about 20 per cent[1] while they constituted some 37 per cent of the labour force in 1971.[2]   A detailed breakdown by nationality is not available but Omanis, according to the 1971 census, constitute the majority, while several thousand Saudis, Yemenis, Jordanians and Palestinians are also found.   In addition, Bahrain has large numbers of non-Arabs, mostly from Iran, India and Pakistan.

From 1959 to 1971 the total labour force increased by 2.1 per cent per annum, evenly distributed over the two sub-periods 1959-1965 and 1965-1971.   However, while average growth rates for the Bahraini and non-Bahraini components of the labour force are similar for the whole period, the rates for the sub-periods clearly indicate an increasing Bahrainisation of the labour force corresponding with a relative decline in migration.   Thus, the Bahraini labour force increased by almost 1.0 per cent per annum between 1959 and 1965 but the rate for 1965-1971 amounted to 4.0 per cent.   The corresponding rates of increase for non-Bahrainis were 3.6 per cent and 0.7 per cent respectively.

While the over-all share of non-Bahrainis in the labour force amounts to 37 per cent, it varies widely for the different sectors.

Table 12:   Distribution of labour force by sector and nationality, 1971

Economic activity	Total employed	Bahraini share %	Non-Bahraini share %
Agriculture and fishing	3 990	76.0	24.9
Mining and manufacturing	8 464	66.3	33.7
of which:			
Mining, quarrying	85	95.3	4.7
Food, beverages	1 240	37.7	62.3
Textile	837	25.8	74.2
Petroleum	4 310	88.0	12.0
Gas and water	1 705	86.8	13.2
Construction	10 404	54.2	45.8
Wholesale, retail, restaurants, hotels	7 706	63.0	37.0
Transport, storage, communications	7 743	65.4	34.6
Finance, insurance, real estate	1 084	68.3	31.7
Community, social and personnel service	18 388	59.4	40.6
Other	817	77.6	22.4
Total	60 301	62.9	37.1

Source: Socknat, Projections of Manpower Supply and Demand, op. cit., p. 89.

It will be noted that Bahrainis have a high share in agriculture, mining, petroleum refining and public utilities, while non-Bahrainis are strongly represented in food, beverage and textile manufacturing as well as in construction.

The occupational distribution of the labour force shows the relatively high share of Bahrainis in clerical and skilled occupations:

---

[1] About 45,000 out of a total population of 225,000.

[2] 22,351 foreigners;   total labour force: 60,301.

Table 13:   Distribution of labour force by
            occupation and nationality, 1971

Occupation	Total Employed	Bahraini Share %	Non-Bahraini Share %
Professional, technical	1 876	40.0	60.0
Technician	4 127	64.5	35.5
Clerical	9 564	80.2	19.8
Skilled	17 681	60.0	40.0
Semi-skilled	13 152	58.3	41.7
Unskilled	12 048	57.6	42.4
Others*	1 853	90.1	9.9
All	60 301	62.9	37.1

* Mostly policemen.

Source: Socknat, Projections of Manpower Supply and Demand, op. cit.,
          p. 91.

Within the occupational groups, occupations in which the highest share of Bahrainis are found are shopkeepers, chemical (petroleum) process workers, farmers, butchers, postmen and the armed forces.   Non-Bahrainis are strongly represented in the following occupations: architects, engineers, medical doctors, aircraft pilots, watchmakers, barbers and launderers.   No details as to nationality are available.

Manpower projections[1] indicate that the trend towards increasing Bahrainisation and decreasing dependence on foreign manpower is likely to continue.   Such trend is caused first, by relative slow increases in employment, 3.4% for the period 1971-76 but only 1.0% for 1982-1986, as a consequence mainly of high gains in productivity, and second, by the high population growth rates.   A third factor, finally, is the increasing level of education of the new Bahraini entrants to the labour force. All these factors combined are expected to lead to replacement of foreigners by Bahrainis and full Bahrainisation of the labour force is expected to be reached by 1986.   During the period 1977-1981 new Bahraini entrants to the labour force will, for the first time, exceed the number of new jobs available and Bahrain, therefore, is likely to become a net exporter of manpower very soon.   At the higher skill levels Bahrain may continue to be a net importer of foreign manpower for a little longer and will only start pushing out its skilled and professional foreign manpower during the 1980s.   While these general trends are in all probability correct forecasts of the future, the tentative nature of these and all other manpower forecasts should be remembered and the validity of the two basic assumptions of the study - continuing high population growth rates and declining output growth rates combined with increased gains in productivity to yield sharply-decreasing growth rates in employment - should constantly be reviewed.

5. Lebanon

The situation in Lebanon is somewhat unique as Lebanon is both a manpower-importing and a manpower-exporting country.   However, statistical information is hard to get and only two sources of data actually exist.   One is the sample survey of the active population, carried out in 1970 by the Central Statistical Agency[2], the other the information collected by the statistical section of the Ministry of Labour, of which the work permit statistics are of relevance.   The 1970 survey is

---

[1] Socknat, Projections of Manpower Supply and Demand, op. cit.

[2] Ministère du Plan, Direction Centrale de la Statistique, L'Enquête par sondage sur la population active au Liban, vols. 1 et 2, Beyrouth, juillet 1972.

restricted to resident population and is becoming out-dated, while work permit statistics probably have a rather limited coverage only (modern sectors). Thus a great number of mostly seasonal migrants from Syria working in agriculture and construction are excluded and little is known about the number of persons involved.

The 1970 survey estimates total population to be 2,126,325 persons, 178,700 or 8.4 per cent of whom are foreigners, while 184,000 persons (8.6 per cent) were born outside Lebanon. The total labour force is estimated at about 572,000 persons, 5.8 per cent of whom are unemployed. Of the employed population of 538,000, 68,000 persons (11.9 per cent) have migrated from abroad - almost 75 per cent of whom from Arab countries.[1] A separate classification of economically active foreigners by nationality, economic activity or occupation is not available. An indication of the nationality composition of the non-Lebanese labour force can however be obtained from the nationality of all immigrants in Lebanon, 49.7 per cent of whom are from Syria, 11.9 per cent are Palestinian and 6.6. per cent are from Egypt.

Work permit statistics indicate that the number of work permits issued is far below the number of economically active foreigners. The total number of work permits in 1970 amounted to no more than 18,230, about 26 per cent of the number of non-nationals working in Lebanon. About 70 per cent of these work permits were issued to Arabs, some 50 per cent of which to Syrians. The occupational distribution of the work permits issued in 1970 is as follows:

Table 14: Occupational distribution of work permits issued

Occupation	1970		1973	
	Number	%	Number	%
Professional, technical	2 705	14.8	2 678	13.9
High level cadre	553	3.0	472	2.5
Administrative	1 033	5.7	973	5.1
Commercial	3 366	18.4	3 170	16.5
Service	4 317	23.6	6 280	32.7
Farmers, hunters, etc.	90	0.5	134	0.7
Production and processing workers	6 195	33.9	5 494	28.6
All	18 259	100.0	19 201	100.0

Source: Ministry of Labour and Social Affairs.

The number of persons holding work permits, compared with the occupational distribution of the total labour force, is particularly high in professional/ technical, commercial and service occupations, but very few are found in agricultural occupations where, however, it is known that many non-Lebanese work as seasonal labourers.

6. Oman

Statistical information about population and manpower in the Sultanate of Oman is scarce and differs widely. Recent population estimates put total population at

---

[1] See Audroing and Vernières, The Working of the Labour Market in Lebanon.

450,000 (including 15,000 foreigners) in 1971[1], 600,000 in 1972[2] and 750,000 also for 1972.[3]   More recent information assembled by Ghaleb[4] for 1973 still indicates total population of 600,000.   Labour force estimates quoted by Ghaleb range from 110,000 (7,000 foreigners) for 1971 to 214,000 (62,000 foreigners and 6,000 unemployed) for 1973, whereas Fischer and Muzaffar use a figure of 150,000 for 1972.   The dominance of agriculture is self-evident, though percentage estimates range between 50 per cent and 83 per cent.

More reliable statistics are available for Government, where most of the non-Omani manpower is considered to be employed.   Increases in both Omani and non-Omani Government employment have been very rapid, between 1972 and 1973, almost 50 per cent for the former and 200 per cent for the latter as indicated in the following table:

Table 15:   Government employment by nationality

Date	Omani	%	Non-Omani	%	Total
31.12.71	4 082	94.1	255	5.9	4 337
31.12.72	4 990	89.9	553	10.1	5 453
31.12.73	7 403	81.6	1 670	18.4	9 073

Source: Fischer and Muzaffar, op. cit., table 21, p. 44.

Non-nationals appear to be employed in the middle positions in Government with relatively heavy concentration in education.   The non-Government modern sector, possibly employing another 10,000 persons in 1973, could employ some 5,000 foreigners.[5]   Contrary to other countries the share of Indians and Pakistanis in expatriate employment in Oman is considered to be high.

Both the absence of reliable and comprehensive statistical information and the extremely rapid developments in Oman render forecasts impossible.

7.   Qatar

The total population of Qatar is estimated at 111,000 for 1971[6] and 130,000 for 1972.[7]

Fischer and Muzaffar, in a paper for a seminar held in Bahrain in February 1975, estimated the total labour force in 1970 at 48,330 persons, 8,240 (17 per cent) of whom were Qataris and 40,090 (83 per cent) non-Qataris.   The extreme dependence on foreign manpower is further illustrated by occupational data presented by Fischer and Muzaffar:

---

[1] World Bank estimate quoted in National Census Bureau, Census Yearbook, 1972.

[2] Whitehead Report, 1972, quoted by M.A. Ghaleb, Employment Problems and Policies in the least-developed countries (PDRY, Oman, ARY), E/ECWA/ILO/Wg.4/10, July 1975, mimeographed, p. 18.

[3] Gerard Fischer and Abdul Muhsin Muzaffar, Some basic characteristics of the labour force in Bahrain, Qatar, United Arab Emirates and Oman, mimeographed, February 1975, p. 10.

[4] Ghaleb, ibid.

[5] Indicated in Fischer and Muzaffar, op. cit., p. 54.

[6] Robert A. Mertz, Education and Manpower in the Arabian Gulf, quoted by James A. Socknat, Labour Market Conditions and Prospects in the Gulf States and Saudi Arabia, paper prepared for a seminar in Amman, Jordan, June 1975, p. 24.   Mertz estimated 45,700 Qataris and 65,300 non-Qataris.

[7] World Bank Atlas, 1974.

Table 16: Occupational composition of labour
force by nationality, 1970

Occupation	Total	Share of	
		Qataris %	Non-Qataris %
Professional, technical	2 900	19	81
Administrative, managerial	970	48	52
Clerical	4 830	28	72
Sales	3 870	19	81
Farming, fishing	1 930	5	95
Transport and communications	4 350	34	66
Craftsmen, production process workers	19 815	13	87
Services, sport, recreation workers	9 665	14	86
All	48 330	17	83

Source: Fischer and Muzaffar, op. cit., p. 49.

Contrasting with the high share of non-Qataris in the labour force, it will be
noted that Qataris form a larger proportion in administrative, managerial, clerical
and transport/communications occupations.   Hardly any Qataris, on the other hand,
are employed in agricultural occupations.   According to table 17 below, it appears
that Qataris form a high percentage of those with technical education.

Table 17: Educational qualifications of the
labour force by nationality, 1970

Educational attainment	Total	Qatari %	Non-Qatari %
No education	32 348	15.7	84.3
Primary	8 924	24.3	75.7
Secondary	4 799	13.7	86.3
Technical	750	25.7	74.3
University	1 569	5.1	94.9
All	48 390	16.9	83.1

Source: Socknat, ibid.

Clearly few Qataris have completed university education and though they constitute
a relatively high percentage of those with technical education, the absolute number
of those is small, small enough to doubt the reliability of the occupational classification given in table 16 above.

Available information points to extremely rapid growth of the labour force
during the last few years.   Population, probably more as a consequence than a
cause, has grown at rates approaching 10 per cent per annum.   Labour force growth
has been particularly rapid in the Government sector where employment rose from
about 6,000 in 1970 to 11,000 in 1974 (15-16 per cent per annum).[1]   Details of
Government employment are given by Fischer and Muzaffar[2] who indicate that Qataris
occupy 64 per cent of all Government jobs.   This finding is difficult to reconcile

---

[1] James A. Socknat, ibid, p. 25.

[2] Gerard Fischer and Abdul-Muhsin Muzaffar, Some basic characteristics of the
labour force in Bahrain, Qatar, United Arab Emirates and Oman (mimeographed),
February 1975, p. 38.

with the information given in tables 16 and 17 above where the share of Qataris in total employment is given as 17 per cent and the absolute number of those in the labour force in 1970 is only slightly higher than those in Government employment in 1974, implying that very few Qataris work in non-government sectors. The nationality composition given by Fischer and Muzaffar for government employment indicates that Arabs constitute 60 per cent of non-Qatari employment, the remaining 40 per cent being composed of Pakistanis, Indians, Iranians and Europeans.

Formal projections of manpower requirements and labour supply have not been made. Future labour supply is, however, relatively fixed because of high natural growth rates of population and rapidly increasing enrolments. Whether this will lead to replacement of foreign manpower by Qatari nationals essentially depends on the rate of growth of the economy. Projections of one category of manpower, teachers, have been prepared by Sinclair.[1] The total number of non-Qatari teachers increases slightly, from 1970 to 1975, to drop sharply thereafter as the increase in Qatari teacher supply exceeds increase in total teacher requirements. As the figures given represent stocks of teachers and replacement needs are not calculated, the actual manpower flows cannot be estimated with accuracy but clearly the net inflow of teachers will eventually turn into a net outflow and the likely date would be around 1975.

8. United Arab Emirates

Most of the information on population and manpower in the United Arab Emirates has been pulled together by Fischer and Muzaffar and the main characteristics are briefly summarised below. Total population of the United Arab Emirates is estimated at 320,000 in 1972 and may have grown at 9.6 per cent per annum between 1968 and 1972. Expatriate population increased at 15 per cent per annum during the same period, with concentrations in the two emirates of Abu Dhabi and Dubai.

Between 1968 and 1973 the labour force (employed persons) grew from 78,000 to 114,000 at a rate of close to 8 per cent per annum. Employment growth was particularly strong in oil, trade and in government services.

The difference between the educational background of employed foreigners and UAE nationals is illustrated in the following table:

Table 18: Employed population by educational qualification and nationality, 1968

Educational level	Number	Percentage share of	
		Nationals	Non-nationals
No formal education	60 218	49	51
Primary completed	9 516	34	66
Secondary completed	6 047	18	82
Post secondary	2 290	7	93
All	78 071	43	57

More detailed information is available about government employment by ministry, indicating that 45 per cent of government employment is accounted for by the Ministry of Education.

Unlike other countries, however, the share of UAE nationals in Government employment is similar to the share in over-all employment, indicating that either UAE nationals are not sufficiently available for the jobs required by the Government or the Government has no strong preferences for the employment of nationals.

---

[1] C.A. Sinclair, The Future Development of Highly-Qualified Manpower in Gulf States, paper presented to the Conference on "Human Resource Development", Bahrain, February 1975 (mimeographed).

The share of non-nationals in government employment (April, 1974) equals 54 per cent.   Of these, about 25 per cent are Egyptians, about 15 per cent each are Jordanians, Palestinians and Omanis and some 20 per cent are non-Arab (Indians, Pakistanis, Iranians).

The pattern of employment by nationality and economic sector differs widely. The following table, derived from 1968 census data, gives the relevant information.

Table 19:   Employed population by economic
sector and nationality, 1968

Economic sector	Total	Percentage share of	
		Nationals	Non-nationals
Agriculture, fishing	13 270	93	7
Manufacture, mining	3 125	19	81
Construction	20 300	18	82
Oil	3 125	49	51
Commerce, banking	8 590	43	57
Transport, communications	8 590	47	53
Government services	12 490	44	56
Other services	8 590	26	74
All	78 071	43	57

Source: Calculated from Fischer and Muzaffar, op cit., p. 51, table 27.

It will be noted that nationals are strongly represented in agriculture and fishing, the traditional activity par excellence, and participate very little in secondary activities (manufacturing, mining and construction, but not oil).

Later data, for 1973, are only available for Abu Dhabi which, in 1968, represented almost 38 per cent of all UAE employment but increased its share of total employment to about 44 per cent in 1973.   The 1973 nationality shares are as follows:

Table 20:   Employment population (Abu Dhabi) by economic
activity and nationality, 1973

Economic activity	Total	Percentage share of	
		Nationals	Non-nationals
Agriculture, fishing	3 222	63	37
Manufacture, mining	1 239	5	95
Construction	8 911	4	96
Oil	2 528	28	72
Trade and banking	5 550	9	91
Transport, communications	2 041	28	72
Government services	14 950	20	80
Other services	7 716	9	91
All	46 157	17	83

Source: Extracted from Fischer and Muzaffar, op. cit., table 28, p. 53.

Clearly the above table indicates, first, the concentration of non-nationals in Abu Dhabi and, second, confirms their relative importance in manufacturing, mining and construction but also in trade, banking and other services.

Manpower projections for the UAE do not exist save calculations of teacher requirements based on certain assumptions regarding population growth and enrolment trends.[1]   Based on these assumptions, the number of teachers needed by 1980 would amount to about 4,000, an increase by about 2,200 over 1971-72.   As the UAE has only two teacher training institutes with small enrolments, the maximum possible output will not exceed 500 teachers and a continued inflow of foreign teaching staff will therefore be required.

9.   Other countries

None of the other countries in the region, with the exception of Iraq, for which no information is available, can be considered a real manpower-importing country.   Rather, they should be characterised as exporters of manpower to the other countries of the region as well as, in the case of Algeria, Tunisia and Morocco, to European countries.   Nevertheless, all of the remaining countries do also import manpower though in smaller numbers.   In Syria the 1970 census enumerated a total of about 42,000 non-Syrians working in the country, representing 3 per cent of the labour force.[2]   A majority of these, 30,000 persons, are Palestinians engaged in various economic activities and occupations.

Tunisia is estimated to have an expatriate labour force of around 5,000 to 6,000 persons, mostly teachers, doctors and technicians.   On the other hand, 165,000 Tunisians were working abroad on 1 January 1974, close to 100,000 of whom are in France and another 35,000 in Libya.[3]

France alone employed another 450,000 Algerians and 200,000 Moroccans in 1974.   Both Algeria and Morocco have sizeable expatriate (though mostly non-Arab) communities, some 50,000 of whom in each of the countries are thought to be engaged in economic activities.   Foreign manpower in the two Yemens might number some 10,000 persons though recent estimates are not available.   Jordanian studies indicate as few as 400 non-nationals to be working in Jordan in 1973.[4]   A study by Azar, on the other hand, estimates the total number of Jordanians working abroad at 250,000, 80 per cent of whom are said to be working in Arab countries.[5] Egyptian sources estimate 75,000 persons to have left Egypt during 1969-1972 to seek employment elsewhere in Arab countries[6] while Syrian estimates put the outflow of technical and scientific personnel during the period 1956-1969 at 8,000 persons; the 1970 stock for such personnel is 8,700 only.[7]   Clearly, statistics of importing and exporting countries do not match and, in the absence of better and more comprehensive statistics, cannot be reconciled.

---

[1] C.A. Sinclair, The Future Development of Highly-qualified Manpower in Gulf States, op. cit.   Teachers constitute approximately half of all professional manpower.

[2] Central Bureau of Statistics, Population Census in the Syrian Arab Republic, 1970, Vol. I, p. 310.

[3] Ministère du Plan, Charactéristiques de l'Emigration Tunisienne, Tunis, 1974, p. 51.

[4] National Planning Council, Manpower Planning Section, Reports on Manpower (various issues), Amman, 1972 and 1973, p. 128.

[5] Azar, Wasef Y., The Population of Jordan, paper presented at the First Regional Population Conference, Beirut, 18 February - 1 March 1974 (ECWA/Pop./Conf.1/ SP.17/E), p. 14.

[6] Central Agency for General Mobilisation and Statistics, Population Movements Across the Borders of the UAR, (quarterly reports), Cairo, various years.

[7] Central Bureau of Statistics, Estimation of Manpower Supply and demand by Scientific and Technical Specialisation in Syria, p. 16.

PART II

AN OVERVIEW

Having reviewed the situation in the individual countries we will try and add up the situation. Table 21 below presents the over-all situation with regard to migrant workers in the whole region. The figures should of course be read with caution, if only because they are mostly derived from censuses in the receiving countries. The total number of migrants shown, about 900,000, is most probably an underestimate.

Several reasons can be cited for this: first, a number of countries has been excluded for lack of information. Among the more important such countries are Iraq, which might well have some 50,000 migrants, and the Maghreb countries, which have a substantial expatriate (though mostly non-Arab) labour force. Second, some of the countries included in the tabulation have understated their foreign labour force because of lack of reliable information. Thus, Lebanon is reported to employ up to half a million Syrians as seasonal workers in agriculture, in addition to a large number of Palestinians, both groups being excluded from the main survey. Similarly, Libya and Saudi Arabia are thought to have large, unregistered, often illegally residing populations of migrants. For instance, Yemeni sources indicate around 1.5 million Yemenis to reside outside their country, but Saudi Arabian estimates of Yemenis working in Saudi Arabia do not exceed 250,000 persons. Similarly, a gap exists between Tunisian and Libyan estimates of the number of Tunisians working in Libya.

These reasons lead us to believe that the actual number of Arab migrants working in other Arab countries might be close to 2.5 million, i.e. about 4 to 6 per cent of the total Arab labour force. This figure applies - by and large - to 1970.   Later figures are very scarce. Indications are, however, that labour force growth rates - and rates of immigration - have been high in Libya, the United Arab Emirates and Oman in the past few years, and average or low in Kuwait, Saudi Arabia, Bahrain and Qatar. Actual flows of migrants are almost impossible to determine as most of the available information is derived from censuses which measure stocks rather than flows.   There is, therefore, a great need for improving the information base.

Of more interest than the over-all magnitude of the phenomenon are the more detailed observations that can be inferred from the available information. Such more detailed observations can be made with regard to such criteria as nationality, occupation and economic activity.

The indications of nationality composition of migrant population are somewhat ambivalent and it is difficult to draw pertinent conclusions. Distance plays some role as one finds relatively more Tunisians and Egyptians in Libya, Yemenis in Saudi Arabia and Syrians in Lebanon, but most of the Gulf States also have substantial numbers of Indians and Pakistanis, which, inter alia, suggests a weak preference for Arabic-speaking migrants. The larger numbers of migrants originate from Syria, Palestine and Egypt. Syria probably has the largest percentage of its labour force outside the country though Lebanon and Jordan also score high. On the whole, the available information only permits negative conclusions: first, there is no strong preference for any one nationality in any one country and, second, apart from distance, particular patterns of migration cannot be detected.

Though data for most of the countries are lacking with respect to economic activity, certain indications of the relative concentration of the expatriate labour force can nevertheless be obtained from tables presented in the country profiles. In all of the countries for which data are available, the share of non-nationals is particularly high in manufacturing and construction; the picture is less clear in mining as nationals appear to be strongly represented in oil and oil-related industries but not necessarily so in other mining activities. By and large, non-nationals form a higher proportion in secondary activities, their share in such activities ranging from 50 per cent for Saudi Arabia to 85 per cent for Kuwait and the United Arab Emirates, against over-all shares of 30, 75 and 57 per cent respectively. In contrast, the primary and tertiary sectors exhibit dissimilar tendencies in the different countries. The concentration of non-nationals in agriculture ranges from close to nil to close to 100 per cent. At the same time, agriculture and fishing have only minor significance in the smaller countries concerned, e.g. they employ not more than 1.7 per cent of the labour force in Kuwait.

Concentration of foreigners in agriculture is somewhat stronger in the smaller countries, such as Lebanon and Qatar (though not in the United Arab Emirates and Oman), than in the more populated ones such as Saudi Arabia, Libya and, presumably, Iraq.   In the latter countries it might be hypothesised, employment growth in the modern sectors has not (yet) been rapid enough to absorb part of the labour engaged in traditional agricultural activities.

The service sectors, like agriculture, show greatly varying shares in total employment - more or less inversely related with agriculture - as well as of non-national employment.   The more advanced countries such as Kuwait and Bahrain have a relatively low concentration of non-nationals in services, in particular government services.   Less advanced countries have much higher shares, presumably because the educational systems have not expanded in line.   The tendency - over time - would then be for the concentration of outsiders in the services sectors to diminish.

The broad occupational distribution of migrants is possibly even more revealing than the sectoral distribution.   Typically, non-nationals appear to have higher than average shares in professional occupations and low shares in clerical occupations.   At a more detailed occupational level, the picture is similar: occupations requiring longer periods of education and experience have stronger concentrations of foreigners; administrative, clerical and teaching posts have far less foreigners presumably because nationals are available in larger numbers, their education and training requiring less time.

At the lower skill levels, the situation varies widely between countries.   The less populated and more developed countries of the region, in particular Libya, have relatively many non-nationals in lower skilled occupations; less developed countries whether with high or low population densities have few.   The relative concentrations of non-nationals in the four countries for which more detailed information is available is shown in the graph overleaf.

Clearly then, two categories of migrants can be distinguished.   The bulk of the migrants are little or not skilled, neither organised nor regulated, and work primarily in private sectors in construction, manufacturing and agriculture. Recruitment probably takes place through private agents and the whole process is regulated through impersonal market forces.   No information exists about the way this system works nor about conditions of work, wages, etc.

The second category of migrants is composed of skilled and professional workers, working both for governments and for private employers in secondary and tertiary sectors.   Teachers most probably constitute the biggest group.

Manpower projections for individual countries of the region are very scarce, the only country having attempted a more or less comprehensive forecast of manpower supply and demand being Bahrain and, more recently, forecasts of teaching manpower having been prepared for the Gulf area.   Further attempts at forecasting are underway in Saudi Arabia, Qatar, Kuwait, Libya, etc.   Useful though such attempts are, their limitations have to be realised.   Indications are that the initial manpower deficits caused by the rapid development during the last ten or so years are easing somewhat as output from the different educational systems is beginning to catch up. Furthermore, because of the extremely heavy investments in education over the last decade there is likely to be an educational explosion in the not too distant future. Indications are that not enough suitable job openings may **become** available in a majority of the countries concerned.   Already countries like Libya and Saudi Arabia are creating more government jobs, of an administrative low-productivity type, than are necessary for the functioning of the government.

However, while migration streams will probably diminish for the higher skill levels, it is not certain that migration of unskilled persons will also diminish. Great numbers of persons will probably continue to be required in spite of the general capital-intensity of investments because of the heavy investments, in particular in construction.   The region as a whole obviously does not suffer from over-all manpower shortages.   The opposite would sooner be true though particular areas may suffer from shortages as a consequence of heavy investments in labour-intensive sectors in relatively under-populated areas.   Some of the countries of the region appear, however, to have reached a stage where immigration of manpower is no longer necessary.   Projections for Bahrain and Qatar in particular indicate net outflows of manpower to have started, or to begin soon.

TABLE 21: MIGRANT WORKERS BY ORIGIN AND DESTINATION

Origin / Destination	Date	PDR Yemen	Egypt	Syria	Palestine	Lebanon	Jordan	Oman	Other Arab Countries	All Arab Countries	Non-Arab Countries	Unknown	
Saudi Arabia	1970	200 000 250 000	n.a.	(40 000)	(50 000)	(30 000)	n.a.	n.a.	n.a.	(345 000)	n.a.	(65 000)	(400 000)
Kuwait	1970	6 898	17 714	12 659	*	8 419	41 299	10 483	24 467	121 514	53 925	-	175 439
Libya	1973	-	60 752	6 162	4 324	8 324	4 324	-	24 215	108 100	20 300	-	128 400
Lebanon	1970	n.a.	4 500	33 800	8 100	-	n.a.	n.a.	n.a.	46 400	n.a.	21 600	68 000
U A E	1968	n.a.	11 100	6 640	6 640	n.a.	6 640	6 640	4 430	35 450	8 819	n.a.	44 269
Qatar	1970	n.a.	n.a.	n.a.	n.a.	n.a.	n.a.	n.a.	n.a.	(24 000)	(16 090)	n.a.	(40 090)
Bahrain	1971	(2 000)	n.a.	n.a.	(2 000)	n.a.	(2 000)	(5 600)	(4 000)	(15 600)	(6 000)	(751)	(22 351)
Oman	1973	n.a.	n.a.	n.a.	n.a.	n.a.	n.a.	n.a.	n.a.	(2 000)	(3 000)	n.a.	(5 000)
	1970 circa	233 898	94 066	99 261	91 064	46 743	34 263	22 723	57 112	652 089	107 709	87 351	883 549

Source: see under country profiles.

Notes: * included with Jordanians
n.a. is not available
figures in brackets denote rough estimates.

Graph 1: Relative concentration of non-nationals by
occupational category: Qatar, Kuwait, Bahrain and Libya

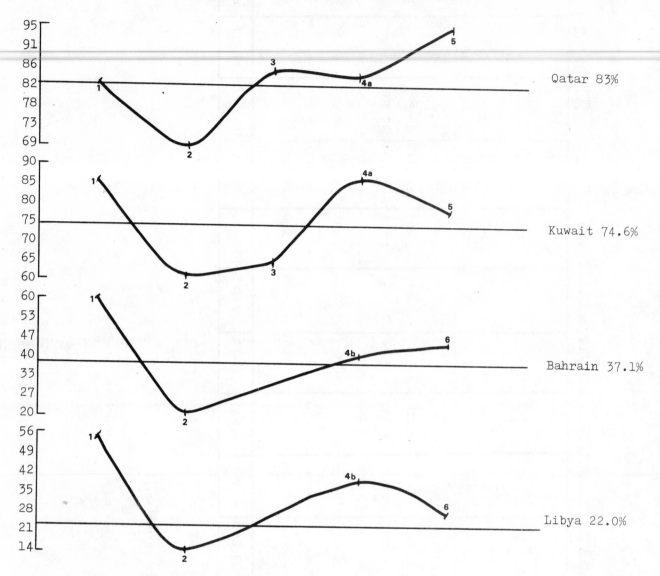

Qatar 83%

Kuwait 74.6%

Bahrain 37.1%

Libya 22.0%

Notes: 1 = Professional, technical workers;
         2 = Administrative and clerical;
         3 = Sales and services;
         4a = Production process workers;
         4b = Skilled and semi-skilled;
         5 = Agricultural workers;
         6 = Unskilled workers.

Sources: see text.

The existing arrangements covering migrant workers are mostly of a bilateral nature and primarily deal with skilled and professional workers. Thus, there exists a system whereby teachers, trainers, doctors, nurses, etc. are provided from Arab countries which can supply them to those which require them. In the case of Egyptian teachers, for example, an annual request is submitted in March or April to the Egyptian Government from other Arab and African countries. More than 10 per cent of the stock of Egyptian teachers is teaching outside Egypt (20,000 teachers). These are on loan to Libya, Saudi Arabia, Kuwait, United Arab Emirates and Sudan in this order. This arrangement is done by formal bilateral agreement between each of these governments and the Government of Egypt. There exists between Arab countries other systems of manpower transfers which are based mostly on personal recruitment and application. Group recruitments in certain occupations are made by individual contractors. This is particularly true of construction workers. This means that in this case the two governments concerned do not enter into direct deals with each other or with the individual worker as such.

Meanwhile and regardless of the existence of any formal multilateral agreement among all Arab countries on labour movements, people seem to be moving among these countries either on their personal initiative or under government auspices. The term migration is commonly used to describe these movements. In this way certain Arab countries are actually contributing to the development of others and conversely relieving pressures on the employment market in labour surplus countries. The latest and most spectacular move in this regard is the agreement reached between Egypt and Iraq, whereby half a million Egyptian peasant families will each receive 20 acres of land near Baghdad to cultivate under a system of permanent private ownership. Similar bilateral agreements should be encouraged as the outcome of such agreements will certainly be to the advantage of countries with surplus labour of certain manpower categories and those who are short of that type of labour. Practical arrangements for this type of movement are not difficult to make. Living and working conditions for peasants are hardly dissimilar in the different Arab countries.

Any broader or more extensive scheme of labour movements among Arab countries would necessitate, however, more specific arrangements and provisions. This is particularly true in the case of industrial and service workers. In such cases the need arises for more detailed formal agreements between the different bilateral or multilateral parties.

The League of Arab States may wish, therefore, to produce a model or a standard agreement which can serve as a basis for any two or more Arab countries, to enter into agreement with regard to temporary and permanent migration for employment purposes. This model agreement may, if so desired, be inspired by, but not necessarily be a replica of, specific ILO Conventions and Recommendations.[1] Any bilateral or multilateral agreement of this type should be adapted to the real needs and reflect the real situation in each of the parties concerned. It is important to emphasise in such agreements, for example, the need for the countries of immigration to guarantee certain basic rights for the migrant worker in order to enable him to be integrated in the stream of life in these countries.

A model agreement should be structured around the following aspects:

(a) exchange of information among countries of immigration and countries of emigration, concerning the legislative and administrative framework, the numbers and categories desired, etc.;

(b) the type of formalities which are to be followed by migrant workers including the validation of necessary documents, medical and job certificates, etc.;

---

[1] Particularly Convention No. 97 and Recommendation No. 86 both concerning Migration for Employment, revised 1949, as well as the Convention and Recommendation on Migration adopted at the 60th Session (1975) of the General Conference of the ILO.

(c) procedures of selection, testing, screening, recruitment, placement, dismissal and compulsory return;

(d) training, education, travel arrangements, cost of travel, maintenance expenses, return journey, etc;

(e) transfer of funds: amount and frequency;

(f) working conditions, living conditions (e.g. housing, hygiene, etc.), facilities and the procedure of settling differences and disputes between a migrant and his employer;

(g) equality of treatment, e.g. in social security, medical treatment, supply of food, employment stability, and avoiding double taxation.

II. <u>A S P E C T S</u>

UNDER-EMPLOYMENT IN EGYPTIAN AGRICULTURE

by

Dr. Amr Mohie-Eldin *

I. Introduction

Agriculture is the largest sector of the Egyptian economy. It absorbs over 55 per cent of the labour force and contributes around one-third of national income. As a result of the increase in cultivated area to keep pace with population increase over the last five decades, there has been mounting population pressure on land and a severe decline in per capita cultivated area. This increasing population density was coupled with the failure of non-agricultural sectors (particularly industry) to expand and hence provide adequate employment opportunities. This means that much of the increase in the labour force (resulting from the increase in population) has had nowhere to go and has had to remain on the land (in agriculture) where social institutions permit the absorption of labour beyond what is actually needed for the existing level of output. This has led many economists to assume the prevalence of permanent under-employment and disguised unemployment in Egyptian agriculture, and there have been several attempts to measure such phenomena. This paper is devoted to an examination in quantitative terms of whether under-employment exists in Egyptian agriculture and on what scale, and to an investigation of the factors lying behind such phenomena.

II. Definitions

It is important at the outset that one should define clearly the concepts to be used to avoid confusion. Thus by under-employment we mean the difference between "the amount of work performed by persons in employment and the amount of work they would normally be able and willing to perform".[1]

This definition differs considerably from the traditional concept that dominated the literature on under-developed countries known as "disguised unemployment". That concept meant "that even with unchanged techniques of agriculture, a large part of the population engaged in agriculture could be removed without reducing output.... In technical terms the marginal productivity of labour over a wide range is zero".[2] The consensus among those favouring that concept is that a reorganisation in agriculture is necessary if we are to remove disguised unemployment from agriculture.[3]

The differences between these two concepts are significant. First, while under-employment implies that all labour input is necessary and indispensable for production, disguised unemployment assumes that labour is wastefully applied, in the sense that more labour is applied than is actually needed by the existing level of output. Disguised unemployment assumes a situation where rationalisation in the use of labour is needed.

---

* Faculty of Economics and Political Science, Cairo University. Abridged version.

1/ I.L.O., Measurement of Under-Employment, Ninth International Conference of Labour Statisticians, Geneva, 1957, p.22.

2/ R. Nurkse, Problems of Capital Formation in Under-developed Countries, Oxford, Basil Blackwell, 1958, p.32.

3/ A. Lewis, "Economic Development with Unlimited Supplies of Labour" in Agarwala and Singh, Economics of Under-development, Oxford, 1958, pp.400-450; Rosenstein-Rodan, "Disguised Unemployment and Under-Employment in Agriculture", in F.A.O. Monthly Bulletin of Agricultural Economics and Statistics, Vol. VI, July-August 1957; Georgescu-Raegen, "Economic Theory and Agrarian Economics", Oxford Economic Papers, Vol. 12, February 1960, pp.1-40.

The second difference is that, with disguised unemployment, the marginal productivity of labour as well as labourers is zero over a wide range, whereas the concept of under-employment implies that the marginal productivity of labour can only be zero at the margin. This confusion arises out of the failure to distinguish between labour and the labourer.1/ It is not "that too much labour is being spent in the production process, but that too many labourers are spending it".2/

However, applying labour till its marginal product falls to zero should not be looked at as irrational economic behaviour. On the contrary, this type of behaviour seems to tally with the nature of organisation prevailing in under-developed countries. In economies where family farms predominate, where no wages are paid, and where labour is free within the family, labour members of the household do not evaluate their labour input in terms of its market value, due to the absence of alternative employment opportunities. Hence labour is applied till its marginal product falls to zero. It would in fact be wasteful not to squeeze the most out of the scarce factor, i.e. land, until the marginal product of the abundant factor falls to zero.3/ Consequently peasant families in their attempt to maximise output from a limited piece of land try to utilize to the utmost the scarce factor i.e. land, by liberal use of the abundant factor i.e. labour.4/ The only waste that arises out of such a situation is not because marginal product falls to zero, but because the total number of working days is distributed among members of the family so that each member is working few hours a day or few days per month - less than he is able to supply.

The situation on large capitalist farms is quite different. The aim is to maximise profits. Labour input is evaluated according to its market value. It would be irrational in this situation to apply labour beyond the point where the value of its marginal product equals the wage rate.

This under-employment can take different forms. It can be of a seasonal kind, in which periods of inactivity recur regularly every year at the same time, even though their importance may not be felt to the same extent from year to year. At the peak period of the demand for labour, however, the labour force is fully employed. The second type can be described as permanent under-employment. It comes into existence when a certain section of the labour force is still under-employed, even at the peak periods of the demand for labour. Those who are unemployed at the peak agricultural season represent the volume of surplus labour available. However, in peasant economies where the family is the unit of production, under-employment within the family is disguised, in which case it can be termed disguised under-employment as distinct from open under-employment of outside wage labour hired on large farms.

Thus under-employment is due to both the physical factors which govern the sequence of agricultural operations and the social factors, i.e. institutional arrangements which govern the organisation of production over the farming area as a whole.

The most important of the physical factors is the seasonality in agriculture. By this we do not imply, as is generally supposed, that there is a marked season during which there is continuous and full time work, and seasons in which there is total unemployment. The situation is rather one of alternate rushes of work

---

1/ A.K. Sen, The Choice of Techniques, Basil Blackwell, Oxford 1960, p.13. Also see H. Myint, The Economics of the Developing Countries, Praeger, New York, 1965, p.86.

2/ A.K. Sen, Ibid, p.14.

3/ Statistical surveys carried out in both Egypt and India seem to corroborate the fact that input of labour per unit of land decreases as the size of the farm increases and that family farms are characterised by a high degree of input of family labour compared to large farms. See, for India, Studies in the Economics of Farm Management in Madras, Government of India, Ministry of Food and Agriculture, Report of the Years 1956-1967, pp.57-62. For Egypt, see Monthly Bulletin of Agricultural Economics, Ministry of Agriculture, Department of Economics and Statistics, Cairo, February 1964, No.2.

4/ Monthly Bulletin of Agricultural Economics, Ibid, No.2.

and idleness in constant succession. It is the time lag between different agricultural operations (of the same crop) which necessitates a stand-by labour force. Among the physical factors one could mention the limited availability of cultivated land, and absence of alternative investment opportunities.

By social factors we mean the predominance of the family as a unit of production and consumption in developing societies, which permits the absorption of labour beyond what is really needed to supply the required volume of labour hours. The institutional framework in these societies permits the absorption of labour to any extent, their customs techniques, and conventions adapting themselves to the required extent.1/ The family is also the unit of consumption, i.e. income sharing is the rule. This means that wages (consumption) have the nature of a fixed cost. It is paid irrespective of the member's contribution to output, i.e. irrespective of his labour input. On large capitalist farms, however, wages take the form of a variable cost.

Any attempt to investigate the problem of under-employment in Egyptian agriculture requires the examination, first, of the two important factors of production in agriculture, i.e. farm land and labour power, their development and structure. It requires, secondly, the examination of the prevailing mode of production in agriculture, i.e. the way in which both factors of production are combined in the production process. One can then go a step further towards a quantitative estimate of under-employment.

III. The Agricultural Labour Force

Given a fixed amount of agricultural land, two factors determine the volume of under-employment or surplus labour. The first is the demand for labour, which is in turn determined by the size of the farm, the type of crop and the method of cultivation. The second is the supply of labour, which is determined in turn by the growth of population, its age structure, and institutional factors which determine the participation of different groups in the labour force.

In tracing the development of the agricultural labour force two sources are available: the population censuses and the agricultural censuses. However, great difficulties are encountered in tracing this development due to the non-comparability of the data over time and among different sources. The population censuses present data based on varying definitions, so are of limited usefulness. They do imply however, that the agricultural labour force has been roughly constant between 1960 and 1970, with little change since 1937.

TABLE 1: The Agricultural Labour Force Since 1917 2/ (000)

Year	Male		%	Female		%		Total	
1917	2130		81.0	496		19.0		2626	
1927	3001		85.0	524		15.0		3526	
1937	3605		83.6	703		16.4		4308	
1947	3656		48.3 (86.0)	3899	(591*)	51.7	(14*)	7555	(4247)
1960	4136		93.8	271		6.2		4407	
1970	4145	(4311*)	96.4	153	(159)	3.6		4298	(4464**)

    * Adjusted figures for 1947 by removing the number of farmers' housewives.
  ** Adjusted figures for 1970 by increasing the Sample figure by 4%.

Sources: For 1917, The Population Census of 1927, Government Press, Cairo 1930, Table XVI, p.74; for 1937 and 1947, see Population Census of 1947, Government Press, Cairo, 1954, Table XXI, p.110; for 1960, The Population Census 1960, Government Press, Cairo, 1963, p.15; for 1970 see Labour Force Sample Survey 1970, May round 1970, Cairo 1972, p.81.

1/ K.N. Raj, op.cit., p.4.

2/ The 1937 and 1947 censuses enumerated all those above the age of 5, while in 1960 the minimum age was 6. The sample survey for 1970 enumerated all those above the age of 12. However, in 1970, we added those between 6-12 years in rural areas as shown by the sample.

The table shows a continuous decline in the percentage of women in the agricultural labour force. The number of women in the labour force fell by about 54 per cent between 1947 and 1960, and by another 44 per cent between 1960 and 1970. Women as a proportion of the agricultural labour force declined from 14 per cent in 1947 to 6.2 per cent in 1960 and 3.6 per cent in 1970.

However, the above figures are not strictly comparable as age-limits and definition of economically active differed between the censuses. Therefore an adjustment was made to obtain comparable figures.

TABLE 2: Agricultural Labour Force (Adjusted Figures) (000)

Year	Agricultural Labour Force (1)	Rural Population (2)	Total Population (3)	Participation Ratio (1:2) (4)
1937	4020	11429	15921	35.1%
1947	4086	12604	18961	32.4%
1960	4406	16120	25984	27.3%
1970	4298 (4464*)	19460	32816	22.0%

* Adjusted figure for 1970 by raising the original figure by 4%.

Sources: Population Census of 1960, Vol.II General Tables, Government Press, Cairo, 1963, pp.1,2,333. For 1970, Labour Force Sample Survey 1970, Cairo 1972, p.81.

This table shows that the labour force has remained constant since 1937. This has induced some economists to conclude that there is no permanent under-employment or surplus labour in Egyptian agriculture.[1] Their argument is based on, first, the constancy of the agricultural labour force since 1937, and secondly, that with an unchanged labour force output continued to increase and hence both average and marginal products of labour increased. This argument seems to us to be unfounded, for while it is true that the labour force remained constant since 1937, this does not exclude the possibility that there was surplus labour in 1937 and still in 1970.

Such disputes are however difficult to resolve given the problems involved in measuring the agricultural labour force. The first problem is related to the statistical treatment of women members of farm families, which varies a great deal even in advanced countries and does not always correspond to their actual participation. The second is the inadequacy of the census definition of the labour force. The census of 1960 defines members of the labour force as "the individuals who, by their physical or mental effort, contribute to any activity related to the production of goods and services".[2] But many goods and services do not enter the market, and it is not clear to what extent they are counted.

Also, the census includes only those who are in a state of continuous employment. However, it is known that members of the agricultural household in peasant societies are associated in varying degrees with production. Female members do lend a hand when they are needed. Their employment is part-time, in specific days or specific seasons. Moreover, there are special operations which are carried out only by women and children. According to the 1960 census, women in the agricultural labour force constituted 6 per cent of the labour force.

---

[1] Dr. M. El-Imam, The Development of Crop Production In Half a Century, U.A.R. National Planning Commission, Memo 152, January 1959, p.8 and 14.

[2] C.S.O., Population Census of 1960, Government Press, Cairo 1963, Vol.II, Introduction, p.6.

In 1970 the measured ratio was 3.6 per cent. The participation ratio of women in the agricultural labour force was 3.3 per cent in 1960 and 1.6 per cent in 1970. These ratios are very low indeed in a country like Egypt, where, as we shall see later, family farms constitute 84 per cent of the number of farms. We expect that there is substantial under-estimation, but the extent is unclear.

The second source of information on the agricultural labour force is the agricultural census, regularly taken since 1929. The enumeration unit here is the farm and not the household (which is the case in the population censuses). The agricultural censuses, with the exception of the 1961 census, collect information about the permanent agricultural labour force, i.e., those who are permanently employed in the fields.

TABLE 3: Permanent Agricultural Labour Force Since 1939[1]/ (000)

Categories of the Labour Force		1939	1950	1961	1970
Holders working on their holding	) M	778	944	1559	-
	(F	67	51	53	-
Members of the household family	) M	1154	1042	1377	
	(F	351	347	399	-
Permanent wage labour	) M	1347	850	402	-
	(F	281	208	50	-
Total	) M	3279	2836	3338	-
	(F	699	606	502	
General Total		3978	3442	3840	(4,200)[2]/

Sources: Agricultural Census 1939, Ministry of Agriculture, Government Press, Cairo, 1946, Table XXXI, pp.134-136; Agricultural Census 1950, Cairo, 1958, Table XXX, p.412; Agricultural Census 1961, Cairo, 1966, Table XXXXXVIII.

There is a marked increase between 1939-1961 in the category of farmers and members of their families working on farms, and a marked drop in the category of permanent wage labour, a decline that amounts to more than 50 per cent between 1950 and 1961. This development might be due to the land reform since 1952, which resulted in the breaking up of large estates. It is consistent with the increase in the number of family farms and the area they occupy between 1950 and 1961,[3]/ for these farms rely almost exclusively on family labour. However, this decline in wage labour is too big to be accounted for by the land reform only. Many of those who left the ranks of permanent wage labour must have joined the category of casual labour.

The agricultural census of 1961, which is the latest agricultural census, presented for the first time information concerning the distribution of the labour force according to size of farm. This information is very important to an analysis of under-employment and the reasons behind it. We find that family labour decreases as the size of the farm increases, from 96 per cent in farms

---

1/ The 1939 and 1950 censuses set the lower age limit at 12 years. However, in 1961, the lower age limit is 6. We excluded the age group 6-12 years in the 1961 census to make the data comparable.

2/ The figure for 1970 is projected on the assumption of a 1 per cent rate of growth between 1961 and 1970, which was the rate of growth between 1950-1961.

3/ See Section IV.

below 5 feddan to 37 per cent on farms above 20 feddan. Moreover, permanent wage labour increases as the size of the farm increases, from 4 per cent on small farms below 5 feddan to 63 per cent on large farms above 20 feddan. This is quite expected. For small farms are always family farms that rely on family members, and hence non-wage employment prevails, while large farms are operated on a capitalist basis and rely on wage labour, whether permanent or casual.1/

We also find that the agricultural labour force is not evenly distributed over the farming area. Over 73 per cent of the labour force resides on small family farms. This is an important fact in any analysis concerning under-employment and surplus labour in Egyptian agriculture. For it is clear that small farms are over-crowded with labour when compared to large farms. This will become more apparent when we examine the farm structure.

IV. Farm Land and Farm Structure

We have already noted that the cultivated area failed to keep pace either with population or labour force growth, with the result of a severe decline in per capita cultivated land. Even the growth of the cropped area failed to keep pace with population increase, and the result was a severe decline over time in per capita cropped area.

If we examine the structure of farms in Egypt, we find that the farming area is dominated by small family farms (below 5 feddan).

TABLE 4: Distribution of Land by Size of the Farm 1950-1961 (00)

Size Group	1950				1961			
	Number of Holdings	%	Area (Feddan)	%	Number of Holdings	%	Area (Feddan)	%
Below 5 feddan	7867	78.5	14108	23.2	13812	84.2	23544	38.0
5 to less than 20 feddan	1749	17.4	15237	24.8	2267	13.8	18398	29.7
20 feddan and over	414	4.1	31975	52.0	341	2.0	20032	32.3
Total	10030	100	61439	100	16419	100	61974	100

Sources: For 1950, Agricultural Census 1950, Department of Statistics and Census, Ministry of Agriculture, Vol. I, Government Press, Cairo, 1958, Table 3, p.34-35; for 1961, Agricultural Census 1961, General Agency for Mobilisation and Statistics, Ministry of Agriculture, Cairo, 1966, Table 41.

Small farms in 1961 occupy 65 per cent more of the cultivated area than in 1950. This may be explained by the two land reform laws (of 1952 and 1961) and the breaking up of large estates. The number of large farms (above 20 feddan) and the area they occupy declined from 52 per cent to 32 per cent of the cultivated area, while their number declined from 4 per cent to 2 per cent of the number of

---

1/ According to the 1961 census the casual labour force is 1,213,000 (around 899,000 male and 315,000 females). Added to the permanent labour force, the total agricultural labour force in 1961 comes to 5,053,000. This figure represents those in the age group 12 and above. The figure already exceeds the agricultural labour force as defined by the 1960 population census by around one million workers. The difference would be larger if we include those below 12 years as counted by the agricultural census, since the figures of the 1960 population census are presented as the lower age limit is 6 years. The difference between the two censuses comes to around 2 million.

farms.1/ There is no information available since 1961 about the pattern of farm distribution. However, the 1961 census provides us with additional information on the distribution of the agricultural labour force among farms of different size.

TABLE 5: Distribution of Agricultural Labour Force by Size of Farm, 1961
(000's)

Size Group	Labour Force	%	Area (Feddan)	%	Holdings (Number)	%	Density per Feddan	Density per Feddan
Below 5 feddan	27,929	72.7	23,544	38.0	13,812	84.2	1.1	2.0
5 to less than 20 feddan	7,820	20.3	18,398	29.7	2,267	13.8	0.4	3.4
20 feddan and over	2,650	7.0	20,032	32.3	341	2.0	0.1	7.7
Total	38,399	100	61,974	100	16,420	100	0.6	2.3

Source: Agricultural Census of 1961, Ministry of Agriculture, General Agency for Mobilisation and Statistics, Cairo, 1966, Table 58.

Small farms below 5 feddan constitute 84 per cent of the number of holdings, occupy 38 per cent of the cultivated area, and absorb 73 per cent of the agricultural labour force. The medium farms (5-20 feddan) represent 13 per cent of the number of holdings, occupy 30 per cent of the cultivated area, and absorb 20 per cent of the labour force. Large farms (20 and over) represent 2 per cent of the number of holdings, occupy 32 per cent of the cultivated area, and absorb 7 per cent of the labour force in agriculture. On small farms, 96 per cent of the labour force is family labour, while 4 per cent represents wage labour. On large farms 63 per cent of the labour force is wage labour.

Two tendencies are observable as far as density of labour is concerned: density per unit of land decreases as the size of the farm increases, while density per farm increases as the size of the farm increases. Density per unit of land on small farms is over ten times that on large farms, and it is this relationship that is important for our study.

It is also clear that one of the characteristics of Egyptian agriculture is the parallel existence of small family farms with a high density of population dominated by non-wage labour, and large farms operated primarily with wage labour and having low population density. The agricultural sector is divided then into two sub-sectors that exist together - a family farm sector and a capitalist farm sector. It is usually argued that if the non-agricultural sector is organised on a capitalist basis, the residual burden of population falls squarely on agriculture. If, then, a capitalist sub-sector exists within agriculture, the logical consequence would be to aggravate the surplus labour problem in the remaining part of the agricultural sector. If employment opportunities are limited in the non-agricultural sector, and if employment in the capitalist sub-sector is organised on a capitalist basis, the family farm sector in agriculture has to absorb the superfluous labour.

The understanding of this dual character of the agricultural sector is very important for the understanding of the nature of under-employment in agriculture, and cautions against making generalisations concerning the agricultural sector as a whole.

_____

1/ A farm or a holding according to the Census is one or more pieces of land devoted to agricultural activity which is managed by one holder or a farmer whether he is an owner or a tenant or both together. According to this definition the number of farms will be equal to the number of farmers. (See Agricultural Census 1950, op.cit., p.1.)

V.   System of Cultivation

Intensity and seasonality are the twin characteristics of agricultural cultivation in Egypt. There are two aspects of the intensity of cultivation - intensity in the use of land and intensity in the use of labour. The intensity in the use of land was the result of the transfer of cultivation in the last century from basin irrigation to perennial irrigation. The result was the cultivation of more than one crop per unit of land. Most land of Egypt comes under the three crop rotation system, i.e. shitwi (winter) crops, sifi (summer) crops, and Nili (autumn) crops.1/ The piece of land is always divided into three parts to allow the use of the three crop rotation. Thus the three types alternate on the same plot of land year in and year out, with a fallow period of maximum five weeks in two years. However, intensity in the use of land differs among farms according to size. This could be indicated by comparing the ratio of cropped area to cultivated area in farms of different size. Thus in family farms below five feddan the ratio is 1.8, in medium farms (5 to less than 20 feddan) the ratio is 1.6, while on large farms the ratio is 1.4. This is perhaps due to the attempt of small farmers to get the maximum out of their small plot of land - i.e. to use land more intensively.

Labour is also used intensively in cultivation. Cotton growing - which occupies one third of the cultivated area - as practised in Egypt is, in fact, one of the most labour-intensive forms of agriculture known. The extraordinary demand for labour is mainly due to the succession of agricultural operations, some of which are extremely labour consuming. Thus the number of mandays2/ (labour input) spent in cotton cultivation in 1970 represented over 25 per cent of total mandays spent in the agricultural sector as a whole.3/ Labour input in cotton and rice (another labour-intensive crop) represented around 40 per cent of the total man-labour input in agriculture in 1970. Moreover, non-man days4/ spent in cotton cultivation represented 62 per cent of total non-man days spent in agriculture. Cotton and rice together used 82 per cent of the total non-man labour input.

However, labour input differs greatly among farms of different size for the same crop. Intensity in the use of labour decreases as the size of the farm increases.5/ The same applies to the input of animal manure - there is an inverse relationship between the size of the farm and its use.6/ The situation would be different in the use of chemical fertilizers. Small farmers try to obtain maximum output from small plots by more intensive use of the factors which to them are free or have no opportunity cost, e.g. labour and animal manure.

Seasonality is the second characteristic of agricultural cultivation in Egypt. The succession of agricultural operations with different labour requirements, with time lags between them, leads to a seasonal pattern of demand for labour. The distribution of labour time shows peaks at certain periods and troughs at others. This is exemplified by the time-lag between sowing and hoeing, and between patching and harvesting. Every operation has to be performed within the time span for it. The time lag between some operations is very short, between

---

1/ Winter crops are from November till May, summer crops from February-March till September, while autumn crops are from July to the end of November.

2/ Mandays means male labour input only.

3/ See Appendix, Table 3a.

4/ By non-men, we mean women and children; see Appendix, Table 3b.

5/ For example, in cotton, the input of labour in small farms below 5 feddan is 39 mandays and 97 non-mandays, on farms between 5 and 20 feddan it is 34 mandays and 85 non-mandays. (See Ministry of Agriculture, Department of Economics, Agricultural Economy, Vol.15, No.2, Cairo, February 1964, p.20.)

6/ Ministry of Agriculture, Agricultural Economy, op.cit., p.24.

others quite long.1/ While the separation in time of certain operations flattens the demand for labour, a bunching together of others where the completion is necessary within the same time span results in a considerable pressure on the labour force. Moreover, there may be coincidence of operations for two crops at the same time. Thus, while there might be a time separation in the demand for labour, the continuous presence of the farmer is needed near the field.

The peak demand for labour can be divided into two kinds: 1) the normal peak resulting from the biological cycle of plant growth, like harvesting; 2) a sporadic and sudden peak, best exemplified by the demand for labour due to the spreading attack of the cotton worm, which comes irregularly and suddenly some-time between the end of May and the end of July.

In a system of cultivation where the timing of labour requirements is both uneven and sporadic, the absence of appropriate organisational measures may necessitate a much larger number of labourers as a stand-by labour force than is reflected in the total number of days actually worked. In such cases members of peasant families find a sense of security with regard to their need for labour in having their relatives close at hand in case of emergency. Continuity in the availability of labour provides a hedge against labour shortage in peak-agricultural seasons. Thus, members of the household who could find employment outside do not always attempt to do so because sudden need may arise.

Two important points concerning the system of cultivation remain to be mentioned. The first point is related to the pattern of work allocation in agriculture. Within the family unit certain farm operations are carried out by men, others are within the sphere of specialisation of women and children ("non-man"). This pattern of work allocation is determined by the prevailing system of social relations and the way in which production is organised. In general, the work performed by one group (men) cannot be carried out by the other group (non-men). Thus individual members of the work force are not homogeneous factors perfectly substitutable for one another. Every category, men, women and children, has a specified operation to perform, and convention militates against the use of male or female labour in farming operations which have always been the traditional preserve of the other sex. This stereotyped pattern of work allocation to men, women and children of a predetermined and well defined task is, while wasteful from the point of view of labour utilisation, ineradicably part of the rural way of life. In such a situation the contribution of any single member of a farming family, however intermittent, may still be acutely needed. This fact has to be borne in mind in analysing the reasons behind under-employment and the factors that determine the supply of labour outside the family farm.

The second point is related to the fact that there is no co-ordinated plan for the utilisation of labour resources of a number of farming units in a certain area. Every farm is considered an "autonomous" unit so far as labour resources are concerned. This is very important in understanding the fact that a large work force might exist on the farm beyond that which is technically needed.

VI. Under-Employment and Surplus Labour

In this section we attempt a quantitative estimate of seasonal and permanent under-employment. The level of employment is determined on one side by the size of the labour force available and on the other side by the amount of labour time actually spent in farming operations. The latter depends on the type of crop and the method of cultivation. There are other variables that affect the level of labour input in agriculture, but will be neglected for the time being. We have calculated the actual labour input for 25 field crops which together occupy 9,680,000 feddans that represent 91 per cent of the cropped area in Egypt in 1970. The rest of the cropped area is under fruits and vegetables and was excluded from this study, since no information is available concerning its labour inputs.

1/ For the time distribution of farm operations, see: Ministry of Agriculture, Rural Information Department, Farm Diary for Field Crops, Cairo, October 1972.

As for the size of the labour force, there is no information for 1970. The only source available was the 1961 agricultural census. It reports a permanent agricultural labour force (6 years and above) in 1961 of 4,758,000. This labour force was distributed as follows: 3,338,000 males 12 years and above, 502,000 females 12 years and above, and 918,000 children between 6 and 12 years. We carried out an estimation of seasonal employment for men and non-men (women and children) on the assumption that the labour force remained constant between 1961 and 1970. However, two assumptions were made concerning the size of the men and non-men labour force, and hence two estimates of seasonal employment were made.

The first assumption was that the man labour force includes males 12 years and above (3,338,000), and the non-man labour force includes females 12 years and over (502,000) and children in the age group 6-12 (918,000). The second assumption was that the man labour force includes only males 18 years and above (2,530,000), while the non-man labour force includes females 12 years and over (502,000) and males in the age group 12-18 (808,000), thus excluding children 6-12 years.

Using the first assumption, the seasonal demand for men is much flatter than that for non-men.1/ This is due to the fact that the number of farm operations where men are involved is large and spread throughout the year. However, the peak demand for man's labour is in April and May when the harvesting of shitwi (winter) crops takes place. The increasing demand in September and October is due to both the harvesting of Seifi crops and the preparation of the land for winter crops. Chronic permanent under-employment and seasonal unemployment prevails in the case of men. Permanent under-employment or surplus labour at the peak agricultural season (May) amounts to 39,474,000 man days of work, which represents, in terms of labourers, 1,518,000.2/ Thus permanent under-employment or surplus labour represents 45 per cent of the male labour force in Egyptian agriculture.

The male labour force experiences heavy seasonal under-employment. The total number of working days per man is 85 days. If we assume that every man can work the whole year with the exception of Fridays (i.e. 313 days in 1970), seasonal under-employment of men will be equal to 766,438,000 mandays or 73 per cent of the amount of labour days the labour force is able to supply throughout the year. This is equivalent to the work of 4,449,000 men. However, it should be remembered that seasonal under-employment includes here the surplus labour time mentioned before. Yet those who are in a state of seasonal under-employment cannot be removed from agriculture. Those who could be withdrawn from agriculture represent the surplus labour at the peak season, i.e. 1,518,000 male labourers.

Seasonal fluctuations in the demand for non-men's labour is much sharper than for men. This is due to the fact that their labour is demanded for specific operations at specific times. The most notable examples of these are the attack against cotton worm, the harvesting of cotton, and the cultivation of rice. The peak demand for non-men's labour is in September, due to the harvesting of cotton in this month. The increase in the demand in May and June is due to the mobilisation of the labour force for counter-attacking the cotton worm and the cultivation of rice. However, there is an acute shortage of non-men's labour at the peak of the agricultural season.3/ Yet there is widespread seasonal under-employment among them. The shortage of labour time at the peak season comes to 20,682,000 non-man days of work. This is equal to the work of 795,000 non-man labourers.

Using the second assumption (excluding children 6-12 years), the seasonal demand for both groups is the same as in the previous case.4/ Yet the amount of unemployment per month is higher now, due to the reduction in the size of the labour force.

1/ See Appendix, Tables 4-6 and Charts III and IV for seasonal employment patterns.

2/ For the method of calculation, see Appendix.

3/ See Appendix, Table 4 and Chart IV.

4/ See Appendix, Table 5 and Charts V and VI.

The seasonal employment profile of men still shows severe permanent and seasonal under-employment. Permanent under-employment at the peak agricultural season is equal to 18,466,000 mandays or 710,000 labourers. Thus permanent under-employment or surplus labour represents in this case 28 per cent of the male labour force which could be withdrawn from agriculture. As for seasonal under-employment, the volume is equal to 513,534,000 mandays, on the assumption that a labourer is able to work the whole year with the exception of Fridays (i.e. 313 days a year). This represents 65 per cent of the total supply of men's labour throughout the year.

The shortage of non-man's labour in the peak agricultural season is much more acute in this case (where we exclude children 6-12). The volume of shortage equals 23,542,000 days of non-men's labour. This amounts to a shortage of labourers equal to 905,000 non-men. Therefore "non-men" cannot be withdrawn without an effect on output. Yet there is also widespread seasonal under-employment. The number of working days per labourer throughout the year is 174 days, while each member of the working force can supply 313 days of work. The volume of seasonal under-employment is equivalent to 182,752,000 days of work, which is equal to the work of 584,000 workers.[1]

This analysis of the seasonal employment profile of the agricultural labour force in 1970 shows widespread surplus labour in the case of men, and an acute shortage of labour at the peak season in the case of non-men. The surplus labour in the case of men exceeds 30 per cent of the labour force in agriculture. Moreover, widespread chronic seasonal under-employment exists among both men, and women and children.

However, if one looks at the volume of surplus labour and the extent of shortage, one could easily conclude that the surplus labour could easily meet the shortage and still leave a certain volume of permanent under-employment of men. This is based on the assumption that one day of man's work is equal to one day of non-man's day and that mobility between tasks exists. Such might not be the case. Even if we assume that one man's day of work is equal to two days of work of a non-man, the surplus labour in the case of men can very easily meet the shortage of non-men and still leave a large volume of surplus labour among men. But we are still left with the problem of mobility, and non-homogeneity of the labour force, due to the social and institutional barriers.

However, the estimated acute shortage of non-men's labour at the peak season is due largely to the small size of the permanent female labour force in agriculture, which we suspect is a great underestimation of reality. This is likely due to the definition of the labour force in both the population and agricultural censuses. It is implausible that the females were only 3 per cent of the agricultural labour force in 1970,[2] or that they represented only 13 per cent of the permanent agricultural labour force.[3] All these represent in our opinion a great deal of under-estimation in a sector dominated by family farms and non-wage employment. Measurement of the female agricultural labour force is hindered because they participate irregularly in farm operations and do not offer their labour outside their family farms, due to institutional barriers.

Still, to the extent that there is a problem of labour shortage at the peak season, it can be solved by resorting to casual labour. According to the 1961 Agricultural Census, there were 1,213,000 casual or temporary labourers - 26 per cent females and 74 per cent males.[4] This is more than sufficient to meet the shortage at peak seasons if we ignore the separation of tasks by sex.

---

[1] For the calculation of seasonal under-employment in terms of days of work and in terms of workers, see Appendix.

[2] Labour Force Sample Survey, 1970, op.cit.

[3] Agricultural Census, 1961, op.cit.

[4] 12 years and over. (Agricultural Census, 1961, op.cit., Table 58.)

To complete our analysis of under-employment and surplus labour in agriculture we attempted a third estimation of seasonal employment on the basis of the agricultural labour force as indicated by the results of the Labour Force Sample Survey in 1970. It reports an agricultural labour force in 1970 of 4,120,000 people (12 years and over),1/ - 3 per cent of which are female. Here we assumed that the male labour force represents males above the age of 15 (3,630,000 in 1970), so the non-men labour force includes females plus males in the age group 12-15. And we added children 6-12 years (177,000)2/ to the non-men labour force. The resulting non-men labour force will be equal to 668,000.

The seasonal profile under this third assumption is not changed significantly from the previous results.3/ However, in this case permanent under-employment and surplus labour is much more pronounced, while the shortage of non-men is more acute here than in the previous cases. From the beginning of May till the end of September there is an acute shortage of non-man labour.

Permanent under-employment of men is equal to 47,066,000 days of work. In terms of the number of labourers this is equal to 1,810,000 labourers. Thus surplus male labour is equal to 50 per cent of the male labour force (15 years and over). Seasonal under-employment in the case of men is equal to 857,834,000 labour days, which is equivalent to 76 per cent of the year's total male labour supply.

The shortage of non-men is most acute at the peak season (September) when it amounts to 40,234,000 days of work or the work of 1,547,000 non-men labourers. If we assume that the ratio of one man's day of work to one non-man's day of work is equal to 2:1,4/ then this shortage can be met by the work of men. Thus the shortage in terms of equivalent male labourers is equal to 774,000, while surplus male labour is equal to 1,810,000. This leaves around 1,036,000 surplus male labourers after meeting the peak shortage. This surplus is equal to 29 per cent of the male labour force 15 years and over.

This acute shortage of labour among non-men, which continues for more than 5 months, is due of course to the under-estimation of female members of the labour force (3 per cent of the agricultural labour force in 1970). This implies that surplus male labour force left after meeting this shortage is substantially underestimated.

VII. Qualifications

We have attempted a quantitative estimation of the volume of under-employment and surplus labour. However, this method implied certain assumptions which need to be made explicit in order to evaluate the results. The first assumption was that the agricultural sector was one whole, composed of homogeneous units - farms. The second implicit assumption was that the labour force was evenly distributed among the production units (i.e. farms). The third assumption was that within each category of the labour force, i.e. men and non-men, there was perfect mobility of labour among farms. Consequently, the only variables that were taken into consideration in determining the level of employment were: 1) the types of crops cultivated which in turn determine labour input per feddan; and 2) the size of the labour force.

1/ Labour Force Sample Survey, May round 1970, op.cit., Table 8, p.81.

2/ According to the Labour Force Sample Survey of 1970, children in the age group 6-12 who are part of the labour force come to 215,000 and around 177,000 of them are employed in rural areas (see Appendix, Table I).

3/ See Appendix, Table 6.

4/ This is plausible given the ratio of their money wages. The average daily wage rate for a man in 1970 is equal to 26 piastres, while that for a non-man is equal to 13 piastres. Moreover, this ratio has been roughly constant over time. (Information obtained from the Ministry of Agriculture, Cairo, 1974.)

However, other variables affect labour input per unit of land. First, the size of the farm is an important variable affecting labour input per feddan for the same crop: labour input decreases as farm size increases. There are also regional differences in labour input for the same crop. Even for farms of the same size producing the same crop, one observes wide differences in labour input per unit of land.

Moreover, the labour force is not evenly distributed over the farming area. Neither the farming area nor its labour force are evenly distributed. We have noted the substantial variation according to farm size.1/ And even within each group, the labour force is irregularly spread. In other words, different farms of the same size, in the same region, producing the same crops, have different sized families. And adjacent farms may follow different patterns of crop rotation. Its significance lies in the fact that if every farm is considered an autonomous production unit from the point of view of its utilisation of human and land resources, the phenomena of both shortages and surpluses of labour can coexist side by side. This is due to the absence of a co-ordinated plan for the utilisation of labour and land resources of adjacent farms. There is no mechanism that guarantees that the surplus labour in one farm will be utilised to meet the shortage in another.

We carried out another study on surplus labour in agriculture in 1961, which sheds some light on this aspect of the problem.2/ We calculated seasonal under-employment and permanent under-employment (surplus labour) according to the size of the farm and for the 16 governorates in Egypt. It was found out that for the man labour force in farms below 5 feddan there was widespread surplus labour, equal to 65 per cent of the male labour force in that group of farms. In medium farms (5 to less than 20 feddan), there was widespread seasonal under-employment, yet the man labour force was fully employed at the peak season. On large farms (above 20 feddan), there was an acute shortage of labour not only at the peak season but in the off season as well.

Considering female and child labour we found that on small farms below 5 feddan, there is chronic seasonal under-employment. Yet, the non-man labour force is fully employed at the peak season. Only on farms below one feddan is there widespread surplus labour among non-men. As for medium farms, there is an acute shortage of non-men labour not only at the peak, but during four months of the year. Large farms experience an acute shortage of non-man labour throughout 8 months of the year. However, there are wide differences in the volume of surplus labour and shortage of labour among the 16 governorates in Egypt.

This breakdown - by size of farm and by region - is based on 1961 data. Since we have no more recent data, we could not include these relevant variables in our calculations for 1970. One must be careful in drawing conclusions from our 1970 results.

VIII. Remarks on Other Attempts

In this section we examine other attempts to examine the phenomenon of under-employment in Egyptian agriculture. These studies come to the conclusion that while there is widespread seasonal under-employment, there is no evidence to support the existence of permanent under-employment or surplus labour. In this context we refer to two major studies in this field. The first study was carried out by Bent Hansen,3/ and the second by Mongi and Hanafi of the Institute of National Planning at Cairo.4/ Both studies were based on the results and findings

---

1/ See Section IV of this chapter.

2/ A. Mohie-Eldin, Agricultural Investment and Employment in Egypt since 1935, London, 1966 (typescript).

3/ B. Hansen: Marginal Productivity Wage Theory and Subsistence Wage in Egyptian Agriculture, U.A.R. Institute of National Planning, memo No.547, Cairo, 1965; and B. Hansen, "Employment and Wages in Rural Egypt", American Economic Review, Vol.59, June, 1969.

4/ M. Mongi and M.N. Hanafi, Labour Absorption in the Egyptian Economy, Institute of National Planning, Cairo, 1973.

of the labour force survey carried out by the ILO in co-operation with the
Institute of National Planning in Cairo to examine rural employment problems in
1964.[1] Both studies contradict in a way our findings in this study and in
previous studies.[2]

Hansen reached his conclusion - the absence of permanent under-employment
(surplus labour) in Egyptian agriculture - on the basis of two studies. His
first study concerns wage determination in Egyptian agriculture. According to
his study, marginal productivity theory is the only theory capable of explaining
wage determination in agriculture. There is a perfect labour market in Egyptian
agriculture that responds normally to supply and demand conditions. Moreover,
there are wide seasonal wage differentials in Egyptian agriculture. On these
bases he came to the conclusion that permanent under-employment is almost non-
existent; otherwise how would we explain seasonal differences in wage rates.[3]
According to him "it is a well known observation that during the peaks there is
even a regular shortage of labour in Egyptian agriculture".[4]

His second study is concerned with the examination of the results of the ILO
sample records of rural employment and wages. This research by the ILO selected
some farms from the provinces with 6 different types of crop rotation. For every
type of crop rotation there are different strata of farms that differ in farm size
and in the size of the household. These range from less tha half a feddan to
more than five feddan. His findings from the sample results were: 1) small farms,
even those below 2 feddan, resort to temporary labour from the outside. The
resort to outside labour increases as the size of the farm increases; 2) that
wage rates differ a great deal from season to season. In the peak season the
wage rate for men is, for example, 50 per cent above the average; 3) in certain
instances family labour seeks outside employment. These findings led him to
conclude that permanent under-employment is non-existent, while there is widespread seasonal under-employment.

R. Mabro, in a recent article, tried to provide a compromise between our
findings and those of Professor Hansen. In his opinion, physical under-employment
(surplus labour-time) is consistent with a perfect labour market and seasonal
wage differentials.[5] He constructed a simple model of an agriculture sector,
composed of capitalist farms operated by wage labour, family farms operated by
family labour, and landless labourers offering their labour service in the labour
market. In this case, there is a perfect market for labour determined by the
supply of landless labourers and the demand for labour by capitalist farms.

According to Mabro, family sector individuals aim at maximising "their
utility when they trade leisure for income (say corn) through work".[6] The
failure of some family labour to respond to wage increases and hence of offering
their labour in the outside market may be due to the presence of risks which, at
low levels of income, weigh heavily in peasants decisions.[7] Family members may
like to retain control over their labour services to the family farm and the
outside employer[8] while an important agricultural operation is being performed.
Thus if there are great risks involved as a result of delaying certain tasks, the

---

[1] U.A.R. Institute of National Planning and ILO Research Report on
Employment Problems in Rural Areas, Cairo, 10 Vols., 1965-8.

[2] A. Mohie-Eldin, Investment and Employment Problems, op.cit., pp.74-110.

[3] B. Hansen, Marginal Productivity Wage Theory and Subsistence Wage Theory
in Egyptian Agriculture, op.cit., p.23.

[4] Ibid., p.25.

[5] R. Mabro: "Employment and Wages in Dual Agriculture", Oxford Economic
Papers, Vol.23, No.3, November, 1971, pp.401-417.

[6] Mabro, op.cit., p.405.

[7] Ibid.

[8] Ibid., p.407.

- 124 -

family worker would want to complete the jobs on his farm before offering his labour service outside. Moreover, in other circumstances he may value the convenience of being able to switch back to his own farm should an emergency arise after he has taken some outside job. Thus at the peak season, the probability of finding employment outside his farm "is high but the disutility of outside employment may weigh significantly in the worker's decision".[1]

Physical under-employment at the peak season may exist if family workers who are not employed on their farms for the full duration of the agricultural operation do not offer their labour on the outside market. They may do this because 1) the free time available falls short of the minimum required by the labour contract; 2) they have chosen to remain on the farm because of risks and costs involved in offering their labour outside while certain farm operations are not yet complete.

However, while we appreciate highly Mabro's attempt to explain this contradiction, the explanation does not really need the construction of such an elaborate model. The explanation is actually very simple. The existence of surplus labour does not in any way mean that this surplus is readily available for outside work as soon as there is the demand for it. And surplus labour is consistent with seasonal variations in the wage rate.

What actually determines the supply of labour outside family farms is not the absolute size of the labour force, but rather the degree of imperfection in its supply. There are several technological as well as institutional factors likely to affect its supply imperfections. These factors are: 1) the fact that the labour force is irregularly spread over the area, and farms are operated as autonomous production units; 2) the demand for labour is uneven and sometimes sporadic, which leads family farms to keep their family members ready at hand as a hedge against shortage of labour when the need arises; 3) female members who participate in work on the family farm do not offer their labour outside due to institutional factors; 4) there is the traditional pattern of work allocation based on sex. All these factors contribute to the fact that while physical under-employment might exist at the peak season, it is not necessarily available for outside employment as soon as the demand for it arises. Thus surplus labour is consistent with seasonal differences in wage rates.

However, in any case, information obtained about seasonal wage rates in agriculture does not show great differences in different seasons. The wage rate at the peak season increases by 10 per cent to 15 per cent over the average rate at the slack season.[2] The divergence between the average wage rate at the slack season and at the peak season is not large. Moreover, if we try to examine the behaviour of the real wage rate over time, we observe that the average daily real wage remained more or less constant through time or even declined.[3] While the money wage rate increased between 1966 and 1973, the real wage rate actually declined. Even the increase in the money wage rate is not noticeable during this period. However, a declining real wage rate is inconsistent with the absence of widespread permanent under-employment. One would expect that the real wage rate would increase if the argument of those who deny the existence of surplus labour is correct.

IX. Policies

We have seen that the agricultural sector in Egypt is composed of two sub-sectors, a family farm sector, and a capitalist farm sector. Family farms represent the largest number of farms and absorb over 73 per cent of the agricultural labour force. Most labour (96 per cent) on family farms is family labour. The capitalist farm sector represents a very small percentage of the number of farms, and commands a large percentage of the cultivated area; it also absorbs 7 per cent of the agricultural labour. Capitalist farms are operated by wage labour whether permanent or temporary.

---

[1] Ibid., p.411.

[2] See Appendix, Table 7.

[3] See Appendix, Table 8.

There is widespread chronic, permanent under-employment among men, while at the same time there appears to be an acute shortage of female and child labour at the peak season. There is no mechanism to guarantee that surplus in one area or among one category of workers will compensate for the shortages experienced in other areas or for other categories of workers, as mobility between farms and substitituion between categories of labour is very limited. What would we do, then, with under-employed or surplus labour in agriculture?

The aim of any policy to solve the problem of permanent under-employment is to try to create the means of efficiently utilising surplus labour with the minimum social cost involved. This policy should be carried out in two stages with different aims for each stage.

The first stage would aim at the realisation of such surplus labour (or permanent under-employment). For surplus labour might exist, yet it might not be available for outside employment. It might be trapped within the family farm unit due to institutional rigidities. The first type of policies are those that aim at making this surplus labour available.

Such policies include the consolidation of scattered farm holdings, allowing the enlargement of the planning unit so that there will be unification of the crop rotation over a larger area. This need not in any way affect the private owner-ship of land or the size of the production unit. All that we mean is that the cultivated area of 4 or 5 adjacent villages be unified in a large planning unit that applies the same crop rotation. This would allow the formulation of a coordinated plan for the whole area that coordinates the use of land, labour, and capital resources of the member farms. This would avoid a great deal of waste in the use of labour or capital resources of individual farming families.

It was mentioned in Chapter 4 that there are several factors responsible for the phenomenon of surplus labour or permanent under-employment. First, labour and land resources are unevenly distributed. Second is the autonomy and independence of individual production units in agriculture, which means that there is an absence of a coordinated plan for the utilisation of labour resources of neighbouring farms. That is why the phenomena of surplus and shortages exist side by side. Thus the creation of an organisational framework where land and labour resources are pooled together might have important consequences for surplus labour. For one of the most important characteristics of labour within the family farm is that it represents in a way an indivisible factor (in the sense that while it is available for extra employment within the family farm, it is not immediately available, due to institutional factors, to meet outside demand). The pooling of labour resources of different farms and the establishment of a coordinated schedule of work could ease such a situation. Moreover, the pooling of surplus labour resources, would enable the undertaking of projects outside agriculture which the surplus labour of a single family or small number of farms cannot under-take.

In the second stage, policies should aim at the utilisation of surplus labour with minimum social cost. This means the creation of employment opportunities within the confines of the rural area to reduce the cost involved in the transfer of labour outside the area. These costs include extra consumption due to higher living standards and higher wages in urban areas, expenditure for the creation of social amenities in the new areas of settlement, and costs of the transfer itself. Thus projects for employment of surplus labour should be largely within their localities.

There are many investment projects that could utilise surplus labour with minimum cost involved. These include roads, irrigation and drainage projects, and all types of construction projects in rural areas. Moreover, there are industries which could be established on a small scale basis, such as basket industry, farm processing industries, farm tools and equipment, industry that manufactures tubes from pottery needed in underground drainage, etc. There are other types of industries which could be established on a small scale and scattered in rural areas. The Japanese experience of the late nineteenth and early twentieth century has additional examples of such industries, such as the bicycle, tooth-brush and small machine tool industries. The Chinese experience of the twentieth century is of a similar pattern but in a different social framework.

The most notable feature of both the Japanese and Chinese models is the fact that instead of transferring labour to industry, industry was directed to labour. Manpower was recruited for industrial employment through symbioses of industry with agriculture. The mobilisation of under-employed labour within the confines of the rural areas itself provided a dynamic impulse for a substantial lowering of the wage costs. The peasant is usually attached to the soil, and finds it easier to contribute a portion of his labour in familiar surroundings.

The integration of industry into the rural way of life would delay the trend towards urbanisation, and would help the economy to hold the line against mounting pressures of domestic demand. This again would ease the problem of open unemployment in urban areas, which is due largely to the migration of unskilled labour to urban areas.

APPENDIX

Method of Estimating Under-Employment

In order to estimate permanent under-employment or surplus labour we first have to estimate seasonal employment, i.e. labour input in every month of the year. This requires information about the area cultivated with every crop in 1970. This information was obtained and it is expressed in Table 1. Secondly we needed information about input of labour per unit of land (feddan) by farm operation. That is to say, input of labour per unit of land. This information was obtained from the Ministry of Agriculture, Department of Economics and Statistics, and is expressed in Table 2. It represents a weighted average for the economy as a whole. Input of labour is distributed among men and non-men (women and children). Thirdly we needed information about the timing of every farm operation. That is to say, the time span within which the farm operation is carried out. This information was obtained from the farm diary published by the Ministry of Agriculture.1/ In this diary the timing of every farm operation for every crop was listed. The timing of the farming operations according to this diary is a theoretical one. It is the time when every farm operation is to be carried out. What happens in reality might differ in one way or another. For example, according to the diary the preparation of land for cultivation of cotton should take place in January. Some farmers might carry out the operation in this time. Others who prefer to obtain more than one harvest from the winter crop (fodder) might carry out that operation in February. Moreover, according to the diary the time for the harvesting of wheat (winter crop) is May, yet some farmers, who cultivate their land for winter crops later than the normal time, usually harvest wheat in June.

To calculate the seasonal employment profile, we started by calculating the labour input in agriculture every month of the year. This was done by multiplying the area under every crop by the labour input of the specific farm operation in question. For example, if the area under wheat is 100 feddan and the labour input in the farming operation (preparation for cultivation) is 4 days, we multiplied 4 by 100 to get 400 days of work. If that farming operation is carried out in October, the 400 days were put under October. If 12 days of work represent labour input in harvesting of wheat and if harvesting of wheat is carried out in May, we then multiply 12 by 100 and the result is 1200 days of work under May. In this way the distribution of the labour input for every crop throughout the different months of the year was obtained. This operation was carried out for 25 field crops which occupy 90 per cent of the cropped area in 1970. And it was carried out twice, one time for labour input of men, the other for labour input of non-men (women and children). Then we summed up all labour input for all crops for every month of the year to obtain the total seasonal labour input in every month of the year in agriculture. This was done for both men and non-men. The results of these calculations are presented in Tables 3A and 3B.

Having obtained seasonal labour input in agriculture, we arrived at the seasonal employment profile for men and non-men by dividing the labour input (in terms of man or non-man days) by the labour force in agriculture to arrive at the number of days of employment (or work) for each member of the labour force for every month.

After calculating seasonal employment, we started to calculate permanent under-employment or surplus labour. This represents the difference between the actual labour input at the peak season and the labour input the labour force is able to provide or supply at the peak season. We assumed that every member of the labour force can work the whole month except Fridays. If at the peak month each member of the labour force can supply 26 days of work, we multiplied 26 by the size of the labour force to arrive at the number of working days the labour force is able to supply at the peak season. The difference between the number of days the labour force is able to supply and the actual labour input represents the surplus labour time (in terms of days of work) available. In order to arrive at the permanent under-employment or the surplus in terms of number of labourers, we

---

1/ **Farm Diary for Field Crops**, Ministry of Agriculture, Department of Rural Information, Cairo, October, 1974.

divided the surplus time (in terms of days) by the number of days of work each member of the labour force can supply. In this way we arrived at the surplus labourers. Thus, if the amount of surplus labour time is 260 days of work and each member can supply 26 days at the peak month, the surplus labourers are 10.

The same procedure was carried out to calculate the shortage either in terms of labour time or in terms of labourers. Thus if labour input is larger than what the labour force can supply, we have a case of labour shortage in terms of man-days or non-man days. By dividing the volume of shortage in terms of labour days by the number of days each member of the labour force can normally supply we arrive at the shortage in terms of labourers.

This is for surplus labour or permanent under-employment. As for seasonal under-employment, we assumed that each member of the labour force can work the whole year with the exception of Fridays (i.e. 313 days). By multiplying the labour force by 313 we get the total number of working days the labour force is able to supply throughout the year. The difference between the amount and actual labour input throughout the year represents the volume of seasonal under-employment in terms of days of work. By dividing seasonal under-employment in terms of days by the normal working days for a year each member of the labour force can supply we obtain seasonal under-employment in terms of labourers.

APPENDIX

TABLE 1

AREA CULTIVATED BY DIFFERENT CROPS IN 1970

(000) FEDDAN

Shitwi (Winter) Crops	Area	Sifi (Summer) Crops	Area	Nili (Autumn) Crops	Area
Wheat	1,304,4	Cotton	1,627,4	Nili Rice	2,8
Beans	330,4	Rice	1,139,5	Nili Maize	350,6
Barley	83,2	Sifi Millet	464,7	Nili Millet	35,5
Lentils	47,2	Sifi Maize	1,152,9	--	
Fenugreek	40,0	Sugar Cane	186,2		
Shetwi Onions	34,1	Ground Nuts	42,5		
Garlic	7,2	Sesame	41,0		
Flax	21,4	Henna	0,7		
Lupine	9,9	Sifi Onions	4,0		
Chick-Peas	6,7	--			
Safflower	0,02				
Bersim (Fadder) Prennial	1,227,1				
Bersim (Tahrish)	1,520,5				
Rambling-Vetch	0,9				
Total	4,633,0	Total	4,658,9	Total	388,9

Source: Ministry of Agriculture, Department of Economics and Statistics, The Agricultural Economy, Cairo, December, 1972.

APPENDIX

TABLE 2

LABOUR INPUTS PER FEDDAN FOR DIFFERENT CROPS

Crop	Men	Women and Children
Cotton	42	87
Sugar Cane	98	31
Rice	35	40
Maize	25	10
Beans	19	5
Fenugreek	20	2.5
Chick Peas	22	2
Flax	34	17
Bersim prennial	19.5	1
Bersim tahrish	11.75	-
Millet	42	9
Sesame	28	4
Ground Nuts	41	35
Wheat	27	4
Barley	18.25	3
Lupine	20	2
Lentils	21	2
Garlic	39	43
Onions	33.5	70

Source: Ministry of Agriculture, Department of Economics, Agricultural Economy, Vol.15, No.2, Cairo, February, 1964.

APPENDIX

TABLE 3A

TOTAL INPUT OF LABOUR (MEN) PER CROP PER MONTH, 1970 (000 MAN DAYS)

Crop	Jan.	Feb.	March	April	May	June	July	Aug.	Sept.	Oct.	Nov.	Dec.	Total Year
Ground Nut	–	–	–	85	287	308	266	213	191	394	–	–	1,744
Sifi Millet	–	–	3,253	4,414	2,556	929	929	6,970	465	–	–	–	19,516
Sifi Maize	–	–	4,611	–	8,646	7,494	2,306	5,764	–	–	–	–	28,821
Rice	–	–	–	4,558	6,837	6,837	1,994	2,564	1,140	11,395	4,558	–	39,883
Cotton	14,647	1,090	5,973	5,184	7,047	7,047	2,164	2,164	13,020	–	–	–	68,336
Garlic	14	14	7	–	115	–	–	–	72	22	–	14	258
Barley	–	83	83	915	–	–	–	–	–	333	21	83	1,519
Beans	–	165	83	2,974	–	–	–	–	–	1,322	330	1,404	6,278
Bersim (Prennial)	6,082	4,561	4,561	–	–	–	–	–	6,082	3,001	–	4,561	29,649
Bersim (Tahrish)	–	–	–	–	–	–	–	–	5,522	1,534	3,681	3,681	14,418
Lentils	12	12	236	401	–	–	–	–	–	236	35	12	943
Fenugreek	20	20	200	320	–	–	–	–	–	120	80	40	800
Lupine	10	5	5	49	74	–	–	–	–	15	30	10	198
Chick-peas	–	–	27	65	–	–	–	–	–	53	2	–	147
Sifi Onions	14	40	10	2	2	2	32	52	–	–	–	–	155
Wheat	–	2,283	987	987	20,871	–	–	–	–	4,892	1,631	2,283	33,915
Flax	21	43	21	438	43	–	–	–	43	86	11	21	727
Rambling Vetch	1	2	1	18	2	–	–	–	2	–	4	1	30
Sugar Cane	1,304	1,304	2,095	2,095	419	419	372	372	372	372	6,890	1,862	17,878
Shetwi Onions	17	17	273	273	–	–	–	–	119	341	85	17	1,142
Sesame	–	–	–	266	164	61	61	594	–	–	–	–	1,146
Henna	–	–	–	5	3	1	1	10	–	–	–	–	20
Nili Rice	–	–	–	–	–	11	3	10	6	6	39	6	81
Nili Maize	–	–	–	–	–	1,403	701	2,980	1,929	526	1,753	–	9,292
Nili Millet	–	–	–	–	249	338	196	71	71	356	178	–	1,458
Total	22,142	9,640	22,417	33,041	47,314	24,850	9,027	21,767	29,032	25,805	19,325	13,996	278,356

Source: Based on Tables 1 and 2.

APPENDIX

TABLE 3B

TOTAL INPUT OF LABOUR (NON-MEN)* PER CROP PER MONTH   (000 NON-MAN DAYS)

Crop	Jan.	Feb.	March	April	May	June	July	Aug.	Sept.	Oct.	Nov.	Dec.	Total Year
Ground Nut	-	-	-	-	128	-	-	-	-	1,361	-	-	1,489
Sifi Millet	-	-	-	1,162	1,162	465	-	929	465	-	-	-	4,182
Sifi Maize	-	-	-	2,306	576	576	-	8,070	-	-	-	-	11,529
Rice	-	-	-	-	18,802	17,663	2,849	2,279	570	2,279	1,140	-	45,581
Cotton	-	4,882	3,255	3,255	18,715	18,715	18,715	18,715	55,333	-	-	-	141,586
Garlic	38	38	29	-	187	-	-	-	79	31	-	14	415
Barley	-	20	-	208	-	-	-	-	-	-	-	21	249
Beans	-	-	-	991	-	-	-	-	-	-	330	331	1,652
Bersim (Prennial)	-	-	-	-	-	-	-	-	760	760	-	-	1,520
Bersim (Tahrish)	-	-	-	-	-	-	-	-	-	-	-	-	-
Lentils	-	-	47	47	-	-	-	-	-	-	-	-	94
Fenugreek	10	-	20	40	-	-	-	-	-	-	20	10	100
Lupine	3	2	-	-	-	-	-	-	-	-	10	3	20
Chick-peas	-	-	3	10	-	-	-	-	-	-	-	3	13
Sifi Onions	-	97	20	20	20	20	32	53	-	-	-	-	262
Wheat	652	652	-	-	3,913	-	-	-	-	-	-	-	5,217
Flax	64	86	64	86	-	-	-	-	-	-	-	64	364
Rambling Vetch	2	4	2	4	-	-	-	-	-	-	-	-	15
Sugar Cane	1,304	1,304	372	-	-	-	-	-	-	-	3,166	3	6,146
Shetwi Onions	171	171	443	443	-	-	-	-	-	818	171	170	2,387
Sesame	-	-	-	-	123	41	-	-	-	-	-	-	164
Henna	-	-	-	-	2	1	-	-	-	-	-	-	3
Nili Rice	-	-	-	-	-	-	3	47	45	6	8	3	112
Nili Maize	-	-	-	-	-	-	701	351	351	-	2,454	-	3,857
Nili Millet	-	-	-	-	-	89	89	36	-	71	35	-	320
Total	2,243	7,256	4,259	8,571	43,629	37,570	22,389	30,480	57,602	5,326	7,335	618	227,278

* Women and children.

Source: Based on Tables 1 and 2.

APPENDIX

TABLE 4

SEASONAL EMPLOYMENT OF MEN AND NON-MEN IN

AGRICULTURE IN 1970

(DAYS PER PERSON)

	Jan.	Feb.	Mar.	Apr.	May	June	July	Aug.	Sep.	Oct.	Nov.	Dec.	Total
MEN	7	3	7	10	14	7	3	7	9	8	6	4	85
NON-MEN	2	5	3	6	31	27	16	21	41	4	5	.5	161.5

Sources: Tables 3A and 3B.

TABLE 5

SEASONAL EMPLOYMENT IN AGRICULTURE 1970 (DAYS PER PERSON)

2nd ASSUMPTION

	Jan.	Feb.	Mar.	Apr.	May	June	July	Aug.	Sep.	Oct.	Nov.	Dec.	Total
MEN	9	4	9	13	19	10	4	9	12	10	8	6	113
NON-MEN	2	6	3	7	33	29	17	23	44	4	6	.5	174.5

Sources: Tables 3A and 3B.

TABLE 6

SEASONAL EMPLOYMENT IN AGRICULTURE 1970 (DAYS PER PERSON)

3rd ASSUMPTION

	Jan.	Feb.	Mar.	Apr.	May	June	July	Aug.	Sep.	Oct.	Nov.	Dec.	Total
MEN	6	3	6	9	13	7	3	6	8	7	5	4	77
NON-MEN*	3	11	6	13	65	56	33	46	86	8	11	1	339

* Women and children 12 years and over.

Sources: Tables 3A and 3B.

APPENDIX

TABLE 7

SEASONAL WAGE RATE IN EGYPTIAN AGRICULTURE IN SELECTED YEARS
(PIASTRES)[1]

		Jan.	Feb.	Mar.	Apr.	May	June	July	Aug.	Sep.	Oct.	Nov.	Dec.	Average
	1963	14	14	14	15	15.5	15.5	16	16	16	16.5	16.5	16	16
	1966	24	24	24	24	26	26	26	26	27	25	25	25	25
MEN	1968	24	23	24	24	25	25	25	24	25	24	24	24	24
	1970	25	25	25	25	26.5	27	26	26	25.5	26	25	25	26
	1972	26	26	26	25.5	26	26.5	27	26.5	28	28.5	26.5	26	26.5
	1963	7	7	7	7	7	7.5	8	8	9	9	8.5	8	8
	1966	12	12	12	12	12	12	12	12	13	13	12	12	12
NON-MEN*	1968	12	12	11	11	12	12	12	12	11	12	12	12	11.5
	1970	12	12	12.5	12.5	12	13	13	13	13	13	13	12.5	13
	1972	13	13.5	14	13	14	13.5	13	14	14	14	14	14	14

*   Women and children

1/ These are daily average money wage rates in Egyptian piastres.

Source: Information obtained from the Ministry of Agriculture, 1974.

APPENDIX

TABLE 8

DAILY WAGE RATE IN AGRICULTURE AT CONSTANT PRICES

(1966/67 = 100)

Year	Average daily money wage rate		Average daily real wage rate1/		Index of Consumer Goods Prices in Rural Areas2/
	Men	Non-Men*	Men	Non-Men*	
1966/67	25	12	25	12	100
1967/68	24.5	12	24	12	102
1968/69	24.5	12	23	11	106
1969/70	25.5	13	22	11	114
1970/71	25	12.5	21	10.6	118
1971/72	25.5	12.5	21	10.5	119
1972/73	27.5	13.5	21	10.7	126

* Women and children.

1/ These are money wage rates deflated by a cost of living index for rural areas.

2/ A new cost of living index for rural areas 1966/67 = 100. It is based on the family budget survey of 1965. See National Bank of Egypt, Economic Bulletin, Vol. 27, No.1, Cairo, 1974.

Source: Information obtained from the Ministry of Agriculture, 1974.

CHART I
SEASONAL EMPLOYMENT OF MEN 1970
(1st Assumption)

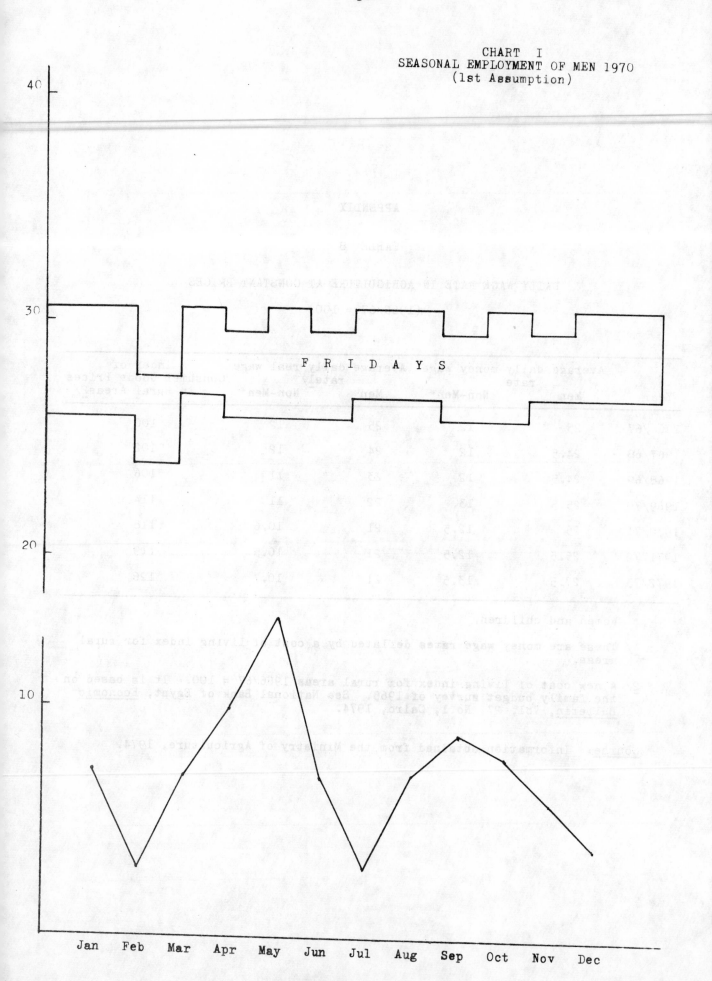

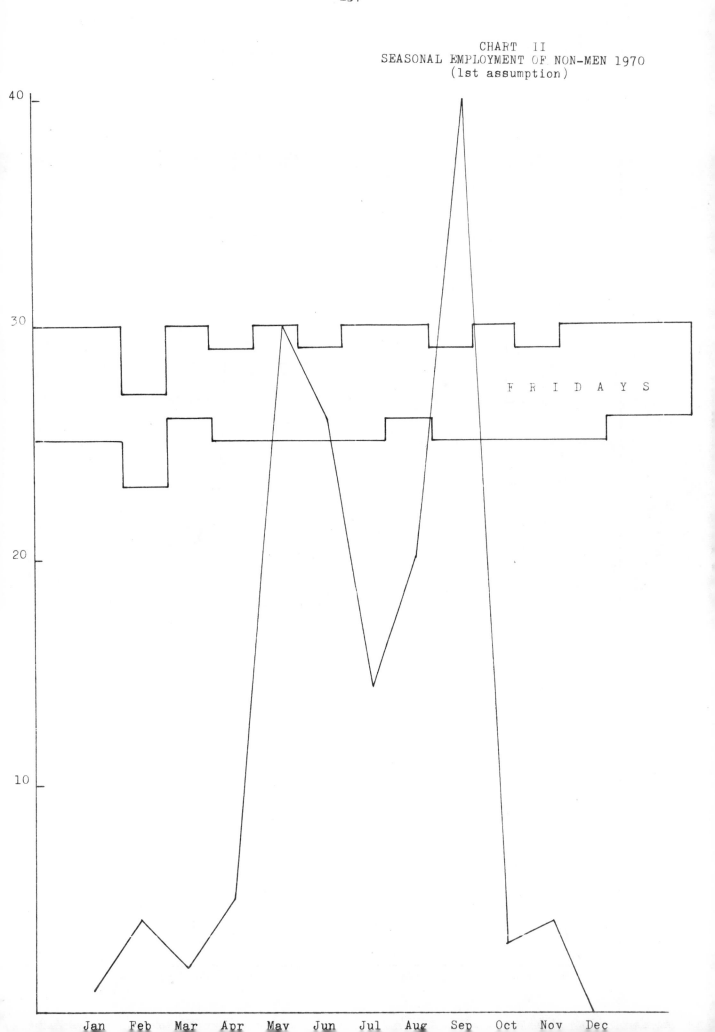

CHART   II
SEASONAL EMPLOYMENT OF NON-MEN 1970
(1st assumption)

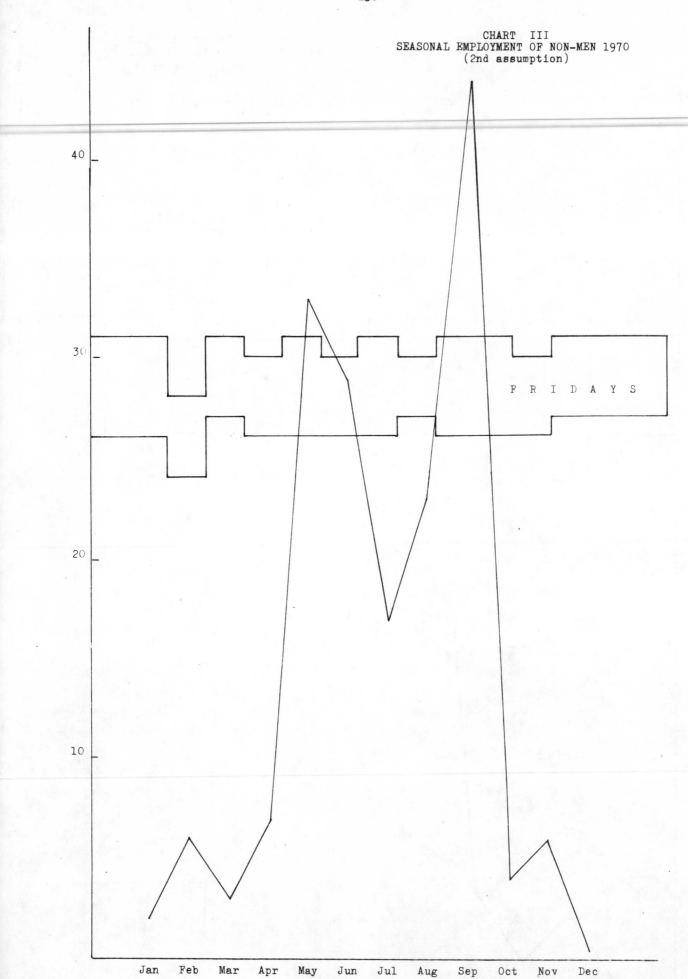

CHART III
SEASONAL EMPLOYMENT OF NON-MEN 1970
(2nd assumption)

F R I D A Y S

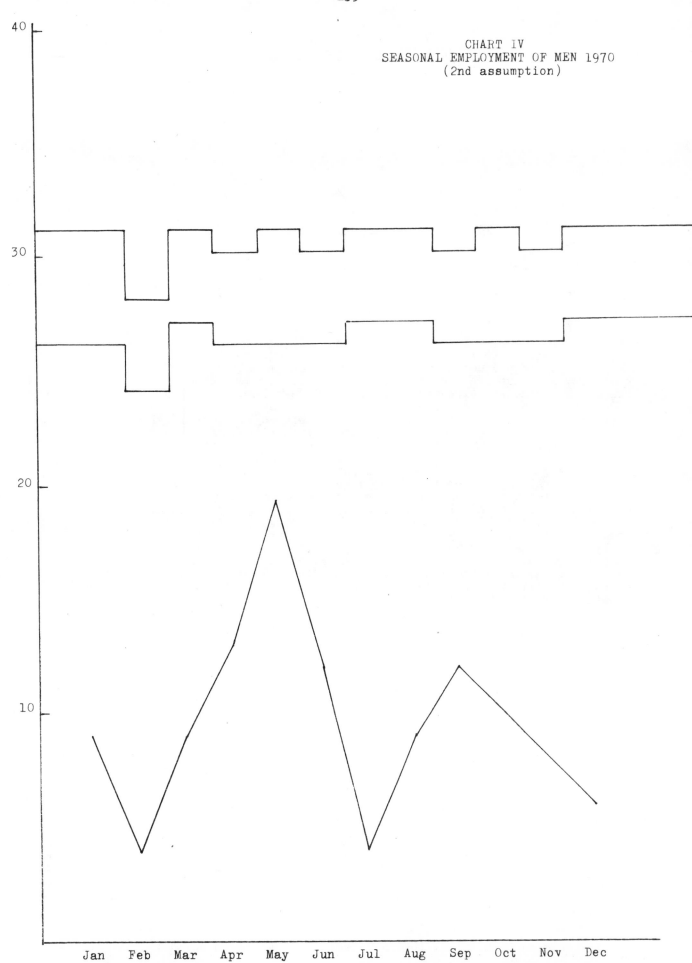

CHART IV
SEASONAL EMPLOYMENT OF MEN 1970
(2nd assumption)

MANPOWER AND EMPLOYMENT PLANNING IN
IRAQ AND THE SYRIAN ARAB REPUBLIC

by

K. Hameed[1]

INTRODUCTION:

The transformed economic situation and prospects

As in several other countries in the region, the economic situation and prospects in Iraq and the Syrian Arab Republic have recently been radically transformed and continue to change.

In both countries, the financial resources and possibilities for investment have, in the last year or two, made an appreciable leap upwards. In Iraq, the austerity programme, which was imposed in 1972 in preparation for dealing with exigencies arising from the nationalisation of the Iraq Petroleum Company (IPC), has given way to phenomenal expansion in planned investment for which the boost in oil revenues has provided finance of a wholly new magnitude. During 1974, Iraq's oil income was expected to approach US$8 billion, which amounts to nearly US$800 per capita, by itself more than twice the Syrian per capita GNP in 1973-74. It is quite obvious that the constraint on implementation of development programmes in Iraq is not at present financial, but is primarily a matter of manpower training and deployment. This situation could continue for more than just a few years.

In the case of the Syrian Arab Republic, the increase in oil income has helped but has naturally been relatively much less significant than in Iraq. However, since the October War, and particularly since the military disengagement, the country has received offers of finance which altogether make the financial limitation on development much less important than it used to be. Here as well, the operative constraint on execution of investment projects and programmes is more likely to centre on the question of manpower training and utilisation. Of course, financial resources availed from external sources, apart from those in outright grant form, have a higher real cost to the Syrian economy than Iraq's increased revenue from oil exports. Any underemployment or misallocation of manpower will certainly inflate the real cost of external finance and impede progress.

In the two countries, the relatively rapid growth of recent years has been accompanied by fast expansion in education and training, rapid migration to larger towns exerting pressures on urban services, and rising employment expectations. The rapid growth in education has sacrificed some quality for the sake of quantity and, in several important respects, has not been geared to development requirements, although a noticeable movement in this direction is already in progress. Despite their drawbacks, these processes have had obvious social and national advantages, in so far as more widely-spread education means a lessening of economic and social inequalities, and a greater contact between town and country people would reinforce social change and feelings of nationhood, and enhance awareness of citizens' rights and responsibilities.

Constraints and bottlenecks have been identified in both countries in the supply of technical and specialised skills; such scarcities have been dramatic in, for instance, the construction industry. Simultaneously, school-leavers and graduates in literary subjects and the humanities have experienced difficulties in obtaining appropriate employment. The rectification of such imbalances and the production of a more suitable array of skills must be one main goal of a transformed system of employment, education, research and training facilities. However, the system also needs to be directed towards contributing a growing amount of endogenous technical progress. A country is hardly developed until it generates a good deal of technological innovation suited to its own resource endowments and economic

---

[1] Economics Department, London University. **Abridged version.**

opportunities.   Imported technology, crucial as it is in bridging the technological gap, cannot alone achieve the transition to a developed economy.

Despite their enormous agricultural potential, both countries have, in recent
years, tended to become net importers of food; Iraq noticeably more than the
Syrian Arab Republic.   This clearly demonstrates the importance of pursuing the
emphasis on agrarian development already evident in the two countries' development
plans.   Technical progress in agriculture has proved to be much more complex than
in industry.   The so-called "green revolution" has not yet made any material
impact in either country.   The problem of imbalance in the distribution of services
between town and country has pointed towards the necessity of integrated rural
development programmes.   Both countries are planning large agricultural projects;
in the Syrian Arab Republic the investments planned in the Euphrates basin could
accompany a far-reaching transformation in the country's agricultural potential.

Iraq and the Syrian Arab Republic have both had to shoulder a heavy burden
of defence expenditure; this has obviously been more onerous in the latter
country, where defence has accounted for 25 per cent of the state budget (1973).
But the manpower deployed in the armed forces has evidently been making a substantial indirect contribution to training and development, where a greater
emphasis has been laid on the armed forces' dual responsibility of reconstruction
as well as defence.

The Iraqi economy will continue to be primarily propelled by the oil revenues
for a good many years.   The long-range problem here will be the transformation
from this situation without allowing the eventual diminution of oil revenues to
administer too severe a shock to economic activity and growth.   In a little over
two decades, Iraq will be supporting twice the present population at a per capita
income perhaps five times as great, and will be requiring several times the
present inputs of raw materials and capital equipment.   Industrialisation and
the creation of a modern highly-productive agrarian sector are the major developments expected to alleviate the impact of oil exhaustion in the long-term.   In
the Syrian Arab Republic, besides industrialisation and the growth of agriculture
especially in the Euphrates basin, tourism has been identified as a major potential
growth pole, relatively much more significant than in Iraq.

In both countries, cyclical fluctuations in the general level of employment
have been superimposed upon both a structural shortage of productive jobs for
existing skills and acute shortages of many manpower categories, in particular
trained operators, craftsmen, technicians and trainers.   Planned investments
imply potential scarcities of skills of an almost overwhelming magnitude.

The public enterprise economy in both countries has been the leading sector
and the main source of unprecedented growth, modernisation and dynamism, with a
considerable impact on the rest of the economy.   Less than one-third of the
civilian employed manpower is within the public sector, but the significance of
this part of the national economy in manpower and employment planning is out of
all proportion to its ratio of the employed population.   This paper will therefore
concentrate on the role of the public sector in the two countries concerned, within their over-all manpower and employment planning framework.

PART ONE:

The role of the public sector

The existence of a large and rapidly expanding public sector in Iraq and the Syrian Arab Republic, with a certain degree of co-ordination and planning, has probably made over-all national planning easier, especially when the impact of this sector on the rest of the economy has systematically been reviewed and taken into account.   In the earlier period of turning over to the public sector exist- ing organisations, there were naturally pressing management and organisation problems.   Since then, a systematisation of national planning and of policy- making processes has been assisted by the more organised and detailed information and data which have been built up about the public enterprises.

Of course manpower and employment planning (MEP) covers the whole economy and not just the public sector.   Employment in the public sector will probably continue for some years to come to expand faster than in the private sector.   The latter still contains more than three-quarters of the employed labour force in both countries, excluding the military sector.   It is wrong, however, to assume that the economic significance of the public sector is proportionate to its ratio of total employment.   It is obvious that in both countries the public sector has had a much higher share of the highly trained and educated manpower.   Moreover, the public sector supports a considerable amount of private sector activity through contracting and subcontracting business and through the provision of services and infrastructure.

Employment planning in the public sector and
the economy as a whole

When MEP is more effectively instituted, a review will have to be made of the criteria used in planning employment in the public sector and in the economy as a whole.   Such criteria will have to be related to manpower availabilities and the expected outputs of educational and training institutions.

Perhaps an instance from the Iraqi experience is worthy of quotation here. It was expected in the 1965-1969 national development plan that employment would expand by 8 per cent, creating 261,500 jobs in all sectors.   In 1970 the plan appraisal indicated that this expectation had been overfulfilled: employment was reported to have increased by 20 per cent or 427,000 over the 1964 figure . However, this expansion was not sufficient for reaching the full employment target mentioned among the objectives of the plan.   Thus the subsequent plan noted:

"Full employment as one of the main objectives of the Plan was not achieved
along the desired lines for the projects executed in the Plan Years ...
could not absorb all the outputs of the educational system during the Plan
years.   Consequently many persons capable of work were left without employment opportunities.   There was, at the same time, a shortage in some
technical specialisations, a fact which hindered the growth of some economic
sectors, particularly the industrial sector.   Such contradictions, surplus
on the one side and shortage on the other, are actually a reflection of the
lack of the element of manpower planning (short and long-term) at sectoral
and occupational levels, despite the fact that this planning must go side
by side with economic development planning. "

The 1970-1974 national development plan has estimated the increase in total employment at 619,500 new jobs, or 24.3 per cent, distributed by sector.   Prelimi- nary figures for the 1976-1980 plan, based on the modified UNOTC projections (1970-1980) indicate an expected increase of some 780,400 in the numbers employed during the plan period.   This is likely to be an underestimate in view of the phenomenal expansion in investments planned.

Until recently insufficient co-ordination existed between the planning or estimation of the number of new job opportunities in the economy and the recruit- ment policies of the public sector.   On the whole, the link was through some rough-and-ready estimation of manpower required for expansion and for new projects in the public sector.   Thus the public sector, especially in the Syrian Arab Republic, based its employment planning on estimated requirements.   This does not of course mean that the public sector organisations were able to find all the trained manpower they required; frequently there were acute shortages. The remainder of the new jobs were presumably to fall within the private sector; no more detailed investigation or follow-up was carried out.

As we have seen, the planned creation of new jobs, whether achieved or not, did not always match the growth in the labour force. Official attitudes have varied over the question of the government's responsibility for providing employment for various categories of workers such as university graduates. In recent years the tendency in Iraq has been towards expanding employment in the public sector sufficiently to absorb the educated unemployed in the expectation that further expansion will redeploy them more effectively while, in the meantime, they will have gained some in-service and on-the-job training. Thus, in 1974, all unemployed university graduates were quickly absorbed in the public sector. In the Syrian Arab Republic a tendency in the same direction has been resisted and the matter seems to be under discussion. Expected expansion in the Syrian public sector will probably soon absorb most if not all the remaining unemployed university graduates. Competitive selection by state organisations, rather than centralised allocation, has been used in recruitment. There still remains in both countries a good deal of unemployment among graduates of secondary schools.

In both countries, it has been reported that frequently the pressure of unskilled and semi-skilled workers seeking jobs in the public sector has encouraged overemployment in public enterprises and organisations in these categories with the result that productivity has not increased as fast as it could have done, and workers' norms of production have been set noticeably below the usual standards in, for instance, the countries from which the equipment was imported. In the Syrian Arab Republic, some observers have noted a tendency of unskilled and semi-skilled workers to move into the public sector, obtain scarce skills through training and then move back to the private sector in order to increase their earnings as employees or, sometimes, as small subcontractors or self-employed; or they might emigrate. No estimation of the numbers of such cases seems to have been made.

Recently both countries have taken interest in similar manpower movements. To stop the flow of trained and professional workers to the private sector, a regulation has recently been considered in Iraq which forbids private-sector firms from employing a person who has resigned from the public sector. In the Syrian Arab Republic strong penalties have been legislated against those who quit their public jobs before their resignations are officially accepted. This uneasiness over the movement of trained manpower into the private sector seems to reflect the lack of a clear policy concerning training in the economy as a whole, and the division of responsibility between the public sector and private firms. An arrangement by which individual firms would make financial contributions to state training establishments has been suggested; this could go some way towards solving the problem.

Such difficulties indicate the need for unambiguous criteria in the planning of manpower, employment and training for the economy as a whole and for the private as well as the public sector. While planning for the private sector is more likely to be of the indicative type, planning for the public sector will be much more direct especially when co-ordination, implementation and follow-up are more adequately developed. The relationships and linkages between the two sectors need to be adequately investigated. If the private sector is to fulfill the role assigned to it tacitly or explicitly in the national plan, some means must be found for involving it in the process of planning and implementation. Without such co-ordination and a clarification of the attitude of the central planners towards the role of the private sector in the economy, conflicts of interest are bound to remain unresolved and to lead to costly frictions.

Employment in the public sector

The Iraqi survey of employed manpower in the state organisations (May 1972) has provided extensive and detailed information which will be of considerable usefulness in future planning. No comparisons with the Syrian Arab Republic are possible since no similar detailed and comprehensive survey seems to have been conducted there yet although the Syrian Mobilization Administration has surveyed some categories of higher-level manpower.

The Iraqi survey counted 385,978 employees in all state organisations (14 per cent of total employment). The total included 62,052 (16 per cent) with higher-level qualifications varying from diploma to doctorate; 76,797 (20 per cent) having completed secondary school; 18 per cent having completed intermediate or primary school; and 46 per cent having completed no stage in school. Nearly 25 per cent of the total were illiterate. Public sector employment has thus provided work for practically all classes of people. The phenomenal expansion in public sector employment is indicated by the fact that 41.9 per cent of government employees were recruited between the end of 1968 and the end of May 1972, less than three and a half years. Since then expansion has probably been even faster.

In the Syrian Arab Republic the 1971 total employment figure of 1,522,334 was estimated to contain 36.2 per cent wage and salary earners and 60.4 per cent unpaid, paid in kind or self-employed. Obviously not all the 36.2 per cent were in the public sector. A figure of 15 per cent of total employment (i.e. 228,350) would probably exceed the number employed in the public sector (excluding the military); perhaps a figure of 200,000 is more likely, about 13 per cent of total employment. Since then there has been a rapid expansion in public sector employment, which may have increased its share of total employment.

Underemployment and organisations concerned

It is of course extremely difficult to estimate the extent of underemployment in the public sector. However, many observers would not rule out the existence of such underemployment and some would suggest it is a significant phenomenon which should be systematically investigated in order to reduce misallocation of scarce human resources, to encourage manpower development and to promote organisational efficiency. Iraq's 1972 survey of public sector employment concluded:

"It is worthy of mention that many employees in the state organisations do not work in their area of specialisation nor in jobs consistent with their obtained qualifications."

A similar opinion has been voiced in the Syrian Arab Republic as well.

It seems that there is no good alternative to a systematic evaluation of manpower utilisation on a continuous basis, both by the employing organisation itself or by a high-powered outside agency which offers technical assistance in management development and productivity promotion.

Both Iraq and the Syrian Arab Republic have instituted national centres of management development and productivity. Iraq's centre appears to have had a greater impact on the public enterprise sector than that of the Syrian Arab Republic, perhaps largely due to two important differences. First, Iraq's National Centre for Consultancy and Management Development (NCCMD) was transferred in 1970 from the Ministry of Industry and attached to the Ministry of Planning, while the Syrian Arab Republic's Management Development and Productivity Centre (MDPC) is still part of the Ministry of Industry, which may have limited the scope of its activities and its authoritative link with the public sector as a whole. Secondly, and perhaps more importantly, Iraq's National Centre has been given greater prestige by support from higher political leadership. In 1972 the Revolutionary Command Council (decree No. 333) required the NCCMD to prepare a national administrative reform plan to deal with the managerial and administrative implications of national development planning and to raise and develop implementation capability and promote productivity in all organisations of the public sector.

The main link recommended is through the institution of organisation and methods units in government establishments, and productivity development units in the firms of the public sector. These units were to be attached directly to heads of organisations under the technical direction of the NCCMD. The units have been charged with the tasks of information processing, revision of administrative processes and regulations, stream-lining of existing procedures, follow-up of work implementation, improvement of work methods in the various divisions, and development of management information services for appropriate decision-making. Although the challenges of effective implementation implicit in the proposed administrative plan are still enormous, considerable progress has already been reported in the development of management information services in many public-sector enterprises. The Centre is currently engaged in developing the over-all administrative reform plan as part of the 1976-1980 economic and social development plan.

The Syrian MDP Centre has perhaps tended towards laying greater emphasis on strictly more technical-industrial problems such as industrial standardisation and quality control; it has also had to restrict its activities to the modern public industrial sector, or a segment of it.

Even if underemployment is not considered at any one time a serious problem in the public sector, it seems essential in conditions of expansion and dynamic change to have a well-supported national organisation which not only offers consultancy services and trains personnel in the various techniques and practices necessary for management development and productivity promotion, but also contributes to organisational innovation and development. The activities of a management development and productivity centre are of course no substitute for efforts at the establishment level to innovate and to promote productivity and organisational efficiency. On the contrary, the national centre is supposed to provide its services through catalytic units within each and every establishment.

Both national centres could rapidly institute and develop training programmes in manpower and employment planning for the central planning organisation as well as production and service establishments. No such programmes have yet been offered on a systematic basis; the development of national MEP is unlikely to be effective without trained cadres. In the Syrian Arab Republic the Institute of Social and Economic Planning (attached to the State Planning Commission) has given some instruction in manpower planning and was expecting to institute more extensive training courses in this field from September/October 1974. Iraq took a decision in July 1974 to establish a national centre for manpower planning, to be attached to the Planning Board; once established it may take interest in developing MEP courses.

Training and shortages of skills

The role of the public sector in developing the formal training of manpower for the alleviation of skill shortages, has undoubtedly been of major significance in reshaping the employment structure. Besides the very rapid expansion in schools, colleges and universities, there has been an upsurge recently in several forms of technological and vocational training centres, programmes and institutions. The greater the planned and achieved investments, the greater the requirements for training. Training is clearly considered a key investment in both countries. Paradoxically, shortage of skilled manpower (due to inadequacies in training facilities) is itself instrumental in producing unemployment and handicapping progress towards full employment. The utilisation of semi-skilled and unskilled manpower and the generation of jobs depend to an appreciable extent on the availability of trained workers.

The following major tasks may be identified in this field: (a) the planning of training requirements and resources on a national basis; (b) the restructuring of the educational system in order to gear it to development needs and to facilitate the tasks of training; (c) the effective training of trainers; (d) the institution and encouragement of on-the-job and in-service training in all establishments and organisations throughout the economy; and, (e) the spreading of basic forms of training and skills which facilitate the acquisition of skills and the enhancement of the individual's development role, such as functional literacy, general education particularly in rural areas, mother-and-child care, motor vehicle operation and maintenance, etc., through intensive and speedy training programmes at appropriate centres. In all these fields appreciable progress and efforts have been made in both Iraq and the Syrian Arab Republic, but the tasks ahead are even more challenging.

In Iraq, at the beginning of the academic year 1973-1974, there were some 5,221 pupils enrolled in the 17 industrial secondary schools and some 904 enrolled in the two main technical institutes. A survey has recently been carried out as part of the national training programme to estimate requirements of skilled manpower and to relate these to expected availabilities. Although the coverage was not comprehensive, it revealed considerable shortages of trained manpower in practically all levels of skills.

In view of the acceleration of planned development investment in Iraq since the above survey was conducted, the shortages will probably accentuate unless training can be expanded much faster than hitherto. For instance, the planned capacities of the technical training institutions for the late 1970s will hardly produce a sufficient number of trained technicians to meet the present estimated level of demand; by then the need for technicians will have further expanded. The estimated requirements for training skilled workers during 1971-1974 are nearly double the number of training places available, and planned new training capacity is unlikely to keep pace with demand. A severe constraint here is the supply and training of trainers. This is one reason why Iraq has recently allowed and encouraged all ministries and state organisations to seek bilateral technical arrangements, embodying training programmes, with technically advanced countries. Such bilateral arrangements are mushrooming. Perhaps co-ordination of these agreements and programmes will increasingly be an important task in the future in order to avoid unsystematic proliferation which might defeat the very objectives of training endeavours. In the meantime, the main aim is as speedy implementation of investment projects as possible without undue cost inflation.

In the Syrian Arab Republic, detailed surveys and estimates of training capacity and expected requirements of trained manpower have not yet become available. A study by the Central Bureau of Statistics outlined estimates of university graduates in medicine, dentistry, veterinary medicine, pharmacy, engineering branches, fine arts, science and agriculture for certain recent years. But when it came to estimating requirements, it was simply suggested that, for medical specialists, a comparison with their incidence in the populations of developed countries showed that there would be deficits all around. However, a better way of obtaining reliable estimates is to investigate the actual and estimated future requirements of the employing organisations for use in planning.

Of course, in both countries great strides can be expected in estimating and planning skill requirements and training facilities; the more speedily and effectively this is accomplished, the smaller will be the development sacrifices arising from sudden emergence of acute shortages.

Income distribution

The distribution of income in Iraq and the Syrian Arab Republic appears to have been radically reshaped by developments in the public sector. The over-all picture is, however, unclear due to lack of comprehensive information. To the extent that the public sector has generated productive employment, it has helped in spreading the benefits of development more widely. On the whole, some observers would suggest that the use of up-to-date technology, by the public sector, the more rapid generation of employment for educated and trained manpower than for the unskilled, and the faster growth of social services and investments in the towns relative to rural areas, may have hindered the process of more even income distribution. However, better and more equal opportunities in education and training and migration to towns would have countered these processes. In Iraq, for instance, 60 per cent of large industrial establishments by the end of the 1960s and 50 per cent of all industrial employment are reported to be located in Baghdad, while small towns and rural areas are observed to have experienced relative stagnation in employment and incomes. This seems to have accelerated migration to the Baghdad area and to have accentuated the social and economic dualism between the modern and the traditional sectors. Damascus has had a similar but perhaps relatively smaller impact.

On the other hand, in both countries there has been a large-scale redistribution of agricultural land, long periods of pay freeze for public sector employees and an unprecedented growth of education, public health, communications and other services throughout the two countries. It would seem unlikely that any sizable population group has had an absolute deterioration in its real income. None the less, in Iraq, large differences between rural and urban incomes have been observed. In the Syrian Arab Republic it has been estimated that non-agricultural incomes averaged more than four times agricultural incomes during 1970, and that this ratio had hardly changed during the previous decade.

In Iraq, where revenues from oil shot up and are likely to form a dominant proportion of total income, the narrow dispersion of income growth might turn out to be more problematic. Continual examination of investment projects, of adopted technology and of the dispersion of social services may be essential in order to prevent any sizable section of the lower income groups from falling behind appreciably. Otherwise development incentives may be blunted.

In the Syrian Arab Republic some observers would suggest that the tendency towards equalisation of incomes throughout the economy by means of pay freezes in the public sector has probably already adversely affected motivation, and differentials need to be widened to improve development incentives and reduce emigration and the so-called "brain drain". For the first time in recent years, the Syrian Government granted a 10 per cent pay increase, subject to a maximum of 100 Syrian pounds, plus 25 Syrian pounds to all state employees in July 1974 (Legislative Decree No. 44, dated 17 July 1974). The already described mobility of unskilled workers from the private sector to the public sector and of skilled workers in the reverse direction may also have helped to reduce income inequalities.

While the private sector probably contains a wider dispersion of incomes, many state employees, especially in the clerical and administrative grades, have had to supplement their incomes with overtime and part-time jobs in the private sector. Evidently, a noticeable number of state employees managed in the past to resign and left their jobs even before their resignations were officially accepted. Thus another Legislative Decree (No. 46, dated 23 July 1974) stipulated severe penalties for any public employee who left his job before his resignation had been judicially accepted.

Impact of the public sector on the private sector

It is not easy to ascertain the impact of the public sector on the private sector, which still accounts for over two-thirds of total employment and at least as many paid jobs as the public sector. The impact seems to have gone through ups and downs. It appears that, on the whole, the part of the private sector which managed to obtain contract work from the public sector has been at a considerable advantage. Outstanding in this respect would be building and construction firms and suppliers of local building and other materials, although in both Iraq and the Syrian Arab Republic the shortcomings of such firms have induced increased public sector participation. In Iraq, the public sector recently expanded its share in foreign trade and distribution; following this, underemployment has been reported in the commercial private sector.

In Iraq and the Syrian Arab Republic it is reported that many small-scale industries have been appreciably limited in their prospects by competition from large modern public-sector organisations and by too much legal restriction on and regulation of their operations. In the latter country especially, the small-scale sector has not maintained a reasonable rate of investment for quite some years. It seems that both countries are beginning to recognise the role of small-scale establishments in providing employment, informal training and potential recruits for the modern sector, quite apart from the often efficient services they provide and the investment they can generate. Recently the Syrian Arab Republic has declared what amounts to a new outlook and strategy, the so-called "open door" policy, in which not only is the private sector to be encouraged to grow, but it is considered a national duty of those employed in this sector to contribute to the development of the economy as a whole. Already there are indications that the Syrian private sector has responded positively to this new trend in government policy, but it seems that there needs to be extensive study of the influences and impacts of the State on the operations and opportunities of the private sector.

Obviously no effective comprehensive MEP could be performed without some coverage of the private sector. The effectiveness of such coverage will very much depend on the working relations between the organisations of the two sectors and on the possible co-ordination. Not infrequently in the past, especially during periods of rapid extension of the public sector, the private sector as such seemed to have been assigned a more or less residual role. Development in this context may have been seen as very much related to the rate at which the modern state economy absorbed the economic activities of the private sector. This undoubtedly enhanced instability and uncertainties in the expectations and plans of private firms, with a more or less direct effect on the rate of their investments. When a high proportion of manpower is employed within this sector, as has been the case in both Iraq and the Syrian Arab Republic, such an outcome magnifies the employment and development tasks of the public sector and may immobilise the growth potential outside it. More workers tend to prefer secure employment in the public sector; thus, greater pressures for accelerating this form of employment are generated. Hence the capacity of the public sector to generate completely new and productive jobs is partly dissipated in providing jobs for workers who want to move from productive employment in the private sector.

An alternative approach is to identify and publicise a sectoral "territorial" division of economic activities and specialisations between the two sectors, acknowleging legitimate areas of competition and endeavouring to improve co-ordination where this is necessary. This is likely to provide a more stable basis for private sector growth. Such a framework to which state policies could be related may be necessary if, for instance, the fulfilment of the Syrian expectation of accelerating the development contribution of the private sector is to fully materialise. The indications are that this issue is likely to remain a problematic area.

PART TWO:

The machinery for manpower and employment planning

Iraq and the Syrian Arab Republic have pursued rather different paths in their search for the structure most appropriate for their individual circumstances and needs for manpower and employment planning (MEP). Generally, the need is for a dynamic organisation within which experience and awareness of realities are cumulatively built up and which develops an effective capability for formulating, implementing and evaluating plans, for co-ordinating related activities, for systematically appraising the relevant data and for anticipating and tackling problematic situations.

Some general issues

There is perhaps too little room here to enumerate all the organisations which will need to co-operate in central manpower planning. In a sense, every organisation and production unit of any import will need to look ahead and consider seriously its future requirements of manpower and its in-service and on-the-job training programmes, and budget its manpower development in a more detailed fashion than has been implicit in financial budgeting. Unless this kind of manpower planning at the establishment level is developed, sectoral, regional and national manpower planning is less likely to be realistic or effective.

There is also the question of the need to co-ordinate policies determining pay and price structures throughout the economy with manpower training and allocation programmes since pay and price structures determine the hierarchy of incentives and of real rewards for various kinds of skill and hence influence occupational mobility. In the past, for obvious reasons, the Syrian Arab Republic, and also Iraq to a lesser extent, has had to follow a policy of general freeze on public wages and salaries with occasional increases whenever circumstances were considered favourable. No central body as such was given the task of regularly investigating and rationalising the structures of publicly-determined pay and prices and relating these to the rest of the economy. The question of relative rewards for skill hierarchies and work performance could obviously be a sensitive issue and needs to be not only scientifically evaluated but also sanctioned, promoted and explained to the public by the higher political leadership as is already done with respect to general pay increases in the public sector.

Of the many other important issues which must come within the over-all activities of MEP, the following are worth mentioning. First, in attempting to estimate the rate at which productive jobs are generated and to match this with changes in the labour force in order to ensure maximum utilisation of human resources, account must be taken of the private sector - often in direct competition with the public sector - and providing more than two-thirds of total employment about which information has been much more scarce and patchy. Second, the educational and training system, the structure of its output, the content of curricula and the resources deployed need to be systematically reviewed and geared to the developmental demands of the country. Third, underemployment, disguised unemployment and sub-productive employment are no less relevant for optimal allocation of manpower than unemployment and may indeed be trickier to deal with. It is desirable to have an unambiguous allocation of responsibility for appraising these issues and others that may arise. Under the present system it is not always clear which authority is charged with their investigation and how the work of such a body is to be effectively co-ordinated.

It is obvious that the whole gamut of economic and social policies comes under review and scrutiny when central manpower planning is attempted. The complexity of these activities needs to be borne in mind when one considers the following issues: (a) Is the present organisation of manpower planning likely to develop the capability necessary for effectively performing such complex tasks? (b) Has this organisation the appropriate authority, personnel and information channels to enable it to obtain co-operation and perform the necessary co-ordination? (c) Has it the dynamism which enables it to generate initiative and motivation at all levels, to change attitudes, to innovate, to forecast and anticipate problematic situations, shortages and bottlenecks and to spearhead effective programmes to avert these?

Manpower and employment planning in the
Syrian Arab Republic

In the Syrian Arab Republic a significant event in the mobilisation of public concern was the Conference of Public Mobilisation for Development and Defence held in 1971, in which a large number of institutions and individuals participated. Public discussions of manpower deployment, training, education, etc., and of socio-economic problems, such as the "brain drain", appear to have spread and strengthened interest in the subject. Although political party conferences in both countries do discuss topics related to the subject, the Syrian public mobilisation conference appeared to be a unique and useful experience which could beneficially be turned into a regular event.

Subsequently the Ministry of Labour and Social Affairs, which itself includes a budding unit for manpower and employment planning, formulated and put forward for consideration and approval a comprehensive programme for establishing an integrated hierarchy for manpower planning. According to this proposal, which is quite detailed, a central manpower planning commission would be attached to the Council of Ministers; under this a central manpower planning administration would be charged with manpower planning and implementation according to the Commission's policies within a set-up in which the existing labour and employment offices would be developed into area manpower survey units.

At the preliminary discussion stage this proposal of the Ministry of Labour and Social Affairs ran into difficulties. Perhaps inevitably, the State Planning Commission (SPC) saw in it an encroachment on its own legislated planning powers and prerogatives. The matter appeared to have been resolved by setting up early in 1974 a division of manpower and employment within the SPC. This was of course a good beginning but it could not be expected to satisfy the aspirations behind the proposals of the Ministry of Labour.

The idea of attaching a new commission to the Council of Ministers was rejected perhaps on the basis that such a link could readily be forged through the SPC; perhaps there was also a tendency to discourage attaching too many bodies directly to the Council of Ministers. With a view to assisting in the co-ordination necessary for manpower planning, a committee of experts from various ministries and central organisations was set up as a temporary co-ordinating forum.

Several countries have experienced a similar conflict over the same issue between the central planning agency and the Ministry of Labour. It is thus important not to exaggerate the area of disagreement and duplication in this question of organisation which was originally brought up in the Syrian Arab Republic by the Ministry of Labour. Rather, the whole series of events reveals keen interest and an active dialogue aimed at establishing a dynamic organisation specialised in MEP. The formation of the manpower division in the SPC need not necessarily discourage the Ministry of Labour from using its expertise and experience to build up an effective implementation capability through developing area manpower survey units, etc. The problem might then be confined to co-ordination between the SPC and the Ministry of Labour. Some observers, however, doubt whether the present resolution of the issue is entirely satisfactory and fear that the initiative of the Ministry of Labour may have been thwarted and rebuffed without the SPC manpower division managing to develop a sufficiently effective manpower planning capability. Such a danger needs to be guarded against lest the necessary co-ordination between the two authorities is sacrificed at the expense of effective MEP.

Although the SPC manpower division is quite recent, having been set up early in 1974, it seems to have already made rapid progress. In mid-1974 it consisted of a nucleus of five specialists and this number was ideally expected to reach 16 by 1976. Although the division did not include any specialist with long experience in manpower planning (these are everywhere quite scarce), it was expected that a national manpower plan would be prepared and integrated with, or attached to, the 1976-80 five-year plan. Previous development plans did include some estimates of manpower and new jobs, but not in a sufficiently detailed or comprehensive manner to allow effective national manpower planning. Although time is very short for a detailed manpower plan to be embodied in the third development plan and the task is very challenging, the effort as an initial endeavour using very limited resources is likely to prove useful provided other concerned bodies are induced to co-operate in the performance of this task.

There are, of course, many organisations directly involved in manpower planning; among these are notable the Mobilization Administration and the Science Council. The former is a military organisation, which must have accumulated appreciable experience which could make a valuable contribution. It has, for instance, surveyed and estimated certain categories of highly trained manpower in the country. The latter organisation has concerned itself with estimating the manpower with higher-level scientific training and has formulated a scientific manpower plan. Mention should also be made of the Central Statistical Bureau which has regularly surveyed and investigated demographic and manpower statistical data, the Ministries of Education and of Higher Education, the Ministry of Industry, and various other ministries and organisations which supervise and control training activities and which influence the whole dynamic structure of skill availabilities and requirements. Very soon, for instance, the General Authority for the Development of the Euphrates Basin (GADEB), or the Ministry of the Euphrates Dam, will need to concern itself in greater detail in estimating and planning the manpower requirements for the enormous development which is scheduled to take place stage by stage in that part of the country.

Manpower and employment planning in Iraq

The same questions need to be raised in the light of the experience of Iraq, where there has also been considerable activity and debate which may be considered to have paved the way for greater concerted action. Interest in the subject has not been less keen than in the Syrian Arab Republic, and the National Charter has stipulated the objective that it is every able citizen's right and obligation to work and that unemployment should be eliminated.

Attempts at planning manpower training at the sector level have been made for quite some time. The Ministry of Industry, for instance, where scarcity of skills had been most strongly felt, has had a manpower planning unit since 1960. This unit has been reduced in size in the last few years, although it is still active and has recently put forward a preliminary study based on manpower requirements and availabilities in the public industrial sector for the period of the coming development plan 1976-1980. Recently the Ministry of Labour and Social Affairs and the Ministry of Planning expanded their interest in this field. In 1971 the Workers' Establishment for Employment, Training and Rehabilitation (WEETR) was set up within the Ministry of Labour and Social Affairs partly as a response to the needs revealed by phase I (1969-70) of the national vocational training programme supported by UNDP/ILO; the Ministry of Labour and Social Affairs was designated as the co-operating government agency and later the Ministry of Planning participated in implementation.

The WEETR has developed valuable experience in vocational training and in dealing with mainly urban employment problems through its contact with the labour market. In 1971 Labour Law No. 151 charged the Central Bureau of Vocational Training under the WEETR with the responsibility of planning and co-ordinating training activities. At the national level, and in the context of the development plan, responsibility for these was ascribed to the inter-ministry Industrial Training Co-ordinating Body, supported in its task by the technical secretarial services of the Education and Social Department of the Ministry of Planning which has also been concerned with planning manpower and training. Phase II (1972-) of the project supported by the UNDP/ILO aimed, among other objectives, at strengthening the implementation capability of the Central Bureau of Vocational Training (under the WEETR) with respect to:

"(i) assessment on a continuous basis of the country's manpower situation to determine needs of trained personnel at various levels,

(ii) formulation of training policies and training standards for the various programmes".

The project also formulated the objective of helping:

"to develop the capabilities of the concerned staff of the Ministry of Planning's Education and Social Department in its capacity as the technical secretariat of the Industrial Training Co-ordinating Body and as the organ responsible for the formulation of vocational training plans within the context of the National Development Plan".

Subsequently there appeared to be some overlap of authority and duplication of effort between the WEETR of the Ministry of Labour and the Educational and Social

- 152 -

Department of the Ministry of Planning in the field of manpower planning and training.   A formula for the resolution of any potential inter-ministry conflicts over this issue seemed to be centered on the idea that the planning activity was the function of the Education and Social Department of the Planning Ministry, while the implementation was the responsibility of the Ministry of Labour.   In the field of training some overlap of functions was also noticed between the Industrial Training Co-ordinating Body which handles planning and co-ordination at the national level, and the Central Bureau of Vocational Training with more limited coverage. Recently there has been a proliferation of training schemes and centres which has not always been sufficiently co-ordinated to ensure consistency in the hierarchy of training programmes and qualifications obtained.

The Education and Social Department had in mid-1974 about six specialists concerned with education, vocational training and manpower planning (in the sections: labour force, educational planning and vocational training project).   Two of these specialists were concerned with manpower planning;   as in the Syrian Arab Republic, no specialist with long experience in MEP was available.

Within the Ministry of Planning, the Long-Range Planning Commission and the Regional Planning Commission are also becoming increasingly concerned with MEP from their specialised points of view;   their work is expected to assist in this field thus making for a more pluralistic structure in the organisation of MEP. But the institutional set-up so far does not suggest that an effective capability for comprehensive MEP has been developed in a manner which could satisfactorily answer the questions previously raised.   This is natural in view of the phenomenal growth of investment that has been planned and is being implemented in Iraq.   Some observers, noting the increasingly strategic nature of the manpower constraint on development in Iraq and the continuing need for strengthening and streamlining the organisation of MEP, go to the extent of suggesting setting up a human resources plan and a ministry of human resource development.

As in the Syrian Arab Republic, and probably more pronouncedly, co-ordination of manpower planning with the structures of pay and prices has been lacking.   This has produced an unsystematic pay and prices structure.   In July 1974 a central prices organisation was set up to study and supervise prices.   This is obviously a step forward.   As part of MEP, price structures and policies will then need to be related to the system of salaries and wages since it is real pay patterns which shape incentives and influence manpower mobilities.

Since 1973, there has been a strong tendency in Iraq towards developing a man-power plan but it is doubtful whether a detailed and comprehensive one will be prepared in time to be integrated into the 1976-80 national development plan. Emphasis may thus be laid on studying the expected manpower and training constraints and bottlenecks in order to plan action to avert these as much as possible.   A national manpower and employment plan consistent with the national development plan may have to await the completion in both countries of a comprehensive employment study and the strengthening of the MEP organisation.

Manpower and employment planning and
national development planning

Iraq's 1970-74 five-year plan noted that manpower planning "must go side by side with economic development planning".   It has been suggested that no effective manpower and employment planning could be performed independently of over-all national development planning;   the two planning processes are inter-dependent and the institutional structure of central planning should facilitate the functional integration of these two activities.   This is evidently a complex issue;   only a brief outline of the problem can be mentioned here.

Until recently the basic framework of development plans in Iraq and the Syrian Arab Republic, as in most other developing countries, has been set in terms of financial capital resources, the rate of growth being determined by the relationship between the saving ratio, supplemented by external finance and the capital/output ratio.   Subsequently the plan detailed sectoral projects and the trained manpower requirements of the sectors or projects were worked out together with some estimates of the number of job opportunities that would be created.   An alternative or supplement to this approach has been suggested on the basis of a human resources plan which starts from a survey of the employment and skill structure of the labour force and sets out the implications for savings, investment, techniques to be used, various economic policies, sectoral allocations, etc., of attempting to eliminate unemployment and underemployment and to reach a full employment situation within different time horizons. The rate of growth of savings and investment considered most feasible then determines the length of time required for reaching a full employment situation where the expanding labour force will be productively deployed. This forms the longer-range framework of the plan - say ten or fifteen years - and medium-term plans are then formulated to include sectoral and project allocations not only of investment but also of manpower.

There is no doubt that a great deal of uncertainty exists in forecasting and planning, and to start from two different viewpoints (manpower as well as capital), may have the advantage of reducing the margin of error. It seems unrealistic to expect that in a plan adopted on the basis of manipulating only financial resources, a full employment situation will automatically or necessarily be reached during the plan period even though full employment is mentioned as an objective. The evaluation of Iraq's 1965-69 national development plan set out in the 1970-74 plan expressed this clearly. It is important to realise here that the feasibility of projects and of adopted technology may be quite different when reaching full employment within a particular time horizon is introduced from the beginning as a basic objective to supplement the more traditional one of, say, doubling the per capita income or the national income within so many years. The per capita income may be doubled while one-quarter of the labour force is either unemployed or in sub-productive employment. The benefits from development will then be less widely shared, and a pronouncedly skewed income distribution could create serious social and political problems besides blunting motivation and development incentives.

When one comes to the institutional structure of planning which assists in the integration of MEP into national development planning, many solutions are feasible and the choice needs to be at least partly dictated by the organisational adaptations most likely to produce an appropriate structure. Merely creating a new ministry or a new department does not guarantee a solution and may sometimes make the necessary co-ordination even more problematic. This is not to rule out the possibility of extending institutional specialisation through the setting up of new organs.

The problematic nature of co-ordination and implementation in national planning may be partly due to the style adopted in plan formulation, which probably has not adequately involved the various ministries nor encouraged their commitment to their implementation roles as implied in the national plan. Specifically, when ministries do not participate effectively in plan formulation their implied role may be unrealistic and they may also feel that it has been imposed upon them without sufficient consultation. Ideally the Ministry of Planning (or the SPC) would, on the basis of the national and broad objectives, design a general outline of the medium-term plan within a longer-range framework; it would then request each ministry to formulate a medium-term sectoral plan capable of fulfilling these objectives. Such partial plans would not make over-all sense unless they are co-ordinated and harmonised within the Ministry of Planning (SPC) during a process of consultation with the ministries which would enable them to see why their separate plans needed to be modified. Once this process is completed, each ministry would not only be more inclined to commit itself to its sectoral tasks but also would more readily understand the interactions expected with other sectors and ministries. This would facilitate co-ordination in the implementation stage.

One reason usually given for not adopting such a decentralised style of plan formulation is that the ministries, despite their relatively newly instituted planning units, do not possess the planning capabilities to set up initial detailed sectoral plans. This in itself might be a good enough reason for inducing them to make a start in order "to learn by doing", with the assistance of the Central Planning Organisation. Only through endeavouring to formulate sectoral plans would they acquire the experience and expertise.

Repeatedly, implementation and follow-up have been referred to as problematic. In the Syrian Arab Republic recently a system was suggested in which the SPC would organise month-by-month reports on plan execution and progress. In Iraq, the institutional structure of central planning formally includes a central follow-up commission, but it seems that in practice this does not appear to have performed the function of follow-up anticipated. The Economic Department of the Ministry of Planning has been reporting on follow-up from a more general macro and sectoral point of view.

How does all this relate to MEP? If the plan formulation style were adopted (especially in the Syrian Arab Republic) along more decentralised lines and the

Ministry of Labour were to be charged with implementation of manpower and employment plans while the SPC retained its usual functions of follow-up and plan co-ordination, then there need not be any unresolved conflict or rivalry between the two organisations; the Ministry of Labour's initiative in developing manpower and employment planning could be channelled into the implementation function as well as co-operation with the SPC in formulating a manpower plan which the SPC would integrate into the national development plan. One must, however, guard against assuming that such proposed decentralisation in plan formulation can be carried out rapidly, even though it is one of the changes which seem to be both appropriate and easy to introduce provided the central planning agency sees it as assisting its planning functions rather than dissipating its planning authority.

In Iraq it has been suggested that the Steering Committee, which at present co-ordinates the work of the various departments of the Ministry of Planning and consists of the Ministry's directors of divisions, could be expanded, either permanently or intermittently, to include senior representatives from the other ministries. It might then perform the function of co-ordination more effectively both in the formulation of the national plan and in follow-up, without recourse to higher political authority (the Planning Board) which at present might seem to be burdened with a good deal of detailed co-ordination as well as decision-making. For instance, consideration of feasibility studies and suggestions for new project evaluations would be accomplished on a detailed technical basis at the level of the broadened Steering Committee. The time of the Planning Board would be more optimally allocated to reviewing and evaluating recommendations in the light of national political objectives and considerations, as well as dealing with any unresolved disagreements over inter-ministry co-ordination. In this the Planning Board would be acting as co-ordinator of last resort only. This proposed arrangement is worthy of consideration since it might well assist in the integration of manpower and employment planning as well as other sectoral planning with national development planning. A similar proposal could also be appraised in considering the planning hierarchy in the Syrian Arab Republic.

CONCLUSIONS AND SUGGESTIONS

In both Iraq and the Syrian Arab Republic, despite the low percentages of open unemployment, there have been considerable, though unmeasured, over-all shortages of productive jobs which could be manned by unemployed, marginally-employed and underemployed persons. This situation has been accompanied by acute shortages of many categories of skilled manpower, in particular trained operators, craftsmen, supervisory and training cadres, technicians, production-based specialists and trained executives. Planned investments imply potential scarcities of skills of almost overwhelming magnitude. Yet, in both countries the labour force is expected to continue to increase at rapid rates.

These circumstances imply that inadequate manpower training and utilisation is increasingly becoming a key constraint on further development. The main challenges to be met are:

(a) generation of sufficient and appropriate jobs for the rapidly increasing labour force, as well as the currently unemployed and underemployed;

(b) restructuring employment throughout the economy in such a way that manpower at present in sub-productive or marginally productive jobs (whether in agriculture, traditional activities, the private or the public sector) is fully redeployed in productive work; and

(c) organisation of effective and well-co-ordinated training programmes, institutions and facilities which will adequately meet the requirements and challenges of national economic and social development.

In both countries the public sector has a strategic role in economic development and can become a more effective source of leadership, dynamism and technological progress, as well as the key employer.

Development of manpower and employment
planning (MEP) capability

It is suggested that the constraint of trained manpower on development in Iraq and the Syrian Arab Republic justifies the institution of manpower and employment planning at a high level in the central planning system, in a manner which complements and reinforces national development planning and assists in the optimisation of development through accelerating progress towards full employment of manpower resources. The logistics of instituting, strengthening and developing an effective, well co-ordinated MEP sub-system need to be carefully appraised so that its institution is not accomplished at the expense of the development of effectiveness in the economic planning system as a whole.

The MEP agency, charged with the tasks mentioned above, might aim at formulating a detailed human resources development plan (HRDP) to be co-ordinated with the national development plan. The HRDP would devise a realistic employment strategy based on reliable and comprehensive studies of both the employment structure in the country and the manpower and training situations.

A thorough review of economic and social policies needs to be made in order to appraise their implications for MEP. Systematic co-ordination of pay and price structures with MEP decisions and strategies is essential for appropriate motivation and effective implementation. It is suggested that a review be made of the relative real incomes of the poorest 30 per cent of the population in order to ascertain whether they have been falling behind the rest of the population and to reach appropriate remedial steps if necessary.

Studying and evaluating the manpower and
employment situation and potentialities

At present, information on manpower and employment in the economies of both countries is incomplete and has to be pieced together from various sources. A great deal of studying is necessary before an understanding of the structure of employment adequate for realistic forecasting can be built up. Information gathered from such diverse sources as labour and employment offices, agricultural censuses, etc., needs to be collated and co-ordinated; careful investigations in the form of, for instance, sample surveys, are needed to fill in the gaps, such as the private industrial sector and the traditional sector. Employment offices could be developed into area employment and manpower survey units and cover rural areas as well. It is suggested that a detailed monthly national bulletin of manpower and employment be adequately edited and published to assist in the organisation and use of this kind of information.

Iraq and the Syrian Arab Republic may benefit from seeking external technical assistance in order to accomplish the comprehensive inter-disciplinary studies of their employment structures which are vital for evolving a realistic employment strategy.

In the near future some urgent needs are: (a) a study to identify immediate manpower shortages and surpluses, to enable appropriate decisions to be made for rectifying such imbalances through training programmes and changes in short-term employment policies; (b) in the Syrian Arab Republic, concerted action to meet the estimated manpower requirements of the Euphrates basin scheme, working on the basis of detailed survey information concerning current availabilities and short-falls in the relevant skill categories; and (c) studies of the existing and potential employment opportunities for youth and women.

Training

Side by side with the identification of crucial shortages of trained manpower and the estimation of the size of national requirements of various skills, the planning and implementation of appropriate training programmes and schemes are vital. The time-lag before such programmes begin to "deliver" trained manpower should be borne in mind and their output planned in line with future and not just current needs. Training facilities should, if possible, be geared to meet the requirements of the whole economy; and a coherent system allowing for the needs of the private sector should be evolved.

All important organisations need to be supported in their endeavours to develop on-the-job and in-service training programmes and facilities on a continuing basis. It is suggested that all public sector organisations be required to prepare manpower plans estimating training output, requirements and shortfalls.

Progress already made towards basing educational planning on development requirements should be reviewed and appraised for future supporting action. The required transformation in the educational system will need careful investigation.

It is suggested that vocational guidance be introduced and developed in secondary schools. In each school at least two teachers would need to be trained in this field and given adequate backing to provide instruction and advice to pupils at least two years before they are due to leave school.

Iraq's national programme of vocational training needs to be further supported. The Syrian Arab Republic might consider establishing a similar programme. Other involved organisations, such as the Ministry of Labour or Social Affairs, need to be encouraged in their efforts to strengthen their implementation capabilities in the field of employment and training services, under some kind of over-all co-ordination.

Eliminating underemployment

Assistance in such areas as management development, productivity and training of personnel in MEP, should be provided on an increasing scale to as wide a range of organisations and productive enterprises as possible. There should be an effort to publicise and increase awareness of the benefits of such management services.

In Iraq, the National Centre for Consultancy and Management Development (NCCMD) might be encouraged to institute and develop advanced courses in MEP; or the newly-established National Centre of Planning might take an interest in providing such courses.

It is suggested that a centre for management development and productivity promotion in the rural sector be instituted in both countries to supplement existing rural extension services.

Regional co-operation

Neither Iraq nor the Syrian Arab Republic is isolated from manpower mobilities in the Arab region, and both will be increasingly influenced by developments in this area. Further possibilities of regional co-operation in manpower training and employment planning need, therefore to be explored.

THE WORKING OF THE LABOUR MARKET IN LEBANON

by

J.F. Audroing[1] and M. Vernieres[2]

INTRODUCTION

The Lebanese economy has two characteristics, a limited state sector, and a determination on the part of the authorities to leave as much initiative as possible to individual agents, which makes it impossible to co-ordinate individual decisions otherwise than through the market. To be more accurate, in a free economy adjustment of intended supply and consumer demands is achieved through price variations, by the mechanism of increases and decreases. If we regard labour as one among a number of economic goods, then variations in the price of labour services should bring about an adjustment between labour supply and demand, with pay differentials guiding individuals in their choice of occupation.

This theoretical view of the working of the labour market in a free economy offers some justification for regarding any employment policy as pointless. The purpose of this paper is to explore the validity of this kind of conclusion in the case of the Lebanese economy, and to do this we must study the working of the labour market in Lebanon. Difficulties have been encountered owing to the inadequacy of the information available on employment, but it nevertheless seems possible to indicate a number of shortcomings in the working of the Lebanese labour market, and to show that optimum allocation of labour resources has not been achieved. Judging by these conclusions, there is a need for an employment policy.

Before submitting some recommendations on this point, in Part Three, it would appear necessary, as a first step, to undertake an over-all analysis of the labour market in Lebanon. Careful study of labour force participation rates and the structure of unemployment reveals the need for a breakdown of this over-all market into a number of sub-markets.

The second stage will help us to define these sub-markets in terms of the comparative immobility of manpower either in its geographical context, or between one economic sector or occupation and another, or as regards levels of skills. This last criterion of difference will be found to be the most important and the most operational.

The third step consists in studying possible ways of adjusting labour supply and demand through market mechanisms, in the absence of an employment policy. The limitations of these mechanisms give rise to a number of recommendations, put forward at the end of this study, for the adoption of such a policy.

---

[1] Faculty of Law and Economics, Saint Joseph University, Beirut.

[2] University of Paris I.

PART ONE:

AN OVER-ALL ANALYSIS OF THE LABOUR MARKET IN LEBANON

In this first part, the labour market is studied as a whole, and we must therefore begin by explaining the nature of it and of the data from which it can be studied. Secondly, we shall consider the statistical information available in Lebanon, which to all intents and purposes is confined to the results of the Economically Active Population Survey carried out by the Central Bureau of Statistics in 1970. A study of labour participation rates and of the unemployment structure in Lebanon, however, provides evidence of the inadequacy of over-all analysis, and of the need to differentiate between several labour sub-markets, as defined by various criteria to be described later.

1. Conditions for over-all analysis

A labour market study presupposes a knowledge of the pay scales applied and the numbers of jobseekers and vacancies, at a given time or over a period, since any quantitative imbalance is shown by a discrepancy between jobs offered and jobs sought. In the case of prices, an imbalance may also appear from pay differentials.

In the absence of data on pay scales, a labour market study can only be carried out in quantitative terms. In the case of Lebanon, however, the lack of employment bureaux, labour exchanges or a national employment agency to register job vacancies and applications, and the absence of any specific inquiry into the subject, make it necessary to confine the analysis of the labour market essentially to a mere study of information concerning unemployment.

An unemployed person is anyone who is available and in search of work. This definition does not necessarily restrict the idea of unemployment to the wage-earning section of the active population (60 per cent in Lebanon), but the unemployment problem takes different forms depending on professional status: for instance, the self-employed are seldom unemployed in the true sense of the term, but may be very much subject to under-utilisation of their work capacity. It follows that non-wage earners seldom register as jobseekers, and unemployment is difficult to estimate for that particular social category. The volume of unemployment actually registered must therefore be regarded as only a very approximate indication of the labour resources not being put to use in Lebanon.

Lastly, in order to interpret data on unemployment, its nature must be specified. It may be the result of an economic recession, in which case jobseekers far outnumber job vacancies in all the various sectors of the economy. There can be no question there of laying the blame on the working of the labour market as a mechanism for allocation of labour resources. If there is unemployment, it is for general economic reasons relating to the existing situation.

If, on the other hand, the unemployment noted arises from maladjustment between the type of jobs offered and the type of jobs being sought, manpower surplus may be equal to the unsatisfied demand for labour. In this case, unemployment is due to the unsatisfactory allocation of labour resources by market mechanisms.

It is important from the point of view of eliminating unemployment to make the distinction between these two types, for the methods to be adopted are very different in the two cases. In this report dealing with analysis of the working of the labour market in Lebanon, attention will be concentrated mainly on the second of the two types of unemployment defined above.

2. Available data

Regular periodic statistics on employment in Lebanon are non-existent. The only statistics compiled by the Ministry of Labour and Social Affairs relate to work permits granted to foreigners, grouped by nationality and occupation (published by the Central Bureau of Statistics in its monthly statistical bulletin). It would seem, however, that these statistics do not convey the whole truth about the employment of foreign manpower in Lebanon.

Practically the only real source of information on the subject is the Sample Survey of the Economically Active Population in Lebanon which was carried out by the Central Bureau of Statistics in November 1970. It was done on a household basis, and in addition to demographical information (sex, age, marital status, place of birth, last migratory move, etc.) it collected particulars regarding school enrolment, level of education and professional activity (unemployment, occupation engaged in, activity sector, professional status, work duration and so on). The results of the survey, which were first published in aggregate form, and then in detail in a second volume, make it possible to obtain a general picture of the employment situation in Lebanon. However, we must emphasise the limitations of the survey with respect to the labour market analysis which concerns us here.

In the first place, the survey covers only residents (persons who reside in Lebanon for more than six months of the year, with the exception of members of the diplomatic corps, students, members of the armed forces, hospital patients who are regarded as residing in their place of origin no matter how long they have been away from it). This means, among other things, that Syrian workers from just across the border who are temporarily employed in Lebanon do not come within the scope of the survey.

Secondly, the survey does not cover persons living in the Palestinian refugee camps.

Thirdly, the particulars obtained from a sample survey are not all significant. It should be mentioned, however, that a considerable number of households were visited (about 25,000) so that a reliable analysis of the main aspects of employment is possible: thus population categories numbering more than 3,000 persons have in general been depicted with a fair degree of accuracy.[1]

The findings of the survey regarding labour force participation rates and the structure of unemployment bring to light some interesting characteristics of the labour market in Lebanon.

3. Analysis of labour force participation
   rates[2]

According to the Active Population Survey, the labour force participation rate (members of the labour force/total population) is only 27 per cent, which is far from high compared with findings in other countries. This can be explained partly by the high proportion of young people (42.6 per cent of the population are under 15), but is also due to the low participation rates noted both for women and men.

In the first place the female participation rate is 15.8 per cent (female active population/total population for the 15-64 age group). It varies considerably with age and reaches a maximum of 23.8 per cent in the 20-24 age group, after which it shows a regular decrease. This can be ascribed to the fact that in Lebanon the traditional place of women and girls is at home. A change of attitude can be observed among the younger generation in this respect, however, and in the years to come this may alter the conditions for achieving equilibrium on the labour market.

---

[1] It should be mentioned that the sampling was done on two levels: the first included all large towns and a stratified sample of villages. After a complete census of residential premises in these localities, a second-degree sampling of the premises was done to obtain a sample of households uniformly representing the total resident population in a ratio of 1:15. Incidentally, the report on the survey findings calculates that the population was systematically underestimated by 4 or 5 per cent owing to faults in the sampling basis and that this led to a slight distortion (in fact negligible) in the form of under-representation of marginal population groups.

[2] For a more detailed study, see the Economically Active Population Survey, Vol. 1, Methods, Analysis and Presentation of Results, p. 108.

The male participation rate of 78.4 per cent is low in comparison with the rates observed in other countries.[1] A study of the curve representing participation rates according to ages shows that young people are late in beginning their working life (the average age for beginning work is 20) and that adults tend to retire early. The low participation rate among young people must be taken to indicate hidden unemployment, for many young people in Lebanon begin working life late because they take a long time to find suitable employment. During the survey, not all these young people declared themselves as jobseekers.

Thus the study of participation rates suggests that there are quite a large number of job demands not satisfied, and also not expressed; the figures for job demands not satisfied are believed to be higher in actual fact than those indicated in available data on unemployment.

4. Analysis of unemployment in Lebanon in November 1970

In the Active Population Survey, the aggregate unemployment rate in Lebanon is broken down into three elements: the unemployed in the narrow sense of the term, i.e. workers who have lost their jobs and so far failed to find new ones (3.1 per cent of the resident active population), persons seeking their first job (2.7 per cent) and temporarily unemployed or seasonal workers (2.3 per cent). This aggregate unemployment figure (8.1 per cent) covers situations that differ considerably according to age, occupation and level of education.

The distribution of unemployed persons by age groups shows that more than half of the unemployed are aged between 15 and 24. Incidentally the figure for that group is particularly high since 12.8 per cent of the total number are unemployed as against 3.7 per cent for old workers. This situation, which prevails in many countries, arises out of the large numbers of young people looking for their first job. It should also be noted, however, that the unemployment rate is also higher[2] among young people who have already had jobs than among older workers. Seniority is probably a factor of some importance in stability of employment in Lebanon.

The distribution of the unemployed by occupation gives an opportunity to stress the very special position of agricultural workers: permanent (and declared) unemployment is very low (1.1 per cent of the total number), but seasonal unemployment is very high (9.8 per cent of the total). These results are not surprising in view of the fact that considerable underemployment, of a seasonal nature at least, is often found among agricultural workers. They suggest that the present survey should go on to deal separately with employment problems in agriculture, which would thus constitute a fairly self-contained "sub-market" in the aggregate labour market.

Still in connection with the distribution of the unemployed by occupation, attention should also be drawn to the comparatively high unemployment rate among non-agricultural labourers and production workers (4.1 per cent) and the comparatively low rate for technicians and professional workers (2.7 per cent). According to observations made in many countries, workers are affected more or less by unemployment according to their level of skills. In the case of Lebanon, this trend is confirmed by the information on unemployment by level of education. Graph 1 represents permanent unemployment rates (excluding temporary or seasonal unemployment) by levels of education.

---

[1] The authors of the survey note (page 112) that "out of the 21.6 per cent not in the labour force, 14.1 per cent are studying, 1 per cent are physically handicapped, and there remains a sizable proportion of men (6.5 per cent) who are not in the labour force for no apparent reason: 2.8 per cent have retired before the normal age and 3.7 per cent have never worked and do not seek to work. This high rate of non-active people may be partly explained by the existence of persons of independent means, for it should be noted that anyone declaring that he lived on the income from his property without doing any specific work was classified as non-active".

[2] The rate of unemployment in the narrow sense is 3.9 per cent for the 15-24 age groups as against 2.9 per cent for workers aged 25-64 (the difference between the two percentages is significant from the statistical point of view).

The lowest rate is obtained for workers with no schooling, which is partly explained by the large numbers of farm workers included in this category, with their low rate of permanent unemployment; another contributory factor, however, is the refusal of workers with some schooling to accept certain types of job which are considered inferior, and which are filled by recourse to foreign manpower, Syrian in particular. This attitude would go a long way towards explaining the particularly high rate of permanent unemployment (over 9 per cent) among workers with primary or junior secondary schooling, the categories most affected by permanent unemployment in Lebanon. Unemployed persons with senior secondary or university education who have already held jobs are comparatively few in number, but attention must be drawn to the high percentages (3.2 per cent and 4 per cent respectively of the total numbers) of persons with a university or senior secondary education seeking their first job. These percentages throw into relief the difficulties encountered by young Lebanese graduates and secondary school leavers in finding suitable employment. The situation may be partly attributed to the inadequate number of posts available corresponding to these levels of education, and it may also arise from unsatisfactory distribution among the different types of courses (literature, law, technology ...). There is a marked contrast between the high percentage (3.2 per cent) of graduates seeking their first job and the lower figure for workers of university level who are unemployed (1.9 per cent). This contrast may be explained either by the gradual adaptation of the latter to the types of job available, or by the fact that some have emigrated.

This rapid review of the data concerning unemployment in Lebanon would suggest that there is a misfit between manpower needs by skill levels and the output of the Lebanese educational system, and this hypothesis is strengthened by the magnitude of international migration movements in Lebanon. If our analysis is to go forward, however, it cannot continue simply to treat the matter as a whole. The study of Lebanese unemployment rates alone has shown the need to distinguish between several labour sub-markets according to activity sector (specificity of agriculture) or according to skills.

Part Two will seek to establish criteria for differentiating between these various sub-markets.

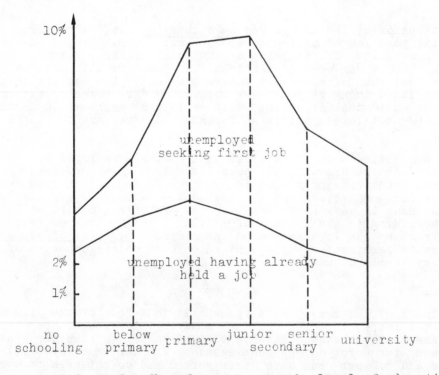

Graph 1. Unemployment rates by level of education

Source: Economically Active Population Survey (table 78)

PART TWO:

ANALYSIS IN TERMS OF SUB-MARKETS

In this second part, the labour market in Lebanon is divided up into sub-markets showing comparative immobility of the labour factor. While it is acknowledged that there may be a relationship between one sub-market and another, the aim here is to find criteria by which comparatively self-contained sub-groups may be defined, and their workings analysed. Three lines of research are proposed: a geographical division, a division by sectors or by occupations, and a division by levels of skills.

Section I - Regional labour markets

Although Lebanon covers an area of only 10,000 km^2 and Beirut acts as a magnet for all the rest of the country, it is possible to consider a geographical division of Lebanon based on the analysis of manpower movements from one region to another. A regional labour market can be defined in the same way as the nation in the study of international economic relationships: it is a zone of comparative immobility of the labour factor. This definition may be arrived at either from the pay differentials that may exist between similar professional activities, or from the study of internal migration movements. Available data allow us to adopt only the second criterion, which is established from observations on the difference between declared place of residence and declared place of work, and on changes of residence.

1. Available data

The Active Population Survey shows two tables relating to internal migrations: one is concerned with daily or weekly migrations (or to put it more accurately the distribution of residents according to their place of residence and place of work), while the other deals with more or less permanent migrations (or more accurately the distribution of migrants according to their previous place of residence and present place of residence). This second table covers all migratory movements (active and non-active), however, and is therefore of little value as far as this study is concerned. The Central Bureau of Statistics has kindly made available to us the unpublished data on migrations of active persons only.

(a) Daily or weekly migrations

The distribution of Lebanese residents according to their place of work and place of residence highlights the magnitude of the daily or weekly movements of workers, since out of 100 workers employed in Beirut, for instance, only 63 actually live there, with a further 25 living in the immediate outskirts. With Lebanon divided up into four regions (Beirut - outer suburbs - Mount Lebanon; North Lebanon; South Lebanon; the Bekaa), satisfactory immobility figures can be obtained for daily or weekly migrations. Thus 98.2 per cent of the workers employed in North Lebanon live in North Lebanon (for each region, the corresponding percentage is over 95). Thus the study of daily or weekly migrations suggests a division of the labour market in Lebanon into four sub-markets.

(b) Changes in workers' place of residence

Data were collected on changes of residence for active persons according to date of migration: less than one year from the date of the survey of November 1970, one to four years from that date, five years or more. They show a very high rate of immigration into the Beirut - outer suburbs - Mount Lebanon area. In a single year, November 1969-November 1970, the net increase in manpower is 9,300 persons, the equivalent of 2.9 per cent of the active population of the area.[1] Two features of this movement are noteworthy:

_____

[1] If we consider only Beirut and its outer suburbs, the figures are still more impressive: the net inflow of labour is 9,135 persons, which represents 3.71 per cent of the active population of the agglomeration.

- The large number of active persons from abroad (5,265), mainly from the Arab countries (4,335). It should also be noted that these data do not represent the entire inflow of migrants, since the survey does not take into account temporary migrants.

- The number of active persons drawn from other areas of Lebanon. In the year before the survey alone, 3.34 per cent of the active population of South Lebanon, 1.70 per cent of that of the Bekaa and 1.06 per cent of that of North Lebanon emigrated to Beirut - outer suburbs - Mount Lebanon.

At the same time, internal migratory movements vary greatly from one region to another. While the movement of workers is almost entirely internal for the Beirut - outer suburbs - Mount Lebanon area, the percentage of internal migration as compared to the total is 58 per cent for North Lebanon, 50 per cent for South Lebanon and 26 per cent for the Bekaa. These differences are due to the fact that the towns in the different regions vary greatly in size. The towns of the Bekaa do not serve to any great extent as a migratory screen, as compared with the Beirut area. On the other hand, there is a tendency for migratory movements towards Beirut and its immediate surroundings to increase.

2. Conclusions

Four regions have been considered in this study:

(a) Beirut - outer suburbs - Mount Lebanon, in which the principal activities are the various services, trade and the hotel business, business services and industry;

(b) North Lebanon, which forms a well-balanced region where agriculture, industry and services all have their place;

(c) the Bekaa, which is mainly agricultural;

(d) South Lebanon, also mainly agricultural.

The power of attraction exercised by Beirut is very marked and appears to be growing. Must we conclude from this that any subdivision of the Lebanese labour market is pointless? The example of North Lebanon enjoins caution; this well-balanced region is less vulnerable to the attraction of Beirut. In our view, however, the geographical division of the labour market cannot be regarded as a vital factor, but is rather of secondary importance compared with the subdivisions by sectors or by skills which must now be discussed.

Section II - Sectoral and occupational markets

Where the pay is the same, it is probably not a matter of indifference to a worker in which activity sector he is employed - agriculture, construction, services and so on. Some sectors are unpopular (refusal to do farm work, manual labour ...) while others have considerable drawing power (some services, in particular "social services"). Our task here is to find criteria for a grading of the various sectors which will reflect the preferences of jobseekers as regards sectors looked upon as privileged.

Sectoral grading rests, however, on a classification of business concerns (and not of workers) according to the nature of the product manufactured, and must therefore be accompanied by occupational grading. A worker tends to be drawn more towards a particular occupation than towards a particular sector of economic activity, and all occupations do not attract jobseekers to the same extent. Our aim here is therefore to suggest criteria for grading sectors and occupations in such a way as to divide up the over-all labour market into more or less self-contained sub-markets. These criteria are sometimes economic, sometimes psycho-sociological in character; we have for instance:

- sector-specific skills (sectors requiring particular qualifications);

- pay and fringe benefits, including social benefits;

- security of employment and work status (self-employed workers, wage earners);

- working conditions (noise, accidents);

- social standing (a factor which is probably more inherent in the occupation than in the sector, but which is also linked up with the nature - national or foreign - and the size of the companies);

- place of work (urban or rural).

1. Steps for building a system of sectoral grading

In the absence of specific surveys, we shall have to be content with the information provided by the Active Population Survey on which to base our system of grading economic activities. The material used consists of double-entry tables in which the distribution of workers by sector of activity is tabulated along with:

- work status: self-employed workers, permanent wage earners (usually paid by the month), wage earners paid by the day, tenant farmers (paying rent in kind), family helpers;

- rhythm of work: work on a permanent basis (no stoppages, except for weekly time off), seasonal or casual work;

- age of workers, which in the absence of data on trends in the active population can be a dynamic indicator for the sector. Such an indicator is not always reliable, however, since young workers may simply pass through a particular sector while waiting for a job more to their taste in another sector.

In addition to these findings, production per worker and per sector (for the year 1970) has been included, as an indicator of efficiency and, very roughly, of pay differentials.

In table 1, the first column indicates the structure of the active population: we can see the important place occupied by the tertiary sector, which comprises 55.3 per cent of the working population; next come the secondary sector (25.3 per cent) and agriculture (18.9 per cent). The other columns in the table bring together the available data from which a system of sectoral grading for Lebanon can be built up: these include in particular the percentage of day labourers and family helpers and the percentage of permanent workers, in relation to the total active population of the sector concerned.

At the bottom of the scale comes agriculture: agricultural work is in fact regarded by the Lebanese as one of the inferior jobs (low pay, non-existent social benefits, social standing nil), and owing to the localisation of the jobs, in rural areas, and the specific nature of the work done, agriculture probably constitutes a fairly self-contained labour sub-market.

Next comes the building industry, a special feature of which is the high rate of day labourers employed (over 50 per cent), and then the extractive and manufacturing industries. The position is less clear for the other sectors, which in any case cover widely different activities: for instance, the heading "other services" includes among other things domestic services and government services. However, business services might be regarded as coming at the head of the scale.[1]

It would thus appear that, in spite of the inadequacy of our criteria, some sectors are less favourably placed than others. Indeed, the fact that agriculture and building come at the bottom of the sectoral scale is confirmed by the employment in these sectors of large numbers of foreign workers, who are not generally taken into account in the survey.

---

[1] The "electricity and water" sector is not very large compared with others: its high rating by our criteria is due to the fact that the companies in this sector are usually public ones.

TABLE 1

AVAILABLE DATA FROM WHICH TO ESTABLISH A GRADING OF SECTORS

		Structure of the active population %	Work status			Percentage of permanent workers	Percentage of workers under 35	Gross domestic product per worker in LP (1970)
			Day labourers, family helpers %	Monthly wage earners %	Self-employed, owners of businesses %			
1	Agriculture	18.9	55.5	2.0	42.5	17.0	35.8	4 400
5	Construction	6.5	53.4	10.6	36.0	32.9	48.5	6 200
2-3	Extractive and manufacturing industries	17.8	43.4	27.9	28.7	81.2	60.9	7 300
6	Commerce, hotel industry	17.0	16.7	29.8	53.5	89.4	44.6	10 000
9	Other services	27.8	15.3	71.4	13.3	85.6	59.3	10 500
7	Transport	7.1	18.8	47.8	33.4	86.5	42.4	9 000
8	Business services	3.4	3.6	69.5	26.9	93.4	59.4	
4	Electricity, water	1.0	11.5	87.2	2.2	98.2	38.8	14 200
	Miscellaneous	0.5						
	TOTAL	100.0	30.6	37.8	31.6	-	-	-

Source: Economically Active Population Survey, Vol. 1.

2. Steps for building a system of
    occupational grading

    The foregoing sectoral grading is based on the nature of the product manufactured by the firms. A worker, however, tends not so much to choose a production sector as to take up an occupation: for instance, other things being equal, an accountant will be prepared to use his capacities in industry, the building trade or in services, attaching only secondary importance to the nature of the final product of the firm which may use his services. To arrive at a more detailed analysis of the labour market, therefore, it may prove more useful to establish a scale of occupations.

    In the absence of specific inquiries into reasons for the choice of an occupation, and of data on earnings by occupation, we have selected only two not very satisfactory indicators: work status and unemployment. As regards the first, a high percentage of workers rated as day labourers or family helpers is interpreted as indicating an "inferior" occupation. As regards the second, a high unemployment rate (including seasonal and casual unemployment) is also a sign of instability of employment and therefore of an inferior occupation.

    As was to be expected, the categories "administrative and managerial workers", "technical and professional workers", "clerical and related workers" come at the top of the scale, while non-agricultural labourers and production and farm workers come at the bottom.

    If we examine the data using the detailed lists of the International Standard Classification of Occupations, we find considerable disparities within the major groups 4 (sales workers), 5 (service workers) and 7, 8 and 9 (production and related workers). Therefore, the criteria used here are inadequate for an accurate classification. However, they do indicate a rough grading of occupations which might serve as a starting point for more penetrating and exhaustive studies. These would have to take into account the essential criterion of skill, which we must now consider in the light of a few available data.

Section III - Labour markets according to the skill criterion

    The importance of taking skills into account in any analysis of the labour market can be brought out by means of one simple fact: some jobs require, for technological reasons, specific qualifications which cannot be quickly acquired. Thus any division of the over-all labour market based on skills derives from the ability of some workers to fill specific jobs. This brings to light a number of graded sub-markets, each one open only to workers with the requisite skills. For the jobseeker, therefore, the market contains "no-access areas".

    Segmentation of the market may result, however, from the behaviour of economic agents who, when they have reached a certain level of skill, refuse certain jobs. We then have, for many agents, "refusal areas" on the market. In Lebanon, this attitude largely explains why foreign labour is employed in farming, the building trade and certain service industries. Before trying to assess the number and size of these various labour sub-markets in the Lebanese economy, we must define the concept of skill and the criterion by which it can be assessed.

1. Choice of a skill criterion: training

    An individual's level of skill can be judged in three ways: by his contribution to production, by the remuneration received and by length of training.

    The principle of using remuneration received as a basis is highly debatable, and in any case this is out of the question in Lebanon for want of data.

    Estimating the individual worker's contribution to production is made very difficult by the collective nature of the production process, which is the outcome of the united efforts of many groups. This type of estimate is very difficult to make in industry, and much more so in the service sectors which bulk very large in the Lebanese economy.

Work skill also features as a good produced through a training process.
The market does not permit of isolating the price of this good, so its value has to
be estimated from its production costs, i.e. from the cost of training.   This may
be calculated by adding up the direct and indirect financial costs met by the
trained individual and by the community.   The higher the cost of training a worker,
the more highly qualified he will be considered to be.   A simpler but still less
satisfactory criterion of skill may also be adopted: time spent on training.
The longer this is, the more highly qualified the worker is said to be.   Thus
various categories of skill can be recognised from the information available about
manpower training in Lebanon.

The data concerning the workers' educational levels are inadequate.   Training
acquired in establishments other than schools, by private study or from experience
on the job must also be taken into account.   The last two means of acquiring skills
are not to be discounted, but they are very difficult to estimate in a general study,
and their comparative importance varies greatly according to occupations and activity
sectors.   Thus surveys carried out in the French chemical industry reveal that
81 per cent of engineers were engaged in that capacity.   In the case of technicians,
on the other hand, out-of-school training and seniority play an important part.[1]

On the whole, experience features primarily as a means of reaching higher
grades within a broad skill category (engineers, technicians, skilled workers and
foremen) by holding positions of responsibility and authority rather than jobs
requiring very different technical qualifications.   Thus we appear to have skill
thresholds which it is almost impossible to cross without lengthy additional
training.

In view of these findings, it seems advisable in studying the Lebanese labour
market to limit ourselves to distinguishing between a few broad skill categories
which must be defined.

2.   Definition of broad skill categories

In Lebanon, as in other countries that are not highly industrialised, on-the-
job training, even if quantitatively important, cannot be regarded as adequate.
Where there are no long-established technical traditions, assimilating a new
technology calls for specialised training for the personnel involved, and this
implies a given level of general education.   This being so, we can take as our
starting point in the case of Lebanon the survey findings relating to the general
educational level of the working population.

These findings show that the occupational structure varies very considerably
according to the level of schooling.   They justify the view that a mix among
workers holding secondary certificates and higher diplomas might be acceptable.
Indeed, this kind of mix is validated by the work of S. Bowles[2] who has calculated
a very high elasticity of substitution between workers who have completed 8 to 11
years of schooling and those who have completed more than 11 years.   This author
thus reaches the same conclusions as can be drawn from an important OECD publication dealing with the relationship between occupational and educational structures
and levels of development.[3]   It appears from a large number of regression analyses
carried out by the OECD that the most significant correlation that can be established
between the level of development and the educational attainments of workers is
obtained where a distinction is made between workers with more than eight years of
schooling and those with less than eight.   This limit of eight years corresponds
to the junior secondary level.

---

[1] Cf. Butler, Gaudemar, Pitoeff, Tourreau, "Formations et Carrières
professionnelles", Sociologie du Travail, No. 1, 1974.

[2] Cf. "Aggregation of labour inputs in the economics of growth and planning:
experiments with a two-level CES function".   Journal of Political Economy,
Jan.-Feb. 1970, pp. 68-81.

[3] OECD, Paris, 1970.

These results give us ground for assuming that a worker may be termed "skilled" when his level of general educational attainment corresponds at least to the junior secondary level.

3. Analysis of the Lebanese data

The lack of organised information other than the sample data supplied by the Active Population Survey makes it impossible to do more than draw up a list of the skilled workers in the Lebanese active population. From a general analysis of these data we can specify the grading of occupations already referred to, before estimating the number of technicians available.

(a) General analysis

Skilled members of the labour force, i.e. those with a level of schooling at least equal to the junior secondary represent about one-fifth of the Lebanese active population.[1] It is important to know this over-all figure, for even if these people are at present being inefficiently used in jobs which theoretically do not call for such a level of education, they constitute a potential reserve of technical personnel, who can acquire the necessary specific qualifications by experience or through additional training.

A study of table 2 would seem to indicate a very definite grading of occupations according to the criterion of schooling. The first four groups of occupations (0, 1, 2, 3 of ISCO) comprise from 61 per cent to 87 per cent of skilled workers as against 20 per cent in the total active population.[2] It is in these groups that the technical and administrative personnel of the country are registered. However, the not insignificant number of workers with schooling of primary level or below reminds us of the heterogeneous nature of these occupational groups, as far as skills are concerned. For a more accurate study of the skilled manpower resources of the Lebanese economy, these broad groups will have to be broken down into smaller ones.

(b) Analysis of skilled manpower resources[3]

To reach a certain level of skill, a particular level of educational attainment is often necessary, but on-the-job experience, or training courses, can help some workers to reach a higher level of skill than that indicated, a priori, by their level of schooling. Special surveys would be needed to provide fuller information on this factor.

Failing these, it would seem possible to assume that for a given occupation the level of schooling required is that of the "modal" class, in other words the class which shows the biggest numbers of workers of that occupation in the distribution by levels of schooling.[4]

It seems reasonable to assume, however, that the workers in the educational class immediately below this one have acquired, by experience or by out-of-school training, qualifications comparable to those of the better educated workers in the same occupation. Thus there will be more skilled workers than are indicated by reference to the criterion of education alone, and in fact workers with primary schooling but doing a job for which the modal class is the junior secondary level (i.e. in this case rather more than 10,000) are counted as skilled, on the basis of that assumption.

---

[1] 107,925 as against 538,410 for the total labour force.

[2] These four groups comprise 70 per cent of the so-called skilled workers.

[3] The definition of skilled personnel adopted is only a rough approximation of the real thing, and must be taken as a working hypothesis.

[4] E.g. for occupation 32 (stenographers, typists ...), in which the figure of 1,705 workers is broken down as follows: 3.2 per cent higher level, 27.5 per cent senior secondary, 47.7 per cent junior secondary, 17.4 per cent primary and 4.0 per cent below primary, the modal class is the junior secondary level.

TABLE 2

LEVEL OF SCHOOLING BY OCCUPATIONAL CATEGORY
(in %)

	Occupational group	Higher level	Junior + senior secondary + higher	Primary + below primary	Illiterate	Unknown
0	Professional and related	22.5	86.6	12.6	0.5	0.3
1	Scientific and technical personnel	47.8	75.1	22.1	2.5	0.3
2	Administrators	27.6	62.0	33.1	3.3	1.6
3	Clerical personnel	5.3	60.9	36.7	1.7	0.7
4	Sales workers	2.7	21.2	54.6	20.7	3.5
5	Service workers	0.3	6.9	50.0	40.4	2.7
7-8 9	Production and related workers and labourers	0.1	4.4	63.9	27.8	3.9
6	Agricultural workers	0.1	1.3	39.0	58.3	1.4
	Over-all	4.3	20.1	48.9	28.4	2.6

Source: Active Population Survey (unpublished data).

Table 3, based on the distribution of Lebanese workers according to the detailed classification of the ISCO, comprises "skilled occupations", i.e. those for which the level of schooling required (that of the modal class) is at least the junior secondary.   The big percentage of skilled workers engaged in an occupation which does not as general rule call for a high level of education may appear to be evidence of difficulties on the Lebanese labour market.   A considerable number of skilled workers are apparently not finding the jobs for which they are qualified.   However, a careful study of the occupations of the "other skilled personnel" (not included in table 3) gives reason to estimate that only half are actually in an occupation where their particular level of education may be required.[1]   In the end, the rate of under-utilisation of skilled manpower would only be in the neighbourhood of 13 per cent.

In the case of personnel with higher education, it would seem that they should be regarded as under-utilised if engaged in an occupation for which the modal educational level is not at least equivalent to secondary.   As before, however, we have to add the workers engaged in occupations with very heterogeneous skill levels, but in which this higher qualification may prove necessary at times.[2]   The figure obtained is again in the neighbourhood of 13 per cent.

---

[1] We refer to sub-groups 07, 14, 16, 41, 43, 44, 50, 51, 61, 70.

[2] We refer to sub-groups 14, 16 for the total number of workers with higher education, and sub-groups 41, 43, 44, 50, 51, 61 for half of them.

TABLE 3

SKILLED WORKERS BY OCCUPATION

ISCO number	Modal class	"Skilled occupations"	No. of higher level workers in the occupation	% of total no. of workers in the occupation	Number of skilled workers	% of total no. of workers in the occupation
01	(1)	Physicists-chemists	210	56.0	330	88.0
02	(1)	Architects-engineers	2 850	98.4	2 895	100.0
03	(3)	Draughtsmen, industrial technicians	30	1.1	2 235	67.2
04	(2)	Pilots, deck-officers, ship's engineers	90	37.5	240	100.0
05	(1)	Biologists, agronomists	360	41.4	735	65.5
06	(1)	Doctors, dentists, pharmacists	2 355	91.3	2 535	97.3
08	(1)	Statisticians, mathematicians	75	83.3	90	100.0
09	(1)	Economists	60	100.0	60	100.0
11	(1)	Accountants	360	60.0	570	95.0
12	(1)	Lawyers	2 160	96.6	2 175	97.3
13	(3)	Teachers	5 025	16.9	29 475	91.8
15	(2)	Authors, journalists	300	22.0	1 230	91.2
17	(2)	Musicians, actors, producers	90	12.5	360	50.0
18	(2)	Athletes, sportsmen	15	3.6	315	75.0
19	(2)	Prof. and tech. personnel (0 and 1) not classified elsewhere	225	29.4	660	86.3
20	(1)	Government administrators	450	75.0	540	90.0
21	(1)	Managers	2 475	24.8	6 030	60.4
30	(2)	Clerical supervisors	465	24.8	1 530	81.6
31	(1)	Government executive officials	360	23.6	990	64.7
32	(3)	Stenographers, typists, punching machine operators	210	3.2	6 420	78.4
33	(3)	Book-keepers, cashiers	495	3.8	11 370	70.1
34	(3)	Data processing machine operators	30	11.8	255	82.4
35	(3)	Transport supervisors	135	11.1	960	65.2
39	(3)	Clerical personnel not classified elsewhere	690	4.4	12 405	54.3
40	(2)	Managers (wholesale and retail trade)	210	18.7	900	80.1
42	(3)	Sales supervisors and buyers	45	10.4	420	86.2
		Armed forces	315		1 605	
		Other skilled personnel not engaged in "skilled occupations"	2 985		30 790	
		TOTAL	23 070		118 120	

Notes on table 3

<u>Source</u>: Active Population Survey (unpublished data).

1.   Modal class: higher level (1)

      Modal class: senior secondary level (2)

      Modal class: junior secondary level (3)

2.   In calculating the percentages, workers whose level of educational attainment
      is unknown have not been included.

      Thus it would appear that a quite considerable proportion of Lebanese skilled
manpower, whatever the level of educational attainment, is not engaged in occupations requiring the level of qualifications offered.   This seems to provide
confirmation of some of the conclusions reached after studying unemployment and
participation rates in Part One.

      The classification used is not sufficiently homogeneous to permit of going
further with this analysis and so there is justification for being content to make
a distinction between skilled and unskilled labour in any general study of the labour
market in Lebanon.   It would seem desirable, however, to make a further distinction
between "scientific and technical" personnel and other skilled workers, since the
"scientific" category is made up of quite highly specialised workers, while other
skilled personnel are more multivalent.   Moreover, while it is comparatively easy
for a scientific worker to switch to administrative work, the reverse is more
difficult.   The survey's data show the relatively small number of technicians
employed in the Lebanese economy (less than 6 per cent of the total number of
skilled personnel, 16 per cent of the workers with higher education).   The
explanation for this lies in the overriding importance of services in the Lebanese
economy.   In view of the vital part played by technicians in any policy of industrial
development, however, it seems right to devote special attention to this subsection
of the labour market.

PART THREE :

NEED FOR AN EMPLOYMENT POLICY IN LEBANON

This study has been almost entirely based on the Economically Active Population Survey made in November 1970 by the Central Bureau of Statistics. It would be worth while to continue this survey over a period in order to determine the pattern of change, but the incomplete information at our disposal is more in the nature of a series of anecdotes than of a scientific document to be used as a basis for serious quantified analysis. It is nevertheless possible to arrive at some conclusion from Parts One and Two, and we think we can say that they are still valid at the present time.

(a) There are large numbers of unemployed. In 1970 they represented 8 per cent of the active population, and this percentage does not take into account the hidden unemployment corresponding to the employment of workers on unproductive jobs. In addition, the Survey probably did not register the marginal unemployed whose motives for seeking employment do not arise from economic pressures and who do not spontaneously declare themselves as unemployed, although they are prepared to take a job.

(b) Young people have great difficulty in finding jobs to suit them. The 1970 Survey reveals that young people enter working life late (20 is the average age for beginning work) and that more than 50 per cent of the declared unemployed are aged between 15 and 24.

(c) The growing rapidity with which jobs are being concentrated in Beirut leads to imbalances in the regional labour markets; some predominantly agricultural regions, with needed manpower draining away, are obliged to fall back on foreign labour.

(d) In the sectoral grading, the fact that the industrial sector comes after an already overcrowded tertiary sector does nothing to promote the orientation of employment towards rapid industrialisation.

(e) Similarly, the limited number of scientific and technical personnel constitutes an obstacle to industrial development.

It can also be added that a rapid increase in the number of jobseekers is to be expected. This is due to several factors, and in particular to a considerable increase in population and to a rise in female participation rates (among young women). Furthermore, owing to increases in school enrolment in the sixties, young people will be coming on to the labour market with higher degrees than the older generation and will thus be likely to refuse certain categories of job. A single figure will be enough to illustrate the extent of the phenomenon: in 1970-71, almost one third of the resident population was at school or university. Lastly, an expansion of wage-earning employment must be expected[1]; individual initiative will thus be less likely in future to contribute as much as it does at present to the creation of jobs.

There is, therefore, every probability that the various labour markets will be subject to varying degrees of disequilibrium. What adjustments can be expected in a free economy which relies on market mechanisms? What action should be contemplated with a view to gradual introduction of an employment policy in Lebanon?

---

[1] In the Active Population Survey 68 per cent of the resident workers are registered as day labourers or wage earners, but the percentage varies noticeably with age: it goes from 43 per cent for the 60-64 age group to 85 per cent for the 15-19 age group.

Section I - The limitations of adjustments
brought about by market mechanisms

What are the remedial mechanisms by which the anticipated imbalances on the various Lebanese labour markets can be eliminated? We shall consider four adjustment processes: wages, out-of-school training, under-utilisation of skills and migration movements; we believe the last two are likely to be of major importance.

1. Adjustment by wage differentials

In a country like Lebanon the existence of large professional classes (lawyers, doctors, engineers ...) with effective professional organisations prohibits the assumption that the labour market for those with the highest qualifications is anything like competitive. In reality pay scales depend much more on the comparative strengths of the different social groups concerned than on their contribution to production, which in any case has yet to be measured. The comparative insignificance of industry, in which the link between productivity and pay is easier to determine (at least in the case of personnel directly involved in production) goes some way towards explaining this. Fundamentally, wage scales are determined by social factors, such as occupational grading which rests on the social standing attached to a particular type of work or level of schooling ...

It is true that scarcity of a particular skill is bound to have some effect on pay. In this connection, mention may be made of the wage increases which occurred during 1973 for some building trades, domestic staff and programmers. Investigation would be needed to find out whether these rises produced by a market mechanism are sufficient to eliminate labour surplus conditions. This does not appear to be generally the case because of the refusal to accept certain jobs associated with less satisfactory working conditions, lower social standing, limited prospects of advancement, and so on. In Lebanon, as elsewhere, wage scales have only a limited influence on the attitudes of jobseekers.

All in all, while the adjustments likely to occur as a result of wage differentials cannot be entirely discounted, they will not of themselves ensure that the balance between labour supply and demand is restored. One of the reasons which frequently prevents this happening is that as workers having the desired qualifications are not always available, provision has to be made for additional training.

2. Adjustment by out-of-school training

As the Lebanese economy is at present organised, out-of-school training is certainly an important factor in the acquisition of various skills, particularly for manual workers, but the absence of accurate information makes it impossible to assess the precise extent and nature of the phenomenon. Besides, it derives essentially from on-the-job apprenticeships and this procedure is not adequate in the event of swift technical advances, accelerating growth and changes in earlier productive structures.

The fact that establishments providing continuous training for adults are practically non-existent leads to the conclusion that it is impossible to achieve notable adjustments by out-of-school training if the imbalance between supply and demand involves skills that are scarce for the time being in Lebanon, or that call for a sound general education plus specialised training.

Thus out-of-school training, like wage differentials, can only permit of limited adjustments in the present state of the Lebanese economic system. An essential step would be to carry out surveys among firms to find out what internal training schemes they offer. Banking appears to be well organised in this respect.

3. Adjustment by under-utilisation of existing skills

It is not possible on the basis of available data to measure the situation with regard to under-utilisation of existing skills. Only specific inquiries relating to well-defined occupations would provide an answer, and the comments which follow simply place the problem in its Lebanese context without attempting to solve it.

If a doctor in physical science with fairly lengthy research experience is only doing the work of an average technician it is obvious that his qualifications are being under-utilised. On the other hand, the fact that a law graduate is engaged as a bank clerk is not necessarily a sign of under-utilisation of skills. A degree in law does not constitute specialised preparation for a career in banking, and it is therefore conceivable that the graduate will receive the necessary special training on the job. There would only be a waste of skills if the level of efficiency and the banking career of the graduate were the same as those of an employee without higher education.

There are many such examples and they serve to draw attention to the fact that a university course is a means of reaching a certain level of general education and culture, but must be supplemented by specialised training, possibly on the job, to provide qualifications that are of use to production. Graduates in general subjects constitute as it were a stock of "semi-finished" products that cannot be put to direct use in production. It is therefore not surprising that many students who hope to find high-grade jobs are disappointed when they leave the university. The phenomenon is all the more marked when, as is the case in Lebanon, the distribution of students by type of general education is weighted in favour of certain courses (law, literature).

From the cultural point of view it is an excellent thing that as many people as possible should have access to higher studies, and the long-term effects on development may be beneficial. It is natural for the individual to wish to pursue his studies as long as possible, and this can only promote his personal advancement. It is therefore quite normal that there should be a strong social demand for education. From the standpoint of the national interest, however, it is important to give priority in allocating available educational resources to the types of training most appropriate to the development choices made by the political authorities. Where there is no genuine training policy closely linked to development policy, the under-utilisation of potential skills is inevitable. The consequences of such a situation, especially the psychological effects, can only be to drive those concerned to emigrate.

4. Adjustment by immigration and emigration

Lebanon has for long been at once a haven for immigrants and a land of emigrants, and the capital sent home by Lebanese emigrants does much to maintain Lebanon's balance of payments. Is that a reason for concluding that these migration movements are a natural phenomenon and a beneficial one?

For this to be the case it would have to be accepted that the skilled workers who emigrate cannot be profitably employed by the Lebanese community, and that expenditure on their education is offset to a great extent by the returns of foreign currency from their work abroad. In the absence of systematic studies on this question no firm conclusion can be put forward, but it would seem to be a distinguishing feature of Lebanese emigration, and one that is more marked now than in the past, that it means highly skilled workers leaving the country for good. According to a report issued by the United Nations General Secretariat[1], the number of Lebanese engineers leaving annually to settle in Canada, the United States and France from 1962 to 1966 represented 35 per cent of the number of engineers graduating per year, or about 5 per cent of the total number of engineers, technicians and the equivalent who were registered in the November 1970 Survey. The extent of this phenomenon which seems, from incomplete and not too reliable particulars available, to be gaining momentum, is an undeniable indication of the maladjustments affecting the Lebanese labour market.

At the same time, there is a very strong current of immigration of unskilled manpower into Lebanon. For a long time these unskilled immigrant workers came from Syria, but they have recently begun to include Egyptians in service industries (restaurants, petrol stations, etc.) and Turkish and Pakistani labourers in the building industry. The extent of this new trend cannot be measured in figures, nor is it possible to say whether these workers are replacing manpower from Syria or supplementing it.

---

[1] The drift of skilled personnel from the developing countries, 5 November 1968, Document A/1794.

These two-way migration movements highlight the imbalances of the Lebanese labour market. Because residents refuse to do many types of poorly-paid, unpleasant jobs requiring minimum skills, the tendency for demand for this kind of workers to exceed supply is met by encouraging the immigration of unskilled workers from the Arab countries. At the same time, large numbers of skilled workers are leaving the country either because they cannot find jobs or because the conditions of employment offered them do not appear satisfactory. Adjustment therefore only comes about by the departure of the workers whose qualifications are most needed for the modernisation of the productive structures of the Lebanese economy.

This situation further emphasises the need to set up a genuine employment policy in Lebanon.

Section II - Recommendations for setting up an employment policy

Any employment policy has to meet the problems of manpower skills and therefore of training. Because of the length of time involved in training, a first pre-requisite is to prepare forecasts of future, probable or desirable trends in man-power supply and demand according to skills. However, it is common knowledge that the statistical data on which such forecasts could be based are inadequate as yet in Lebanon[1], and that is why, before dealing with recommendations concerning the broad outlines of an employment policy, we shall indicate what statistics should be compiled and what studies carried out in order to provide better information on manpower problems.

1. The development of information on employment

The development and distribution of information about employment should certainly have priority in any plan of action by the Lebanese Government. Whether or not the State wishes to intervene on the labour market, information is in itself one of the essential conditions for the smooth working of the adjustment mechanism of decisions taken by various independent centres: firms seeking the manpower they must have if they are to expand, individuals looking for a career, etc. Besides, the publication of statistics, studies and analyses of employment problems creates a public awareness of such problems, and this in turn, in a liberal democratic regime like that of Lebanon, leads the authorities to take action.

Statistics should be compiled regularly on employment so as to define its structure, medium-term trends and variations due to the general economic situation. Specific studies are also needed to throw light on special aspects for the benefit of one or other of the "centres of decision".

(1) A programme of regular statistics

In addition to basic statistics such as population and establishments censuses, which it is advisable to carry out every five years, a programme of regular monthly or at least quarterly statistics should be set on foot in order to monitor trends in employment, unemployment, wages and worker migrations. Here are some suggestions regarding the statistics which could be compiled in a structural framework such as that of Lebanon.

(a) Sample survey of the population

If there is no census sample surveys like the Sample Survey of the Economically Active Population of November 1970 should be carried out every five years so that changes in the structure of the active population may be observed.

(b) Census of industrial and commercial firms

A census of this kind carried out at the same time as the population census will provide a picture of the economic structure on which employment depends. It would be advisable to classify the firms concerned according to sector of economic activity,

---

[1] Cf. in this connection the interesting statistical and methodological research done by Mr. Nabil ABBOUD on the problem of forecasting employment by skills, in "Croissance économique et besoins d'éducation au Liban", doctor's thesis, University of Clermont-Ferrand, France, 1974.

numbers of workers employed, legal status, geographical area, etc. The preparation
of a card index of firms would also be of immense value for any future study of
within-firm employment.

(c) Statistics on the establishment of new firms or the closing down of existing firms

These statistics, which should be made up quarterly (or monthly) - for instance
in conjunction with the systematic bringing up to date of the card index of firms -
would make it possible to keep a regular check on trends in manpower demand at the
source, as related to the general state of the economy. At the same time it is
essential to follow developments in economic activities not covered by a study of
business firms - like construction and agriculture - by means of special statistics.

(d) Movement of wage earners registered under the National Social Security Scheme

Social security, covering as it does almost half of the workers, is nowadays
one of the main sources of statistics on wage-earning employment. With a few
changes in the registration cards it should be possible to compile regular
(quarterly) statistics on:

- Wage earners newly registered under the Scheme, their distribution by sex,
  age, level of schooling, occupation and activity sector.

- Wage earners who have changed employer, distributed according to sex, age,
  old and new occupation, old and new activity sector and place of residence.

- Wage earners who have ceased to belong to the wage-earning category, distributed by sex, age, last occupation and activity sector.

In view of the high proportion of wage earners (85 per cent) among young
workers, statistics on new registrations under the Social Security Scheme are of
great importance as a source of knowledge about the employment of young people just
arriving on the labour market. The other statistics make it possible to measure
labour mobility.

(e) Statistics on jobs offered and jobs sought

With no national employment office and no adequately developed labour exchanges
it is difficult to compile statistics on jobs offered and jobs sought, and yet
information about the kind of jobs offered (by work sector, place of work) and about
jobs sought can be very useful. It would therefore be worth while to try and
obtain data through a system of permanent surveys carried out in firms and in the
centres where workers are recruited.

(f) Wages

As wages play no small part in the adjustment of supply to demand, it is
advisable to observe wage trends. Statistics on wages by occupation, skills,
activity sector, place of work and other factors should be compiled annually on the
basis of establishments' sample surveys. Indications regarding changes in a few
selected pay rates (unskilled labourers employed by the day, trainee office
workers, etc.), obtained from monthly surveys, can also be very useful as a means of
observing market trends.

A final recommendation is for systematic study of the statements of earnings
made quarterly to the National Social Security Scheme or the annual returns sent in
to the Ministry of Finance.

(g) Migratory movements of workers

The real proportions of the foreign labour force are little known in Lebanon.
It is known that most of the unskilled labourers working on building sites or in
agriculture and even in some service industries are Syrians, or, a recent development, Egyptians, Turks or Pakistanis. Failing any strict check on the entry and
length of stay of these labourers, it is difficult to compile statistics on immigration movements of foreign workers. Regular surveys can be recommended, however, on
building sites, agricultural holdings and in other establishments where temporary

labourers are likely to be employed, so as to establish the numbers and the precise nature of this workforce. The State Police Department could also be asked to consider separate registration of temporary workers in the records of foreigners entering and leaving the country.

The emigration of Lebanese workers to other countries is another phenomenon that has not yet been accurately assessed. A big effort must be made to study the nature (skills), magnitude and destinations of this flow of emigrants (statistics from the reception countries, periodical inquiries at the frontier posts among Lebanese leaving the country, and so on).

(2) A programme of special studies and surveys

If labour problems are to be solved by a coherent programme of action, the facts and figures mentioned above must be accompanied by a thorough-going knowledge of certain mechanisms or relationships of a socio-economic nature which affect employment: complementarity of substitutability between certain types of work, potentialities for the absorption of certain types of skills by developing particular sectors or particular types of production process, part played by education in vocational guidance, etc. Here are some suggestions as to the main fields of study.

(a) Employment structure within the firm

A good or a service is produced within a firm, thanks to a group of persons carrying out certain specified tasks. The composition of these tasks and the way in which they are distributed among workers with various qualifications determine the employment structure within the firm. This structure is not uniform from one firm to another within a particular branch of economic activity. It depends specifically on the type of production process used (degree of mechanisation) and on the size of the firm. Obviously workers employed in a big industrial concern will not have the same skills or carry out the same tasks as those in a craft-type industry of the same sector. While workers in the small firm are usually multivalent, division of labour is carried to greater lengths in the big production units. In addition, some forms of work that do not exist in the small units are found in the large ones (e.g. marketing and survey departments).

A knowledge of the employment structure, acquired by means of specialised establishment surveys, is essential if the intention is to make employment forecasts by occupation or skill and to determine the nature of vocational training (should the choice be multivalent training or specialised training, and to what extent?).

(b) The possibilities of developing the use of certain skills

Manpower supply and manpower demand are not independent. It is obvious that the availability of certain qualifications leads to some extent to an expansion of the activities making use of these qualifications. It is worth while to study the mechanisms of this kind of interaction and explore the possibilities of extending given skills or types of work. There are two possible lines of investigation here:

- study of the possibilities of developing branches of activity likely to employ the qualifications proposed;

- study, within each sector, of production methods which will appeal more to Lebanese workers (for instance mechanisation of building work, the replacement of unattractive assembly-line work with a production system calling for some individual initiative, and so on).

(c) The links between education and employment

It is obvious that the kind of education received by a child from his earliest days plays a great part in deciding what occupation he will want or be able to engage in later on. Apart from purely educational research to bring out these links, statistical studies should be undertaken on the occupations actually taken up by young people going through the various streams of the educational system, and the way in which young workers are trained. Studies of this kind are essential to the drawing up of an education policy that will take employment problems into account.

(d) The influence of workers' pay and of income distribution on employment

The pay rates for certain types of work (unskilled labour, or at the other end of the scale, highly skilled work) are a very important factor in migration movements of workers: the immigration of foreign labourers willing to accept lower wages than the Lebanese, and the "brain drain" due to the low salaries offered. It would be desirable to know the wage "demands" of the Lebanese, that is to say the lowest pay limits at which they are prepared to engage in a particular occupation. There must also be investigation, on a concrete basis, into the wages which a developing economy can afford to pay to workers with scarce qualifications to keem them in the country.

(e) Projections of employment in the region

Lebanon "imports" manpower, in the main unskilled, from neighbouring countries, and "exports" skilled manpower. It is highly advisable to prepare projections on economic and social trends throughout the region, in order to know how far this movement may continue.

2. Steps for an employment policy in Lebanon

The statistics and studies suggested above, if properly carried out, might make it possible to perceive the real problems of employment in a country like Lebanon, and to put forward appropriate solutions. They should be synthesised, with the addition of forecasts on medium-term trends in employment. The production of a document of this kind would make it possible for state action - in co-operation with private "centres of decision" - to be undertaken on sound and coherent bases. Meanwhile, a few suggestions can be put forward regarding measures which might improve the employment position in Lebanon.

(1) Action on manpower demand

(a) In a free economy like that of Lebanon, it is only possible to act indirectly on the manpower demands of private businessmen. Such action cannot be divorced from the development policy chosen by the authorities, and it is at this level that problems relating to employment must be considered. In particular, the choice of sectors to be given priority must take into account, among other factors, the skills required, so as to make the best possible use of the skilled manpower available in the country or the manpower it can train. Seen in this light, employment policy is directly linked to taxation, customs and financial policy, but we cannot go further into these questions in the limited framework of this report.

(b) There is, however, one sector in which the authorities do directly determine the demand for labour, namely the public sector. At the present time, civil servants and contractual staff are taken on from one day to another according to the needs and political influences of the moment. An essential step would be for the Government to draw up a detailed programme of appointments of staff with various qualifications for a period of three or five years. With such a programme it would be possible to direct new arrivals on the labour market towards administrative and civil service careers at the right time, and ensure that they received adequate vocational training.

In an economy like that of Lebanon, where the general level of activity is satisfactory, labour demands tend to adapt to available supply, although the disparity between the kind of jobs offered by firms and those sought by the workers must not be too great if this ex-post adjustment is to take place. There can be no question of any measures of coercion being applied to the active population, but the authorities can act by offering incentives, provided they set up an incomes policy and a training policy.

(2) Incomes policy

Taking the studies suggested above as a starting point, a genuine incomes policy should be introduced so as to attract the workers, by higher pay, towards the skills in short supply and the jobs that are difficult to fill. There are many psycho-sociological and political obstacles in the way of a policy of this kind.

(a) Thus in the case of government officials and public servants it would seem advisable to offer a special bonus to the technicians who are not available in sufficient number to meet the needs of the public services. A measure of this kind has already been applied in Lebanon in the form of a premium for technical capacity. This solution has two disadvantages, however; the public servants who do not receive this bonus do everything they can to obtain equivalent benefits so as to keep their place in the wages scale; in addition, when there is no longer a scarcity of technicians with those particular qualifications, those who are receiving the bonus quite naturally object to its being abolished.

(b) In order to put a brake on immigration into the Beirut area, it would be worth while to pay special allowances to public servants (agronomists, teachers, doctors, etc.) who are prepared to live in remote parts of the countryside.

(c) Where the private sector is concerned, the authorities can only exert an indirect influence, in particular through taxation policy and social legislation. Thus a tax policy which favours the traditional independent professions (lawyers, doctors, etc.) by under-taxing them will hardly do much towards attracting students to the technical and scientific courses which are becoming relatively less popular in Lebanon.

Social legislation is another means of influencing labour supply. The privileges enjoyed in this respect by personnel in the modern tertiary sector, e.g. banks, as compared with most industrial workers can only strengthen the drawing power of administrative-type training.

(d) Any drive to promote the development of the industrial sector in Lebanon would have to include, beside the measures indicated above, suitable publicity campaigns to enhance the social standing of the so-called technical jobs.

Even assuming that all these considerable obstacles could be overcome and an effective incomes policy implemented, success would not be achieved without a genuine training policy.

(3) Training policy

A training policy should concentrate on improving basic education and promoting permanent education. According to the choices made as regards the country's development policy (e.g. emphasis on a particular type of industrial sector or service industry) the curricula of primary and secondary schools should be adapted so that pupils are not diverted in advance from work considered essential for the development of the country.

In addition, a programme of vocational training would be needed to help to draw young people in school to the careers in which there is a manpower shortage. Another desirable step would be the introduction of a study grants policy to go hand in hand with the training policy.

However, action with regard to basic education is not enough. Technical change is very rapid nowadays, so that permanent education is a necessity. It is essential to set up re-training centres, with the co-operation of firms and professional associations. As an example of the sort of thing we mean, mention could be made of the Centre for Banking Studies set up in 1967 by the Bankers' Association and the Law Faculty of St. Joseph University. The authorities could encourage such ventures or provide the necessary impetus for them by introducing a special tax and creating specialised agencies, in close liaison with the education sector.

These partial measures (influencing labour demand, incomes policy, education policy) have to be specified and quantified, which is no easy task in the present position regarding statistical information. They will have to be considered in the framework of a Human Resources Development Programme arising out of a general analysis of manpower problems in Lebanon. The aim of this Programme would be to co-ordinate the various measures adopted regarding employment by the different departments of the Ministry of Labour and by other ministries.

Until such time as the machinery for carrying out such a programme gradually comes into operation, the State should make itself responsible for setting up Labour Exchanges where people seeking work and people seeking manpower could be brought together in more satisfactory conditions than at present. This would be a first step towards ensuring, at least in the short run, a better adjustment of labour supply and demand; these labour exchanges would also be a source of information which would bring into greater relief the problems of the labour market in Lebanon.

EMPLOYMENT AND PLANNED DEVELOPMENT OF THE ALGERIAN ECONOMY

by

Abderrahmane Remili

I. Introduction: the political, economic and social situation in Algeria before and after Independence

The background to the planning of employment and of the Algerian economy is marked by two features:

- the burden of the colonial past weighing on the economic and social structures inherited at Independence;

- the emergence of a national revolution, essential basis for the building of Algerian socialism.

(a) The burden of the colonial past

Once Independence had been obtained, the economic and social situation inherited after 132 years gave serious concern, for several reasons: in the first place, the economy was a colonial one, structured with the French economy in mind and directed towards satisfying the needs of a privileged minority; in the second place, it was affected by the war.

The colonial economy showed all the characteristic symptoms of under-development:

- a low level of industrialisation and very few links between industry and the national economy, particularly agriculture, with 50 per cent of supplies for industry coming from outside. Industry provided only 200,000 jobs for 11 million inhabitants;

- the preponderant part played by agriculture in providing employment (60 per cent of the active population was engaged in it, but produced only 20 per cent of the gross domestic product);

- low individual incomes, particularly among the rural population (6 million Algerians), a great proportion of whom only worked a few days per year;

- limited knowledge of modern techniques owing to illiteracy in the countryside and in the towns;

- an excessive dualism at inter-sectoral, sectoral and territorial levels. Two systems were operating simultaneously, first of all at inter-sectoral level: industry in Algeria was absorbing only 15 per cent of agricultural production and agriculture made little demand for industrial goods. Sectoral dualism was to be found particularly in the agricultural sector, where there were alongside each other a modern sector (3 million hectares) responsible for 60 per cent of production and aimed at foreign markets, and a traditional sector (over 4 million hectares) geared to a subsistence economy. The territorial economic dualism was typified by the existence along the coasts of Algeria of developed economic areas, veritable enclaves which contrasted with the poverty-stricken remainder of the territory.

This weak and non-integrated economy which Algeria inherited was also extremely dependent as regards trade, technology, financing and human resources, and vulnerability was one of its marked characteristics. In the field of trade, France absorbed more than 80 per cent of Algeria's exports while Algerian imports mostly came from the French market. Exports were by their nature (similar Mediterranean products) dependent on the French market. In the technical field, dependence was due to the nature of Algeria's equipment (of French manufacture), which made it necessary to maintain existing links. Financial dependence was apparent at the level of government finance (French aid to Algeria) and linked with foreign currency payments (currency transferable without restrictions between Algeria and France until 1963).   Dependence in the field of manpower was due to the number of Algerians working in France (over 350,000) and the number of persons brought in under the technical co-operation scheme whom Algeria needed to replace the French managers and executives who left the country in great numbers immediately after Independence.

As for the vulnerability of the economy, it lay in the foreign trade structure (not enough diversification, and also too high a proportion of domestic production involved).   This weak, non-integrated and dependent economy had to stand up to the effects of the war, which lasted seven and a half years, caused enormous destruction in human lives (over a million dead) and in material resources, and brought about major population changes.

When Independence came, Algeria, with a population of 10 million inhabitants, had to "face a very heavy reckoning and a tragic inheritance"[1]: over a million dead, "hundreds of thousands of widows and orphans, 2 million people released from prisons and resettlement camps, hundreds of thousands of refugees repatriated and 8,000 villages destroyed".   Making provision for widows, orphans and the disabled and helping in the rehabilitation of ex-prisoners, refugees and resettled persons represented far-reaching social problems.   Besides, as Independence led to the departure of the majority of French technicians and managerial personnel, the economy was drained of its skilled manpower in a matter of a few days.   All these economic and social upheavals resulted in an economic recession.   Algeria had to deal with difficult problems of management in the first five years, and undertook structural reforms in conformity with the fundamental political choices she had made.

The weakness of the colonial economy had repercussions in the field of employ-ment, which was also affected by population increase.   As a result of the fall in the death rate, the population of Algeria, which amounted to 5,150,000 in 1926 and 5,588,000 in 1931, had risen to 8,450,000 in 1954 (8,700,000 if we include temporary emigrants).   The natural rate of population increase, which was under 1 per cent before 1914, had risen to 2.85 in 1954.   The number of fully unemployed persons in the rural areas was estimated at 400,000 by the colonial authorities (Delavignette Report).   Other sources reported a million rural unemployed in 1954.   This situation explains the drift from the countryside of a population which was soon to find no more work in the towns.

However, it was in the field of education and training that the past weighed most heavily.   The educational system adopted, which was geared to the schooling needs of the European minority and the skilled manpower requirements of the colonial modern sector, was little concerned with the education of Algerians and the economic sectors from which they earned a bare living.

(b) The emergence of a national revolution,
     essential basis for the building of
     Algerian socialism

Algeria could not but be deeply marked by such a heavy inheritance.   At the same time, however, the national liberation achieved at the cost of great sacrifices had the merit of mobilising the country's energies and making it determined to satisfy its aspirations for independence, democracy and socialist development.

As regards political and institutional changes, the national goals chosen were the gradual socialisation (through various forms of social management) of all the sectors vital to development, and the sharing of the citizen and the producer in the management of affairs within various administrative, economic and socio-cultural units.   In existing conditions in Algeria, where the working class was still small, the socialist choice "does not and cannot mean the immediate setting up of a socialist system.   Indeed, no socialist system can be built without first developing the productive forces of the country, which have been wasted by the colonial regime".[2]

---

[1] In Conference - debate of 29 July 1969 ("El Moudjahid" of 1 August 1969).

[2] See Akkache: "Capitaux étrangers et libération économique: l'expérience algérienne", Maspéro, Paris, 1969, p. 127.

The characteristic feature of the Algerian revolution, apart from the setting up of a system of participation and efforts put into the planned development of a strong and independent economy, has been the gradual socialisation of the means of production of goods and services.[1] As regards direct or indirect taking over by the State of production and trading assets, it should be noted that more than 80 per cent of industrial production, more than 60 per cent of modern agricultural production (with the implementation of the agrarian revolution), 60 per cent of transport and 50 per cent of services have been socialised.

By assigning genuine responsibilities at the various levels, it became easier to set up mobilisation structures. This same concern to assign genuine responsibilities to the grass-root levels, and to accustom them to relying on their own efforts, determined the general trend of the reforms involving local communities: the latter are important political, economic and social agents.

In economic and social sectors where worker-management has not been adopted as the modus operandi, arrangements have been made to ensure that the workers are responsible partners in the running of firms. Indeed, the transformation of existing social conditions "with a view to setting up a new order governed by the law of socialist democracy" is aimed at in the Charter concerning the Socialist Organisation of Firms and in the Orders of 16 November 1971, one dealing with the socialist management of firms and the other one with collective labour relations in the private sector.

II. The labour force: situation in 1966 (immediately before the adoption of the development strategy) and trends and prospects for 1966-1985

The extent of structural unemployment and underemployment at the time of Independence (1962) explains why, four years later, these basic features of the social situation were still of considerable concern, together with the low educational and skill levels of the active population.

(a) Low levels of labour force participation

The active population generally includes those individuals who are contributing to the production of goods and services, whether they are actually employed or seeking employment. There are also age criteria: it is usual to count only those between the ages of 15 and 64. As this United Nations definition was ill-adapted to the case of Algeria, the 1966 census defined "the real active population" as comprising:

- children of 6 to 14 years who are employed;

- persons aged 15 years and over, whether employed or seeking work.

---

[1] In 8 years, the State has taken control of most of the direct or indirect means of production. There has been extensive decolonialisation and socialisation in the agricultural sector, in particular. The change to worker-management in the richest (2,300,000 ha.), most productive and best equipped agricultural sector was the first revolutionary act carried out by the country. On the eve of the Revolution of 1 November 1954, agrarian demands constituted one of the deepest roots of the national liberation movement. The Tripoli manifesto had denounced the existing situation as regards land tenure, and proclaimed the need for an agrarian revolution. When the great mass of the French colonists left at Independence, the Algerian agricultural workers spontaneously took over the running of the vacant farms and ensured that there was no break in production. Worker-management has made it possible to avoid creating another class of large-scale farmers. In spite of its weaknesses, due primarily to the lack of trained managerial staff on the farms and in the supervisory bodies, it has been a positive step towards the establishment of a socialist system based on the democratic running of farms, and of an agricultural sector better geared to domestic needs. In the industrial sector, a large proportion of existing firms have been socialised and new public corporations have also been set up as a part of the industrialisation programme. In 1971, the Charter of the Agrarian Revolution gave further impetus, along more radical lines, to changes in agrarian structures in the private sector.

According to this definition, the real active population as determined by the 1966 census, and excluding Algerians working abroad (233,691), reached a total of 2,798,354.

In recent years, Algerian planners have preferred to use a new concept, that of the labour force. This term comprises persons of working age (18-59) who are **working or** seeking work. It includes essentially the male population aged from 18 to 59, minus students over 18 years of age, persons who have given up[1] professional activity before reaching the age of 59 and persons unfit for work.

The distribution of labour force participation rates by sex and by wilaya (see table 1) shows:

- generally low participation rates (only 21.7 per cent for Algeria as a whole);

- very low female participation rates which are higher in more urbanised areas;

- contrast between rich and poor regions (in particular, participation rates are lower in the east of Algeria than in the west).

---

[1] The General Report on the Second Four-Year Plan (1974-1977) gives the following particulars on page 44:

- "The male labour force: men aged 18 to 59 who are fit for work. This group represented in the past, and still represents, the main element of manpower supply and, therefore, constitutes the predominant indicator of the employment situation.

- The female labour force: in the past, female manpower supply in non-agricultural economic activities was almost nil, but in the future the impetus given by compulsory schooling will certainly bring about new trends in this supply. The projections therefore contain, assuming changing attitudes, an estimate of the numbers of educated women who could take up employment in the non-agricultural sector and who wish to work.

- Lastly, other workers: old people over 59 and young people. As a result of increasing school enrolment, the employment of young people under 18 should tend to be eliminated in the agricultural and non-agricultural sectors of the economy.

The concept of "active" is used to measure actual pressure on the labour market. The student population and young people doing National Service are not included among active persons, but their numbers can be expected to increase considerably. They therefore appear separately in the over-all forecasts for the active population."

Table 1: Participation rates by wilaya and sex, 1966

Wilaya	Total	Men	Women
Algiers	23.5	43.7	3.2
El Asnam	22.5	43.3	2.2
Médéa	23.5	45.2	1.0
Tizi-Ouzou	17.7	38.4	0.8
North Central Region	22.2	43.0	3.1
Mostaganem	22.0	42.8	1.6
Oran	23.7	44.8	2.8
Saïda	23.8	46.0	1.4
Tiaret	24.5	47.0	1.4
Tlemcen	21.3	41.1	3.2
Western Region	23.0	44.1	2.2
Annaba	21.6	41.4	1.7
Aurès	20.5	43.0	1.4
Constantine	19.9	39.6	1.3
Sétif	18.2	37.1	1.2
Eastern Region	19.9	39.5	1.4
Oases	24.8	46.5	1.6
Saoura	24.7	46.6	2.8
Southern Region	24.8	46.6	1.9
All Algeria	21.7	42.2	1.8

Source: 1966 Census.

Table 2 shows the distribution of the active population by branch of economic activity in 1966. Labour force patterns were very traditional: most of the active persons were in the primary sector and only a small proportion were involved in the secondary sector.

Table 2: Distribution of the total active population
by branch of economic activity and sex, 1966

Branch	Men	Women	Total	Percentage
Agriculture, forestry, hunting and fishing	853 800	19 800	873 600	50.6
Extractive industries	20 800	300	21 100	1.2
Manufacturing industries	127 600	13 200	140 800	8.2
Construction and public works	70 400	500	70 900	4.1
Electricity, gas, water and sanitary services	10 100	400	10 500	6.0
Trade, banking, insurance and real estate	136 500	3 600	140 100	8.1
Transport, warehousing and communications	73 300	2 200	75 500	4.4
Governmental and other services	289 200	47 600	335 500	19.5
Undetermined	54 000	2 900	59 900	3.3
TOTAL	1 634 480	90 500	1 724 900	100.0

Source: 1966 Census.

(b) Low educational and skill levels of
the active population

Low educational levels at the time of Independence are illustrated by the following data:

- 75 per cent of the population were illiterate;

- school enrolment figures were very low.

Table 3: School enrolment data 1962

Date	Pupils in primary schools	Primary teachers	Pupils in general secondary schools	Pupils in technical secondary schools
October 1962	746 937	12 696	31 900	18 100

Low levels of skills are revealed by the skills structure in the manufacturing sector in 1971, in spite of considerable efforts made since 1962 in the field of education and training.

Table 4: Skills patterns in manufacturing, 1971

Levels of skill	Number	Percentage
Managers and higher administrators	7 296	2.6
Foremen and middle-level administrators	10 822	3.8
Skilled and highly-skilled personnel	109 807	38.4
Specialised and auxiliary personnel	61 225	21.5
Labourers and unskilled personnel	96 138	33.7
TOTAL	285 288	100.0

(c) Labour force trends and prospects (1966-1985)

The theoretical male labour force, estimated at 2,530,000 persons in 1973, should reach 3,005,000 in 1977, 3,420,000 in 1980 and 4,296,000 in 1985 (in other words, an increase of about 4.4 per cent per annum, the same as during the seven-year period 1966-1973).   The biggest increase should occur between 1980 and 1985, when the rate of growth of the labour force is expected to rise from 4.25 per cent per annum during 1973-1980 to 4.5 per cent per annum between 1980 and 1985, due to the arrival on the labour market of the young people born during the "population explosion" period which followed immediately after Independence.

As regards increases in the non-agricultural labour force, the Second Four-Year Plan (1974-1977) gives the following estimates:

"As for the theoretical female non-agricultural labour force, which was assessed at 80,000 in 1966 and estimated at 131,000 in 1973, it is likely to increase at more or less the same rate as the numbers leaving school; it will number 181,000 in 1977 and 237,000 in 1980, growing at the rate of about 8.5 per cent per annum.

As regards old and young workers, the main feature of the trends expected in these two categories is the gradual elimination from 1973 to 1980 of the employment of young people under 18, which should be nil by 1985. The number of old workers in the non-agricultural sectors, which reached 66,000 in 1966 and was estimated at 74,000 in 1973, will amount to 76,000 in 1977, 82,000 in 1980 and 92,000 in 1985, whereas the number of young workers under 18 in the non-agricultural sectors will drop from 26,000 in 1973 to 14,000 in 1977 and 8,000 in 1980, and will be nil in 1985".

For the theoretical agricultural labour force, the same source gives the following indications, separately for males and for females, old and young workers.

- Males: the figure is low as compared with the total labour force. This is primarily due to the drift from the countryside and to emigration, which affected this category mainly before 1973. There is also a considerable proportion of households in the agricultural sector where the head is not active (25 per cent as against 17 per cent in the non-agricultural sector). Thus, in 1973, the agricultural labour force amounted to 1,155,000 persons, corresponding to 45 per cent of the total labour force; it would amount to 1,239,000 in 1977 and 1,275,000 in 1980, which implies a very low rate of increase, in the neighbourhood of 1.75 per cent per annum during 1973-1977, and about 1 per cent from 1977 to 1980. It is believed that the additional labour force will be, from 1973 onwards, exerting pressure mainly on the non-agricultural sectors.

- Females, old and young workers: this part of the labour force was estimated at 320,000 persons in 1966 and it is characterised by two different trends, "first a reduction in the number of young workers, and then an increase in old and female workers. This led us to assume that the two flows will offset one another, so that the over-all figure of 320,000 persons will remain unchanged".

Table 5:   Trends in the total theoretical labour force (TLF)
(1966-1985)

Sector	(In thousands)					
	1966	1969	1973	1977	1980	1985
Non-agricultural TLF	1 180 (1)	1 376	1 606	2 037	2 472	3 499
Agricultural TLF	1 290 (1)	1 370	1 475	1 559	1 595	1 595
Total TLF	2 470 (1)	2 746	3 081	3 596	4 067	5 094

(1) The figures differ from Table 2 because of differences in concepts.

Source: Second Four-year Plan (1974-1977).

Thus, forecasts of the active population, established according to the concepts of Algerian planners, assume the arrival on the labour market of 475,000 men aged 18 to 60 from 1973 to 1977, including 391,000 in non-agricultural sectors and 84,000 in the agricultural sector. During the same period, the additional supply of old and young workers and of women would amount to 40,000 only for the non-agricultural sector. The increase in the labour force is particularly marked for the non-agricultural sector, especially during the period 1980-1985, when it would amount to 1,027,000 persons, that is to say the total additional supply of labour, since the agricultural sector is assumed to be saturated from 1980 onwards.

III. Development strategy and its implementation during the First Three Plans (Three-year Plan 1967-1969, first Four-year Plan 1970-1973, second Four-year Plan 1974-1977)

The political choice of planned development for the country derives as much from the socialist path chosen as from the organisational requirements for building up an economy to meet the vast needs of a very rapidly growing population. Algeria had to wait for five years after obtaining her Independence before all the conditions were present for setting up a national development plan.

A plan could not be drawn up before instruments had been provided for economic analysis and for the assessment of the organisational capacity of the newly-created administrative machine. Up to 1967 capital equipment budgets made it possible both to complete some of the operations specified in the Constantine Plan and to start new operations suited to Algerian goals and realities (particularly in the industrial sector). There was no risk of serious error in choosing the latter operations without reference to a plan, both because of the magnitude of the action required and because of the state intervention in sectors hitherto neglected by the colonial authorities.

Four years of experience permitted laying the material and technical foundations for planning. In 1966, structures had become more definite. The basic administrative, economic and social institutions were already set up or coming into existence. In addition, studies and statistical data had been prepared during the years 1963, 1964 and 1965, which provided valuable guidance and made possible the next step of inserting development schemes into the framework of a plan.

(a) The development strategy

Algeria's will to develop was expressed in the adoption of a development strategy aimed at transforming economic, social, political and mental structures in order to improve the living standards and the quality of life of the population as a whole. This strategy implied a double struggle, abroad and at home.

Abroad, Algeria's aim was and still is to break with existing forms of international specialisation, in other words to free herself gradually from the world market and organise a self-oriented (independent) and self-sustained process of development (without systematic recourse to foreign assistance, financial or human).   Her position in favour of transforming international economic relation-ships was made clear on the occasion of the "77" and the "non-aligned countries" conferences that were held in Algiers, and in a practical manner during the two "oil battles" in 1971 and 1973.

At home, the objective of launching a development process directed to the masses and which enabled them to reach tangible results was achieved by putting into practice options for socialist development.   This is illustrated by the choice of patterns of economic growth in favour of industrialisation and economic diversi-fication and by the adoption of socialist measures, e.g. the implementation of the agrarian revolution and the taking over of the principal means of production of goods and services.   The growth targets for the various sectors were fixed in accordance with their contribution to a strong and integrated economy, to the expansion of employment which is of major concern to the authorities, and to the promotion of a more just society.

(b) Implementation of the strategy through planning

The seven-year development prospects included in this strategy[1] were centred on four themes:

- the initiation of economic integration;

- the expansion of the productive capacity;

- the adaptation of the educational system to the needs of the economy; and

- the redistribution of incomes.

(i) The initiation of integration of
     the various branches of the economy:

For many years, the main characteristic of the Algerian economy was the lack of integration of the various branches with one another, and their integration with the economy of the colonial power. This meant that all industrial activities needed for complementing the existing economy had to be created, to make possible exchanges and thus start the process of economic integration. In the case of manufacturing, a brake had to be put on exports of raw materials and an iron and steel industry, engineering and petro-chemical factories had to be set up to process these materials locally.   In the case of agriculture, the creation of a food-processing industry could make it possible to integrate the agricultural sector into the Algerian economy. This integration is important for three reasons: in the first place, value added arises primarily at the processing stage, not simply at the stage of extraction or production of raw materials; secondly, investment in a particular branch and the expansion of its production would make itself felt, not on foreign economies through an increased demand for foreign intermediate products (imports), but on the national economy through an increased demand for domestic products, and there would be a snowball effect; finally, at the foreign trade level, the balance of payments would benefit from the limitation of imports to the capital goods needed to set up additional branches of the Algerian economy.

(ii) The expansion of the productive
      capacity:

The creation of these new branches of the economy called for the production or the importation of capital goods, in other words the formation of a national industrial capital. In existing conditions in Algeria, most of these capital goods had to be imported.   The huge sums required for these imports justified the need for a policy of export expansion, particularly in the field of oil, so as to make con-siderable sums available for foreign payments. The main source of foreign currency

---

[1] And covering the period 1967-1973.

is the export of oil and gas products. Thus, the expansion of the productive capacities of the economy as a whole depended on increased production in the oil sector.

(iii) <u>The introduction of a new educational system adapted to economic
requirements</u>:

Here, there were two essential requirements: the democratisation of education, and a general system of training, the contents and methods of which should be geared to the needs of the economy. The process was to go forward in two stages: first, accelerated vocational training schemes to meet the most urgent manpower needs, and then a reorganisation of the educational system in order to prepare great numbers of young people for the tasks of the future.

(iv) <u>The redistribution of incomes</u>:

This goal was to be achieved in the long run by the gradual elimination of unemployment, i.e. by the creation of new jobs. In the short term a policy of redistribution of incomes through taxation, subsidies, etc., should bring about an expansion in the domestic market, a basic factor for economic growth.

The First Four-year Plan (1970-1973), which is part of the seven-year development prospects, made use of several schemes to achieve this basic aim of redistributing national incomes with special reference to the underprivileged as indicated by the Secretary of State for Planning: "With regard to investments, this is the aim to bear in mind in introducing such forms of intervention as investments for rural development, human investment schemes and the policy of loans to the traditional agricultural sector".

The price policy included in the First Four-year Plan also comprised a number of important provisions relating to the redistribution of incomes. There was to be a price policy for such aids to production as fertilizers, seeds, implements, aimed at making them available to agricultural producers, especially those of the traditional sector, on the most favourable terms possible. Were also provided guaranteed prices together with upgrading for some products. As far as the consumer is concerned, it should be noted that prices were to be stabilised or reduced for a number of basic products.

The policy of social allowances represented another aspect of the redistribution measures. Besides, the steps taken to organise trade and the various professions were aimed at eliminating parasitism in sectors where profiteers were believed to be making money at the expense of the great mass of consumers.

Lastly, it must be mentioned that a considerable increase was projected in investments directed towards the satisfaction of social needs. This applied particularly to water supplies, to the electrification of rural areas and, to a much smaller degree, to housing and the sanitary system. The policy of decentralising social amenities and production equipment was another indication of the will to redistribute wealth.

The creation of a thousand villages as part of the agrarian revolution before the end of the decade should make it possible to offer people living scattered in unsatisfactory conditions opportunities for free housing and other socio-cultural equipments (water, electricity, gas, schools, health centres, markets and so on).

(c) <u>The investment policy</u>

To show how development was fostered, it is useful to have a quick look at the ambitious investment policy which has resulted in a very heavy demand for skilled manpower.

(i)   The First Four-year Plan (1970-1973):

The average annual **growth** rate for the gross domestic product during the First Four-year Plan (1970-1973) was fixed at 9 per cent. The various factors contributing to that production (investments and full utilisation of production capacities) were assessed as follows:

- over 30 per cent of the increase in production over the four years would derive from intensified valorisation of oil products;

- 20 per cent of the production increase would derive from value added in construction and public works as a result of the capital equipment programme;

- over 25 per cent would derive from new industrial and agricultural production schemes;

- a little less than 20 per cent would represent effects induced by the expansion of transport, services and trade.

If we look at the structure of public investments (table 6 below), we find that nearly three-quarters (72 per cent) were provided for agriculture, manufacturing, education and training.[1]

---

[1] The policy of development financing followed four guiding principles:

- financing was to be effected, to a great extent, from the country's own resources; the aim being to maintain economic independence and achieve development at the lowest possible costs; foreign credits were regarded as purely supplementary;

- national savings (deriving from the profits of public corporations, national companies, worker-managed sector) were to be allocated in priority to financing development schemes. Giving priority in this way to capital equipment expenditures over the State's routine expenditures was in keeping with the directives of the First Four-year Plan;

- all productive investments were to be made in the form of loans, except for equipments for the economic and social infrastructure, investments in research activities and those taking a long time to mature;

- the issue of currency was subjected to the implementation of production and investment programmes, in order to avoid any inflationary process.

Table 6: Structure of public investments projected
for the First Four-year Plan (1970-1973)

Sector	(in millions of Algerian Dinars)				
	1970	1971	1972	1973	Total 1970-1973
Manufacturing	3 100	3 100	3 100	3 100	12 400
Agriculture	720	910	1 100	1 400	4 140
Infrastructure	494	500	600	713	2 307
Education	650	665	683	721	2 720
Training	135	160	160	132	587
Housing	238	368	438	476	1 520
Transport	368	208	131	93	800
Tourism	165	170	180	185	700
Welfare	190	213	243	288	934
Collective equipments	165	175	195	225	762
Administrative equipments	210	210	220	230	870
TOTAL	6 435	6 679	7 563	7 563	27 740

Source: First Four-year Plan (1970-1973).

    To achieve modernisation with a policy involving the majority of the population, however, it is not enough for the State to have taken over most means of production, to be making a correct use of planning mechanisms and to aim at agro-industrial development and the integration of the traditional sector; there should be a simultaneous drive to promote action at intermediate levels. Thus, decentralisation, which presents political and psychological advantages, also permits the optimal utilisation of the human and material resources which can be used only at the local level. As a result of special programmes and of preparations for the Second Four-year Plan (1974-1977), wide-ranging measures were carried out at the level of those who were the most concerned and also the most deprived.

    The special programmes which were drafted, adopted and carried out, either entirely or in part, for eight underprivileged wilayates and two daïrates were very often specific projects supplementing the centrally-planned efforts to eliminate regional disparities. They called for simultaneous action in the field of productive equipments and in that of socio-cultural equipments. The goal of these government schemes was to bring into use material and human resources by implementing investment programmes which had not found their place within the framework of central planning. Moreover, at the time of preparing the Second Four-year Plan (1974-1977), an innovation in the planning process led in 1973 to an interesting experiment. It consisted of the drafting by those directly concerned of plans for their own communes and wilayates. These plans were based on analyses of the socio-economic conditions in the latter. They included series of proposals as to desirable investments.

    (ii) The Second Four-year Plan (1974-1977):

    Since the main goals of the First Four-year Plan had been reached, the Second Four-year Plan aimed at pursuing all the important long-term objectives at the centre of political thinking. Indeed, the increased financial resources available as a result of the rise in oil world prices, along with the progress made by the economy, had made it possible to raise the level of priority investments and also give attention to relatively neglected sectors.

The amount of investments indeed has tripled as compared with the figures for the previous plan. It represents about 40 per cent of the GNP. It is distributed as follows:

Table 7: Structure of public investments projected for the Second Four-year Plan (1974-1977)

Sector	(in millions of Algerian Dinars)		
	Total expenditures authorised for 1974-1977	Percentage	Cost of the new programmes
Manufacturing	48 000	43.5	65 350
Agriculture	12 005	10.9	9 224
Hydraulic schemes	4 600	4.2	4 840
Tourism	1 500	1.4	1 200
Fishing	115	0.1	54
Economic infrastructure	15 521	14.0	16 718
Education/training	9 947	9.0	8 988
Social welfare	14 610	13.3	16 330
Administrative equipments	1 399	1.3	1 304
Studies-miscellaneous-unforeseen	2 520	2.3	2 463
TOTAL	110 217	100.0	126 471

Source: Second Four-year Plan (1974-1977).

Greater importance has been attached to changing general social conditions: through an intensified incomes policy on the one hand, and by applying a more active policy of improving living conditions on the other (housing, health, welfare). There are already signs of more widespread development in the interior of the country, thanks to a more refined policy of regional planning, especially through the new communal plans conceived as instruments for activating all local human and material resources.

IV. Employment planning during the last two plans (1970-1973 and 1974-1977)

Employment, major objective of the development strategy, received great attention from the planners during the First and especially the Second Four-year Plan. During the First Plan, the authorities were primarily concerned with adapting the educational system to skilled manpower requirements. Although this is still a vital question, more attention is given in the Second Four-year Plan to providing enough employment opportunities.

(a) <u>Adaptation of education and training
to skilled manpower needs</u>

Up to the preparation of the First Four-year Plan (1970-1973), education and employment developed along their own particular lines. Only a limited attempt at relating their needs with one another was made in the Three-year Plan (1967-1969). The latter tried, within the statistical limitations of the first years of Independence, to produce a beginning of educational response to skilled manpower requirements. The enormous replacement needs due to the departure of the skilled foreign personnel at Independence far exceeded the capacity of the inherited educational system, particularly as the majority of pupils had entered schools only after Independence and had not yet reached the stage of entrance into the labour market. This situation was reflected in the seven-year prospects (1967-1973) and the Three-year Plan (1967-1969), which attempted to adapt the educational system to the needs of the economy and of newly-created industries.

With respect to the formation of planning and executive staff, administrators and managers, the formula adopted was that of special training based on four years of schooling distributed as follows:

First year: preparatory courses.

Second and third years: specialised training.

Fourth year: related to actual working conditions.

The training was to be given in newly-created institutions which were to receive as from 1968 1,500 to 2,000 students of senior secondary school level.[1]

In the case of middle-level personnel, the target set was the training of 30,000 persons needed for filling anticipated shortages. This was to be done by imparting skills to 10,000 young people of junior secondary school level and by upgrading 20,000 young people of lower educational levels. Besides, priority was given to the training of primary teachers who could achieve schooling and training objectives.

Over-all planning can only provide preliminary guidelines, which alone are insufficient. An approach at the training institutions level itself can be useful only if each centre of learning accepted the permanent obligation to keep in touch with the needs of the users. This meant a rethinking of the structures, curricula and teaching methods of the educational system that was inherited from the past.

Algeria has taken the first step along this road, since it was decided to reform higher education in such a way as to provide specialised training for operational high-level personnel. The planning of secondary education is retarded, however, by the fact that no reorganisation of its structures has yet been undertaken.

(b) <u>Increasing concern for expanding
employment opportunities</u>

"The aim of expanding employment is the main priority in the country's development efforts. This aim is the keystone of social policy, for employment remains, if not the sole agent, at least the deciding factor in raising the people's living standards".[2]

Because the economic structures of 1966 permitted the creation of only a limited number of new jobs (in the neighbourhood of 30,000 per year, at best)[3], "there was

---

[1] The implementation of that scheme was before 1969 under the responsibility of the Ministry of National Education. Because the Ministry failed to carry it out, the General Directorate of Planning took over in 1969 the task of designing, staffing and co-ordinating a network of special training centres, designated as institutes of technology.

[2] See General Report on the Second Four-year Plan (1974-1977), p. 61.

[3] In other words, less than half of the annual increase in real manpower supply (70,000 persons per year).

thus no alternative to undertaking in-depth long-term action to reorganise completely the country's underdeveloped structures, with a view to finding a lasting solution to the growing disequilibrium between the manpower supply of young persons and the capacity of the economy to absorb them".[1]

During the first development phase (1967-1973), the investment structure had given more priority to heavy investments aimed at exports, in order to ensure that the country was financially independent. The investment orientation has changed in the Second Four-year Plan (1974-1977): "by means of a new distribution of resources, the second phase (1974-1980) should develop three main lines of action:

- the speeding up of the integration schemes set up during the first phase, which are to take the form of intensified development of manufacturing industries geared to meeting domestic needs for equipment and consumer goods;

- the consolidation and strengthening of educational and training schemes at all levels;

- and, on the basis of the results achieved in expanding resources during the first phase, the adoption of a much more decisive policy of improvement of living standards."[2]

This means that, as the Plan goes on, the investment structure will again be altered significantly in favour of sectors which could meet requirements in consumer goods and services, sectors which present a high employment potential.

Employment increases during the first phase, which ended with the First Four-year Plan (1970-1973), are quantitatively satisfactory: "the number of jobs created through the development of non-agricultural activities reached 480,000, 330,000 of which were created during the 1970-1973 Four-year Plan, making an increase of nearly 66 per cent in 7 years, at an annual growth rate of 7.5 per cent. If we add to these new jobs in the non-agricultural economy increases in other activities, of about 72,000 (including 50,000 students and 12,000 volunteers of the National Service introduced at the end of 1968), these satisfactory results meant on the whole a marked reduction in initial unemployment, while making it possible to meet increasing manpower supply in the towns and to absorb some 90,000 rural-urban migrants.

This expansion of employment was due to a number of factors:

- the rapid setting up of state and local community structures, the creation of national corporations and, above all, the fast development of educational programmes. These factors combined accounted for more than 30 per cent of the new jobs (+160,000);

- the effects of investment programmes on construction, public works, services and transport (another 30 per cent);

- more efficient use of the existing production capacity, both in manufacturing and in other sectors (25 per cent);

- and the direct effects of the first productive investment programmes to become operational (about 15 per cent).

The last factor, in which some delay was registered, should constitute the main driving force of future developments".[3]

The progress made in building up the Algerian economy will make it possible to double the number of new jobs to be created between 1974 and 1980, as compared with the results registered during the period 1967-1973.

---

[1] See General Report on the Second Four-year Plan (1974-1977), p. 62.

[2] See General Report on the Second Four-year Plan (1974-1977), p. 63.

[3] See General Report on the Second Four-year Plan (1974-1977), pp. 64 and 65.

"The projected expansion of employment in the Plan depends upon three conditions essential for the implementation of the production and investment programmes:

- adherence to the timetable set for carrying out the priority investment programmes, which will enable new equipments to become operational at the fixed dates, is the most important condition for achieving minimum aims;

- the second condition lies in the progress expected, beyond minimum aims, in improving the output capacities of the national economy;

- finally, the last factor determining employment forecasts will be the satisfaction of consumer needs at rates corresponding to the levels set in the Plan.

Levels of consumption do in fact induce part of the growth in consumer industries, but particularly the trends foreseen for the trade and services sectors".[1]

The aggregate forecast of employment growth during the Second Four-year Plan (1974-1977) involves about 450,000 non-agricultural new jobs for the four years, with an annual rate of increase of over 8 per cent (see table 8):

Table 8: Contribution of the various non-agricultural sectors to the planned expansion of employment, 1974-1977

Sector	Employment increase during 1974-1977	Average annual growth rate (in percentage)
1. Construction and public works	+ 138 000	14.6
2. Administration	+ 106 000	7.9
3. Industry	+ 85 000	7.7
4. Services	+ 60 000	7.5
5. Trade	+ 50 000	5.2
6. Transport	+ 19 000	5.8
TOTAL	+ 458 000	8.3
Source: Second Four-year plan (1974-1977).		

As regards agriculture, the large-scale programmes provided for in the Second Four-year Plan, which include new irrigation schemes and the intensification of livestock production and of the planting of fruit trees, should bring about considerable increases in employment opportunities:

"In worker-managed undertakings, these employment effects should become apparent in a marked increase in the number of days worked, and be manifested not only in improvements in present rates of activity, but also in the creation of about 10,000 additional permanent jobs (new irrigation schemes, intensive livestock production ventures, etc.).

These programmes will also have the effect of providing better opportunities for agricultural work in the agrarian revolution co-operatives, since the implementation of the various agrarian revolution schemes will mean an increase of about 90,000 workers in the co-operatives associated with the agrarian revolution, the land improvement groups and the grazing and forestry co-operatives. As a result, the total number of farmers enrolled in the new co-operatives at the end of the Plan will be in the neighbourhood of 150,000.

___

[1] See General Report on the Second Four-year Plan (1974-1977), p. 66.

The implementation of these programmes, combined with ambitious projects to be carried out in other fields (particularly forestry), should make it possible to meet the additional manpower supply arising out of the expected increase in the active population remaining in agriculture, and also bring about a sensible improvement in the employment situation of those who are at present underemployed".[1]

There will be an increase of about 20 per cent in agricultural employment. If this employment promotion policy is to succeed, four conditions should be given full weight in implementing the Second Four-year Plan:

- "adequate preparation of the non-agricultural sector, by the creation of new jobs at the rates specified in the forecasts, to provide work for those who leave the countryside (this probable drift to the towns is on a relatively large scale; however it corresponds to the continuation of past trends);

- the design of projects aimed at improving the capacity of the agricultural economy to absorb new equipments, and the spread of genuine technical progress;

- much greater attention to be paid consistently to over-mechanisation in agricultural work, which constitutes an obstacle to the expansion of job opportunities;

- the need for a better geographical distribution of some agricultural investment programmes, in relation to areas from which the drift is likely to be extensive".[2]

The aim, beyond the Second Four-year Plan, is to create over a million jobs during 1974-1980 "with the help of the sectors in which growth can be guaranteed over a very long period (integrated and consumer goods industries), and at the same time to ensure that the causes of unemployment and underemployment inherent in economic structures are eliminated in the future".

To this end, the political and administrative authorities are calling upon all agents of the economy for a disciplined effort, not only as regards keeping to timetables and completing current investment and production programmes, but above all:

- with respect to the measures involved in the setting up and running of new schemes, so as to leave more room for manoeuvre on the spot and make it possible to alter the investment structure in favour of those investments which are more employment-creating;

- towards stricter regionalisation in the creation of new jobs, especially by speedily putting into effect communal plans for the underprivileged areas with a strong migration potential.

V. Critical evaluation and desirable
reorientation of the Algerian experience

During the First Four-year Plan, some weaknesses became apparent in the planning of human resources, both at the stages of formulation and implementation. The most serious problems concerned, as they still do, the relationship between educational planning and employment planning. Therefore, our analysis will concentrate on these problems.

Human resources planning was indeed adversely affected by inadequate knowledge of the basic employment situation. It also suffered from the lack of long-term development prospects. In this respect, some action was taken by the Second Plan, at least in the case of primary, secondary and higher education. Nothing was done however to promote a more scientific knowledge of short-, medium- and long-term

[1] See General Report on the Second Four-year Plan (1974-1977), p. 70.

[2] See General Report on the Second Four-year Plan (1974-1977), pp. 70 and 71.

employment prospects. Besides, no multiple strategies of response to manpower demand on the basis of different assumptions regarding school output, occupational mobility, and so on, were devised. The economic growth policy acted as a constraint on the development of the educational system: the present and foreseeable educational levels of the population had no influence on economic choices, e.g. choice of industries or techniques.

In the absence of a permanent committee for educational planning and co-ordination, the implementation of the plan took the form of a large number of separate projects, limited in scope. There was no co-ordination, for instance, to regulate movements or establish well-marked connections between the educational system and the training system.[1] Under these circumstances it was not possible to exercise adequate supervision on the implementation of the various programmes.

(a) Improvements in manpower planning techniques

However, Algeria is perhaps the only country[2], apart from those with a planned economy, which has made an attempt at integrated planning of education and employment. Forecasts of manpower needs, though far from perfect, influenced to some extent educational policy. Skilled manpower shortages (determined by comparison between the outflow from the educational system and manpower demand) have led to the setting up of a new training system (Institutes of Technology), to an increase in centres of higher education and their reform, to the creation of a system of general education aimed at improving human potentials and to measures rationalising the pupils' progress through school (e.g. determining standards for moving up from class to class, and for passing examinations). It was also decided that 35 per cent of secondary school pupils would be directed towards technical education.

On the other hand, manpower requirements forecasts were used for medium-term policy (the period of the Plan), but not for the long term, so that they have not influenced the development of all the educational system. Political choices determined the response to social demand.

For the First Four-year Plan (1970-1973), in spite of theoretical and practical shortcomings in manpower requirements forecasts and the inadequacies of the statistical data used, the exceptional magnitude of the needs (due to a combination of the shortages arising out of the past and the demand for skilled manpower resulting from ambitious development objectives) made it worth-while to use techniques that would at least determine trends. However, now that the economy is becoming more complex, and with the "historic shortage" soon to be eliminated, it is worth questioning forecasting methods which result in the over-estimation of training needs. Shortcomings in forecasting indeed arise from the fact that the relationship between the educational system and the economy is much less simple than it was thought to be:

"There is a relationship between occupational and educational patterns and levels of economic development, but the limits of reliability are not narrow enough for using the parameters of regression equations for the purpose of forecasting manpower needs, especially in the case of detailed forecasts for specific occupational categories or for educational profiles by occupations. There is indeed justification for thinking that it is the unexplained statistical residue that is the most important factor for the planners, for it is the very absence of a fixed correlation between these three fields (economy, occupation, education) that offers possibilities of substitution, i.e of combining occupations or types of training that are more effective than others, and which are the very ones that should be identified and put into operation. Where several combinations are possible, the essential problem lies in deciding on the best strategy, and in considering not only

---

[1] This is also true within each of the two systems: thus the university recognises only three of the technical leaving certificates awarded by the Ministry of Primary and Secondary Education.

[2] See Michel Debeauvais: "Faut-il réviser la stratégie de la planification intégrée de l'éducation et de l'emploi?", document submitted to the UNESCO International Commission on the Development of Education, 1971.

problems of vocational training for young people, but also the further training of workers already in employment and the most efficient possible utilisation of available human resources. From this point of view, present methods of forecasting manpower needs are questionable not only in so far as they systematically over-estimate the need for graduates, but also because, by stressing the purely quantitative aspects of what are supposed to be the predetermined "needs of the economy", they could make us lose sight of the essential problems of human resources planning".[1]

The approach of compulsory schooling for all, the large number of unemployed among pupils leaving school at the level of the junior secondary course and the tremendous increase of university graduates in the next few years should lead the planners to use more refined techniques of human resources planning in order to reduce existing or future tensions on the employment market.

First of all, there must be an improved basis for planning, in particular a statistical survey of employment, using an appropriate classification from which to obtain a thorough knowledge of the correlation between three data fundamental to all programming activities: the real level of skill, the specialisation and the functions performed.

Besides, the analysis of long-term needs which has been started, using inter-national comparison methods,[2] must be improved by means of direct interviews in the various economic sectors. Studies of this kind, although insufficient, help to draw the attention of the authorities concerned with shortages of high-level personnel to the fact that the long-term development of the educational system cannot be con-sidered only from the standpoint of the present labour market, in which important qualitative changes are taking place. Forecasts attempted for 1990[3] give some initial indications concerning the desirable reorientation of the education system. These indications should be the subject of further studies.

Thus, there should be a reorientation of the student flows along the following lines:

- rapid expansion of technical training (both agricultural and industrial);

- moderate expansion of para-medical training;

- stabilisation of the numbers trained in human sciences, except for arts and law, where a reduction in the numbers of graduates should be planned.

A rapid expansion of middle-level technical and vocational training seems necessary for teaching occupations, and the economic, administrative and technical specialisa-tions. For the skilled personnel, considerable expansion will be required for all kinds of skills. Where limited skills or none at all are needed, demand will depend on the results of the measures aimed at reversing, in 1980, the upward trend of unemployment.

It seems indeed likely that employment tensions will be reduced during the Second Four-year Plan (1974-1977). All young persons entering the urban labour market are expected to find work, and urban unemployment is to be reduced (by about 90,000). On the other hand, improvements in rural areas are to result in an increase both in the number of permanent jobs and in the number of man-days worked.

---

[1] See M. Debeauvais, op. cit.

[2] See: "Assessment of skilled manpower requirements and outflow from the educa-tional system during the period 1970-80", July 1972. See also: "Estimates of skilled manpower needs for the period 1974-1977-80 and preliminary indications as to the balance between 'needs' and 'outflow' from the educational system", April 1973.

[3] See: "Développement éducatif", by J. Timar, A. Rovesz and O. Bertrand, UNESCO, June 1973.

Subsequent plans will represent the beginning of a new phase, in which the economy, having completed the preliminary stages in the process of self-sustained development and established the necessary conditions for rapid expansion, will be able to grow at a faster rate and create almost enough jobs to equal the supply of manpower. By bringing the development strategy up to date (present plans do not go beyond 1980), a more subtle approach can be made to employment policy by taking better into account the educational levels of the labour force. Systematic projections should be made of the "supply of graduates" expected to enter the labour market. These "should show variants according to different assumptions concerning the expansion of educational systems, school outputs, occupational mobility, changes in female participation rates, replacement rates by occupation and so on. These supply forecasts are essential to supplement the projections of skilled manpower needs, to which too much importance has been attached so far to the exclusion of other elements. Supply forecasts are less uncertain than projections of the demand for graduates, adjustment mechanisms (or distortions) obtaining on the labour market, the role played by the wage structure, and generally speaking all the problems of more efficient use of manpower".[1]

The relationship "training-employment" should be systematised by means of training agreements to be concluded between industries and training establishments. Additional solutions to the problem of inadequate distribution of skilled manpower are also to be found through the formulation of a national wage policy, the organisation of the civilian and national services and the reduction of the brain drain.

(b) Formulation of a wage policy

The preparation of a national wage scale, which would put an end to earnings disparities between the public, semi-public and private sectors, should make it possible to avoid discrepancies between the posts assigned to high-level personnel and their special qualifications. The social aims of the proposed wage policy are to "give concrete form to the principle of equal pay for equal work, and to promote in general the employment, training, further training and advancement of the workers".[2]

A further aim is to "ensure that priority sectors such as education, health services and public production sectors receive favourable treatment in the allocation of skilled personnel", and to "increase productivity by linking part of the workers' earnings to production".[3]

(c) Organisation of a civilian service

The authorities should also concern themselves with organising the placement of graduates.

The Order No. 71-78 of 3 December 1971, concerning scholarships, pre-employment grants and trainee salaries, specified in article 7 that all pupils and students who have completed a higher education course should undertake 5 years of civilian service in organisations to which they are assigned by the authorities. Another Order of December 1972 made provision for the civilian service scheme to come into force on 1 December 1972. However, the administrative details of the scheme and the practical arrangements for its implementation have still to be worked out, and the new institution has not yet been set up.

The civilian service is compulsory and those taking part in it will have to serve the State, local communities, public establishments/organisations or any other production or service structure. The coming into operation of the scheme should make it possible to utilise highly-trained personnel for eliminating the manpower bottlenecks encountered in carrying out the Four-year Plan.

---

[1] See M. Debeauvais, op. cit.

[2] Interview with the Minister of Labour and Social Affairs in El Moudjahid , 30 April 1974.

[3] Ibid.

(d) Development of the National Service

A more integrated planning of education and employment must allow for the fact that middle- and high-level graduates have to complete two years of National Service before they can enter the labour market.

The establishment of a National Service in 1969 aimed at giving an opportunity to every citizen "whatever his intellectual or occupational level or his social status, or even his physical condition, to share in the work of building a socialist State by serving his country for 24 months, either in the army or in civilian sectors of activity".[1]

The National Service now takes in thousands of young persons. After a preliminary period of enrolment and training, those called up devote their energies, according to their qualifications and to local needs, to rural development schemes (e.g. reafforestation, soil regeneration, etc.) or social services (e.g. teaching, health campaigns, housing, etc.).   Thus, the underprivileged wilayates of the Aurès and Titteri have been helped by thousands of young persons taking part in various development schemes. Similarly, over a thousand national servicemen are helping to build the trans-Saharan highway through which the Sahara regions will be more closely linked with the rest of Algeria, and trade with the countries south of the Sahara can be fostered.

The National Service also gives a great deal to those taking part in it, since it provides them "effectively with national values and gives young people an opportunity to benefit from the latest developments in science and technology" (speech by the Chairman of the Revolutionary Council, 19 June 1970). Politically speaking, this permanent institution is "a melting pot in which our young people are brought together from all over the country, which helps to reinforce the unity of our nation" (idem).

The National Service could be used for a more intensive utilisation of the Algerian human potential, since it combines the essential conditions for mass training at relatively little expense: a considerable material infrastructure, a good number of trainable recruits and adequate cadres from its own ranks (graduate servicemen). In spite of these advantages, it has been decided that the National Service should be directed towards participation in production, with vocational training agreed upon only for one sector (the hotel industry) and in only one training centre.

(e) Reduction of the brain drain

To conclude this review of the education-employment adjustment problem, it is worth mentioning briefly the problems of the "brain drain".

The emigration of professional and technical workers, doctors and the like to the developed countries, a familiar phenomenon in developing countries, ought to receive special attention in Algeria because it may assume greater proportions if suitable solutions are not found to eliminate the causes of the "brain drain" or attenuate their effects.

The basic cause of this phenomenon lies not only in differences in the earnings of high-level workers in their country and the countries to which they emigrate, but also in inadequate research facilities and living conditions in the country of origin. This calls for special incentives. A policy of concrete sharing in the tasks of over-all development can help to keep the "brain drain" down to a minimum. At the same time, the practice of going abroad for training should be stopped, except for a high level of research.

At the end of our analysis, it has become apparent that socialist options have not yet been completely applied to the organisation and workings of the educational system. Some of the maladjustments of the educational system with respect to the over-all guidelines by which it is governed will be eliminated in the next few years. However, greater progress has still to be made in adapting the system to the political, economic and social set-up.

---

[1] Interview with the High Commissioner for the National Service.

III. <u>R E P O R T A N D</u>
      <u>P L A N O F A C T I O N</u>

(Beirut Seminar, 12-24 May, 1975)

REPORT OF THE

SEMINAR ON MANPOWER AND EMPLOYMENT PLANNING

IN THE ARAB COUNTRIES

(BEIRUT, 12-24 MAY 1975)

CHAPTER I

General Review of the Employment and Manpower Situation in the
Arab World

Discussions under this heading were based on five documents reviewing the employment
and manpower situation in Iraq and Syria, Lebanon, the oil-producing countries (Kuwait,
Saudi Arabia and Libya), Algeria and Egypt. A document on employment situation in the
least developed countries in the region (Oman and the two Yemens) was submitted but not
discussed.

A. Manpower and Employment Planning in Iraq and Syria

The background paper on "Manpower and Employment Planning in Iraq and Syria"
pointed to the great improvements made in recent years in the collection of manpower and
employment statistics both quantitatively and qualitatively in the two countries reviewed.
However, it stressed the need for further efforts in that direction, such as better coverage
of manpower and employment statistics in the private sector; systematic and periodic
surveys, population censuses, etc.

The labour force in both countries was growing at an unprecedented rate due, among
other things, to the increase in the size of the population reaching working-age and the
increase in female participation rates. Yet shortages of critical skills, such as high-
level manpower, craftsmen, skilled operators, foremen, technicians, instructors and teachers
were still major bottlenecks.

The public sector had become the major employer in these countries, accounting for
slightly less than a third of total employment. Better planning of manpower utilisation
within the public sector as well as between the public and private sectors was required.

The background document proposed specific recommendations for strengthening the
organisations responsible for employment and manpower planning and stressed the importance
of systematically relating such efforts to the requirements and targets of national development plans in the two countries. In that context, active popular participation in formulating manpower and employment targets was considered a must.

Finally, the document indicated that so far neither Iraq nor Syria have had a
comprehensive employment survey, and consequently both countries were unable to formulate a
comprehensive employment strategy; which explained some of the inconsistencies and conflicts
underlying existing policies.

During the discussion, however, it was indicated that preparations for comprehensive
manpower and employment planning in both Iraq and Syria were already underway and that the
basic studies are being completed; yet, this long-term approach to manpower problems could
not meet the immediate needs of the two countries. For example, the paucity of construction
workers in both Iraq and Syria, which is causing delays in the implementation of vital
development projects, has led the competent authorities to adopt short-term measures of a
restrictive nature in order to minimise, at least partially, the acuteness of such shortages.
These measures include setting obstacles to the movement of the labour force from the public
to the private sector; and discouraging the emigration of critical skills.

It was stressed that planning employment and manpower is not limited to the projection of supply and demand; and that it should include the determination of the level of
employment to be reached and of its impact on productivity, income distribution, and on the
optimal utilisation of scarce human resources. Planning employment and manpower require-

ments must be viewed within the context of an over-all socio-economic development strategy. In the formulation of such plans a dialogue between technocrats and decision-makers (politicians) has to take place.

B. The Working of the Labour Market in Lebanon

The second paper entitled "The Working of the Labour Market in Lebanon" dealt with the workings of the labour market and the necessity of devising measures to improve its functioning. It was indicated in this respect that a low percentage of the population is participating in the labour force. It was also shown that although unemployment has reached eight per cent, it varied with age groups, occupations, education levels, geographic region, etc. The status of different occupations varied considerably and employment stability and level of earnings were important factors in this regard. Labour working in the agricultural sector is paid lower wages than in the construction and manufacturing industries. At the top of the earnings hierarchy come those working for the tertiary sector and in particular banks. Generally, imbalances in the employment situation point to the advisability for the Lebanese authorities to adopt a well-defined employment policy.

Formulating such a policy, however, would not be possible if the information system on the labour market, which is seriously deficient now, is not improved. It was suggested that the establishment of employment offices would improve the exchange of information between employees and employers. In Lebanon, the Ministry of Labour and Social Affairs with the help of ILO has created four employment offices. These offices will provide statistical information on labour and employment, the occupational distribution of workers and other issues pertaining to the labour market. The Lebanese authorities are thinking of expanding the information coverage of these offices to include information on employment opportunities in other countries of the region, and in the rest of the world. It was suggested in this respect that it would be more efficient to classify people not only by their degrees but also by the number of years spent in school, vocational centers or universities, in view of the existing differences in the educational systems and degrees awarded in the region.

It was indicated that basically the labour market in Lebanon is free and that people are, therefore, free to choose their occupations. This causes difficulties in planning the manpower needed for the future development of the country. This contrasts with the situation in certain centrally planned economies where individual preferences have sometimes to be subordinated to the country's needs in the interest of achieving economic and social objectives. In Syria, for example, it was stated that in some professions (medicine, engineering) graduates are required to do their military service and to work for some time for the Government before they obtain their diplomas and the freedom to choose their employment within or outside the country. Yet, it was pointed out that there is not necessarily an incompatibility between planning and full freedom of choice of employment. For example, in Tunisia, which has a planned economy and where 120 employment bureaux are operating, workers are free to turn down or accept offers of employment. It was also argued that the existence of a free labour market does not necessarily mean that all people have equal opportunities.

It was agreed that the establishment of employment bureaux alone does not solve all problems of employment. Employment bureaux can contribute to a better understanding of the labour market but are by no means sufficient.

It was also emphasised that wages are not the only factors determining the supply and demand of labour. Prestige, fringe benefits and other factors play an important role in determining the distribution of labour between different sectors and occupations.

It was also suggested that employment problems in Lebanon would be partly solved by improvements in the training system. The whole region would also benefit since Lebanon exports labour to other Arab countries.

With regard to the market mechanism, it was indicated that while wages do adjust to labour shortage and surplus conditions, this works slowly and ultimately loses its impact in an inflationary environment. It was agreed that labour market policies alone cannot cope with structural imbalances in employment and that over-all development policies are needed to correct them.

C. Employment and Manpower Problems and Policies in Kuwait, Saudi Arabia and Libya

A background paper titled "Employment and Manpower Problems and Policies in Kuwait, Saudi Arabia and Libya", was presented to the Seminar. The document reviewed problems related to: (a) socio-economic structure; (b) work attitudes; (c) education and training; and, (d) administrative structure in the countries in question.

In all three countries a majority of the labour force is composed of expatriates. This situation brings with it socio-economic problems that are peculiar to these countries. In terms of attitudes towards work, the document argued that as a result of assured income (from oil) the national section of the labour force tends to select the most prestigious jobs while rejecting the unpleasant ones, and this tends to increase the countries' dependence on expatriate labour.

Although the three countries reviewed have made commendable progress in organising and expanding educational and training facilities, the traditional socio-economic structure and the attitudes and aspirations of individuals are still major impediments towards an optimal utilisation of such facilities. Individual preferences are still for the fine arts and only small numbers are being trained in engineering, economics and physical sciences.

The concept of planning socio-economic development is new in all three countries; which explains the absence of comprehensive employment and manpower planning. There is a need to shift the emphasis from the assessment of labour supply and demand to an analysis of specific problems in the field of employment and manpower.

Finally the document concurred with the preceeding document on Iraq and Syria, in stressing the need to view employment and manpower planning within the context of the overall socio-economic development strategy of each country; the prerequisite for such an approach is the availability of adequate and comprehensive statistical information on the manpower and employment situation.

It was stressed in the meeting that due to the recent involvement of the Kuwaiti and Saudi Arabian authorities in development planning, the past practice of limiting employment planning to the assessment of supply and demand was inevitable. However, the recent tendency in these two countries is to expand this approach to planning the formation of human capital.

The need to study the economics of existing training facilities in the three countries reviewed was underlined. The type of training facilities offered should be reviewed in the light of an assessment of the types of jobs for which such training facilities are needed. Some doubts were raised, in this context, as to the desirability of training nationals to replace expatriate workers in all types of work, and especially in manual work and jobs that require limited skills.

It was suggested that the feasibility of joint training ventures at the regional level should be studied as a substitute to training at the national level, especially when such training facilities are geared to the training of highly skilled categories of manpower.

Given the fact that the three countries reviewed are, and will remain in the foreseeable future, net importers of labour, it was suggested that investments in education and training facilities should, as far as possible, also be made in sending countries in order to increase the supply of qualified manpower.

Training facilities in immigration countries should, it was suggested, be extended to benefit expatriate labour, whenever this is feasible and beneficial to the host country.

The meeting was warned against concentrating only on the export/import aspect of the labour problem and attention was called to the necessity of improving the labour-absorptive capacity of countries considered to be traditional exporters of labour force. A regional approach to employment and manpower planning was considered a necessity in the absence of which planning at the national level will remain deficient in many respects.

D. Employment and Planned Development of the Algerian Economy

The paper on "Employment and Planned Development of the Algerian Economy", focussed on the need to orient the educational policy in the light of the manpower and employment situation, and to assess the impact of investment, industrialisation and technology on employment in both rural and urban areas. After Independence, Algeria had inherited a weak economy. Its objective was, therefore, to develop an independent, integrated and healthy economy. However, it faced an acute shortage of qualified manpower. To solve this problem, Algeria reformed its educational system encouraging technical and vocational training. Some 35 per cent of secondary students were oriented to technical education. Higher education was also reformed and freed from its academic character, and field and applied work was introduced. A general educational organ was established aiming at improving the human potentialities and regulating the stages of education.

The investment policy in the current Plan was also tuned to meet employment objectives, through establishing a large number of medium and small industries (in addition to some huge projects) that use appropriate technology, i.e., neither obsolete nor of the most up-to-date and labour-saving type. This will create more employment opportunities whereas the huge projects are usually complex and highly capital-intensive.

With a rapid population increase, it is expected that the number of those entering the labour market will increase rapidly in 1980. But employment plans estimate that between 1980-1985 Algeria will be able to greatly reduce unemployment and limit emigration. All the youth entering the urban labour market will find jobs and urban unemployment will be partly absorbed. Moreover, in the rural areas the agricultural projects carried by the State (irrigation, increase in farms and livestock) plus the increase in the number of farmers joining co-operatives will increase employment opportunities and the number of working-days per year. Specialisation and increasing employment opportunities in rural and urban areas are expected to limit rural-urban migration. In the next phase when the economy is on the threshold of an autonomous development and rapid expansion, job creation is expected to absorb all the manpower available.

Discussion of the paper centred on the incentives provided to encourage technical education, in the form of scholarships provided for students at technical institutions, and public information campaigns on radio, TV, in the newspapers and through lectures. As a result, the prestige of academic diplomas was partly eliminated. In addition, the government is trying at present to draw up a policy to provide equal remuneration for equivalent qualifications. The results obtained from training were very encouraging in most cases.

Concerning the return of emigrants to Algeria (specially from France), the limited labour-absorptive capacity of the country led the competent authorities for the present to encourage only the return of those endowed with needed skills. However, the eventual return of most of those desirous to come back to Algeria is desired in the long-run.

E. Employment Problems and Policies in Egypt

This paper dealt mainly with the problem of unemployment and under-employment in the Egyptian economy and the economic policy applied in this context, with special emphasis on employment problems in the agricultural sector.

The paper discussed some of the main characteristics of the labour force in Egypt. The share of the labour force to total population is undergoing a continuous decline due to changing age structure, low female participation rate and rural-urban migration. In general, the labour force has a low level of education and technical skills. Though non-wage employment is declining it is still prevailing.

The industrial sector has a low absorptive capacity. Its share in total employment has been declining as a result of the pattern of industrialisation and of measures of economic policy which lead to the use of more capital-intensive technology. On the other hand, there was an increase in the share of services which are dominated by low productivity occupations.

As revealed in the paper, open unemployment is heavily concentrated in urban areas, especially Cairo and Alexandria and there is considerable rural-urban migration. A study of factors accounting for such migration suggests that the only significant explanatory variable is the degree of unemployment in the area of emigration.

Underemployment in agriculture was defined in the document as the difference between the amount of work actually performed and the amount of work a person is able and willing to supply. Hence, it differs from the concept of disguised unemployment. The author analysed the labour supply distinguishing between adult men on one hand and women and children on the other. He found that underemployment is prevalent among men, where it is both seasonal and permanent, contrasting with an acute shortage of women and children particularly at certain times of the year. The employment situation is affected by the growth of the agricultural labour force and by the preponderance of small farms in the farm structure.

High seasonal peaks of agricultural activity require the maintenance on the farm of a reserve of family labour to meet such seasonal demands. Also, surplus labour in small farms can coincide with shortages on medium and large farms, because the surplus is not necessarily available for work outside the family farm. This is particularly true of women. Moreover, substitution between men and women is difficult because the distribution of agricultural tasks is based on sex.

Calculating the future demand and supply of labour, it was found that if the rate of growth of National Income can be maintained at six per cent and that of industrial income at 8.5 per cent (rates already achieved in the first five year plan and therefore seemingly feasible),the demand for labour will fall short of supply until 1985 when it will catch up with supply but will still not be able to absorb either under-employment in agriculture or the stock of unemployed from the previous period.   Assuming a 7.2 per cent rate of growth of National Income and a 14 per cent rate of growth of industrial income between 1975 and 1980, and a 10 per cent rate of growth of industrial income from 1980 to 1985, the supply is insufficient to meet the demand which must rely on withdrawing labour from agriculture.   To achieve this result, the ratio of investment to National Income should jump to 25 per cent, a target difficult to implement.

It was mentioned during the discussion that the 1960-1975 development strategy in Egypt had aimed mainly at maximising economic growth (at an annual rate of about seven per cent), and that employment growth and the balance of payments position had been subordinated to that target.   However, as from 1976, the priorities would be reversed with full employment as a major objective, to be accompanied by a reasonable GNP growth rate (of say five to six per cent).

It was also argued that the priority given by the Egyptian government to tackling open urban unemployment was correct, including the policy of absorbing university graduates in the public sector, although undue employment resulting from such a policy would need to be dealt with through ensuring a better allocation and utilisation of those graduates.

The study of underemployment in the services sector is a difficult task given the absence of criteria by which to measure labour force requirements for services.   In this context social norms, habits and motivations are major influences determining the number of persons assigned to specific services and the types of services in demand.

It was suggested that the employment problem could be relieved with co-operation and an over-all development strategy covering both Arab countries rich with financial resources and those rich with labour resources.

F.   Least Developed Countries

The paper on the least developed countries in the ECWA region, namely the Yemen Arab Republic, the Democratic Republic of Yemen and the Sultanate of Oman shows that they face many common obstacles and bottlenecks in their development process.   They suffer from a deficiency in statistical data essential for planning and development policies;   an overwhelming part of their population are illiterate or with only preliminary education which is reflected in a severe shortage of skilled and qualified personnel;   and they lack a modern and efficient administrative structure.

Almost 50 per cent of the population in the three countries is beyond 15 years of age.   Accordingly the dependency ratio is very high.   The manpower constitutes 51 per cent of the population of Democratic Republic of Yemen, 59 per cent of the population of the Yemen Arab Republic and around 62 per cent of the population of Oman.   The labour force, however, constitutes only about 25 per cent and 29 per cent of the total population of the two Yemens respectively, while it is about 35 per cent of the total population in Oman since it imports foreign labour.   This reveals the relatively high percentage of those in the working age but outside the labour force.   On the other hand, the majority of the labour force works in the agriculture and fishing sectorswhere there is a high rate of disguised unemployment.   The Yemen Arab Republic suffered in recent years from large emigration of labour toward the rich Arab countries, particularly Saudi Arabia.

To overcome these obstacles ,the three countries are planning to increase the level of education rapidly and eliminate illiteracy.   By improving the skills of their human resources they can expand the absorptive capacity of their economy.   For this purpose, a large number of schools and vocational training centres will be established.   They are also planning to increase the real national income and real per capita income, create more employment opportunities, and modernise the administrative structure.

External aid extended to these countries to develop their educational system was mainly used for the construction of new schools and did not include the provision of trainers or teachers, thus resulting in a wastage of resources.

Finally, the paper suggested that the three countries should co-operate in establishing training and rehabilitation centres to diminish costs and expand training facilities, send more students to study abroad, undertake surveys to provide the necessary statistical information, give financial incentives to attract the qualified people and to prevent the emigration of skills and improve housing facilities and other services.

CHAPTER II

Population, Employment and Economic Development

A background paper entitled "Population, Employment and Development in Arab Countries" was presented to the Seminar. The paper reviewed the general demographic situation in the Region at present and in the future and tried to assess the implications of population growth on the economies of the Arab countries (use of natural resources, income, savings, investment, employment, etc.). The paper stressed that one characteristic of under-development in Arab countries is the low rate of economic activity and this is due to, _inter alia_, low female activity and a young age structure of the population. Although no univer-sal development policy can be applied to all Arab countries, accelerated industrialisation, increasing activity rates particularly for women, facilitating inter-regional migration, reducing mortality rates, regulating fertility in accordance with national purposes and values, and stressing education and training constitute policy issues that should be taken into consideration.

It was indicated that labour force participation rates were low in most Arab countries, although they may not be as low as they appear if statistical reporting and data collection were better. In this connection one is confronted with the problem of assessing partici-pation of certain groups of population in economic life. For example, women and children in agriculture are not fully taken into account. The same stand for the handicraft sector and for small establishments.

It was indicated by some participants that population growth may be desirable for the purpose of development, because it can supply the manpower needed and contribute to a higher economic activity. However, while this may be the case in countries with rich natural res-ources and low population density, it cannot certainly work in countries with high population density.

In this connection it was pointed out that family planning programmes may have differ-ent purposes in different countries. On the one hand, they can be used for encouraging population growth (Libya, Saudi Arabia, Qatar and the United Arab Emirates), while on the other hand it can be used to regulate population growth (Egypt and Tunisia). In any case, family planning does not necessarily mean birth control, because parents have the right to decide on the size of their families.

Looking at the age structure of the Arab population, participation rates of children and youth will be decreased because of advance in education, while in the working age group (20-64) Arab males are as active as those in the rest of the world. The only group that Arab countries can manœuvre with if they wish to increase participation in development is women, since their activity rates are low. Cultural values as well as attitudes of males towards working women, ignorance and illiteracy among them, lack of employment opportunities, and lack of social services for working women have inhibited them from entering into the labour market. In fact, women's employment affects to some extent population growth. Several studies have shown that there is an inverse relationship between female participation rates and fertility. However, this is true only when women work outside the home.

Various problems relating to population mobility were mentioned. First, there is the rural-urban migration which has led to overpopulation in Arab cities and to creation of soc-ial and economic problems beyond the absorptive capacity of these cities and in some cases has also affected the rural areas adversely. Second, there is the intra-regional (inter-country) migration which is contributing to re-dressing the balance of population distribu-tion in the region. This kind of migration was deemed desirable and should be promoted. Third, there is the external migration to countries outside the region. Several countries were not in favour of this kind of migration, in particular when it takes the form of a brain-drain phenomenon, which has been manifested in a loss in terms of capital investment as well as skilled manpower both of which are needed for development. The wish was expres-sed that Arab countries should co-operate to counter-act the effects of this type of migra-tion. Finally, another undesirable form of migration is the forced migration resulting from military aggression and illegal occupation of Arab territories. This forced migration causes unemployment and a great deal of human suffering. It was proposed that the Seminar condems the aggression which leads to this type of migration.

It was also emphasised that the process of development is not only linked to manpower availability and population growth, but also to many economic variables. To effect develop-ment, there is a need for investment and consequently for the securing of the capital needed.

It is through development that employment opportunities are created and participation rates are improved. Thus underemployment and unemployment can be absorbed.

The Seminar emphasised the role of education and training in influencing the economic and social development of the Arab countries. This can be manifested in several ways.

It was indicated, for example, that education and training improve the quality of the population in the short-run (skilled manpower) and influence population growth in the long-run. It can increase the productivity of the labour force, including that·of women in rural areas. The feeling was expressed that educational systems in the Arab countries need revision so that they can meet the requirements of development. Education should be linked to manpower planning. In this respect it was further emphasised that illiteracy eradication in Arab countries is one of the major factors contributing to development and to the improvement of the quality of life.

Development planning has gained roots in all Arab countries. It was indicated that employment should be one of the aims of development plans. In this connection, it was stressed that there is a strong inter-relationship between the various factors influencing development, including population, manpower, education and employment. This inter-relationship should be deeply studied and taken into account in short-term and long-term planning.

The suggestion was made to recommend the creation of a permanent inter-agency team of qualified experts in the fields of economics, demography, manpower and education to study and recommend ways and means of dealing with the questions of population, employment and economic development, and thatECWA in collaboration with ILO should initiate this team.

CHAPTER III

Employment and Technology

A background paper entitled "Employment, Choice of Technology, Sectoral Priorities" was presented. The paper recalls that the employment problem in Arab countries manifests itself not merely as open unemployment but also in many forms of underemployment. It is a part of an over-all development problem which itself is an immediate result of several economic, social and political factors. Imbalances in the economic structure, in particular, constitute one of the principal factors affecting the development of employment.

Actual policies in most Arab countries have favoured industrialisation that has received long-term priority as reflected in development plans, and has been viewed as a means ultimately to develop both incomes and employment. However, industrial development in practice does not seem to have led to very high employment gains or to noticeable changes in the employment structure. In oil economies, the primary sector is the leading sector in terms of income growth, but the tertiary sector shows the greatest employment expansion. In other countries, the share of the tertiary sector is also increasing, both in economies having reached the secondary stage of development and in those which are still at a very early stage. This development of tertiary employment is taking place despite the fact that the tertiary sector does not receive high priority in development plans.

The paper also deals with the question of the choice of technology which is dictated, to a certain extent, by the sectoral priorities of each country and by other technical, economic and socio-political factors. Besides sectoral planning and choice of techniques, manipulation of final demand should be considered as a means of creating more employment. Although choices of technology and reshuffling of sectoral priorities may help, the main thrust on the employment front may only be effected within an integrated development approach which balances various sets of objectives. The paper recalls, moreover, that technology can be defined as a "cultural world which involves knowledge, habits of mind, modes of organisation and social behaviour, education and research".

It was indicated that there was a strong relationship between development, employment and the application of technology. However, imbalances in the economic structure complicate the issue. In this context, reconciling development objectives with employment objectives is a major concern to most countries. To solve the unemployment problem, some governments are resorting to the absorption of manpower into public administration, a phenomenon that may create more problems in the long-run. What is needed, it was pointed out, is a definition of priorities and a transformation of the structure of the economy.

It was pointed out that economic, political, social and cultural factors are involved with respect to choice of technology. In some countries, the abundance of primary resources coupled with a shortage of manpower makes the choice of sophisticated labour-saving technology both feasible and necessary. In any case, flexibility in the choice of technology is often limited. Thus, investment in heavy industry, a first priority in many countries, requires the use of advanced technology. In other sectors, the situation is different and there is more scope for adopting appropriate labour-intensive techniques. One constraint, however, is that available technologies developed in industrialised countries are usually of a labour-saving nature, and consultants and engineers trained abroad tend to recommend them in preference to labour-intensive ones where these exist. Moreover, many technical factors need to be considered in choosing between labour-intensive and capital-intensive techniques, such as respective requirements for inputs in relation to output, for investment in fixed capital and for skilled manpower, and the types and quality of goods (e.g. nutritional value of food products) actually required for different markets and the techniques best suited to produce them.

Other factors include political goals and systems, which play an important role in influencing the choice of sectoral priorities and technology, and the prestige often attached to advanced technology. On the other hand, the absence of a technological tradition in Arab countries may deter its adoption. Problems of assimilation and co-ordination of technology are faced by many countries, which also consider the effects of its introduction on existing industries. Sometimes, the adoption of technology leads to the creation of "enclaves" or islands of modernity in an ocean of backwardness. In order to avoid this, attention must be given to developing linkages and complementarities with the rest of the economy and furthering an industrial milieu in which the effects of modern technology may become diffused.

Generalisations about the choice of technology should be avoided. Decisions need to be taken on a project-by-project basis, and individual projects, themselves, can be sub-divided into processes and operations some of which may lend themselves to labour-intensive techniques and others not. Moreover, attention should not centre only on importing new technology, but also on improving existing local technology. Generally speaking, it was emphasised that Arab countries need to develop a technology that meets their needs and fits into their situation. Imported technology, including that provided under aid programmes, leads the Arab economies to dependence on foreign ones and limits their freedom of movement. In addition, it is highly expensive and raises problems of keeping up with the continuous line of new inventions, including the problems of maintenance and re-training. However, in the short-run, technology will continue to be imported but this should be done within a well planned developmental framework. In particular, countries should expand their training facilities at all levels in order to cope with the introduction of technology and avoid any imbalances which might result.

It was also indicated that history reveals that leading industries are not necessarily heavy industries. The history of technological evolution elsewhere also shows that time is an important factor, and that technology must become an element of culture. The provision of an environment likely to lead to the creation of a technically-minded generation requires an educational system, culture and social attitudes conducive to this objective.

To solve problems of choice of technology as well as many other problems associated with the application of technology for development, it was maintained that regional co-operation is of utmost importance. It should strengthen the bargaining power of Arab countries and facilitate the development of appropriate technologies. It should further the creation of a new International Economic Order in co-operation with other developing countries. Research, planning and training on a regional basis were also stressed, as well as the need for adopting a common terminology and standards in regard to technology. In this context, it was suggested to put forth a resolution requesting Arab states through the Arab League to create a regional centre endowed with adequate resources, to undertake research for identifying, adapting and/or developing appropriate technology, with due regard to employment and development needs, and to disseminate informations about such questions in the Arabic language. Such a body should be established in consultation with the United Nations specialised agencies and in the light of the resolution 1636 (LI) of the Economic and Social Council as well as the resolution adopted by the Second General Conference of the United Nations Industrial Development Organisation (ID/CONF.3/RES.2) and taking into consideration the recommendations of the United Nations Advisory Committee on the Application of Science and Technology to Development of ACAST (ID/CONF.3/11).

It was also indicated that an important barrier to development in the Arab countries is the Israeli aggression which has prohibited a whole nation from contributing to technological and social progress in the Region and forced Arab states to allocate huge amounts of money for defence which could have been used for the creation of employment and appropriate technology.

CHAPTER IV

Employment and Trade

A document entitled "Trade Policy, Relative Prices and Employment" was submitted to the Seminar. The study is concerned with the impact of tariffs, quantitative restrictions, export taxes and subsidies, and of other commercial policy measures on employment objectives. It assessed the implications for employment of protection-induced distortions in the price relationships among particular categories of goods and among sectors, and concentrated on the characteristic bias of tariff structures of many developing countries against agriculture, the bias against exports, and the apparent tendency of systematic relative under-pricing of imported capital goods and industrial inputs to favour sophisticated labour-saving technologies.

These have been major themes in the literature on development economics of the past five to ten years. Most of the empirical work has been based on the experience in Latin America and South Asia. The lessons learned and the implicit policy prescriptions are perhaps completely irrelevant to those of the oil-producing Arab states whose development is at present constrained by neither a surplus of labour nor a shortage of finance. The degree to which they may be applicable in the other Arab countries is a matter for case-by-case study in the context of their particular problems.

All protective measures alter the relationships between domestic prices and international prices. The varying levels of these discrepancies for different kinds of goods can be expressed as ad valorem rates of so-called nominal protection. In analysing a trade-policy system, it is useful to look at the profile or array of the average rates for the various categories of goods.

However, apparent legal tariffs, taken by themselves, tend to give a very misleading picture of the real pattern of a country's protective structure; since these tariffs are frequently not collected at all because of fiscal exemptions given to encourage investments and for other reasons. Or they may be irrelevant or redundant, e.g. where the product is a characteristic export of the country and unlikely to be imported.

The "true" profile of protection may be different from the legal tariffs schedule. The apparent tariffs alone do not measure protection. In many developing countries there are high apparent tariffs on primary agricultural products, but these may be largely meaningless. In reality, agriculture enjoys little protection in developing countries and frequently the protection is negative. That is, the sector is penalised by holding the domestic prices received by farmers below the international prices. Since much higher real protection is given to industrial goods, including perhaps the inputs needed by farmers, this results in what is often called a bias of the protective system against agriculture. Yet, about 60 per cent of the active labour force of the Arab region as a whole is engaged in agriculture. Therefore, a strong tendency for the domestic terms of trade to be tilted against agriculture should perhaps be a matter of concern. This could be especially serious if this reinforces similar adverse relationship in the international terms of trade.

Turning to industrial goods, it had been brought out on several occasions at this meeting that the secondary sector tends to be a disappointing source of employment; however, important industrialisation may be needed for other reasons. Therefore, one should be on his guard against any possible perverse effects of well-intentioned policies that might reduce further the contribution of manufacturing industries to the absorption of excess labour. The highest levels of nominal and effective protection normally apply to finished durable and non-durable consumer goods. Assuming that the protection is non-redundant and in the absence of strict wage and price controls, one of the most important effects is to provide a monopoly shelter over payment of abnormally high money wage rates. This appears to contribute to "wage dualism", discouraging use of labour in the modern sector. The use of ultra-modern technology in the import-substitution consumer-goods sector is of relatively little interest to industrialisation strategy, but it can have vicious effects on the competing artisanal activities (and small-scale industry) that have traditionally absorbed much labour. Super-high protection on consumer goods frequently benefits mainly the multinational companies that own the trade-marks and licenses in finished consumer-goods industries. For this and other reasons, there may be effects on the distribution of income that could be indirectly adverse to employment objectives.

Considerable attention was devoted to the bias in favour of labour-saving technologies that is created by the general practice of assigning low duties to equipment imports, a

point already emphasised during discussions of the previous topic.   Even these are often
not collected because of the investment incentive laws that are common in Arab as well as in
Latin American countries.   Together with artificially low interest rates and other discriminatory advantages given to encourage foreign investors, this results in subsidisation of
the use of the capital factor of production, while use of the labour factor is simultaneously being penalised by wage dualism.

The relative under-protection of capital goods also discourages domestic production of
equipment.   It was shown that import-substitution in this sector may be particularly useful
from an employment standpoint.   Similar observations can be made with respect to the relative under-protection of inputs for industry.

An ironic side effect of extreme import-substitution policies is that they tend to
increase external dependence.   The protection system may make it more profitable to process foreign raw materials and intermediate inputs than to export domestic raw materials in
processed form.   Admittedly, this choice may raise complicated problems that are not sus-
ceptible of simple answers.

Reform of protection systems cannot be a panacea for the problems of absorbing excess
unskilled labour.   Moreover, reckless dismantlement of all protection was not advocated.
Yet it is always useful for all governments to examine all aspects of their policy for
possible undesired side-effects with a view to correcting these if due consideration indicates that this is feasible without sacrifice of the really important objectives.

There are both structural and market reasons for the bias of some modern technologies
against employment which sheds some skepticism as to generalisations about choice of technology.   The the extent that the bias comes from the market side, however, it is worthwhile
trying to reduce this bias by correcting systematic relative price distortions, to the extent
that these are within the province of governmental jurisdiction as is the case with commercial policies.

During the course of discussion following the presentation,it was pointed out that the
differentiation in the rate of tariffs for different imported goods results in a set of
differentiated prices within a country, which would lead to an industrial structure and a
division of labour different from what would have prevailed in the absence of such a set of
tariff rates.   Also, the manifold repercussions of bilateral agreements on the domestic
system of prices (product, factor and foreign exchange prices) make evaluation as to gains
from bilateral trade a difficult task.

In order to study the real rate of protection, international prices are used as bench-
marks.   It was pointed out, however, by a number of participants that these do not emanate
from an equitable, competitive, and efficient world market, and that the impact of international prices on the choice of the type of industrial development a country may adopt
depends on the weight given to such prices by the country in question.   On the one hand,
a country may adopt a development path oriented towards, and mainly based on, international
trade, thus allowing international prices to play a major role in the process of decision-
making;   while on the other hand, this country could adopt an internally-oriented development path based on its proper needs, where international trade has a residual role, thus
attaching low weight to international prices in the process of decision-making.

Import-substitution policy is a special kind of protective system, whose most important
disadvantage is that very frequently it destroys the only standard available for measuring
the gains from international trade, in the sense that it becomes impossible to assess the
real cost to be attached to decisions pertaining to specialisation.   When import-substitution policy ignores the pattern of international specialisation in terms of factor endowments,
it becomes misleading and soon enough runs out of dynamism.

Import-substitution policy does not eliminate dependence on imports but simply changes
the composition of such a dependence, with an aggravation of such a dependence when the
import-substituting industries are in turn dependent on imported inputs.

The move away from import-substitution policies, if decided, in favour of more liberal
policies is to be done gradually.   A combination of an import substitution system with
export promotion measures may increase the complexity of the situation and lead to unfavourable side-effects.

Although it was recognised in the meeting that import-substitution policies may have
little advantages for isolated, economically small, countries, it was stressed by a number
of participants that such policies, when seen in the context of the whole Arab world, could
have significant advantages, and could be considered as one of the major contributors to the

development of the region as a whole.   In this context, the product-mix and technique-mix on the basis of which the countries of the region industrialise should be selected in such a way as to lead to a more equitable income distribution.

With respect to oil-producing countries, where most of the imports are financed by oil revenues, revenues which are expected to wither away, the attempts to build up a productive diversified economy should be geared in such a way as to avoid balance of payment problems and their repercussion on these economies in the post-oil era.

Thus intra-Arab trade should be expanded in order to enhance the viability of invest-ment projects in the region by widening their markets.   Regional economic co-operation and integration (or at least some sort of a customs union) would enhance the ability of the region as a whole to absorb its labour force while accelerating the process of development.

The paucity of statistical information on the profile of tariffs and other protective measures was once more deplored in the meeting.   Improvement in the collection and analysis of such information was recommended.   Attempts to develop averages and to measure price changes attributed to protective policies should be encouraged and generalised.

Planning the foreign sector has in the post consisted mainly of calculating the resi-dual needs and surpluses of a country;   it was stressed in the meeting that the planning of the foreign sector should take place in the light of its impact on employment, and the choice of technology in the respective countries, and in the region as a whole.   Some balance should be adopted between the major objectives with special emphasis as to the trade-off between employment objectives and foreign trade targets.

The remaining salient points raised and discussed at the meeting are:

a) The trade relations between Israel and the occupied territories and their impact on employment were briefly reviewed in the meeting.   The trade balance between Israel and the occupied territories was found to effect a continuous increasing surplus in favour of the former.   Occupied territories are forced to import 90 per cent of their needs from Israel, which permits the latter to export 25 per cent of its total exports to the occupied territories.   The occupied territories are also suffering from a contrived deterioration of the terms of trade with Israel.

The Palestinian labour force working in Israel is paid half the wage received by non-Palestinian workers;   and in addition the Palestinian worker's pay is subject to income taxes and other cuts, without benefiting from any social or health insurance schemes.

b) With respect to Multilateral Trade Negotiations (MTN),some skepticism was voiced as to the product-by-product bargaining approach.   Some of the tariffs in some countries of the region may already be relatively too low.   Their decrease, if it occurs, should be in the context of national reform rather than through item by item bargaining.

c) The Generalised System ofPreferences (GSP) tends to exclude textiles and other labour-intensive products from the benefits offered while greater advantages are given to products which are not produced in significant quanti-ties by developing countries.

d) On the agricultural sector in the Arab world and the bias against it result-ing from protection of industry, the opinion was expressed that the non-protection of agriculture in the region reflects the particular characteristics of this sector.   Most agricultural products have no difficulty in finding outlets within the region (vegetables, etc.) and/or in the rest of the world (cotton).

e) It was also mentioned that the discussion on the effects of tariffs and other trade policies in distorting prices should be expanded to include similar effects resulting from aid and loans.   Food aid seems to have been responsible for low productivity in South Asia.   Such aid may well have had adverse side effects on incentives in the agricultural sector of some recipient countries.

CHAPTER V

Employment and Education

A paper entitled "Employment and Education in the Arab Countries : the Data and their Interpretation" served as a background for the introduction of the subject of education and employment. The paper is divided into two main sections. The first section surveys the recent international evolution of ideas and problems concerning employment and educational policies. The second section makes a critical analysis of some relevant statistical data for some Arab countries and attempts to indicate ways of better use of these statistical data.

Both the Report of the International Commission on Education (UNESCO) and the World Employment Programme (ILO) have stressed the shortcomings of policies, concepts and methods of human resources development and the necessity of an over-all revision. In particular, the relationship between employment and education cannot be satisfactorily studied through the method of forecasting qualified manpower needs using technical coefficients nor through the method of calculating the rate of return to education. In fact, these planning methods have not yielded satisfactory results. Serious imbalances have been developing in a great number of countries: the quantitative development of educational systems has increased the cost of education without being always accompanied with qualitative improvement, and shortages of qualified manpower still prevail, although some countries enjoy a surplus of graduates who have not been absorbed totally by the labour market. The results of the measures taken in the field of training and employment were not sufficient to remedy these problems; sometimes they had negative consequences in other fields. Nor did they yield the expected results in regard to the objectives of democratisation and equality of opportunities.

Several questions may be raised. Should one limit the development of education to the capacity of the labour market to absorb the output of different levels and different branches of the educational system? Is this technically possible? Is it politically acceptable? Should one respect people's desires for various kinds of training and, thus, accept a measure of autonomy of the educational system? Would this not imply the existence of looser ties, between diplomas and occupations? Are the objectives of the equality of opportunities entirely compatible with an efficient allocation of scarce resources? Do the priorities of plans correspond to the real distribution of resources (growth rate of different branches of education, structure of remuneration of qualifications and diplomas in the labour market)?

The second section of the paper relating to statistics aims at presenting some concrete examples of information which seem indispensable such as a) evaluation of the situation of each country and of the existing imbalances; b) defining the objectives of development ,taking into consideration education, employment and the economy; c) operationally defining the policy measures needed to achieve these objectives; and d) evaluation of the results obtained.

The introductory statement presented many practical methods for gathering a minimum of statistical data related to: levels of education of the workers, occupations and wages. It also suggested the establishment of a regional data bank which would permit the exchange of information and experiences among Arab countries.

In the course of the discussion, many disparities in the present educational system of Arab countries were pointed out. There has been a quantitative expansion in education at the expense of its quality. There are great differences between male and female enrolments. In many countries, a big gap between general and technical education exists and also between primary education and secondary and higher education. There are imbalances between urban and rural education ,both quantitatively and qualitatively. In fact, this is reflected in an unequal distribution of educational facilities at the regional level within each country and among Arab countries as well. Often there is also a gap between the implementation of educational plans and the targets specified in those plans.

It was also pointed out that present systems of education in Arab countries allow for much wastage. It is reflected in high repetition rates and a great number of drop-outs. This represents a waste in human resources as well as in investment ,thus inflating the cost of education.

It was emphasised that education, although it is a means for economic improvement and national development, is a basic human right. It should lead to the development of more open human beings. However, it was indicated that merely quantitative expansion of education, particularly at the primary level, has in fact led to greater rates of expansion at higher levels, stimulated rural-urban migration, and fed the economy with a great number of drop-outs, few of whom joined technical education, while many others were not productively employed. This expansion has not always promoted greater equality of opportunities. Moreover, expansion in free public education cannot go on endlessly, as it is limited by the availability of capital, facilities and qualified manpower. What is needed is a system of universal education which imparts at least basic essential skills such as functional literacy, hygiene and civic awareness. In essence, it was further stated, primary education should be supplemented by secondary or technical or any other kind of education and training which prepares young people for adult life.

Although one objective of education is to bring about social justice and a better distribution of incomes, it was indicated that existing systems of education in Arab countries are not producing such effects. Privileged classes are in fact reaping the benefits. This is reflected in a surplus of graduates from higher education, particularly in some fields (arts) which are not on high demand in the labour market. Consequently, problems such as expansion of employment in the public administration and emigration with its accompanied brain-drain effects arise. It was suggested, in this regard, that admission policies to higher education and wage incentives should be modified. Stipends and other forms of financial assistance for needy students should be considered. It was further indicated that there are political, social and economic factors involved with the development of education and that the possibility of reconciling these various objectives should be explored.

It was pointed out that many imbalances and disparities in the educational structure of Arab countries are due to a system which is inherited from colonial regimes whose main purpose was to meet the needs of their administration. The educational system has not yet fully adjusted to the requirements of contemporary life. There is a need for a broader concept of education which emphasises development of the analytical capacity of people and their preparation for productive employment. A new outlook to the content of education needs to be adopted. General and technical education should interact and a change in attitude with respect to manual work and other kinds of employment should be elicited.

Other non-academic forms of education should be sought. To illustrate, the industrial growth of Europe was not linked to formal education but to various forms of on-the-job training. Informal education, therefore, must be part of this broad concept. In this connection, the utilisation of mass media as well as various kinds of social groupings and centres is very important. Defined as a life-long learning activity, education is in fact a continuous process which utilises a variety of means and instruments.

Education, it was indicated, cannot be divorced from the whole socio-economic system. There are links and inter-relationships between education and other variables such as population, technology, trade, development and employment. Therefore, the question is not whether to adjust education to the needs of development or to adapt the economy to the educational system, but to achieve a balance among a number of objectives that need to be realised. This requires integrated planning and integrated policies which take into consideration the importance of comprehensive development, particularly the informal sector (agriculture and small enterprises). Within this framework, provision of basic social services, mobilisation of existing resources, and co-ordination at the national level were stressed. Emphasis was also given to regional co-operation as a means for absorbing surplus capital thus creating more employment, training needed manpower and checking the brain-drain.

The question of women's education and employment was highlighted. Active participation of women in development is desired and it is correlated with their level of education. However, opportunities for their employment are scarce, particularly in the absence of services which enable them to leave their home. In this regard, it was suggested that a regional bureau responsible for studying women's problems be established.

The problem of inadequacy and lack of statistics and information pertaining to employment and education was brought out. However, it was indicated, the main problem is to utilise available information and to improve it first. Moreover, re-organisation of data collection and presentation is needed. This should include information on characteristics and qualifications of the labour force, on the structure of the labour market, and on wages and incomes. It should also include follow-up studies on school leavers and graduates. Research on the attitudes and desires of young people should also be undertaken. In this connection, the establishment of a data bank which would facilitate the exchange of information and experiences among Arab countries was suggested. Furthermore, a seminar on improving and developing data collection, to be jointly sponsored by ECWA and ILO, was also proposed. Moreover, it was suggested that the Arab Labour Organisation should work in consultation with Arab governments on developing common standards related to classifications of occupations based on International Standard Classification of Occupations and adapted to the Arab environment.

To foster a more equitable social system and to redress the balance between education, employment and development, great emphasis was given to adult education and training which should be an integral part of education policy. It was indicated that this calls for considering a number of training activities including training of school drop-outs, on-the-job training, retraining, skill upgrading, accelerated training and provision of refresher courses. Consequently, it was suggested that recommendations should deal with the development of various forms of training programmes and training facilities at both the national and the regional levels. The establishment of an Arab fund to finance a regional institution which would be responsible for planning training activities in the Arab world was also suggested.

A great deal of wastage of resources is taking place as a result of the displacement of Palestinians. Therefore, it was suggested that Arab countries should support the education and training of Palestinians and give them the same employment privileges that nationals enjoy.

CHAPTER VI

Employment and Regional Co-operation

In the paper entitled "Employment and Regional Co-operation", the author indicated that regional co-operation in the field of employment will have to take into consideration the following three difficulties.   First, it seems questionable that such regional co-operation can take place regardless of the adequacy of regional co-operation in the fields of physical and capital resources.   The second constraint projects itself once regional co-operation in employment is viewed in terms of a set of institutions and instruments required to facilitate the movement of workers among Arab countries with the fullest maximisation of the social and economic benefits to all parties.   The third difficulty stems from the fact that the data required for such a study are either lacking, or if available they are not adequate or not adequately classified.   And, above all, to say the least, data if relevant are contradictory and suffer from both internal and external inconsistencies.   Very few statistical systems in Arab countries take the movement of workers inside or outside the country as one of their central concerns.

The author indicated in this respect that although in recent years some manpower importing countries have attempted an inventory of their foreign manpower, they do not always distinguish between Arabs and non-Arabs, and if they do, they do not show individual or even major individual nationalities.   In all cases, the statistics of the country of origin never coincide with the statistics of the country of destination.   While the data in exporting countries are current statistics, those of the importing countries are stock statistics, i.e. an accumulation of the manpower stock in the country over a number of years.   Thus the data presented in this paper is only an honest exercise.   The data were manipulated as appropriate in order to draw a broad picture of regional co-operation in the field of manpower in Arab countries.

This picture has revealed that the main manpower host countries, namely Libya, Kuwait and Saudi Arabia, receive the majority of their respective manpower each from 6-7 guest Arab countries.   These exporting Arab countries contribute no less than 70 per cent of total Arab or total expatriate manpower in the host countries.   The exporting countries contribute mostly professional and skilled manpower.   The skill mix varies from one exporting country to another and the nationality mix varies from one importing country to another.   This nationality mix varies mainly with distance as is the case with Lebanon and Syria and with Tunisia and Libya.   The nationality mix also varies ,especially in the ECWA region,according to easy access to road transportation, as is the case between Jordan, Syria and Saudi Arabia.

A generous guesstimate of all these inter-Arab workers movements,excluding accompanied families,perhaps may be given as only one to two million based partly on official data and partly on some guess work.   This does not take into account, however, the one-half million Syrians who are allegedly working in Lebanon rather informally.

In attempting to identify reasons for such movements, the document stressed that one should distinguish between the general economic, social and employment characteristics in the respective countries concerned on one side and the motives of the individual on the other.   If we fail to make this distinction, the reasons behind these movements risk to be very grossly stated.   The author indicated in this respect that, in order for workers to move from the country of origin to the country of destination, at least three conditions must be fulfilled:

a) there must be an expressed need for his services in the country of destination;

b) there must be willingness on the part of his country of origin to release him , especially if he is employed, which incidentally is the case of some workers outside their home countries;

c) there must be a motive for the individual himself to move.   The prime motive for the individual to work in a country other than his own is the higher wage.

The author added that at the national level, in both the importing and the exporting countries, the official responsibility for migration statistics is divided among a variety of ministries, departments, agencies.   It seems, therefore, that in order to ensure better and stronger co-operation with other countries in the field of manpower, it is essential to establish co-ordination at home between the different ministries.   At the regional level, namely within ECWA, within the Arab League, the ALO, the ICATU, ALESCO, IDCAS, the Arab Councils, the Arab Banks, the Arab Funds, etc., the author felt that there is need to clarify and settle some of the issues relating to regional co-operation in the different fields of say manpower, finance, agriculture, industry, etc.

A major policy issue related to complementarity in human resources development to the benefit of the region as a whole. To begin with, a system should be established whereby the receiving and the delivering countries would exchange information, well in advance, with respect to the respective supply and demand of the different categories of manpower, and with a view to alert the countries of delivery to the possibilities of lay-off in the future. Apart from attempts on each side to make both ends meet through some provisional measures of rotation of certain categories of manpower in order not to aggravate over-all shortages and also to avoid the under-utilisation of valuable manpower as has been the case for University Professors and construction workers, there also should be some agreement with regard to regional training and educational policies. As an interim measure, it may be found very economical to both sides that a programme of fellowships could be launched whereby a short-age country would finance the training or education of a national of another Arab country in his own home country provided he undertakes to serve the granting country for a period of say five years after graduation.

Another policy issue relates to the proper allotment of training activities at the national and at the regional levels. The dilemma might be resolved if we could consider the training of trainers and teaching the teachers as a regional activity as against training the trainees at the national level.

A third policy issue might relate to wage fixing and the determination of wages and remittances. Here again a wide area of choices for wage fixing based on relative scarcity or relative abundance may have to be discussed. Various indices will have to be developed with a view to measuring some sort of the terms of trade in manpower on the basis of shadow prices and the like.

The wealth of international experience in this field is really indispensable. The ILO, for example, has developed the World Employment Programme within which it intends to develop a comprehensive strategy suited for a few regions of the world. It has been suggested by one of the delegates in an earlier session that the Arab Region should be considered by the ILO for a resident integrated team of the sort they see fit for this region from the Arab Gulf to the Ocean. The author mentioned that the ILO has also developed recommendations and conventions which can be adopted or adapted bilaterally or multilaterally between countries. He also added that an adaptation of an ILO convention regarding the movement of workers between Arab countries has already been concluded by the Arab Council for Economic Unity (ACEU). It was issued by the Council on the 28.1.1969. It contains 16 articles and was ratified by five Arab countries, namely Jordan, Syria, Iraq, Sudan and Egypt. It was also discussed in Libya in March 1975. A model bilateral agreement has also been adapted to suit the purposes of any two Arab countries in co-operating together in the field of employment.

A number of participants indicated that the emigrating Arab workers, and even non-Arab workers, enjoy the same privileges and rights as the national workers in the host countries of the region. It was also indicated that one should differentiate between immigration and movement of workers as being two distinct phenomena when studying the flow of labour in the Arab World. Current problems concerning the immigration of the labour force to Arab countries consist among other things of the right to obtain the nationality of the host country, the right to own property and real-estate and other difficult issues that need to be studied. While the movement of workers from one country to another has its own different set of problems.

Governmental bilateral agreements on the movement of labour, such as the agreement between Qatar and Egypt for the utilisation of five thousand Egyptian labourers, could be resorted to in order to encourage the flow of Arab labour in the Arab labour-importing countries while safeguarding the economic and social interests of the labour-exporting countries. In this context, it was also stressed that there is no incompatibility between resorting to bilateral agreements and the freedom of the employer in selecting his workers.

So far, the flow of the labour force in the Arab world has been motivated by individual-istic interests, with wage considerations being one of the major factors taken into account by workers such as social security, working conditions and the like. Regional co-operation in the field of information on employment opportunities, working conditions and fringe bene-fits would enhance the efficiency of such a flow.

The composition of the set of critical skills demanded by the various countries in the region is changing with the changes in their socio-economic conditions. Thus, the Meeting stressed the need to re-train redundant human resources in order to meet the demand for new types of skills (automated industries, petrochemicals and the like).

While recognising the beneficial demonstration effect that expatriate workers have on national workers in the host countries, it was also recognised in the Meeting that there is a need to study the positive and the negative effects of a country's dependence on expat- riate workers. It was also stressed in the Meeting that expatriate experts should train their national counterparts as quickly and efficiently as possible.

It was stressed in the Meeting that the term "surplus labour" should be used with some caution. Egypt and to a lesser extent Syria do not have an absolute surplus in the various professions demanded by the labour importing countries, but only a relative surplus, mainly resulting from the non-availability of financial resources. In certain cases, these econo- mies are suffering from shortages of critical skills that have been attracted by the oil- producing countries. The draining of critical skills led some countries to adopt restric- tive measures against the free movement of labour in order to guarantee the implementation of its own crucial development projects.

A number of participants voiced their apprehensions concerning the future development of the Arab world by indicating that if the rich oil-producing countries continue to attract parts of the critical skills available in the relatively poorer countries, then the current distribution of wealth will certainly be accentuated in the future with the rich countries becoming richer and the poor becoming poorer. This trend, it was indicated, would lead to an unbalanced growth that may not be to the best interest of the region. It was also indi- cated that if the current trends in distributing jobs between nationals and expatriates in the rich countries were to continue, the future picture would consist of having expatriates doing the undesired jobs while the most sophisticated professions would be held by nationals, a resultant of the accentuation of the trend mentioned above, namely that the rich become richer and the poor poorer.

In order to avoid unbalanced growth, it was suggested in the Meeting that the flow of human skills should be accompanied by a flow, in the opposite direction, of financial res- ources. In this way all Arab countries would have a chance to develop simultaneously. However, it was indicated that the simultaneous development of all Arab countries could lead to conflicts of interest as to the flow of the labour force and specially as to the need for critical skills; a conflict that would necessitate co-ordination and planning at the region- al level.

Thus, the Meeting stressed the need for an integrated strategy for the socio-economic development of the Arab world. Preliminary steps in that direction, it was pointed out, had already been taken. On the invitation of the Arab Labour Organisation, the preliminary meeting held in Cairo brought together the Arab regional organisations and the Economic Commission for Western Asia (ECWA) to discuss the launching of an integrated strategy for development. One of the immediate results of that meeting was to enhance the role of the Arab Fund in the field of co-ordinating financial flows and extending technical assistance to Arab countries.

In the context of an integrated approach to the development of the Arab world, it was pointed out in the Meeting that the site, or geographical location, of any project should be determined by economic considerations with special attention being paid to the distribution of the labour force and the realisation of full employment.

In order to make fuller use of the region's human resources, the Meeting recommended that a stock taking of available skills be undertaken, with each country indicating its needs and/ or relative surpluses by categories of jobs and professions needed for the implementation of its development plans. On the occasion of the formulation of a number of development plans in the region in 1976, it was suggested that the planners concerned meet among themselves with a view to realising a beginning of regional co-ordination in their development efforts.

The participants in the Meeting stressed the need for the Arab League and its special- ised agencies to draw on the accumulated experience of the United Nations' System. In this context, the Meeting invited the International Labour Organisation to study the possibility of establishing a regional employment team for the Arab world. The co-operation of the ILO with the Arab Fund in studying the manpower aspects of development projects in the agricul- tural sector in Sudan was noted with appreciation. It was, therefore, recommended in the Meeting that the International Labour Organisation (ILO) establishes a liaison unit between the ILO and Arab regional organisations for the co-ordination of technical assistance projects in the manpower and employment planning field.

CHAPTER VII

Approaches to Employment and Manpower
Planning in the Arab Countries

A short introductory statement indicated that the purpose of this discussion is to arrive at a knowledge of the manpower planning mechanisms in the Arab countries : what organs are responsible for manpower and employment planning and how these organs are linked to the economic and development planning machineries in each country ? Within this context several country statements were made.

In Tunisia, employment is a major objective of the Fourth Development Plan. This required the integration of employment policy with the over-all development policy and the provision of the necessary measures needed to solve the employment problems. These measures included (a) improving statistical data on employment; (b) adjusting the educational system to the needs of the economy; (c) increasing investment within the framework of a labour-intensive policy; and (d) industrial development through decentralisation, rural development, and protection of export industries. In addition, new organs were created to deal with human resources, educational planning, employment and training, and family planning. Co-ordination among those organs is secured through the family planning department.

In Egypt, the principal organ responsible for the process of long-term manpower planning is the Central Department for Manpower Planning in the Ministry of Planning. This department operates in co-operation with the other concerned organs. On the supply side, it solicits the co-operation of the Ministries of Education and Higher Education. The Central Statistical Organisation, in this respect, is expected to undertake a study which will estimate projections for the supply of labour force by occupational status and at the over-all level for periods of five or ten years. On the demand side, the Department co-operates with the Ministries of Agriculture and Industry as well as with other ministries and other government organisations concerned. Within the over-all framework of manpower planning, and consistent with the over-all National Development Plan, the Central Department for Manpower Planning makes estimates of the supply of and demand for labour force for periods of ten to fifteen years. Projections of supply are constructed on the basis of certain available variables such as population, education, graduation and drop-out rates, and the like. The demand projections are reviewed by the ministries concerned, and approved. Then the Department proceeds with laying down the detailed plan on a project-by-project basis within each sector, co-ordinating it with plans for the other sectors.

As far as short-term planning is concerned, the Egyptian Ministry of Labour is the principle organ responsible for this process. It receives from the employment offices the necessary information concerning those who are seeking jobs. The employment offices, on the other hand, provide companies and establishments that have vacancies with the appropriate lists that would help them to meet their needs on the basis of selection.

Three main problems were basically encountered in Egypt in the course of formulating and implementing manpower planning. The first of these problems encountered has been in the process of striking a balance between demand and supply for the main occupational categories. Here lies the difficulty of harmonising between the occupational classification and the educational levels. The second problem encountered relates to the establishment of a manpower balance for each specialised occupational group. Although lack of information for some groups, like technicians, prevented producing such balances, it was possible to establish balances for occupational groups like doctors, engineers, teachers, etc. This exercise revealed shortages in teachers mainly attributed to the unattractiveness of the job despite acceptable rates of graduation. As to doctors and engineers, it is found that there are shortages and this is mainly due to emigration to the developed world. In the last five to seven years it is estimated that around 16,000 doctors and engineers emigrated. Statistical information related to below university levels, classified by industrial activity, occupational and educational qualifications were not given enough attention in the statistical tables. However, a new survey was launched in 1972 in order to meet these needs. The third problem confronted with in Egypt was the increasing role of women in the economic activity of the country, which required a corresponding investment policy that would create for them new employment opportunities. Around 76 per cent of female university graduates, 52 per cent of female secondary and vocational graduates and 12 per cent of female elementary graduates at present participate in the various economic activities. Compared with the female participation rates obtained from the 1966 to 1970 censuses, these higher rates constitute a new variable for determining the supply of the labour force that requires to be

taken into consideration in planning for human resources within over-all planning and investment needs.

In Syria, full employment has been a major objective of all socio-economic development
plans. However, manpower planning is a recent phenomenon. It is carried out within the
framework of meeting the needs of development. Planning of manpower passes through three
stages. The first stage consists of planning the demand for manpower followed by planning
its supply while the third stage involves planning the balance between the demand and supply
of manpower. The State Planning Board is the major body responsible for manpower planning.

In Saudi Arabia, development planning is recent, and it is the responsibility of the
Central Planning Organisation. This body co-operates with all the ministries in setting up
the plan. It is also in charge of the follow-up of the plan implementation as well as
evaluation. The Central Planning Organisation takes care of manpower planning while other
governmental bodies are also involved, particularly in the development of manpower through
education and training (Ministry of Education and Ministry of Labour and Social Affairs
mainly). In this connection, the Second Development Plan provides for policies and measures
necessary for the development of Saudi Arabian manpower. Policies related to periodic population censuses and labour surveys have also been adopted.

The Arab Organisation for Education, Culture and Science (ALESCO) presented a paper on
population growth and its relationship to problems of the labour force in the Arab countries.
The paper stressed the need for manpower planning and claimed that the Arab world needs a
new strategy in this respect. This includes a population policy which should involve
redistribution of the population, sedentarisation of bedouins and organising migration.
This strategy should also include the upgrading of planning machineries in Arab countries,
the provision of more information on manpower through surveys and censuses, and the expansion of training programmes at all levels in order to meet the needs of development and to
cope with technological progress.

In the course of the discussion, the inter-relationship between employment and other
socio-economic factors was again brought out. It was also expressed that employment has
social, political and economic implications.

It was indicated that the problem in manpower planning is the traditional approach to
planning which most Arab countries take. This approach has not solved many problems including the brain-drain problem. It has not achieved full co-ordination among various government bodies. In many instances, only quantitative aspects were considered in planning.
Qualitative aspects are also important and they should be taken into consideration. Studies
are needed on productivity and on the quality of available social services. More and better
statistical data should be supplied. In this connection, regional co-operation to facilitate the exchange of experiences is of great value.

POINTS FOR PLAN OF ACTION IN THE FIELD OF

MANPOWER AND EMPLOYMENT PLANNING

AS ADOPTED BY THE SEMINAR
ON MANPOWER AND EMPLOYMENT PLANNING IN THE
ARAB COUNTRIES
(BEIRUT, 12-24 MAY 1975)

I. ACTION BY ARAB COUNTRIES

A. General Principles

1. Arab countries should declare and vigorously pursue policies designed to eliminate unemployment, to reduce both visible and disguised under-employment, and gradually to absorb a growing proportion of their population of working age in productive work.

2. The immediate objective of such employment policies should be to raise the standard of living of the population as a whole and to eliminate poverty.

3. In order to achieve this, Arab countries should:

(a) adopt full, productive and freely-chosen employment as a major goal of their national development policies and in accordance with the ILO's Convention and Recommendation on Employment Policy, 1964 1/;

(b) orient all aspects of their development policies towards the objective of full employment in a context of sustained economic growth;

(c) review national legislation, policies and practices that may limit or hamper the employment of manpower.

B. Elements of an Employment Policy

1. Population and Employment

In the effort to mobilise productive forces for development and to tap unutilised human resources:

(a) measures should be taken to organise certain economic sectors, such as agriculture, small crafts and services, which employ large numbers of workers who could be released or diverted to other sectors in accordance with the growth of employment opportunities in the latter sectors;

(b) due attention should be paid in particular to enhancing the contribution of women workers, both through making it possible for increasing numbers of women to participate in development tasks (including the promotion of rural development) and through enabling them to acquire the requisite skills;

(c) the promotion of women's employment should take place on the basis of equality of opportunity and treatment for men and women workers in regard to access to employment, education and training, as well as terms and conditions of employment, in particular equal remuneration for work of equal value;

(d) in developing educational and training facilities and programmes, due regard should be paid to the needs of women as well as men both in the rural and traditional sector (in particular agriculture) and in modern-type activities;

1/ The Convention has been ratified by Algeria, Iraq, Jordan, Libya, the Sudan, Syria and Tunisia.

(e) governments wishing to encourage the employment of women should provide or encourage the provision of child care and other facilities making it easier for women to meet their dual responsibilities and to ensure the welfare of their families;

(f) efforts should be made, through appropriate agreements between the countries concerned, to ensure that Arab countries suffering from labour shortages can draw on Arab workers employed in European countries in order to meet these shortages.

2. Choice of Technology and Employment

(a) In those economic sectors offering some technological flexibility, every effort should be made to select technologies appropriate to national conditions, with due regard in particular to absorbing surplus labour where it exists and avoiding undesirable labour displacements in existing activities.

(b) Possibilities of applying labour-using technologies should be identified on a project-by-project basis or for specific processes within a project.

(c) Fiscal and investment policy and legislation should be reviewed with a view to correcting any bias that may favour capital-using rather than labour-using techniques in an undesirable manner.

(d) Suitable measures should be taken in introducing advanced technology to avoid creating wasteful excess capacity of production and to insure that quality and other specifications of goods produced satisfy actual economic and social needs including family, collective and intermediate consumption and exports.

(e) In the case of important industrial projects using advanced technology, such as the creation of basic industries, efforts should be made to develop linkages and complementarities with the rest of the economy, within a well-planned development framework.

(f) Training facilities at all levels should be expanded to cope with the skilled personnel requirements resulting from the introduction of technology.

(g) Steps should be taken, in particular through the educational system and mass media, to influence social attitudes and create an environment conducive to the creation of a technically minded generation.

(h) In order to solve problems related to the choice, identification and development of appropriate technology and the acquisition of technological know-how, Arab States should promote co-operation on a regional basis as well as with other developing countries seeking to achieve a New International Economic Order.

3. Trade and Employment

(a) In planning the foreign sector, governments should take into consideration the impact of trade policies on employment in various sectors and on the choice of technology, and seek to achieve a satisfactory balance between employment objectives and foreign trade targets.

(b) Arab countries should agree on a common policy of industrial specialisation relating to the processing of, and trade in, local raw materials, so as to avoid competition between countries that have similar local resources. This should be done within a framework of economic co-operation designed to achieve the full and effective utilisation of Arab human resources and to ensure that all parties concerned benefit from the development of exports and imports.

4. Education and Employment

(a) In order to ensure that the development of education and training contributes to the achievement of employment and development objectives, to the furtherance of greater equality of opportunity as well as to the self fulfilment of individuals, governments should pay particular attention to the following points:

(i) Programmes of basic universal education should be conceived so as to impart as a minimum essential skills such as functional literacy, hygiene and civic awareness. They should be related to local needs and conditions. They should emphasise the development of analytical skills. They should infuse positive attitudes vis-à-vis manual work and types of education and training which prepare for such work.

(ii) Such basic education should be supplemented by further programmes of education and training; designed so as to ensure an interaction between general education and technical and vocational education and training.

(iii) A proper balance should be maintained between the development of primary education, with a view to achieving as soon as possible the goal of universal primary education, and secondary and higher education.

(iv) Stipends and other assistance should be provided as necessary in order to remove any financial obstacle to the education and training of needy children and students.

(v) In order to avoid the emergence of surpluses of educated personnel, educational and vocational guidance and admission policies to higher education should be reviewed, as well as the structure of wages, salaries and other incentives which induce people to select certain courses of education in numbers that exceed the capacity of the economy to absorb them in productive employment.

(vi) Education should be planned as a lifelong process covering initial education and training during youth as well as adult education, literacy, and various forms of retraining, skill upgrading and refresher courses.

(vii) To supplement the existing network of educational and training facilities, maximum use should be made of informal media such as youth centres, farmers' clubs, etc. The provision of training by employing establishments should be encouraged through the provision of incentives as necessary. Accelerated training programmes should be introduced or expanded in order to meet the requirements for skilled manpower of development projects through adapting or improving available skills in the labour force. Special attention should also be paid to the problem of school drop-outs and to enabling them to have access to further education and to vocational training.

(viii) With a view to meeting the need for specialised qualified personnel responsible for undertaking the tasks of manpower and employment planning, specialised courses in this field should be provided by national universities.

(b) With a view to avoiding a wastage of human resources, efforts should be made to harmonise education and training policies with employment policies so that the former may better meet the needs of the labour market and of economic and social development.

C. Statistics and Research

1. Considering that many effects of population trends are only felt after a considerable lapse of time, governments should conduct studies on long-term population trends as a basis for defining population policy in harmony with their objectives in other fields of development policy including employment policy.

2. Adequate programmes should be developed to train statisticians specialised in the collection of data pertaining to employment, unemployment and under-employment, the composition of the labour force and the distribution of incomes.

3. In view of the importance of the profile of tariffs and other protective duties in determining the patterns of growth of different sectors and the relative capital/labour intensiveness of development in those sectors, as well as the expansion of employment opportunities in different sectors, governments should study those relationships and, for that purpose, improve the collection and analysis of information on such tariff profiles and their

effects, and seek to measure in particular price changes attributable to protective policies.

4. Arab countries should, with the assistance of the Arab Labour Organisation (ALO) and ILO envisage the possibility of preparing an Arab standard classification of occupations, with due regard to the International Standard Classification of Occupations (ISCO) and local experiences and circumstances.

5. In order to promote co-operation in employment between Arab countries, efforts should be made to improve the exchange of information and statistical data on the characteristics of employment in the countries concerned and on respective policies in the fields of population, education and training and employment in the light of over-all regional development policies.

D. Palestinian People and Occupied Territories

1. The Seminar condemns the Israeli aggression and illegal occupation of Arab territories which compel Arab populations to forced emigration. It condemns further the annexationist trade policy practised by Israel vis-à-vis the occupied territories, as well as the deprivation and destruction by Israeli authorities of Arab Palestinian assets as well as the repeated infringements of civic and trade union rights and discrimination in employment and wages affecting all Arab workers and in particular skilled workers.

The Seminar recommends that:

(1) Arab countries should treat Palestinian workers on the basis of equality of opportunity and rights with their own citizens in all matters relating to employment and conditions of employment, including trade union rights and social security.

(2) Arab countries should accept Palestinian students in their technical institutions in order to enable them to improve their technical and scientific qualifications, with a view to limiting the brain drain to countries outside the region and ensuring that the Arab world can benefit from their skills.

(3) Specialised agencies in Arab countries should collect data and conduct studies on the Palestinian labour force present in these countries and provide this information to the Palestine Liberation Organisation (PLO) that will benefit from it in planning that will serve the Palestinian people.

II. ACTION BY REGIONAL AND INTERNATIONAL ORGANISATIONS

1. The ILO and ECWA should consider the possibility of convening a meeting of experts in manpower planning and in manpower and employment statistics with a view to recommending to Arab states a desirable standardisation of statistical concepts and data classification systems, with due regard to existing international standards in this area, including recommendations concerning the concepts to be used in measuring the intensity of labour force utilisation.

2. The ILO and ECWA should consider the establishment of a regional inter-disciplinary employment team specialised in the fields of economics, demography, manpower and education, to undertake a full-scale study of the employment situation and prospects in the context of population and over-all economic and social development in Arab world, and to provide advisory services.

3. Arab states should, through the Arab League, recommend the establishment of a regional centre endowed with adequate resources and responsible for research designed to identify, adapt and develop appropriate technology, with due regard to employment and development needs, and to disseminate information about such questions in the Arabic language. Such a body should be established in consultation with ECWA and other United Nations specialised agencies and in the light of the resolution 1636 (LI) of the Economic and Social Council as well as the resolution adopted by the Second General Conference of the United Nations Industrial Development Organisation (ID/CONF.3/RES.2) and taking into consideration the recommendation of the United Nations Advisory Committee on the Application of Science and Technology to Development of ACAST (ID/CONF.3/11).

4. The League of Arab States should, in consultation with Arab countries and with international and regional organisations, study the feasibility of establishing a regional fund to help countries to meet their requirements for trained personnel, including the replacement of skilled and high-level personnel lost through migration. The objective of such a fund should

be to develop national and, where appropriate, regional facilities, and to plan the development of vocational training at the regional level. This Fund should also provide resources to help sending countries to expand their educational and training facilities so as to meet the requirements of receiving countries. Particular attention should be given to help those countries that require training facilities but lack the necessary financial resources.

5. ECWA, ILO and ALO should co-operate with other international organisations to provide specialised technical training programmes either within or outside the Arab region and allocate quotas for such training to the respective Arab countries, so as to enable them to adjust their manpower at high and intermediate levels to the pressing and urgent requirements of development projects.

6. In the field of education and training policy as related to employment, the following action should be taken:

(a) With a view to promoting a better understanding of the objectives, forecasting methods used, measures adopted, reforms introduced and results obtained in different countries, a thorough-going examination and comparison should be undertaken of national policies aiming at harmonising education and employment within the framework of economic and social development plans.

(b) A **quantitative** evaluation of the present situation and prospective trends in regard to skilled manpower supply and demand should be carried out, with due regard to the development plans of individual countries. This evaluation, which should be supplemented by an inventory of training facilities in the region, should bring out fields in which regional co-operation would be possible and desirable.

(c) A list of indicators of employment (including its structural, occupational, educational, income characteristics, etc.) and of education (including out-of-school education and training) should be prepared. Such indicators should provide a basis for the collection of data needed in order to achieve a better understanding of the relationships between employment, education and economic development at the national and regional levels, and facilitate the preparation of national plans and the development of regional co-operation.

(d) Governments should consider in consultation with the Arab League and ILO the feasibility of establishing an Arab regional training institute specialised in the provision of qualified personnel for undertaking the tasks of manpower and employment planning.

(e) ECWA and ILO should follow up on the above recommendations, in consultation with other international and regional organisations concerned, by preparing a programme of work on the above four points, including preparatory studies, meetings and working groups, and the necessary funds should be made available to them for that purpose from appropriate sources.

7. Adequate funds should be provided to enable ECWA and ILO in co-operation with ACA and ALO:

(a) To set up small study groups to assess availabilities and needs of different manpower categories in Arab countries and study the different aspects of employment policy and manpower planning in relation with development planning.

(b) These study groups would meet at regular intervals and finish their respective tasks in two years, at the end of which their reports would be submitted and form the subject of a meeting of Arab technicians and experts, in the different fields of the work of these committees.

(c) This meeting should be followed in the fourth year by a Conference of policy makers to examine the feasibility of the recommendations of the technical meeting in the field of manpower and employment planning and recommend policy measures for implementation to be submitted to the respective executing organs at the national, regional and international levels.

8. The Economic Department of the Arab League and the Council for Arab Economic Unity should co-operate with the Arab League Specialised Agencies, in particular IDCAS, ALESCO and the Center for the Development of Administration with a view to:

(a) Setting up a practical and positive plan of co-ordinated studies and actions designed to ensure the co-ordination and promotion of economic and social development of the Arab world.

(b) Establishing an Arab Bank for Reconstruction and Development (ABRD) whose structure and financial resources would enable it to provide advisory services and technical and financial assistance to member countries, and to recommend to the Arab League and the CAEU strategic projects for the development of the Arab world as a whole; such projects to be selected on the basis of economic and social criteria, including geographic location, economic return and employment creation, and to contribute to the movement of Arab capital and human resources within the Arab world in the interest of balanced and rapid growth.

9. Arab countries should consider the feasibility of merging the greatest possible number of national development funds into a unified Arab bank which will further the development of the Arab world in the way mentioned above.

10. Fully aware of the resolution adopted by the International Labour Organisation on 20 June 1974 with regard to the policy of discrimination, racism and violation of freedom and trade union rights which is practised by the Israeli authorities in Palestine and other occupied territories, the Seminar expresses the wish that the implementation of the said resolution will be accelerated.